AF777443

Effect of Additives/Admixtures on the Properties of Concretes and Cementitious Composites

Effect of Additives/Admixtures on the Properties of Concretes and Cementitious Composites

Guest Editors

Mengjun Chen
Jiwen Bai

MDPI

Basel • Beijing • Wuhan • Barcelona • Belgrade • Novi Sad • Cluj • Manchester

Guest Editors
Mengjun Chen
School of Future Technology
Shandong University
Jinan
China

Jiwen Bai
School of Civil Engineering
Shandong University
Jinan
China

Editorial Office
MDPI AG
Grosspeteranlage 5
4052 Basel, Switzerland

This is a reprint of the Special Issue, published open access by the journal *Materials* (ISSN 1996-1944), freely accessible at: www.mdpi.com/journal/materials/special_issues/LA84U758EJ.

For citation purposes, cite each article independently as indicated on the article page online and using the guide below:

Lastname, A.A.; Lastname, B.B. Article Title. *Journal Name* **Year**, *Volume Number*, Page Range.

ISBN 978-3-7258-3794-6 (Hbk)
ISBN 978-3-7258-3793-9 (PDF)
https://doi.org/10.3390/books978-3-7258-3793-9

© 2025 by the authors. Articles in this book are Open Access and distributed under the Creative Commons Attribution (CC BY) license. The book as a whole is distributed by MDPI under the terms and conditions of the Creative Commons Attribution-NonCommercial-NoDerivs (CC BY-NC-ND) license (https://creativecommons.org/licenses/by-nc-nd/4.0/).

Contents

materials

MDPI

ticle

heological Behavior of Oil Well Cement Slurries with Addition f Core/Shell $TiO_2@SiO_2$ Nanoparticles—Effect of uperplasticizer and Temperature

ovanni dos Santos Batista [1], Francisca Puertas [2,*], Antonio Shigueaki Takimi [3], Eleani Maria da Costa [1] and arta Palacios [2,*]

1 School of Technology, Pontifical Catholic University of Rio Grande do Sul (PUCRS), Avenida Ipiranga, 6681, Porto Alegre 90619-900, Brazil; giovanni.batista@edu.pucrs.br (G.d.S.B.); eleani@pucrs.br (E.M.d.C.)
2 Eduardo Torroja Institute for Construction Sciences (IETcc-CSIC), C/Serrano Galvache, 4, 28033 Madrid, Spain
3 School of Engineering, Federal University of Rio Grande do Sul (UFRGS), Avenida Bento Gonçalves, 9500, Porto Alegre 91540-000, Brazil; antonio.takimi@gmail.com
* Correspondence: puertasf@ietcc.csic.es (F.P.); marta.palacios@ietcc.csic.es (M.P.)

Abstract: This study investigates the rheological behavior of oil well cement pastes (OWCPs) modified with core/shell $TiO_2@SiO_2$ (nTS) nanoparticles and polycarboxylate-ether (PCE) superplasticizers at different temperatures (25, 45, and 60 °C). Results show that nTS particles increased static and dynamic yield stresses and the apparent viscosity of the cement slurries due to an increased solid volume fraction and reduced free water availability. The increase in the slurry dispersion by adding PCE superplasticizers enhanced the effect of the nanoparticles on the rheological parameters. Oscillation rheometry demonstrated that nTS nanoparticles enhanced the structural buildup, while PCE retarded hydration. Furthermore, slurries hydrated at 60 °C experienced higher initial values of the elastic modulus and a faster exponential increase in this rheological parameter due to the acceleration of the cement hydration.

Keywords: oil well cementing; rheology; polycarboxylate ether; temperature; optimization

check for updates

demic Editors: Mengjun Chen and n Bai

ived: 29 November 2024
ised: 30 December 2024
epted: 2 January 2025
lished: 8 January 2025

tion: Batista, G.d.S.; Puertas, F.; mi, A.S.; da Costa, E.M.; cios, M. Rheological Behavior of Well Cement Slurries with ition of Core/Shell $TiO_2@SiO_2$ oparticles—Effect of erplasticizer and Temperature. rials 2025, 18, 239. https:// org/10.3390/ma18020239

yright: © 2025 by the authors. nsee MDPI, Basel, Switzerland. article is an open access article ibuted under the terms and itions of the Creative Commons ibution (CC BY) license s://creativecommons.org/ ses/by/4.0/).

1. Introduction

Rheological properties of cementitious materials play a key role in the petroleum industry [1]. Before pumping into the wellbore, the cement slurry is mixed on the rig in a cementing unit [2]. During the oil well cementing operations, the cement slurry fills the annulus space between the rock formation and the steel casing. The main objectives of the cement sheath are to provide zonal isolation from fluid flow and to protect the steel casing, preventing it from corrosion [3]. Moreover, if the well presents no zonal isolation, it will never reach its best potential as an oil or gas producer [2]. Many problems can be found during cementing operations, such as improper casing centralization, poor bonding between cement formation and cement casing, shrinkage, the inappropriate placement of cement, and fluid loss [1]. Among them, channeling is the most critical one [4,5].

The study of rheological properties of cementitious materials involves the identification of the inherent properties of fluids, including plastic viscosity, yield stress, frictional behavior, and gel strength. Understanding these factors is crucial in determining the flow behavior of cement slurry and establishing the relationship between the flow rate (shear rate) and the pressure gradient (shear stress) that drives fluid movement [6]. Some studies have shown that, in the early stages of insufficient cement hydration, volume shrinkage and external loads contribute to the deformation of the cement stone, leading to oil ar gas well leakage [7,8]. As a result, it is essential to develop oil well cement with suitab rheological properties, a dense hydration product structure, and high early strength. Th rheology of the cement slurry is affected by many factors, such as the chemical compositi of cement, solid volume fraction, the specific surface area of cement, the shape of ceme grains, the type and dosage of chemical admixtures, application methods, the mixing tir and process, the nature of wellbore, etc. [9]. According to Nelson and Guillot [6], the effe of pressure on the rheological properties of oil well cement can be neglected as its effect too small when compared to the temperature. Temperature has a major impact on ceme slurry rheology, but it also depends on the incorporated chemical admixtures.

In recent years, nanoparticles have shown great potential to enhance the properti of cementitious materials, such as the heat of hydration, mechanical strength, microstru ture, shrinkage, and chemical resistance [10,11]. In terms of hydration kinetics, they c accelerate cement hydration by creating additional nucleation sites for the precipitati and increase of calcium silicate hydrate (C-S-H) gel content. This acceleration of hydrati reduces thickening time, facilitating early strength development [12,13].

However, nanoparticles can negatively influence the viscosity of cement-based m terials. Traditional cement without nanoparticles has lower viscosity, leading to a mo brittle cement bond. In contrast, nano-enhanced slurries exhibit higher viscosity due to solid/volume ratio increase and, in many cases, a high water adsorption of water us in the paste preparation, which enhances their flexural performance [14]. The addition nanoparticles, due to their large surface area, typically reduces the workability of ceme slurry. Depending on the type and concentration of the nanomaterial, the slurry's rheolo can change significantly, potentially making it unpumpable [15].

The addition of nanosilica to oil well cement slurry alters its rheological properti such as yield stress and plastic viscosity. Its large surface area increases water and chemi admixture requirements for workability. At constant water content, higher nanosilica co centrations lead to higher solid volume fractions and particle packing, reducing free wa and increasing torque and friction between particles [16]. This reduces cohesion, loweri flow spread and increasing plastic viscosity. Nanosilica particles densify the microstructu by filling voids, though agglomerates may retain free water, reducing workability. Wheth nanosilica affects rheology depends on whether agglomerates act as fillers [17]. Nanopa cles in water tend to agglomerate due to van der Waals interactions, making it challengi to achieve a uniform dispersion when preparing cement nanocomposites [18].

Baragwiha et al. [19] investigated the addition of nano-SiO_2 (15–25 nm) and nano-Ti (20–30 nm) to oil well cement class G in 1, 3, 5, and 7% by weight of cement (BWO Polycarboxylate-ether (PCE) superplasticizer and defoamer dosages were kept constant 1.6 and 0.2% BOWC, respectively. To avoid instant thickening, the w/b ratio varied fro 0.72 to 0.78, depending on the density of the slurries, which was maintained at 1.65 g·cm The authors observed that nano-SiO_2 significantly increased the apparent viscosity a yield stress of the slurries. This behavior was attributed to the increased structure buildi ability of the cement slurries. The effect of nano-TiO_2 was smaller. This was becau while the effect of nano-TiO_2 is purely physical (i.e., more nucleation sites due to a hi surface area), nano-SiO_2 also promoted chemical reactions with calcium hydroxide to fo additional C-S-H due to its pozzolanic nature.

To improve properties both in the fresh and hardened state, core/shell TiO_2@Si (nTS) nanoparticles are a good alternative [20,21]. This material consists of a mixture a non-reactive material (which is the core) covered by a pozzolanic material (being t shell). In previous studies [22,23], we investigated the dispersion of TiO_2 covered w SiO_2 (nTS) nanoparticles of 20–40 nm in water. After adding 1% BWOC of nTS in wa the mean hydrodynamic size of particles was 32.66 nm, indicating that no agglomeration occurred. Additionally, we studied the impact of 0.5% and 1% BWOC of these particles on oil well cement class G hydrated pastes, in the presence and absence of superplasticizers. A decrease in porosity and portlandite content, increased hydration and C-S-H main chain length, and an improvement in mechanical and chemical properties before and after CO_2 exposure were observed. No studies on the rheological behavior of these pastes with PCE have been carried out to date. It is therefore necessary to study the influence of these nTS nanoparticles on the rheology of oil well cement slurries and the effect of temperature in these mixtures. For this reason, the main objective of the present study is to investigate the influence of these nTS particles on the rheological behavior of oil well cement class G slurries in the absence and presence of PCE superplasticizers and at different temperatures.

2. Materials and Methods

2.1. Materials

The cement class G was provided by Lafarge Holcim Brasil S.A., (Rio de Janeiro, Brazil) and its chemical composition was determined by XRF, as presented in Table 1.

Table 1. Cement class G chemical composition.

Oxide	SiO_2	CaO	Al_2O_3	Fe_2O_3	MgO	SO_3	K_2O	Equivalent Na_2O	LOI [1]	IR [2]
wt.%	21.1	64.2	3.8	4.6	1.3	2.6	0.4	0.5	0.8	0.53

[1] Loss of ignition. [2] Insoluble residue.

The commercial core/shell TiO_2@SiO_2 nanoparticles were purchased from SkySpring Nanomaterials. The core consists of rutile phase titanium oxide (TiO_2), which is 99.5% pure. The core is coated with a layer (shell) of silicon oxide (SiO_2). The mean nanoparticle size is 32 nm, measured by Dynamic Light Scattering (DLS) [22]. The TiO_2/SiO_2 ratio is approximately 0.03, and the nanoparticles are highly hydrophilic. The transmission electron microscopy (TEM) image and the X-ray diffraction (XRD) spectrum of nTS are shown in Figures S1 and S2 of the Supplementary Materials, respectively. The amounts of nTS addition were 1, 2, 3, and 4% BWOC. To maintain good workability, a PCE superplasticizer was used (CQ Plast MR 825 superplasticizer admixture provided by Camargo Química S.A., Pomerode, Brazil). This is a polycarboxylate-ether superplasticizer of the third generation and follows the standard C494 [24] as a type F. The Fourier transform infrared spectroscopy (FTIR) of PCE is shown in Figure S3 of the Supplementary Materials. The physical properties of the powders are presented in Table 2.

Table 2. Characteristics of materials.

Material	Size	Specific Mass ($g \cdot cm^{-3}$)	Specific Surface Area ($m^2 \cdot g^{-1}$)
Cement class G	7.30 μm [1]	3.16	0.82 [1]
nTS	32 nm [2]	4.23 [3]	~40

[1] Measured by BET (Figure S4). [2] Measured by DLS in our previous work [22]. [3] Provided by the supplier.

2.2. Mixing Procedures

The mixing proportions of oil well cement pastes (OWCPs) are presented in Table 3. Prior to mixing, the nTS content was added to deionized water. The amount of cement was 100 g, and the w/b ratio was 0.44 for the mixtures without PCE. For the mixtures with the PCE addition, the dosage of PCE used was 0.15 and 0.30% BWOC, and the w/b ratio was reduced to 0.35 to avoid bleeding. Slurries were mixed at 2000 rpm for 60 s. The rheology tests were carried out in a Kinexus Ultra+ rheometer from Netzsch (Selb, Germany).

Table 3. Mix compositions.

Mixture	Cement (g)	Water (g)	nTS (g)	PCE (g)	Solid/Volum Fraction (%)
OWCP0.44_0nTS	100	44	0	0	41.9
OWCP0.44_1nTS	100	44	1	0	42.1
OWCP0.44_2nTS	100	44	2	0	42.3
OWCP0.44_3nTS	100	44	3	0	42.5
OWCP0.44_4nTS	100	44	4	0	42.7
OWCP0.35_0nTS_0.15PCE	100	35	0	0.15	47.6
OWCP0.35_1nTS_0.15PCE	100	35	1	0.15	47.8
OWCP0.35_2nTS_0.15PCE	100	35	2	0.15	48.0
OWCP0.35_3nTS_0.15PCE	100	35	3	0.15	48.2
OWCP0.35_4nTS_0.15PCE	100	35	4	0.15	48.4
OWCP0.35_0nTS_0.30PCE	100	35	0	0.30	47.6
OWCP0.35_1nTS_0.30PCE	100	35	1	0.30	47.8
OWCP0.35_2nTS_0.30PCE	100	35	2	0.30	48.0
OWCP0.35_3nTS_0.30PCE	100	35	3	0.30	48.2
OWCP0.35_4nTS_0.30PCE	100	35	4	0.30	48.4

2.3. *Rheological Test Conditions*

2.3.1. Static Yield Stress

The static yield stress was determined from the stress growth test at 25 °C. To ensu repeatability, a preshear of 200 s^{-1} was applied for 35 s. The stabilization time was set 10 min for structure formation. A constant shear rate of 0.1 s^{-1} was applied, and, with th structure breakdown, the shear stress increased. The static yield stress value was obtaine through the initial peak of the shear stress (Figure S5 in the Supplementary Materials).

2.3.2. Flow Curves and Apparent Viscosity

Flow curves were measured on pastes at 25, 45, and 60 °C using concentric cylinde geometry with roughed surfaces. A preshear was initially conducted at 200 s^{-1} for 35 s. stabilization time of 5 min to reach the target temperature was applied afterward. The upp and lower ramps were from 0 to 100 s^{-1} during 2 min and 15 s each. The dynamic yie stress was determined using the Herschel–Bulkley model (Equation (1)), which present the best fit.

$$\tau = \tau_0 + K\,\dot{\gamma}^n$$

where τ is the shear stress, τ_0 is the dynamic yield stress, K is the consistency factor, $\dot{\gamma}$ the shear rate, and n is the flow index.

The evolution of the apparent viscosity with shear rate was obtained from th down curve.

2.3.3. Oscillation Tests

Oscillation measurements were conducted to study the structural build-up of t slurries at 25 °C and 60 °C and dosages of PCE and nTS. For this, the plate–plate geomet with rough surfaces was used, and the gap between plates was set at 1 mm. The line viscoelastic region (LVER) was initially determined as this is the domain where the r crostructure of the cement paste is preserved. The LVER was determined by increasing t strain at a frequency of 1 Hz [25,26]. For this, small amplitude oscillatory shear (SAC tests were conducted at a strain of 5×10^{-5} up to 2.5 h. To avoid water evaporation duri the measurement, a solvent trap system was used.

3. Results and Discussion

In oil well cementing, understanding rheological properties like static and dynamic yield stresses, apparent viscosity, and oscillation tests is crucial for ensuring the performance and stability of cement slurries. Static and dynamic yield stresses help assess the slurry's ability to resist flow under static and dynamic conditions, impacting placement and preventing fluid migration. Apparent viscosity measures flow resistance, influencing pumpability and placement efficiency. Oscillation tests help evaluate the viscoelastic properties, providing insight into the transition from slurry to solid, crucial for zonal isolation and well integrity. Understanding these properties ensures efficient cementing, preventing well failures, and optimizing production.

In the present study, the nTS content, temperature, and the presence and absence of PCE have been considered as variables in the rheological behavior of oil well cement slurries. The results obtained considering the aforementioned variables are described and discussed below, specifically the following: (i) the impact of nTS and PCE on the static and dynamic yield stress of OWCPs at room temperature; (ii) the impact of temperature and nTS on the dynamic yield stress and apparent viscosity of oil well cement pastes; and (iii) the study of the reactivity of oil well cement pastes containing nTS by oscillation rheometry.

3.1. Impact of nTS and PCE on the Static and Dynamic Yield Stress of Oil Well Cement Pastes at Room Temperature

The static yield stress of the studied OWCPs at 25 °C is shown in Figure 1. This parameter was measured by shear stress-controlled protocols. Static yield stress is the needed stress to initiate flow, and it is associated with a non-disturbed microstructure [27,28].

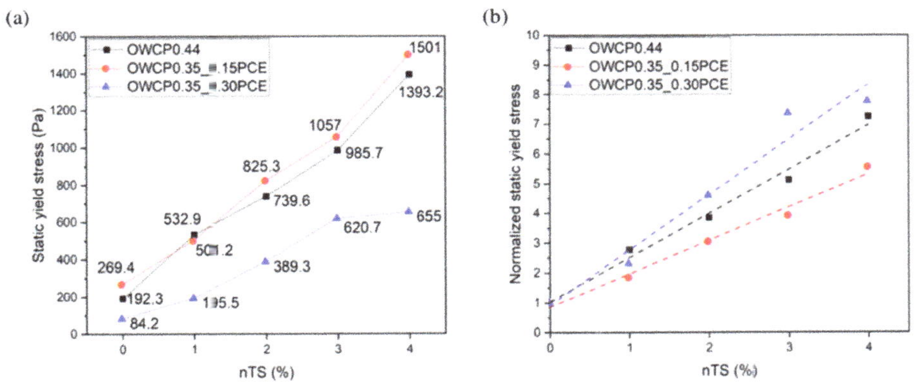

Figure 1. (**a**) Static yield stress values and (**b**) normalized static yield stress at 25 °C.

The addition of 0.15% PCE admixtures enabled the decrease in the water/binder ratio from 0.44 to 0.35 with an increase of around 25% of the static yield stress, regardless of the amount of nTS added to the pastes. This effect of PCE is due to the steric hindrance induced by the adsorbed polymer onto the cement particles [29,30]. The increase in the PCE dosage up to 0.30% led to a decrease of 75% of the static yield stress in the absence of nTS, and this positive effect is preserved when the nanoparticles are added. To compare the impact of nTS in the three cementitious systems, with different water content and polymer dosages, static yield stress values were normalized with respect to the yield stress of the corresponding paste without nTS. From Figure 1b, it can be inferred that the addition of nTS leads to a higher increase in the static yield stress in OWCPs with a l/s = 0.35 and containing the highest amount of PCE, showing that the nanoparticles have a greater effect as the dispersion of particles in the paste increases. This agrees with previous studies that proved that good dispersants are needed to stabilize nanoparticles, such as nano cla or graphene oxide, and preserve their properties as hydration accelerators or viscosit modifying admixtures [31]. At this early reaction time (around 15 min), the amount hydrates can be considered neglectable, and the increase in the static yield stress induce by nTS can be mainly explained by the increase in the solid volume fraction of the paste as shown in Table 3 [32].

3.2. Impact of the Temperature and nTS on the Dynamic Yield Stress and Apparent Viscosity of t Oil Well Cement Pastes

The effect of temperature on dynamic yield stress in the OWCP slurries (with nTS a PCE) is shown in Figure 2. The dynamic yield stress, determined from the flow curve (s Figures S6, S7 and S8a,c,e in the Supplementary Materials), is defined as the minimu stress to maintain or finish the flow of a material that has suffered the breakdown of t microstructure [33,34]. Furthermore, the apparent viscosity of the slurries at differe temperatures (with different nTS content and PCE) is presented in Table 4. All the slurri show a shear-thinning behavior with a decrease in the apparent viscosity as the shear ra increases (see Figures S6, S7 and S8b,d,f in the Supplementary Materials).

The addition of nTS increased both rheological parameters, dynamic yield stress, a apparent viscosity compared to the control samples due to the increase in the solid volur fraction (see Table 4) and the water adsorption by nTS that decreases the amount of fr water needed for flowability [35,36]. For a given nTS content and temperature, mixtur with PCE tend to present lower values of both rheological parameters as the adsorptio of PCE onto the cement surface decreases the attractive interparticle forces that preve particle flocculation and releases the free water trapped within the flocs [37].

The increase in the temperature from 25 °C to 45 °C does not significantly impa the values of dynamic yield stress and apparent viscosity; however, the low flowability most of the OWCPs and OWCP0.35_0.15PCE pastes at 60 °C did not allow us to measu their rheological parameters. This is mainly related to the fast reactivity of the pastes this temperature. In contrast, all OWCP0.35_0.30PCE pastes could be tested at 60 °C, in this case, the higher dosage of PCE led to a higher amount of polymer adsorbed the surface reactive areas of the silicate phases and the consequent retardation of ceme hydration [38,39].

The dynamic yield stress has been plotted versus the apparent viscosity at 10 s^{-1} f most of the studied pastes, containing variable amounts of nTS, PCE, and hydrated at diff ent temperatures. The master curve obtained (Figure 3) exhibits a linear relationship wit high regression coefficient (R^2 = 0.9822), showing a strong correlation between dynan yield stress and apparent viscosity. This further confirms that the observed changes in rh logical behavior can be attributed primarily to the physical effect of added solids rather th chemical interactions associated with hydration. In contrast, the rapid flow loss suffer by OWCPs containing nTS and OWCP0.35_0.15PCE with dosages of nTS above 1% a hydrated at 60 °C did not allow us to measure their rheological properties. For these past flow loss was related to the enhancement of cement hydration induced by temperature a the presence of nanoparticles, as also shown below in the oscillation measurements.

These results show that the addition of PCE is essential to maintain low dynan yield stress values in slurries containing nTS at all tested temperatures. In particular, t synergistic effect of PCE and nTS improved the flowability of the mixtures with low nTS high nTS with high PCE contents even at elevated temperatures, being beneficial for well applications.

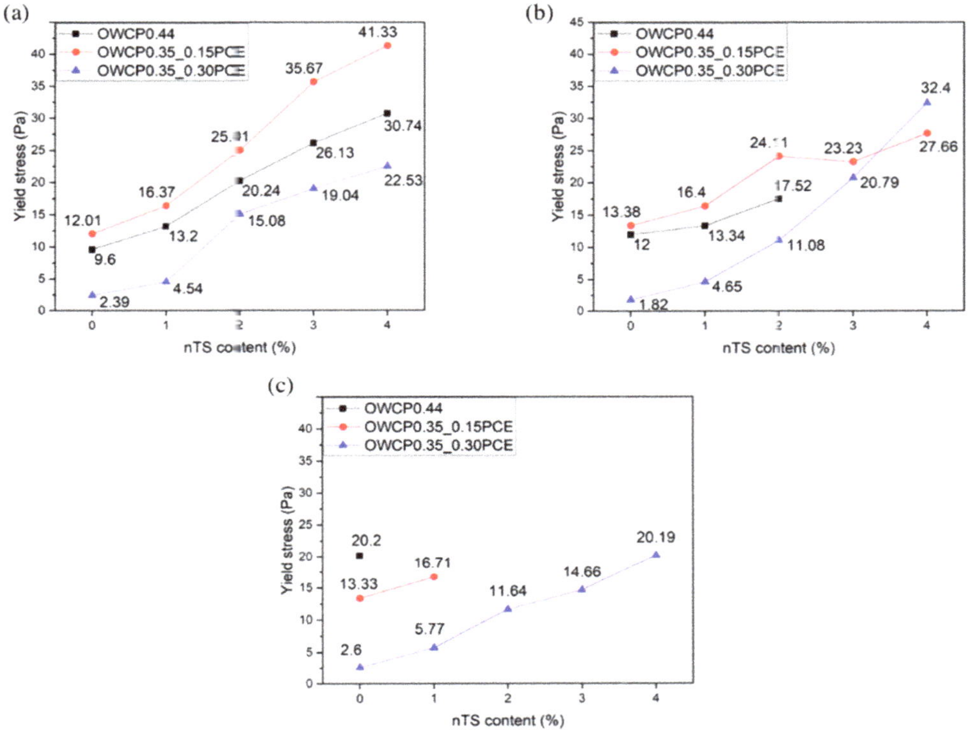

Figure 2. Dynamic yield stress values at different temperatures (**a**) 25 °C, (**b**) 45 °C, and (**c**) 60 °C.

Table 4. Apparent viscosity values at 10 s^{-1} at different temperatures.

Temperature	nTS Content (%)	Apparent Viscosity (Pa·s)		
		OWCP0.44	OWCP0.35_0.15PCE	OWCP0.35_0.30PCE
25 °C	0	2.17	1.85	0.38
	1	2.36	2.08	0.81
	2	2.94	3.68	1.83
	3	3.68	3.80	2.47
	4	4.41	5.55	5.17
45 °C	0	1.95	1.54	0.22
	1	2.31	2.26	0.56
	2	2.76	3.28	1.84
	3	-	3.49	2.47
	4	-	3.65	4.37
60 °C	0	2.65	1.33	0.28
	1	-	2.13	0.66
	2	-	-	1.69
	3	-	-	1.87
	4	-	-	2.02

"-" Measurements could not be taken due to the low flowability of the pastes.

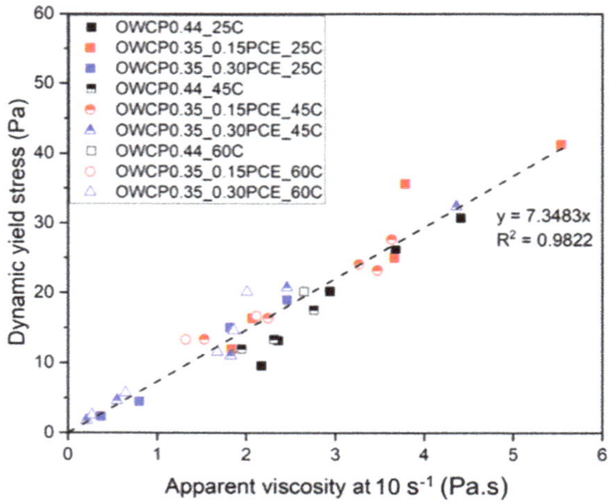

Figure 3. Dynamic yield stress and apparent viscosity relationship.

3.3. Study of the Reactivity of the Oil Well Cement Pastes Containing nTS by Oscillation Rheometry

To further investigate the reaction and structuration of the cement pastes, sma amplitude oscillatory shear (SAOS) measurements were conducted. The LVER graphs 25 and 60 °C are presented in Figures 4 and 5, respectively. The range of strain and stre within the viscoelastic properties of the material remains constant, regardless of the appli strain. Until the yellow line, the material responds predictably to strain and stress and ca return to its original shape. The critical strain was found in the range between 1 × 10 and 5 × 10^{-4} Pa. This region was identified immediately before the G′/G″ values start to decrease and was 5 × 10^{-3}%.

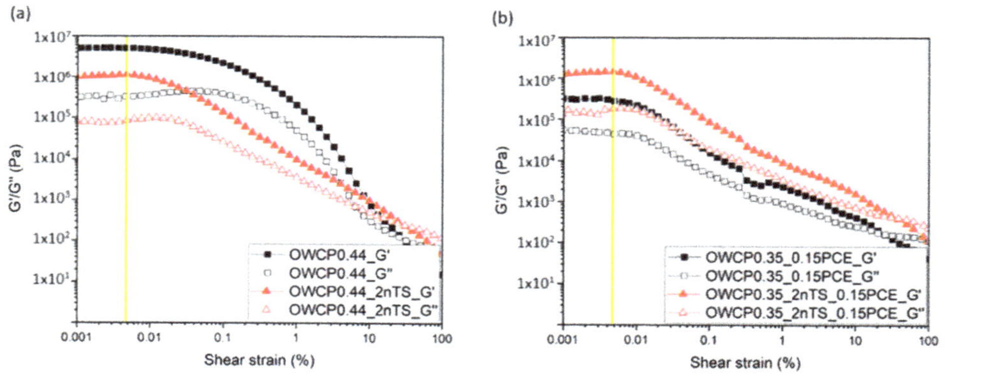

Figure 4. Strain oscillation test conducted on slurries at 25 °C (**a**) without PCE and (**b**) with PCE.

The SAOS was carried out for OWCPs without and with 0.15% of PCE and dosages nTS up to 2% [40]. Figure 6 shows the evolution of the elastic modulus G′ over the reacti time at a constant shear strain at 0.005% (value in the linear viscoelastic regime). At init times, the addition of PCE decreases the elastic modulus of the slurries with respect to t non-admixed one, which confirms the dispersing properties of the PCE superplasticiz In particular, at 25 °C, OWCP and OWCP0.35_0.15PCE showed a G′ of 1.09 × 10^5 a 6.7 × 10^3 Pa, respectively. In contrast, at 60 °C, no significant differences in the G′ valu have been observed for both pastes.

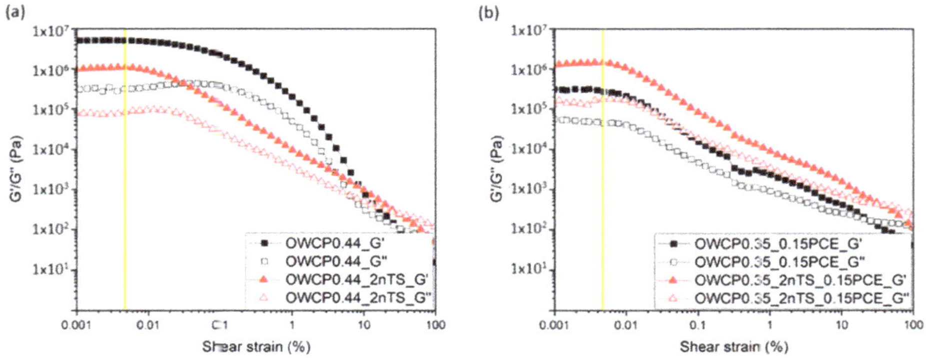

Figure 5. Strain oscillation test conducted on slurries at 60 °C (**a**) without PCE and (**b**) with PCE.

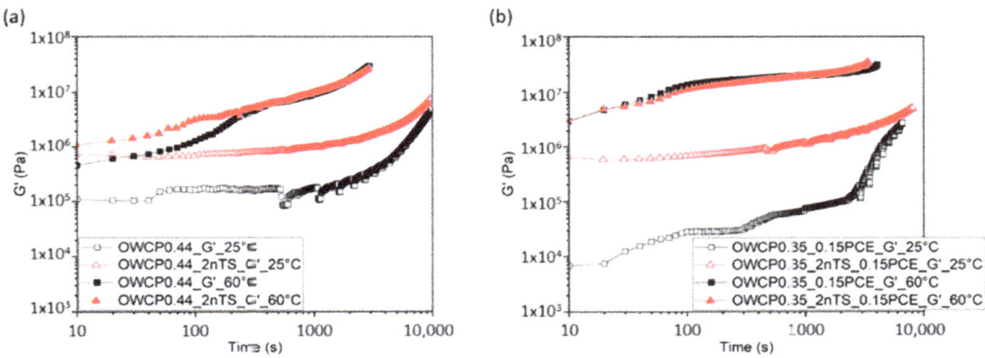

Figure 6. Complex elastic modulus of (**a**) OWCP0.44 and (**b**) OWCP0.35_0.15PCE at 25 and 60 °C.

The addition of 2% nTS to OWCP0.44 increases the initial elastic modulus compared to non-admixed slurries, inferring that the rigidity of the pastes rises with the increase in the solid volume ratio and the consequent decrease in the interparticle distance [41]. At 25 °C, the elastic modulus remains almost constant over the first 15 min of hydration. Afterward, a steep rise in the elastic modulus is observed probably due to the gradual precipitation of reaction products onto the pseudo-contact points between cement particles [25]. The addition of nanoparticles does not modify the time at which G′ increases, but it reduces the slope of the curve after 15 min of hydration. The rise in the temperature to 60 °C in OWCP0.44 slurries with and without nanoparticles leads to an increase in G′ from the very early times due to the acceleration of hydration kinetics with respect to slurries hydrated at 25 °C.

In the presence of PCE, two main stages were observed in the evolution of G′ of pastes hydrated at 25 °C. Over the first stage up to 2000 s, the progressive increase in G′ is associated with the initial flocculation of the cement particles due to colloidal interactions and the initial precipitation of first hydration reaction products [25,26]. Afterward, an exponential increase in G′ is observed and related to the higher amounts of these reaction products over this stage. The addition of the polymer retards the time of appearance of this exponential increase with respect to OWCP0.44 pastes [39] as the polymer adsorption onto the surface reactive sites blocks silicate dissolution. In slurries containing PCE, the rise in the temperature leads to a higher initial G′ value and a faster increase in this parameter; however, the presence of nanoparticles does not modify the evolution of G′ over time, as shown in Figure 6b.

4. Conclusions

This study evaluated the impact of core/shell $TiO_2@SiO_2$ (nTS) nanoparticles a polycarboxylate-ether (PCE) superplasticizer on the rheological behavior of oil well ceme pastes (OWCPs) at different temperatures. The findings reveal that nTS effectively chang the rheological properties of cement slurries by increasing static and dynamic yield stress and the apparent viscosity. This behavior is attributed to an increase in solid volume fracti and a reduction in free water availability. The increase in these rheological paramete induced by the nTS is higher as the PCE dosages increase, which confirms the greater eff of nanoparticles in well-dispersed systems.

The increase in the temperature up to 45 °C induced no significant changes in t rheological parameters. However, slurries hydrated at 60 °C experienced higher initi values of the elastic modulus (measured by oscillation rheometry) and a faster exponenti increase in this rheological parameter.

The synergistic interaction between nTS and PCE emerged as a key finding. Wh nTS enhanced the rheological performance by improving microstructure and partic packing, PCE ensured dispersion and prevented agglomeration, enhancing the over flow properties of the slurries. This combination demonstrates significant potential f improving oil well cement performance in high-temperature environments.

Supplementary Materials: The following supporting information can be downloaded at https: www.mdpi.com/article/10.3390/ma18020239/s1, Figure S1: TEM image of nTS; Figure S2: X spectrum of nTS; Figure S3: FTIR spectrum of PCE; Figure S4: Isothermal graph of anhydrous cem class G; Figure S5: Shear stress graphs for static yield stress determination at 25 °C for the mixtu (a) without PCE, (b) with 0.15 wt.% of PCE, and (c) with 0.30 wt.% of PCE; Figure S6: Shear str and shear viscosity graphs for the mixtures (a,b) without PCE, (c,d) with 0.15 wt.% of PCE, a (e,f) with 0.30 wt.% of PCE; Figure S7: Shear stress and shear viscosity graphs at 45 °C for the mixtu (a,b) without PCE, (c,d) with 0.15 wt.% of PCE, and (e,f) with 0.30 wt.% of PCE; Figure S8: Sh stress and shear viscosity graphs at 60 °C for the mixtures (a,b) without PCE, (c,d) with 0.15 wt.% PCE, and (e,f) with 0.30 wt.% of PCE.

Author Contributions: Conceptualization, G.d.S.B., F.P., A.S.T., E.M.d.C. and M.P.; methodology, and M.P.; software, G.d.S.B. and M.P.; validation, G.d.S.B., F.P. and M.P.; formal analysis, G.d.S investigation, G.d.S.B., F.P. and M.P.; resources, E.M.d.C., F.P. and M.P.; writing—original draft pre ration, G.d.S.B.; writing—review and editing, F.P. and M.P.; visualization, F.P and M.P.; supervisi F.P., A.S.T., E.M.d.C. and M.P.; project administration, F.P. and M.P.; funding acquisition, G.d.S.B., and M.P. All authors have read and agreed to the published version of the manuscript.

Funding: This research was partly funded by Coordenação de Aperfeiçoamento de Pessoal de Ní Superior—Brasil (CAPES), grant number 001 and PID2020-115797RB-I00/AEI/10.13039/50110001 (RHEODUR) project.

Institutional Review Board Statement: Not applicable.

Informed Consent Statement: Not applicable.

Data Availability Statement: The original contributions presented in this study are included in article/Supplementary Materials. Further inquiries can be directed to the corresponding authors

Acknowledgments: This work was supported by the Eduardo Torroja Institute for Construct Sciences (IET-cc). This study was partly financed by the Coordenação de Aperfeiçoamento Pessoal de Nível Superior—Brasil (CAPES)—Finance Code 001. Palacios and Puertas thank PID2 115797RB-I00/ AEI/10.13039/501100011033 (RHEODUR) project.

Conflicts of Interest: The authors declare no conflicts of interest.

References

1. Kumar, S.; Bera, A.; Shah, S.N. Potential Applications of Nanomaterials in Oil and Gas Well Cementing: Current Status, Challenges and Prospects. *J. Pet. Sci. Eng.* **2022**, *213*, 110395. [CrossRef]
2. Hodne, H.; Saasen, A.; O'Hagan, A.B.; Wick, S.O. Effects of Time and Shear Energy on the Rheological Behaviour of Oilwell Cement Slurries. *Cem. Concr. Res.* **2000**, *30*, 1759–1766. [CrossRef]
3. Lootens, D.; Hébraud, P.; Lécolier, E.; Van Damme, H. Gelation, Shear-Thinning and Shear-Thickening in Cement Slurries. *Oil Gas Sci. Technol.* **2004**, *59*, 31–40. [CrossRef]
4. Fink, J. *Petroleum Engineer's Guide to Oil Field Chemicals and Fluids*; Elsevier: Amsterdam, The Netherlands, 2012; ISBN 9780123838445.
5. Shonkoff, S.B.C.; Hays, J.; Finkel, M.L. Environmental Public Health Dimensions of Shale and Tight Gas Development. *Environ. Health Perspect.* **2014**, *122*, 787–795. [CrossRef]
6. Nelson, E.B.; Guillot, D. *Well Cementing*, 2nd ed.; Schlumberger: Houston, TX, USA, 2006.
7. Agofack, N.; Ghabezloo, S.; Sulem, J.; Garnier, A.; Urbanczyk, C. Experimental Investigation of the Early-Age Mechanical Behaviour of Oil-Well Cement Paste. *Cem. Concr. Res.* **2019**, *117*, 91–102. [CrossRef]
8. McElroy, P.; Emadi, H.; Surowiec, K.; Casadonte, D.J. Mechanical, Rheological, and Stability Performance of Simulated in-Situ Cured Oil Well Cement Slurries Reinforced with Alumina Nanofibers. *J. Pet. Sci. Eng.* **2019**, *183*, 106415. [CrossRef]
9. Xu, Y.; Liu, M.; Li, P.; Zhu, L.; Xia, X.; Zhang, C.; Yu, Y.; Guo, J. Effect of Dispersant Types on the Rheological and Mechanical Properties of Oil Well Cement Paste with Nanosilica. *Constr. Build. Mater.* **2021**, *271*, 121576. [CrossRef]
10. Alsaba, M.T.; Al Dushaishi, M.F.; Abbas, A.K. A Comprehensive Review of Nanoparticles Applications in the Oil and Gas Industry. *J. Pet. Explor. Prod. Technol.* **2020**, *10*, 1389–1399. [CrossRef]
11. Zhe, Z.; Yuxiu, A. Nanotechnology for the Oil and Gas Industry—An Overview of Recent Progress. *Nanotechnol. Rev.* **2018**, *7*, 341–353. [CrossRef]
12. Thakkar, A.; Raval, A.; Chandra, S.; Shah, M.; Sircar, A. A Comprehensive Review of the Application of Nano-Silica in Oil Well Cementing. *Petroleum* **2020**, *6*, 123–129. [CrossRef]
13. Atiq Orakzai, M. Hybrid Effect of Nano-Alumina and Nano-Titanium Dioxide on Mechanical Properties of Concrete. *Case Stud. Constr. Mater.* **2021**, *14*, e00483. [CrossRef]
14. de La Roij, R.; Egyed, C.; Lips, J.P. Nano-Engineered Oil Well Cement Improves Flexibility and Increases Compressive Strength: A Laboratory Study. In Proceedings of the All Days, Noordwijk, The Netherlands, 12–14 June 2012.
15. de Paula, J.N.; Calixto, J.M.; Ladeira, L.O.; Ludvig, P.; Souza, T.C.C.; Rocha, J.M.; de Melo, A.A.V. Mechanical and Rheological Behavior of Oil-Well Cement Slurries Produced with Clinker Containing Carbon Nanotubes. *J. Pet. Sci. Eng.* **2014**, *122*, 274–279. [CrossRef]
16. Ahmed, A.; Mahmoud, A.A.; Elkatatny, S. The Use of the Granite Waste Material as an Alternative for Silica Flour in Oil-Well Cementing. *ACS Omega* **2020**, *5*, 32341–32348. [CrossRef]
17. Maagi, M.T.; Lupyana, S.D.; Jun, G. Nanotechnology in the Petroleum Industry: Focus on the Use of Nanosilica in Oil-Well Cementing Applications—A Review. *J. Pet. Sci. Eng.* **2020**, *193*, 107397. [CrossRef]
18. Raki, L.; Beaudoin, J.; Alizadeh, R.; Makar, J.; Sato, T. Cement and Concrete Nanoscience and Nanotechnology. *Materials* **2010**, *3*, 918–942. [CrossRef]
19. Baragwiha, M.B.; Fikeni, K.G.; Zhao, Y.; Cheng, G.; Ge, H.; Pang, X. Influence of Various Nanomaterials on the Rheology and Hydration Kinetics of Oil Well Cement. *Materials* **2023**, *16*, 6514. [CrossRef] [PubMed]
20. Sun, J.; Cao, X.; Xu, Z.; Yu, Z.; Zhang, Y.; Hou, G.; Shen, X. Contribution of Core/Shell $TiO_2@SiO_2$ Nanoparticles to the Hydration of Portland Cement. *Constr. Build. Mater.* **2020**, *233*, 117127. [CrossRef]
21. Han, B.; Li, Z.; Zhang, L.; Zeng, S.; Yu, X.; Han, B.; Ou, J. Reactive Powder Concrete Reinforced with Nano SiO_2-Coated TiO_2. *Constr. Build. Mater.* **2017**, *148*, 104–112. [CrossRef]
22. Batista, G.d.S.; Takimi, A.S.; da Costa, E.M. Hardened Oil Well Cement Paste Modified with $TiO_2@SiO_2$ Nanoparticles: Physical and Chemical Properties. *Constr. Build. Mater.* **2023**, *367*, 130282. [CrossRef]
23. Batista, G.d.S.; Takimi, A.S.; da Costa, E.M. Chemical Changes in the Composition of Oil Well Cement with Core/Shell Nanoparticle Addition under CO_2 Geological Storage Conditions. *Energy Fuels* **2024**, *38*, 22947–22958. [CrossRef]
24. *ASTM C494/C494M*; Standard Specification for Chemical Admixtures for Concrete. ASTM: West Conshohocken, PE, USA, 2017.
25. Roussel, N.; Ovarlez, G.; Garrault, S.; Brumaud, C. The Origins of Thixotropy of Fresh Cement Pastes. *Cem. Concr. Res.* **2012**, *42*, 148–157. [CrossRef]
26. Yuan, Q.; Zhou, D.; Khayat, K.H.; Feys, D.; Shi, C. On the Measurement of Evolution of Structural Build-up of Cement Paste with Time by Static Yield Stress Test vs. Small Amplitude Oscillatory Shear Test. *Cem. Concr. Res.* **2017**, *99*, 183–189. [CrossRef]
27. Xu, Y.; Yu, Y.; Li, P.; Liu, M.; Zhu, L.; Zhang, H.; Zhang, C.; Hu, G.; Hu, M.; Guo, J. Rheological Behavior of Oil Well Cement Pastes Containing Various Types of Dispersants at Different Hydration Temperatures. *Colloids Surf. A Physicochem. Eng. Asp.* **2021**, *624*, 126821. [CrossRef]

28. Qian, Y.; Kawashima, S. Distinguishing Dynamic and Static Yield Stress of Fresh Cement Mortars through Thixotropy. *Cem. Concr. Compos.* **2018**, *86*, 288–296. [CrossRef]
29. Neubauer, C.M.; Yang, M.; Jennings, H.M. Interparticle Potential and Sedimentation Behavior of Cement Suspensions: Effects of Admixtures. *Adv. Cem. Based Mater.* **1998**, *8*, 17–27. [CrossRef]
30. Yoshioka, K.; Sakai, E.; Daimon, M.; Kitahara, A. Role of Steric Hindrance in the Performance of Superplasticizers for Concrete. *J. Am. Ceram. Soc.* **1997**, *80*, 2667–2671. [CrossRef]
31. Yang, H.; Monasterio, M.; Zheng, D.; Cui, H.; Tang, W.; Bao, X.; Chen, X. Effects of Nano Silica on the Properties of Cement-Based Materials: A Comprehensive Review. *Constr. Build. Mater.* **2021**, *282*, 122715. [CrossRef]
32. Kolawole, J.T.; Combrinck, R.; Boshoff, W.P. Measuring the Thixotropy of Conventional Concrete: The Influence of Viscosity Modifying Agent, Superplasticiser and Water. *Constr. Build. Mater.* **2019**, *225*, 853–867. [CrossRef]
33. Moller, P.; Fall, A.; Chikkadi, V.; Derks, D.; Bonn, D. An Attempt to Categorize Yield Stress Fluid Behaviour. *Philos. Trans. R. Soc. A Math. Phys. Eng. Sci.* **2009**, *367*, 5139–5155. [CrossRef]
34. Dinkgreve, M.; Paredes, J.; Denn, M.M.; Bonn, D. On Different Ways of Measuring "the" Yield Stress. *J. Nonnewton Fluid. Mech.* **2016**, *238*, 233–241. [CrossRef]
35. Maagi, M.T.; Jun, G. Effect of the Particle Size of Nanosilica on Early Age Compressive Strength in Oil-Well Cement Paste. *Constr. Build. Mater.* **2020**, *262*, 120393. [CrossRef]
36. Chithra, S.; Senthil Kumar, S.R.R.; Chinnaraju, K. The Effect of Colloidal Nano-Silica on Workability, Mechanical and Durability Properties of High Performance Concrete with Copper Slag as Partial Fine Aggregate. *Constr. Build. Mater.* **2016**, *113*, 794–804. [CrossRef]
37. Phan, T.H.; Chaouche, M.; Moranville, M. Influence of Organic Admixtures on the Rheological Behaviour of Cement Pastes. *Cem. Concr. Res.* **2006**, *36*, 1807–1813. [CrossRef]
38. Palacios, M.; Sanz-Pont, D.; Kunhi Mohamed, A.; Boscaro, F.; Reiter, L.; Marchon, D.; Mantellato, S.; Flatt, R.J. Heating Cement to Slow down Its Hydration: The Unexpected Role of PCE Interpolymer Bridge Formation. *Cem. Concr. Res.* **2022**, *156*, 106765. [CrossRef]
39. Marchon, D.; Juilland, P.; Gallucci, E.; Frunz, L.; Flatt, R.J. Molecular and Submolecular Scale Effects of Comb-copolymers on Tri-calcium Silicate Reactivity: Toward Molecular Design. *J. Am. Ceram. Soc.* **2017**, *100*, 817–841. [CrossRef]
40. Mostafa, A.M.; Yahia, A. New Approach to Assess Build-up of Cement-Based Suspensions. *Cem. Concr. Res.* **2016**, *85*, 174–182 [CrossRef]
41. Chan, S.S.L.; Pennings, R.M.; Edwards, L.; Franks, G.V. 3D Printing of Clay for Decorative Architectural Applications: Effect of Solids Volume Fraction on Rheology and Printability. *Addit. Manuf.* **2020**, *35*, 101335. [CrossRef]

Disclaimer/Publisher's Note: The statements, opinions and data contained in all publications are solely those of the individual author(s) and contributor(s) and not of MDPI and/or the editor(s). MDPI and/or the editor(s) disclaim responsibility for any injury to people or property resulting from any ideas, methods, instructions or products referred to in the content.

materials

MDPI

Article

Study on Performance and Engineering Application of Novel Expansive Superfine Cement Slurry

Xiao Feng [1,*], Xiaowei Cao [2], Lianghao Li [1], Zhiming Li [2], Qingsong Zhang [3], Wen Sun [1], Benao Hou [1], Chi Liu [3,4] and Zhenzhong Shi [1]

1 School of Transportation Engineering, Shandong Jianzhu University, Jinan 250101, China; 2022155138@stu.sdjzu.edu.cn (L.L.); 2023155138@stu.sdjzu.edu.cn (W.S.); 2023155140@stu.sdjzu.edu.cn (B.H.); 2024155112@stu.sdjzu.edu.cn (Z.S.)
2 Xuzhou Metro Group Co., Ltd., Xuzhou 221000, China; caoxiaowei@xzdtjt.com (X.C.); lizhiming@xzdtjt.com (Z.L.)
3 School of Civil Engineering, Shandong University, Jinan 250061, China; zhangqingsong@sdu.edu.cn (Q.Z.); 202420860@mail.sdu.edu.cn (C.L.)
4 Jinan Rail Transit Group Co., Ltd., Jinan 250000, China
* Correspondence: fengxiao19@sdjzu.edu.cn

Abstract: Superfine cement is widely used in building reinforcement and repair, special concrete manufacturing, and environmental protection engineering due to its high toughness, high durability, good bonding strength, and environmental friendliness. However, there are some problems in superfine cement slurry, such as high bleeding rate, prolonged setting time, and consolidated body volume retraction. In this article, on the premise of using the excellent injectability of superfine cement slurry, the fluidity, setting time, reinforcement strength, and volume expansion rate of novel expansive superfine cement slurries with varying proportions were analyzed by adding expansion agent UEA, naphthalene-based water reducer FDN-C, and triisopropanolamine accelerating agent TIPA. The results show that under most mix ratios, the bleeding rate and fluidity of the novel superfine cement slurry initially increase and decrease with rising water-reducing agent dosage. The initial setting time generally decreases with accelerating agent dosage, reaching a minimum value of 506 min, representing a 33.68% reduction compared to the benchmark group (traditional superfine cement). Under normal conditions, the compressive strength of the net slurry consolidation body is positively correlated with expansion agent dosage, achieving maximum strengths of 8.11 MPa at three days and 6.98 MPa at 28 days; these values are respectively higher by 6.7 MPa and 2.6 MPa compared to those in the benchmark group. On the seventh day, the volume expansion rate of the traditional superfine cement solidified sand body ranges from −0.19% to −0.1%, while that for the corresponding body formed from the novel superfine cement is between 0.41% and 1.33%, representing a difference of 0.6–1.43%. After the on-site treatment of water and sand-gushing strata, the core monitor rate of the inspection hole exceeds 70%. The permeability coefficient of the stratum decreases to a range between 1.47×10^{-6} and 8.14×10^{-6} cm/s, resulting in nearly a thousandfold increase in stratum impermeability compared to its original state. Hence, the findings of this research hold practical importance for the future application of such materials in the development of stratum reinforcement or building repair.

Keywords: superfine cement; setting time; reinforcement strength; volume expansion; engineering application

check for updates

Citation: Feng, X.; Cao, X.; Li, L.; Li, Z.; Zhang, Q.; Sun, W.; Hou, B.; Liu, C.; Shi, Z. Study on Performance and Engineering Application of Novel Expansive Superfine Cement Slurry. *Materials* **2024**, *17*, 5597. https://doi.org/10.3390/ma17225597

Academic Editors: Oldrich Sucharda and Geo Paul

Received: 12 October 2024
Revised: 10 November 2024
Accepted: 14 November 2024
Published: 15 November 2024

Copyright: © 2024 by the authors. Licensee MDPI, Basel, Switzerland. This article is an open access article distributed under the terms and conditions of the Creative Commons Attribution (CC BY) license (https://creativecommons.org/licenses/by/4.0/).

1. Introduction

The stable progress of infrastructure construction in China has led to the emergence of projects such as highways, railways, and urban subways traversing the Quaternary sand layer. The loose structure and intricate seepage characteristics often result in disasters such as water gushing, sand collapse, and structural water leakage. Grouting emerges as the predominant technical solution to prevent and manage such disasters. This method involves injecting a solidifiable slurry into the crevices or voids of rock and soil masses to enhance their physical and mechanical properties. However, when grouting in medium-fine sand layers, conventional Portland cement presents issues related to its larger particle size and higher bleeding rate. In contrast, traditional superfine cement is associated with prolonged gel time and susceptibility to volume shrinkage of the solidified mass. Therefore exploring novel superfine cement slurries suitable for grouting in medium-fine sand layers is of significant scientific importance.

Currently, numerous scholars have conducted significant experimental studies on the modification of superfine cement materials. Han Fenglei et al. [1] investigated the effects of the total volume fraction of SiO_2 gas glue and sand particles at 60% on the flowability, dry density, water absorption, thermal conductivity, mechanical properties and microstructure of superfine cement-based materials. The results showed that with the increase of aerogel content from 0% to 60%, the material fluidity decreased by 7.3–22.3% and the dry density gradually decreased while the water absorption increased. Zhang Jianwu et al. [2] explored the influence and mechanism of soluble P_2O_5 on the early-age hydration behavior of superfine sulfoaluminate cement, finding that soluble P_2O_5 has a minor effect on setting time but can significantly increase the formation of early calcarenite. When the soluble P_2O_5 content was between 0% and 1.5%, the early strength of superfine sulfoaluminate cement-based double liquid grouting materials increased with the soluble P_2O_5 content. Zhao Weiquan et al. [3] investigated the pH value of superfine cement slurry at different ages under silica fume content conditions and a water–binder ratio set at 1.4. They determined that when silica fume content is more than 40%, SiO_2 content is more than 50%, and the Ca/Si molar ratio of C-S-H gel is less than 0. 8, the pH value of the consolidation body is less than 11. Tongqiang Xiao et al. [4] to solve the problem of grouting reinforcement of micro-fractures surrounding rock in deep roadways, the influence characteristics of auxiliary materials and additives on slurry flow were analyzed, and the composition and proportion of superfine cement-based composite grouting materials were determined: superfine cement accounted for 89.4%, superfine coal ash accounted for 5%, ultrafine mineral powder accounted for 5%, naphthalene water reducing agent accounted for 3~5‰, and lignin sulfonate calcium accounted for 1~3‰. When the water cement ratio is 1.0 and the water reducer content is 3 ‰, the slurry has the advantages of strong permeability, strong fluidity, and low water bleeding rate. Dongyue Zhang et al. [5] examined the effect of superfine cement content on the strength and microstructure characteristics of solidified materials through uniaxial compression tests, fragment fractal dimension analysis, mercury intrusion porosimetry experiments, and scanning electron microscopy. The results showed that the superfine cement content increased from 0% to 70% when the water–cement ratio was 0.45:1, the compressive strength of the grouted specimens increased from 16.7 MPa to 26.3 MPa, and the fractal dimension decreased from 1.8645 to 1.2301. Shengnan Xu et al. [6] investigated various methods, including mechanical grinding, sulfate activation, and alkali activation, to enhance the reactivity of mineral admixtures. They also analyzed the evolution process of cementitious materials from microstructure to macroscopic mechanical behavior using a laser granularity analyzer and scanning electron microscopy. It is concluded that under the condition that the compressive strength is not lower than that of the control group (without mineral admixture), the content of mineral admixture can be increased to 50%, 70%, and 90% after mechanical grinding, sulfate activation, and alkali activation, respectively. Hao Li et al. [7] utilized oil well cement and superfine cement as raw materials to produce a composite material with excellent compressive and tensile strength by incorporating green carbonation calcium and steel fibers. The strength test results on day 28 showed that the compressive and tensile strength of the material increased from 44 MPa to 74 MPa and from 3.6 MPa to 18.3 MPa compared with the material without the addition of micron-size green silicon carbide. Fei Wang et al. [8] developed the modified coral aggregate concrete, and the effect of using modified superfine cement on its workability and strength is investigated. Experimental results show that the strength of the modified coral aggregates cured for a short duration is slightly lower than that of unmodified coral aggregates, whereas that cured for 28 days is approximately 20% higher than that of unmodified coral aggregates. Longji Wu et al. [9] developed a novel polyacrylate emulsion-modified superfine cement slurry composed of superfine cement, polyacrylic ester butadiene, defoaming agent, and accelerating agent; they compared the workability, mechanical properties, and microstructure of modified superfine cement slurries with different proportions.

Meanwhile, considerable research has been conducted on treating sandy soil layers with superfine cement. Murat Mollamahmutoglu et al. [10] investigated the compressive strength, permeability, expansion potential, and compressibility of high plasticity clay modified by slag-based superfine cement. They observed that wet curing and air drying conditions enhanced the strength of high plasticity clay when treated with slag-based superfine cement while slightly reducing permeability, expansion potential, and compressibility. Xiaoli Liu et al. [11] performed a theoretical analysis on sleeve valve grouting in sandy soil stratum using the discrete element method to simulate the diffusion behavior of Bingham fluids under varying pressures and to establish the relationship between grouting pressure, diffusion radius, and initial fracture pressure. Wenshuai Li et al. [12] enhanced the samples' early shear strength, microstructure, and slurry viscosity by incorporating different particle sizes of cement and nano-SiO_2. Results showed that the optimal superplasticizer dose levels of 1.5% and 0.75% were recommended for superfine cement grouts with and without nano-SiO_2 addition, respectively. Eybhan et al. [13] measured the viscosity, bleeding capacity, setting time, strength, and permeability of superfine cement and fine fly ash mixtures with varying water–cement ratios. Their findings indicated that adding fly ash can enhance the compressive strength of the slurry. Jian Zhang et al. [14] discussed the feasibility of silty fine sand as a substitute sand source for backfill grouting liquid, and research shows that the grouting liquid with the best performance has advantages in terms of 7 d and 28 d strength, bleeding rate, and cementation strength. The stability of this grouting liquid is good, and 44.6% of costs can be saved. Fei Ye et al. [15] investigated the engineering characteristics of wind and sand tunnels using the Shenmu No. 1 tunnel as a case study. They determined the proportion of superfine cement slurry and modified water glass slurry. Yuke Wang et al. [16] compared three traditional grouting materials with a self-developed permeable polymer, analyzing the slurry viscosity, setting time, the strength of the silty sand consolidation body, water stability, and permeability coefficient. Regarding water stability, the specimens reinforced with the permeable polymer showed a minimal reduction of 10.87% after 7 days of immersion, exhibiting excellent water stability. Ying Cui et al. [17] prepared high-performance grouting materials (DS slurry) for water-rich silty fine sand stratum using water glass as the base material and diacid ester as the curing agent. The reaction mechanism between the water glass and the curing agent was studied using infrared spectroscopy and scanning electron microscopy, concluding that DS grouting exhibits adjustable setting time, high strength, and good durability. Grzegorz Ludwik Golewski [18] proposed a most commonly used mineral additive (i.e., fly ash (FA)) combined with nano-silica (NS) as a partial substitute for ordinary Portland cement (OPC) binder. The study found that after adding 15% FA and 5% NS additives to the binder, all mechanical parameters of concrete increased by about 20%.

In the past, another slurry was often introduced to improve the performance of ultrafine cement slurry to form a two-liquid grouting mode. At the same time, the research content is less related to the volume change of net slurry solidified body and solidified sand body of ultrafine cement slurry. This study aims to tackle the challenges of high water bleeding rate, prolonged setting time, and susceptibility to volume shrinkage in traditional superfine cement slurry while ensuring excellent injectability in medium-fine sand layers. By incorporating expansion agent UEA, naphthalene-based water reducer FDN-C, and triisopropanolamine accelerating agent TIPA, the fluidity, gel time, reinforcement strength, and volume expansion rate of novel superfine cement slurries with varying proportions are analyzed. Subsequently, focusing on medium-fine sand, the research investigates the diffusion distance, reinforcement strength, and volume expansion rate of the novel superfine cement slurry within this stratum. Ultimately, the practical application has confirmed the engineering viability of the novel expansive superfine cement.

2. Materials and Methods

2.1. Raw Materials

The cement utilized in the experiment is superfine cement produced by Sino-German Xinya Factory in Jinan, China. The fineness is 800 mesh, the specific surface area is 800 m^2/kg, and the average particle size is 5 μm. The main characteristics of 800-mesh superfine cement include high strength, low permeability, good durability, and environmental protection. Because of its small particle size and large specific surface area, the strength of ultrafine cement is higher than that of ordinary cement.

The expansion agent used was the UEA concrete expansion agent, produced by Huayu Building Materials Factory in Nanchang, China. The main components are calcium sulphoaluminate clinker, alunite, and gypsum. The appearance is a grayish-white powder, the specific gravity is 2.8–3.0, and the specific surface area is not less than 250 m^2/kg. The main characteristics of UEA concrete expansion agents include preventing shrinkage cracking, generating chemical pressure, low dosage, and low alkali content. For example, when the outside completely constrains the mortar consolidation body mixed with the UEA expansion agent, its expansion force will act internally. Ettringite crystals fill the pores to form a very dense, non-shrinkage mortar.

The water-reducing agent used was naphthalene water-reducing agent FDN-C, which is produced by Shandong Wanshan Chemical Co., Ltd., Weifang, China. It is a yellowish powder with a density of 80 g/cm^3, a purity of 99%, a chloride ion content of <0.5%, and a sulfate content of <18%. The main characteristics of naphthalene water-reducing agent FDN-C include solubility in water and stable physical and chemical properties. It also has high dispersion and low foaming, which can significantly improve the fluidity of concrete. The strength and early strength of concrete after adding FDN-C are remarkable; the strength of one day and three days is increased by 60–95%, and the strength of twenty-eight days is increased by 25–40%.

The rapid setting admixture used was the triisopropanolamine accelerating agent TIPA, produced by the Jinyu Chemical Plant in Dehui, China. The molecular formula is $C_9H_{21}NO_3$, a white crystal with a density of 0.994 g/mL and a solubility of 83 g/100 mL in water at 20 °C. The characteristics of triisopropanolamine accelerator mainly include: (1) It can improve the density of concrete by inhibiting the occurrence of hydration reaction, thereby enhancing the strength and durability of concrete. (2) It can increase the ductility and tensile strength of concrete, make the concrete material more flexible, and reduce the occurrence of concrete cracks. (3) It can form a three-dimensional network structure during the hardening process of concrete to prevent cracks in the concrete during drying shrinkage

2.2. Test Methods and Plan

The flowability of the slurry was evaluated using the XN-Φ36 mm × 60 mm × 60 mm Cement paste flow conical die, as described in the Testing Methods of Cement and Concrete for Highway Engineering [19]. The setting time of the slurry was determined with a Vicat apparatus, following the testing method outlined in Test Methods for Water Requirement of Normal Consistency, Setting Time, and Soundness of the Portland Cements [20]. The compressive strength of the consolidation body was assessed using a material strength comprehensive tester, the testing method specified in Test Method for Axial Compressive Strength of Cement Concrete Cylinder [21]. The expansion volume of the specimen was measured using a comparator, following the testing method outlined in the Test Method for Determining Expansive Ratio of Expansive Cement [22]. The test plan is shown in Figure 1

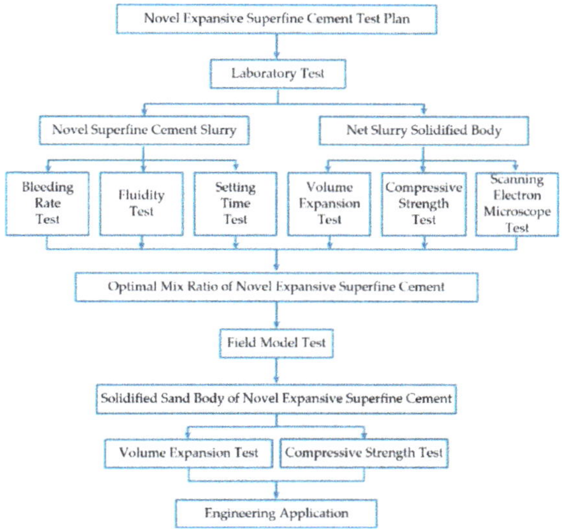

Figure 1. The test plan of novel expansive superfine cement.

3. Laboratory Test and Analysis

3.1. Orthogonal Experiment Design

Under the condition of a water–cement ratio of 1:1 (water 400 g, superfine cement 400 g), after conducting extensive research on the literature, the dosage ranges of the expansion agent UEA, naphthalene-based water reducer FDN-C, and triisopropanolamine accelerating agent TIPA were initially selected (are shown in Table 1). Following the concept and method of orthogonal experimental design, a three-factor, three-level experimental design was implemented (shown in Table 2).

Table 1. Orthogonal test design table.

Level	Factor		
	UEA (Expansion Agent)/g	**FDN-C (Water Reducer)/g**	**TIPA (Accelerating Agent)/g**
1	20 (5%)	0.4 (0.1%)	1.2 (0.3%)
2	30 (7.5%)	0.6 (0.15%)	2.6 (0.65%)
3	40 (10%)	0.8 (0.2%)	4 (1%)

Note: Percentages in parentheses represent each admixture's dosage relative to cement mass (400 g).

Table 2. Experiment scheme.

NO.	U/g	F/g	T/g	NO.	U/g	F/g	T/g	NO.	U/g	F/g	T/g
1	0	0	0	11			1.2	20			1.2
2			1.2	12		0.4	2.6	21		0.4	2.6
3		0.4	2.6	13			4.0	22			4.0
4			4.0	14			1.2	23			1.2
5			1.2	15	30	0.6	2.6	24	40	0.6	2.6
6	20	0.6	2.6	16			4.0	25			4.0
7			4.0	17			1.2	26			1.2
8			1.2	18		0.8	2.6	27		0.8	2.6
9		0.8	2.6	19			4.0	28			4.0
10			4.0								

Note: Expansion agent UEA, naphthalene-based water reducer FDN-C, and triisopropanolamine accelerating agent TIPA are designated U, F, and T, respectively.

3.2. Analysis of Bleeding Rate and Fluidity of Slurry

The study aimed to investigate the influence of naphthalene sulfonate superplasticizer FDN-C on the bleeding rate and fluidity of novel superfine cement slurry. Data analysis was conducted using specific groups (1, 4, 7, 10, 13, 16, 19, 22, 25, and 28) as representatives. Detailed results are presented in Figure 2. In Figure 2, the expansion agent UEA, naphthalene-based water reducer FDN-C, and triisopropanolamine accelerating agent TIPA are represented as U, F, and T respectively. For example, $U_{30}F_{0.6}T_{2.6}$ indicates that the UEA dosage is at a level of 30 g, while the dosages for FDN-C and TIPA are at levels of 0.6 g and 2.6 g, respectively; $U_{20}T_{4.0}$ indicates a UEA dosage of 20 g with varying dosages for FDN-C (ranging from 0 g to 0.8 g) and a TIPA dosage of 4 g.

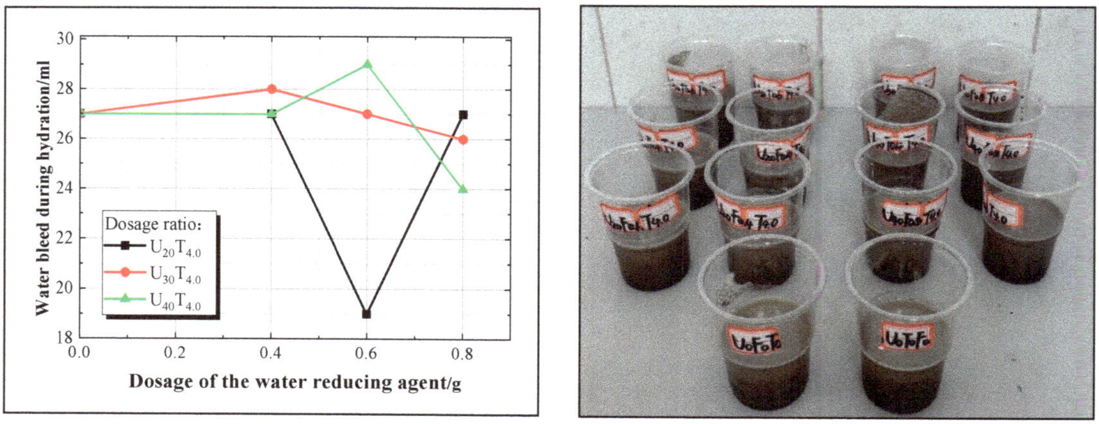

(**a**)

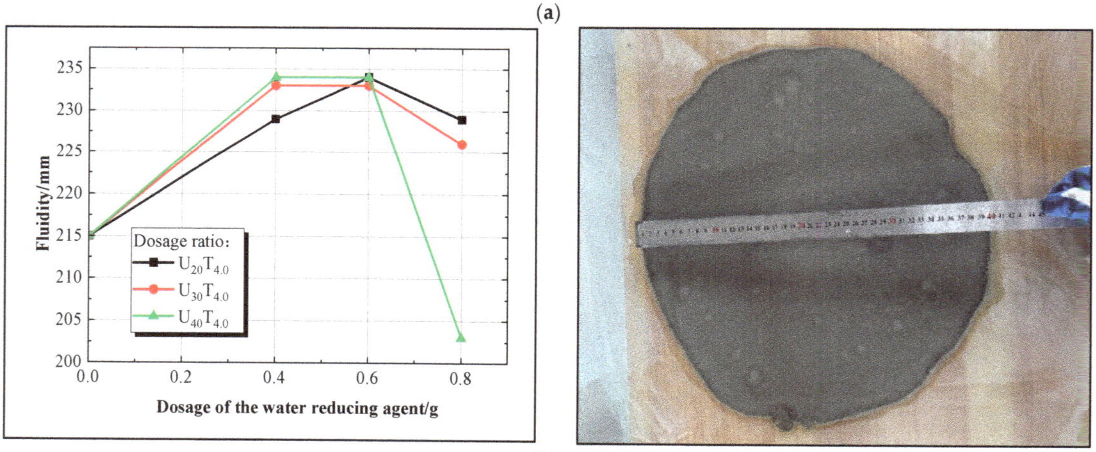

(**b**)

Figure 2. (**a**) Curve of variation in slurry water bleed; (**b**) curve of slurry fluidity variation.

Figure 2a demonstrates that the initial water bleed of the benchmark group (traditional superfine cement) is 27 mL. When considering the $U_{20}T_{4.0}$ ratio, the water bleed rate of the slurry initially decreases, then increases with the rise in water reducer dosage, reaching a minimum of 19 mL. For the $U_{30}T_{4.0}$ and $U_{40}T_{4.0}$ ratios, the water bleed rate of the slurry first increases, then decreases as the water reducer dosage increases, with minimum values of 26 mL and 24 mL, respectively. In Figure 2b, the initial flowability of the benchmark group is 215 mm. The flowability of the novel superfine cement slurry with $U_{20}T_{4.0}$, $U_{30}T_{4.0}$

and $U_{40}T_{4.0}$ ratios all exhibit an increasing trend followed by a decreasing trend with the increased water reducer dosage, peaking at 235 mm. Notably, the $U_{40}T_{4.0}$ ratio shows a significant decrease in flowability, reaching a minimum value of 203 mm, which is 5.6% lower than that of the benchmark group.

The analysis indicates that introducing a water reducer into the superfine cement slurry leads to the dispersion of superfine cement particles, which is attributed to the static repulsion induced by the water reducer. This dispersion improves the suspension stability of the cement particles, thereby reducing the bleeding rate of the slurry. Furthermore, the adsorption film formed by the water reducer on the surface of superfine cement particles demonstrates a favorable lubricating effect, effectively reducing inter-particle sliding resistance and enhancing slurry flowability [16,23]. However, studies have indicated that exceeding a certain threshold in water reducer dosage may decrease slurry flowability. In conclusion, the slurry ratio with a low bleeding rate and high fluidity was initially selected, meeting the requirements in groups 4, 7, 10, 13, 16, 19, 22, and 25.

3.3. Setting Time Analysis

This study conducted a comparative analysis of the test results from groups 1, 2, 3, 4, 11–13, and 20–25 to investigate the impact of the accelerating agent TIPA on the setting time of the novel superfine cement slurry. Detailed findings are presented in Figure 3.

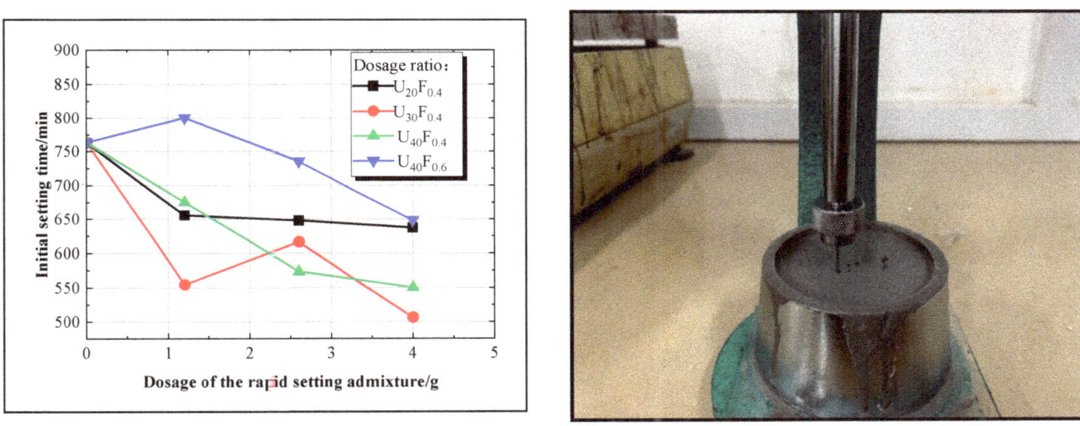

Figure 3. Curve of setting time and its experimental setup.

The analysis presented in Figure 3 illustrates a general reduction in the initial setting time as the dosage of the accelerating agent TIPA increases. Only the slurry with the $U_{40}F_{0.6}T_{1.2}$ ratio exhibited an initial setting time that exceeded the benchmark group (763 min). The $U_{30}F_{0.4}T_{4.0}$ ratio achieved the shortest initial setting time of 506 min, representing a 33.68% reduction compared to the benchmark group. Similarly, the $U_{40}F_{0.4}T_{4.0}$ ratio reached a minimum initial setting time of 550 min, 27.92% shorter than the benchmark group value. Consequently, incorporating TIPA as a rapid-setting admixture significantly reduces the initial setting time of superfine cement slurry.

Analysis indicates that when the dosage ranges from 0.3% to 1.0%, triisopropanolamine (TIPA) diminishes the interfacial tension between superfine cement particles and water, accelerates the hydration process, and interacts with tricalcium aluminate (C_3A) to facilitate the formation of calcium sulfoaluminate (AFt), ultimately reducing the setting time of the slurry [24–27]. Consequently, this study made a preliminary selection for the slurry mixture with an initial setting time shorter than the benchmark group, meeting requirements for groups 2–4, 11–13, 20–22, and 24–25.

3.4. Investigation of Volume Expansion and Compressive Strength of Net Slurry Consolidation Body

3.4.1. Analysis of Volume Expansion of Net Slurry Solidified Body

To address the issue of volume shrinkage in the later stages of the solidification body for net superfine cement slurry, varying dosages of expansion agent UEA were introduced. The expansion rates of specimens at the age of day 3, day 7, day 14, and day 28 for groups 1, 2, 3, 4, 13, 22, and 25 were determined using a comparator, as shown in Figure 4.

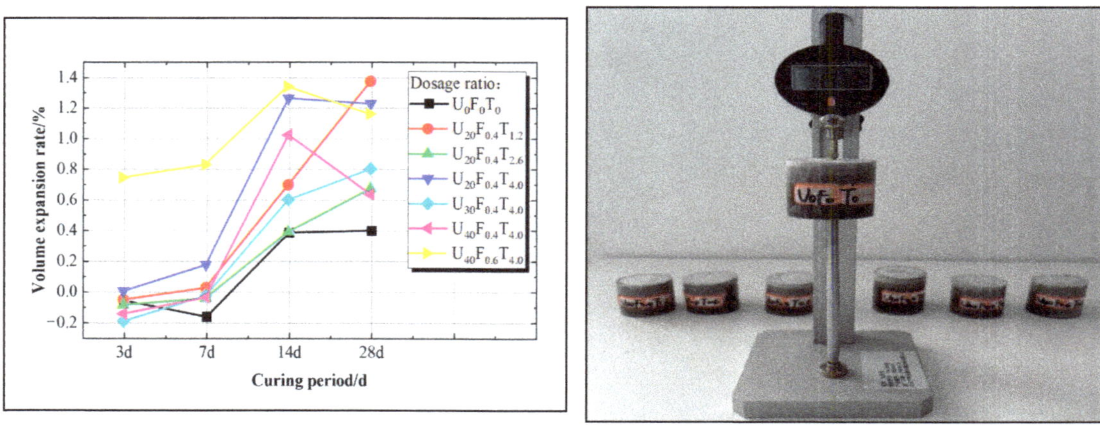

Figure 4. Expansion rate curve of net slurry solidified body and its experimental setup.

Figure 4 illustrates that the volume of the net slurry consolidation body in the benchmark group experienced a slight shrinkage (approximately −0.2%) from day 3 to day 7. In contrast, the volume of the net slurry consolidation body expanded significantly in the $U_{40}F_{0.6}T_{4.0}$ and $U_{20}F_{0.4}T_{4.0}$ groups. The volume of the other groups did not expand compared with the original volume, but compensation for previous volume shrinkage occurred. With the curing period extended, this study significantly enhanced the expansion performance of the novel superfine cement solidification body. For instance, on day 14, the volume expansion rate of $U_{20}F_{0.4}T_{4.0}$ reached 1.2%, which was 0.8% higher than that of the benchmark group, and on day 28, the volume expansion rate of $U_{20}F_{0.4}T_{1.2}$ was 1.4%, which was 1.0% higher than that of the benchmark group. Notably, when using an expansion agent dosage of 40 g (10%), the $U_{40}F_{0.6}T_{4.0}$ ratio exhibited the highest volume expansion, with rates on day 3, day 7, day 14, and day 28 of 0.747%, 0.831%, 1.343%, and 1.164% respectively, which were 0.803%, 0.992%, 0.956%, and 0.528% higher than those of the benchmark group.

Analysis indicates that adding expansion agent UEA to superfine cement slurry enhances the compaction of the net slurry consolidation body by increasing the formation of calcium stones. The delayed formation of calcium scleral crystals mitigates the increase in capillary tension, leading to a significant increase in the volume expansion rate of the solidified body. Moreover, the generation of calcium stone is proportional to the content of the expansion agent, thereby correspondingly enhancing the effect of volume expansion.

3.4.2. Analysis of Compressive Strength of Net Slurry Consolidation Body

After completing the expansion volume test of the net slurry consolidation body for each group of new superfine cement, the compressive strength of the cylindrical specimens at day three and day 28 ages is determined using a comprehensive material strength tester, as shown in Figure 5.

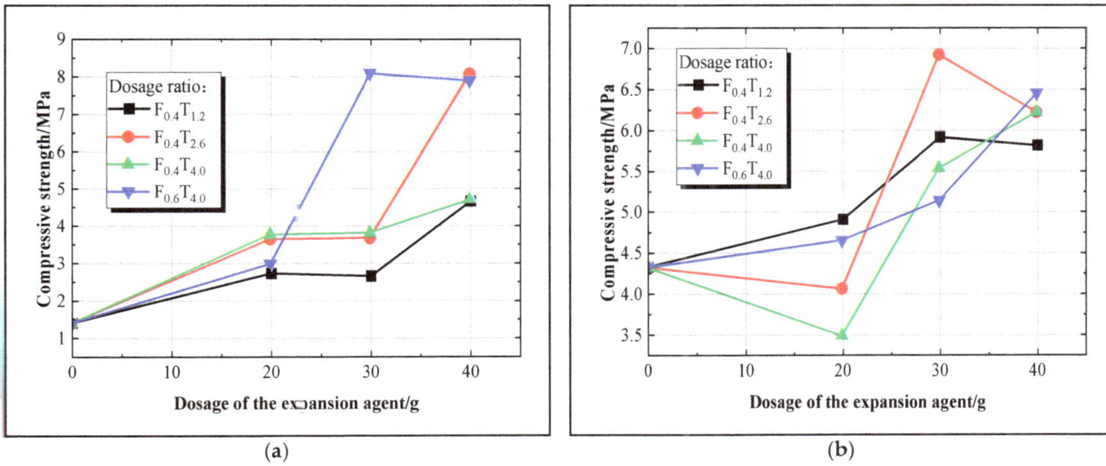

Figure 5. (**a**) Day 3 compressive strength curve of net slurry solidified body; (**b**) day 28 compressive strength curve of net slurry solidified body.

According to Figure 5a, the compressive strength of the benchmark group was 1.41 MPa on the third day of curing age, and it shows a positive correlation between the compressive strength of the new superfine cement net slurry consolidation body and the dosage of the expansion agent UEA. When the ratio is $U_{30}F_{0.6}T_{4.0}$, the third-day compressive strength of the net slurry solidified body peaks at 8.11 MPa. The trend of the $F_{0.4}T_{2.6}$ and $F_{0.4}T_{4.0}$ ratios are essentially similar. As shown in Figure 5b, the 28th-day compressive strength of the benchmark group was 4.33 MPa, while the compressive strength of the $U_{30}F_{0.4}T_{2.6}$ ratio reached a peak of 6.93 MPa, demonstrating a 60% increase in strength compared to the benchmark group. In most cases, there is a positive correlation between expansion agent dosage and 28th-day compressive strength; however, under the specific condition with an expansion agent dosage of 20 g, the strengths of the $F_{0.4}T_{2.6}$ and $F_{0.4}T_{4.0}$ are 4.07 MPa and 3.50 MPa, respectively, which are 6% and 19.17% lower than the initial values, indicating that these ratios are suboptimal.

Analysis suggests that the UEA expansion agent contains active components, such as Al_2O_3 and $CaSO_4$, which react with the $Ca(OH)_2$ in the superfine cementitious material to generate calcium stone (AFt). This process accelerates the early hydration rate of the new superfine cement slurry, increasing the internal stress of the slurry and enhancing the compressive strength of the consolidation body [28–30].

Based on a comprehensive analysis of the indicators, groups 4, 13, 22, and 25 have been selected as the optimal mix ratios for subsequent field testing to assess the actual grouting effect of the new expansion superfine cement material.

3.5 *Scanning Electron Microscope Analysis of Net Slurry Consolidation Body*

Group 1, Group 4, Group 13, Group 22, and Group 25 specimens were cured for seven days and dried at 20~25 °C for one day to make specimens with side lengths < 8 mm and thicknesses < 5 mm. The microstructure was analyzed by scanning electron microscopy (SEM), as shown in Figure 6. Due to space limitations, only the element analysis diagram of Group 22 is shown, as shown in Figure 7.

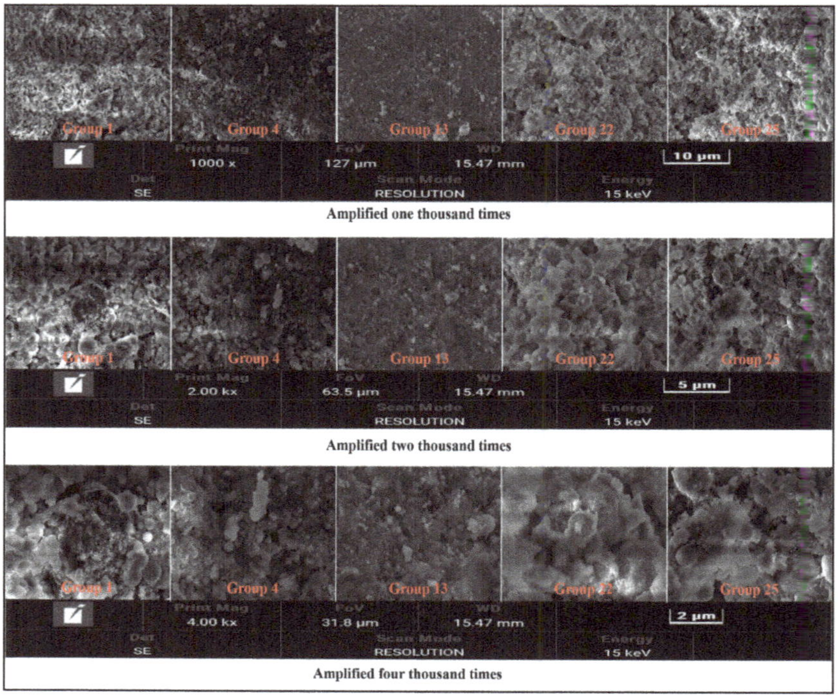

Figure 6. The microstructure of each group under different magnifications.

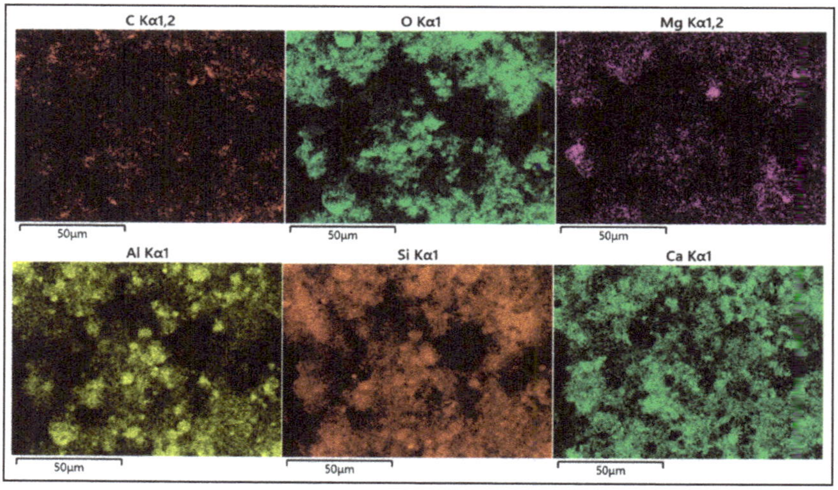

Figure 7. Elemental analysis of No. 22.

Figures 6 and 7 show that Group 1 is the microstructure of a pure cement consolidation body. The matrix contains spherical condensation hydration products, which are considered to be C-S-H gel. The loose gel structure is due to the consolidation body's high porosity under a high water–cement ratio, which decreases strength.

With the increase of the content of the expansion agent and accelerator, the volume of hydration gel decreases, but the number increases and the matrix is denser. On the one hand, the calcium sulphoaluminate clinker in the expansive agent can be rapidly hydrated, generating many hydration products while consuming calcium hydroxide, accelerating the hydration reaction rate of Portland cement. On the other hand, the accelerator triisopropanolamine can accelerate the dissolution of aluminum-containing minerals, significantly promote the hydration process, increase the formation of hydration products, and help improve the microstructure's compactness. When the expansion agent content increases to 10%, the volume of the hydration product increases, the gap between the products cannot be effectively filled, and the compactness of the matrix decreases; this is attributed to the excessive expansion agent (effective components such as calcium sulphoaluminate clinker and gypsum) participating in the reaction. The matrix is subjected to the expansion stress of the excessive expansion product, and defects such as voids appear inside, resulting in a loose structure.

After the content of the naphthalene water-reducing agent increases, the bleeding rate of the material increases, the actual water–cement ratio decreases, and the free water amount involved in the hydration reaction decreases. Compared with Group 22, the internal product structure of Group 25 changed from gel to lamellar, which improved the pores. However, the hydration products could not fill the whole matrix, resulting in more structural voids and lower compactness.

4. Field Model Test

4.1. Test Materials

Sand samples near Xindong Station in Jinan were utilized as test objects for field model grouting tests. Various graded particle sizes were obtained through sieving tests, and the fineness modulus was calculated according to Formula (1). The average value was determined through three calculations, leading to the classification of the field sample as medium sand, as shown in Table 3.

$$M_X = \frac{(A2 + A3 + A4 + A5 + A6) - 5A1}{100 - A1} \quad (1)$$

A_1, A_2, A_3, A_4, A_5, and A_6 represent the cumulative percentages of sieve residue for 4.75 mm, 2.36 mm, 1.18 mm, 0.60 mm, 0.30 mm, and 0.15 mm sieves, respectively.

Table 3. Grain grading of sand sample.

Sand Sample Number	Mass of Particles with Different Particle Sizes (g)							
	≥4.75 mm	4.75~2.3 mm	2.36~1.18 mm	1.18~0.6 mm	0.6~0.3 mm	0.3~0.15 mm	<0.15 mm	Fineness Modulus
1	0	7.6	88.4	98	111.5	137.2	48.8	3.04
2	0	1.7	89.8	133	123.2	107.2	40.7	3.14
3	0	1.9	66.1	137.9	128.2	106.3	45.6	3.0

4.2. Model Test Scheme

The field model grouting tests were conducted using the optimal mix ratio determined from laboratory experiments to investigate the diffusion effect and reinforcement performance of a novel expansion superfine cement slurry in sand layers. The experimental materials included ordinary Portland cement, 800-mesh superfine cement, and novel expansion superfine cement (Groups 4, 13, 22, and 25), with water–cement ratios designed at 1:1, 1.1:1, and 1.2:1 respectively, as shown in Table 4. The grouting final pressure was set at 2.0 MPa to analyze the slurry's diffusion distance, sand body reinforcement strength, and volume expansion rate under varying conditions. The test scheme of the field model is shown in Table 5.

Table 4. Experimental factors and parameters.

Level	Factor	
	Water–Cement Ratios	**Different Materials**
1	1:1	ordinary Portland cement
2	1.1:1	800-mesh superfine cement
3		$U_{20}F_{0.4}T_{4.0}$ (Group 4)
4	1.2:1	$U_{30}F_{0.4}T_{4.0}$ (Group 13)
5		$U_{40}F_{0.4}T_{0.4}$ (Group 22)
6		$U_{40}F_{0.6}T_{4.0}$ (Group 25)

Table 5. Field model test scheme.

NO.	W/C	Materials	NO.	W/C	Materials	NO.	W/C	Materials
A		ordinary Portland cement	A_1		ordinary Portland cement	A_2		ordinary Portland cement
B	1:1	800-mesh superfine cement	B_1	1.1:1	800-mesh superfine cement	B_2	1.2:1	800-mesh superfine cement
C		$U_{20}F_{0.4}T_{4.0}$	C_1		$U_{20}F_{0.4}T_{4.0}$	C_2		$U_{20}F_{0.4}T_{4.0}$
D		$U_{30}F_{0.4}T_{4.0}$	D_1		$U_{30}F_{0.4}T_{4.0}$	D_2		$U_{30}F_{0.4}T_{4.0}$
E		$U_{40}F_{0.4}T_{4.0}$	E_1		$U_{40}F_{0.4}T_{4.0}$	E_2		$U_{40}F_{0.4}T_{4.0}$
F		$U_{40}F_{0.6}T_{4.0}$	F_1		$U_{40}F_{0.6}T_{4.0}$	F_2		$U_{40}F_{0.6}T_{4.0}$

Seamless steel pipes were modified with a diameter of Φ 108 mm and a length of 1~2 m. One end was designed as the slurry inlet with a pressure gauge installed and the other as the slurry outlet with a pressure relief valve installed. Additionally, slurry outlets were set at intervals on the side wall of the seamless steel pipe, each equipped with a one-way valve.

4.3. Experimental Process

First, a layer of mold release agent was uniformly applied on the inner wall of the seamless steel pipe. Subsequently, the initial mass of the steel pipe was measured, and the steel pipe was then filled with on-site sand samples five times, with compaction performed after each filling. The filling mass of the sand sample was controlled to be 16.42 kg. Next, a water pressure test was conducted to evaluate the test device's sealing performance and determine the sand sample's initial permeability coefficient. Finally, a slurry was prepared based on the designed ratios and used to conduct field model grouting tests on the sand samples.

4.4. Test and Analysis of Compressive Strength of Solidified Sand Body

The solidified sand bodies resulting from penetration grouting in each group were numbered sequentially from the inlet to the outlet, the slurry diffusion distance was measured, and the solidified sand bodies were allowed to cure for a specified age of 7 days before conducting the unconfined compressive strength test. For solidified sand bodies with length–diameter ratios not equal to 2, conversion was carried out according to Formula (2).

$$\sigma_C = \frac{8\sigma_L}{7 + 2\frac{D}{H}} \tag{2}$$

where σ_c represents the specimen's uniaxial compressive strength (MPa) with the length–diameter ratio of 2, while σ_L denotes the uniaxial compressive strength (MPa) of non-standard specimens; additionally, D refers to the diameter (cm), and H refers to the height (cm) of the samples.

4.4.1. Strength Analysis of Cement-Solidified Sand Bodies with Varying Particle Sizes

A comparative analysis was conducted utilizing ordinary Portland cement and 800-mesh superfine cement to evaluate the strength of the solidified sand body, with the test results illustrated in Figure 8.

Figure 8. The compressive strength curve of the solidified sand body with ordinary Portland cement and 800-mesh superfine cement.

As illustrated in Figure 8, it is evident that the diffusion range of ordinary Portland cement in Group A is confined to 20–40 cm, whereas Groups A_1 and A_2 exhibit a more comprehensive diffusion range of 40–60 cm. Furthermore, the 800-mesh superfine cement in Group B demonstrates a spreading distance of 60–80 cm, while Groups B_1 and B_2 can spread up to 80–100 cm. Analysis indicates that the spreading distance of the slurry is correlated with its injectability; specifically, higher water–cement ratios or smaller cement particle sizes result in increased spreading distances.

In the 20–40 cm section, Group B_1 exhibits the highest compressive strength at 1.8 MPa, followed by Group B (1.7 MPa), Group A_2 (1.33 MPa), Group B_2 (1.15 MPa), Group A_1 (0.98 MPa), and Group A (0.7 MPa). In the 40–60 cm section, Group B_1 demonstrates a maximum compressive strength of 0.89 MPa, followed by Group B (0.8 MPa), Group B_2 (0.64 MPa), Group A_2 (0.54 MPa), and Group A_1 (0.3 MPa). Comparison of Group B_1 with Group B, or comparison of Groups A_2, A_1, and A under the same type of cement but different water–cement ratios, reveals that a higher water–cement ratio enhances injectability, retains more cement particles, and increases the strength of the solidified sand body. In comparison of Group B_1 with Group A_1, or comparison of Group B with Group A, it is concluded that at the same water–cement ratio but different cement types, smaller cement particle size leads to improved slurry injectability and higher retention of cement particles in the sand medium enhances the strength of the solidified sand body.

Consequently, injectability is directly related to the slurry's diffusion distance and the strength of the solidified sand body. A higher water–cement ratio or smaller cement particle size results in a longer diffusion distance for the slurry. Simultaneously, maintaining a greater mass of cement within a specific diffusion range in the sand stratum leads to increased strength of the solidified sand body.

4.4.2. Strength Analysis of Novel Superfine Cement-Solidified Sand Bodies with Varying Ratios

The solidified sand body strengths of $U_{20}F_{0.4}T_{4.0}$ and $U_{40}F_{0.6}T_{4.0}$ were selected for comparative analysis to study the impact of the novel expansion superfine cement reinforcement sand medium. The experimental results are depicted in Figure 9.

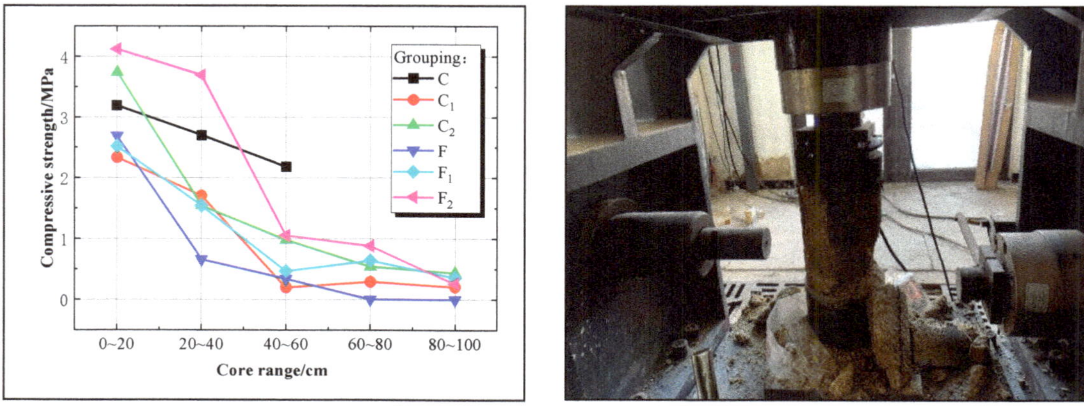

Figure 9. Reinforcement strength curve of novel superfine cement with different proportions.

Figure 9 illustrates that the diffusion distance of Group C is only 40–60 cm, whereas other groups exhibit a diffusion distance of 80–100 cm. Along the slurry's diffusion distance, the overall trend in reinforcement strength of the solidified sand body decreases from Group F_2 (4.12–0.26 MPa) to Group C (3.19–2.18 MPa), followed by Group C_2 (3.74–0.44 MPa), Group F_1 (2.52–0.36 MPa), Group C_1 (2.33–0.21 MPa), and finally, Group F (2.69–0.34 MPa).

When utilizing the $U_{40}F_{0.6}T_{4.0}$ mixing ratio, it was observed that Group F_2 exhibited the highest strength, followed by Group F_1, and then Group F showed the lowest strength. This indicates that under equivalent admixture dosage, a higher water–cement ratio in the slurry leads to increased grouting in the sand and retention of more cement particles within the sand, resulting in enhanced strength of the solidified sand body. In contrast, for the $U_{20}F_{0.4}T_{4.0}$ mixing ratio, Group C demonstrated greater strength than both Group C_2 and C_1 due to its limited diffusion distance of only 40–60 cm; this results in most cement particles accumulating and being compressed within this range, thereby contributing to higher solidified sand body strength.

Furthermore, the comparison between the strengthening effect of Group F_2 ($U_{40}F_{0.6}T_{4.0}$) and Group C_2 ($U_{20}F_{0.4}T_{4.0}$), as well as Group F_1 and Group C_1, under identical water–cement ratio conditions reveals that the dosage of expansion agent exerts a primary influence on the solidified sand body's strengthening effect, followed by the water reducer. The analysis indicates that the expansion agent and water reducer alter the hydration process of superfine cement particles, with a higher quantity of expansion agent resulting in an enhanced strengthening effect in the new slurry.

4.5. Investigation of the Solidified Sand Body Expansion Rate

After curing the solidified sand bodies in each group for 3 and 7 days, the volume of the solidified sand bodies was measured using a comparator. For instance, with a water-cement ratio of 1.2:1, Group B_2 was utilized as the control group, while Groups C_2 and F_2 were designated experimental groups for comparative analysis. Detailed experimental results can be found in Figure 10.

Figure 10 demonstrates that, within the slurry diffusion range, the volume of net superfine cement solidification sand bodies exhibits shrinkage over time. For instance, on day 3, the volume expansion rate of the solidified sand bodies ranged from −0.04% to −0.02%, while on day 7, it ranged from −0.19% to −0.1%, indicating significant volumetric contraction. The shrinkage rate of the solidified sand body at the leading edge of the diffusion distance exceeds that at the trailing edge. For the novel expansion superfine cement material, within the slurry diffusion range, the volume of the solidified sand body expanded with age. In Group F_2, the volume expansion rate ranged from 0.32% to 0.8% on day 3 and from 0.41% to 1.33% on day 7, indicating a significant increase in volume over time. Therefore, it is evident that the expansion performance of the novel superfine cement surpasses that of traditional superfine cement.

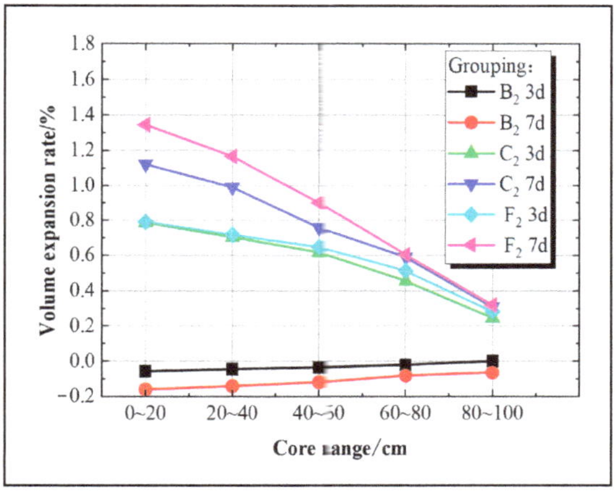

Figure 10. Analysis of solidified sand body expansion rate and its experimental setup.

By the third day of curing, Group F_2 exhibited a higher volume expansion rate than Group C_2, ranging from 0% to 0.03%. However, by the 7th day of curing age, the disparity in volume expansion rates between the two groups had widened to 0.03%–0.23%. Analysis suggests that the content of the expansion agent in Group F_2 ($U_{40}F_{0.6}T_{4.0}$) was double that of Group C_2 ($U_{20}F_{0.4}T_{4.0}$), resulting in a significantly higher volume expansion degree for Group F_2 compared to Group C_2; however, this volume change primarily occurs during later stages due to variations in UEA expansion agent.

5. Engineering Application

5.1. Engineering Overview

In the Tianyuan Avenue comprehensive pipe gallery project at NK2+372–NK2+441.8 in Jinan East Railway Station, a water and sand gushing disaster occurred at the bottom of the pit. The initial remediation plan involved:

1. Utilizing drainage wells with a 700 mm diameter and a minimum depth of 15 m within the confined aquifer, spaced 5 m apart;
2. Reinforcing the pit bottom with double-pipe high-pressure jet grouting utilizing an 800 mm diameter and 550 mm spacing to reach 8.6 m below the pit bottom.

Despite these measures, significant water seepage emerged from multiple points at the bottom of the pit when excavation reached approximately 4 m for the pipe gallery foundation, as shown in Figure 11.

A comprehensive approach involving systematic grouting reinforcement and waterproofing treatment was implemented to address the problem of water and sand gushing into the foundation pit. Initially, grouting holes were strategically positioned around the perimeter of the foundation pit to establish a waterproof curtain, effectively obstructing water pathways surrounding the foundation pit. Subsequently, evenly spaced grouting holes were installed within the foundation pit to seal off water channels and fractures in shallow strata, thereby enhancing the soil layers' waterproofing capacity at the base of the excavation. Finally, structural reinforcement was designed at 33 m to revamp a deep gravel aquifer and mitigate pressure-induced water seepage.

Figure 11. Water and sand gushing in the foundation pit.

5.2. Grouting Pressure and Diffusion Distance

The slurry diffusion distance represents the maximum distance that the slurry can migrate within a given time and pressure and is commonly used for evaluating grouting effectiveness. The grouting pressure is a critical factor influencing slurry diffusion distance. Excessive or inadequate grouting pressure may compromise reinforcement efficacy. Therefore, the permissible grouting pressure P_e can be calculated according to Formula (3):

$$P_e = C(0.75T + Kh\lambda) \times 100\ \mathrm{kN/m^3} \tag{3}$$

where P_e represents the allowable grouting pressure (KPa); C is a coefficient associated with the grouting sequence, taking on values of 1 for the first hole, 1.25 for the second hole, and 1.5 for the third hole; T denotes the thickness of the foundation cover layer (m); K is a coefficient related to the grouting method, taking on values of 0.5 for top-down grouting and 0.6 for bottom-up grouting; h represents the depth from ground level to the grouting section (m); and λ is a coefficient associated with strata properties, which can be selected within a range of 0.5 to 1.5 based on site conditions—lower values are chosen for loose and permeable structures while higher values are chosen otherwise.

The design and treatment depth of the strata in the pipe gallery foundation pit was 33 m, with drilling divided into three sections for progressive grouting from top to bottom. Specifically, the treatment depths were 0–13 m for the first section, 13–23 m for the second section, and 23–33 m for the third section. Substituting C = 1, T = 33 m, K = 0.5, h = 13 m, λ = 1 into Equation (3) yields an allowable grouting pressure of P_{e1}=3.1 MPa for the first section; similarly, calculated values result in P_{e2} = 3.6 MPa for the second section and P_{e3} = 4.1 MPa for the third section.

According to Darcy's law, $q = KiA$. When r = r_0, h = H; r = r_1, h = h_0, this relationship can be derived:

$$H - h_0 = h_1 = \frac{\beta q}{2\pi a K} \ln \frac{r_1}{r_0} \tag{4}$$

$$q = \frac{2\pi a K h_1}{\beta \ln \frac{r_1}{r_0}} \tag{5}$$

Given these, $Q = \pi r_1^2 a n$ and $Q = qt$ are then derived from Formula (5)

$$r_1 = \sqrt{\frac{2Kh_1 t}{n\beta \ln(\frac{r_1}{r_0})}} \tag{6}$$

where q represents the grouting volume per unit time (cm³/s); K denotes the formation permeability coefficient, ranging from 1.20×10^{-3} to 6.0×10^{-3} cm/s; a is the permeation area (cm^2); r_1 stands for the diffusion radius of the slurry (cm); r_0 is defined as the radius of the grouting pipe, set at 5 cm; H signifies the sum of groundwater head and grouting pressure head; h_0 indicates the groundwater pressure head (cm); h_1 refers to the allowable grouting pressure head, set between 31,000 cm and 41,000 cm; β represents the ratio of slurry viscosity to water viscosity, with a dynamic viscosity range of 1.77–2.26 mPa·s for novel superfine cement slurry and 1.0 mPa·s for water; a denotes the treatment section length (cm), set at 1000 cm; n stands for the formation porosity, taken as 0.3; Q represents slurry flow rate (cm^3/s); and t denotes grouting time, set between 5 and 10 min.

According to Formula (6), the diffusion distance of the novel superfine cement slurry in engineering applications ranges from 104 cm to 361 cm. Moreover, with an allowable grouting pressure set at 2.0 MPa, that is, the allowable grouting pressure water head is set to 20,000 cm, the diffusion distance of the novel superfine cement slurry was estimated to be between 86 cm and 96 cm, which aligns closely with the actual diffusion distance observed in field model grouting tests.

5.3. Inspection and Evaluation of Grouting Effect

5.3.1. Inspection Hole Coring and Evaluation

Numerous inspection holes were constructed in the control area to visually and effectively demonstrate the impact of grouting reinforcement, and cores were extracted. Distinct grouting veins are discernible in cores, as shown in Figure 12.

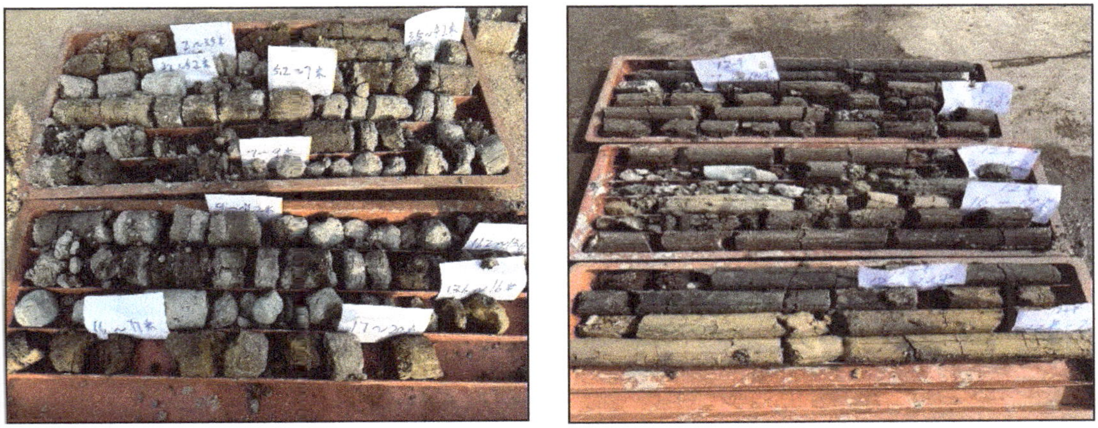

Figure 12. Cores from inspection holes 2 and 12.

Based on the integrity of the rock cores, a favorable overall reinforcement effect is indicated following the injection of the novel superfine cement slurry into the test area, with a core monitor rate exceeding 70% (the core monitor rate is the ratio of the core length to the footage length in a drilling process).

5.3.2. Drilling Variable Head Seepage Test

Through the variable head penetration test, the permeability coefficient of the stratum is calculated according to the relationship between the head drop rate and time in the borehole to evaluate the reinforcement of the bottom layer. Detailed information on the borehole variable head seepage test can be found in Table 6.

The permeability coefficients of each inspection hole range from 1.47×10^{-6} cm/s to 8.14×10^{-6} cm/s, indicating relatively low values. The permeability of the stratum after grouting decreased by nearly three orders of magnitude compared to the pre-grouting value, which ranged from 1.20×10^{-3} cm/s to 6.0×10^{-3} cm/s.

Table 6. Permeability coefficient of inspection hole.

Hole Number	1	3	7	8	9	10	11
Permeability Coefficient k 10^{-6} cm/s	1.90	2.14	5.49	8.14	6.89	1.47	7.30

Note: Surface water level is 2.0 m.

5.3.3. Transient Electromagnetic Detection

Transient electromagnetic methods utilize a non-grounded return line for transmitting pulse current underground. This induces eddy currents in low-resistivity subsurface media under the influence of the pulsed magnetic field, leading to the generation of a secondary magnetic field. Through post-power-off observation using receiving instruments and coils, an analysis of the characteristics and distribution of this secondary field enables the determination of geological body distribution patterns, as shown in Figure 13.

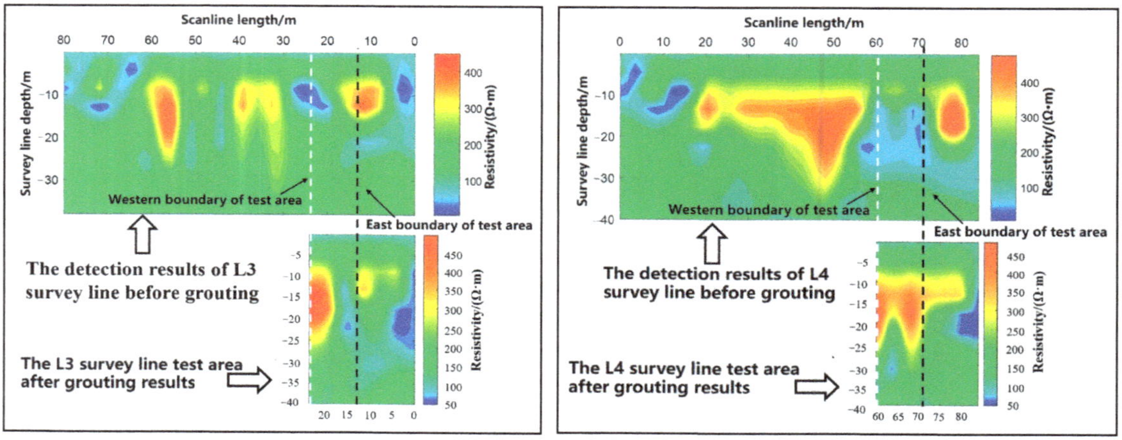

Figure 13. Comparison of L3 and L4 test lines pre- and post-grouting.

By comparing the L3 survey line before and after grouting, it is evident that there was a significant alteration in ground resistivity following the grouting process. The previously low-resistance area transformed into a regional high-resistance zone, indicating successful grouting. Similarly, comparing the L4 survey line before and after grouting, it is apparent that a substantial low-resistance area existed before grouting, suggesting pronounced water enrichment. Post-grouting, this low-resistance region has essentially disappeared, due to the evident filling and consolidation effects of the slurry.

5.3.4. Excavation of Foundation Pit

The comprehensive pipe gallery foundation pit was excavated following treatment with the novel superfine cement slurry. The on-site excavation situation demonstrated excellent integrity of the foundation pit sidewall, a significant increase in bottom layer strength post-grouting, and an absence of water channels or seepage cracks at the base of the pit, ensuring safe excavation of the foundation pit, as shown in Figure 14.

Figure 14. Excavation of foundation pit.

6. Conclusions

1. In most mix ratios, the bleeding rate and fluidity of the novel superfine cement slurry initially increase and then decrease with rising water-reducing agent dosage, reaching minimum bleeding water of 19 mL and maximum fluidity of 235 mm. The initial setting time generally decreases with increasing accelerating agent dosage, reaching a minimum value of 506 min, representing a 33.68% reduction compared to the benchmark group.
2. Between day 3 and day 7, solidified bodies formed from the novel superfine cement slurry are initially unchanged but demonstrate significant expansion as curing progresses. The volume expansion rate reached 1.4% on day 28, 1.0% higher than that of the benchmark group. Under normal conditions, the compressive strength of the net slurry consolidation body is positively correlated with expansion agent dosage, achieving maximum strengths of 8.11 MPa at 3 days and 6.93 MPa at 28 days; these values are respectively higher by 6.7 MPa and 2.6 MPa compared to those in the benchmark group.
3. On the 7th day, the volume expansion rate of the traditional superfine cement solidified sand body is −0.19%–−0.1%, while for the corresponding body formed from the novel superfine cement is 0.41%–1.33%; the expansion effect is significant. Under consistent water–cement ratio conditions, expansion agent dosage primarily influences the strength of solidified sand bodies, followed by the water-reducing admixture. However, the volume changes of solidified sand bodies resulting from variations in expansion agent dosage primarily manifest during later curing stages.
4. After the on-site treatment of water and sand-gushing strata, the core recovery rate of the inspection hole exceeded 70%. The permeability of the stratum after grouting decreased by nearly three orders of magnitude compared to the pre-grouting value, ranging from 1.47×10^{-6} cm/s to 8.14×10^{-6} cm/s. No water inrush occurred during the foundation pit excavation, demonstrating that the grouting performance is commendable.

Author Contributions: Investigation, X.F., Z.L. and L.L.; Methodology, X.C., W.S., C.L. and B.H.; Validation, X.F. and Q.Z.; Resources, X.C., Z.L. and C.L.; Writing—original draft, X.F., L.L. and Z.S.; Writing—review and editing, X.F. and Z.S.; Funding acquisition, X.F.; Supervision, Q.Z. All authors have read and agreed to the published version of the manuscript.

Funding: The authors gratefully acknowledge the financial support from the National Natural Science Foundation of China (Grant No. 52009075), the Natural Science Foundation of Shandong

Province (Grant No. ZR2020QE262 and No. ZR2024ME119), and the Doctoral Research Fund of Shandong Jianzhu University (Grant Number X19018Z).

Institutional Review Board Statement: Not applicable.

Informed Consent Statement: Not applicable.

Data Availability Statement: The raw data supporting the conclusions of this article will be made available by the authors on request.

Acknowledgments: The authors would like to express their sincere appreciation to the reviewers for their valuable comments and suggestions, which helped improve the quality of the paper.

Conflicts of Interest: Authors Xiaowei Cao, Zhiming Li were employed by the company Xuzhou Metro Group Co., Ltd. Author Chi Liu was employed by the company Jinan Rail Transit Group Co. Ltd. All authors declare that they have no conflict of interest.

References

1. Han, F.; Liu, Y.; Liu, T.; Zhang, X.; Lv, Y.; Zhaxi, N. Experimental study on the influence of silica aerogel on the properties of superfine-cement composites. *Mater. Rep.* **2023**, *37*, 22080137-7.
2. Zhang, J.; Guan, X.; Wang, X.; Jin, B.; Zhang, X. Effect and mechanism of soluble P_2O_5 on early hydration properties of superfine sulphoaluminate cement based double liquid grouting materials. *Mater. Rep.* **2023**, *36*, 23010125-6.
3. Zhao, W.; Ren, Z.; Zhang, J.; Li, Y.; Zhang, X. Characteristics of binary low-ph grouting material containing superfine cement and silica fume. *Bull. Chin. Ceram. Soc.* **2023**, *42*, 1156.
4. Xiao, T.; Yu, Z.; Liu, F.; Dai, X.; Sun, J. Study on slurry flow characteristics and diffusion law of superfine cement-based composite grouting material. *Processes* **2023**, *11*, 1906. [CrossRef]
5. Zhang, D.; Ma, Z.; Zou, Y.; Xie, H.; Guan, R. Study on the strength and micro characteristics of grouted specimens with different superfine cement contents. *Materials* **2021**, *14*, 6709. [CrossRef]
6. Xu, S.; Xu, Z.; Ji, Y. Preparation and mechanical properties of low carbon cementitious materials with superfine cement reverse filling high-volume mineral admixtures. *Materials* **2023**, *16*, 4814. [CrossRef]
7. Li, H.; Shi, Y.; Jiao, Z.; Chen, J. Preparation of portland cement with high compressive and tensile strength by the synergistic effect between micron-size green silicon carbide and micro steel fiber. *Earth Environ. Sci.* **2019**, *330*, 042023. [CrossRef]
8. Wang, F.; Hua, J.; Xue, X.; Wang, N.; Yan, F.; Feng, D. Effect of superfine cement modification on properties of coral aggregate concrete. *Materials* **2023**, *16*, 1103. [CrossRef]
9. Wu, L.; Wu, Z.; Weng, L.; Liu, Y.; Liu, Q. Investigation on basic properties and microscopic mechanisms of polyacrylate latex modified cement grouting material for water blocking and reinforcement. *Constr. Build. Mater.* **2023**, *409*, 133872. [CrossRef]
10. Mollamahmutoğlu, M.; Avci, E. Time-Dependent shear strength behavior of superfine cement-stabilized clayey soil. *ACI Mater. J.* **2020**, *117*, 251–258.
11. Liu, X.; Wang, F.; Huang, J.; Wang, S.; Zhang, Z.; Nawnit, K. Grout diffusion in silty fine sand stratum with high groundwater level for tunnel construction. *Tunn. Undergr. Space Technol.* **2019**, *93*, 103051. [CrossRef]
12. Li, W.; Shaikh, F.U.A.; Wang, L.; Lu, Y.; Wang, B.; Jiang, C.; Su, Y. Experimental study on shear property and rheological characteristic of superfine cement grouts with nano-SiO_2 addition. *Constr. Build. Mater.* **2019**, *228*, 117046. [CrossRef]
13. Avcı, E.; Mollamahmutoglu, M. Strength and permeability characteristics of superfine cement and fine fly ash mixture grouted sand. *ACI Mater. J.* **2020**, *117*, 293–304.
14. Zhang, J.; Lu, S.; Feng, T.; Yi, B.; Liu, J. Research on reuse of silty fine sand in backfill grouting material and optimization of backfill grouting material proportions. *Tunn. Undergr. Space. Technol.* **2022**, *43*, 104751. [CrossRef]
15. Ye, F.; Liang, X.; Liang, X.; Zhang, W.; Liu, C.; Feng, H. Grouting technology and construction schemes of a tunnel in aeolian stratum: A case study of Shenmu No. 1 Tunnel. *Sci. Rep.* **2021**, *11*, 23552. [CrossRef]
16. Wang, Y.; Zhang, L.; Liu, M.; Yu, X. Comparative study on the mechanical properties of solidified silty-fine sand reinforced by permeable polymer and traditional grouting materials. *Constr. Build. Mater.* **2024**, *419*, 135485. [CrossRef]
17. Cui, Y.; Tan, Z.; Han, D.; Song, J. Investigation and application of a high performance grouting material in water-rich silty fine sand stratum. *Constr. Build. Mater.* **2022**, *329*, 127100. [CrossRef]
18. Golewski, G. Determination of Fracture Mechanic Parameters of Concretes Based on Cement Matrix Enhanced by Fly Ash and Nano-Silica. *Materials* **2024**, *17*, 4230. [CrossRef]
19. *JTG 3420-2020*; Testing Methods of Cement and Concrete for Highway Engineering. China Communication Press: Beijing, China, 2021.
20. *GB 1346-2011*; Test Methods for Water Requirement of Normal Consistency, Setting Time, and Soundness of the Portland Cements. Standards Press of China: Beijing, China, 2012.
21. *T 0554-2005*; Test Method for Axial Compressive Strength of Cement Concrete Cylinder. China Communication Press: Beijing, China, 2006.

2. *JCT 313-2009*; Test Method for Determining Expansive Ratio of Expansive Cement. China Construction Science and Technology Press: Beijing, China, 2010.
3. Li, Z.; Liu, J.; Qiao, M.; Yu, C.; Xie, W.; Chen, J. Mechanism of viscosity for recycled powder-cement paste based on the adsorption of superplasticizer. *Materials* **2023**, *37*, 21090090-7.
4. Zhang, Q.; Shu, X.; Yang, Y.; Wang, X.; Liu, J.; Ran, Q. Adsorption of superplasticizer and its effect on viscosity of cement-silica fume paste. *J. Chin. Ceram. Soc.* **2020**, *48*, 1716–1721.
5. Xie, W.; Liu, J.; Li, Z.; Yu, C.; Zhu, J.; Li, S. Influence of recycled powders on yield stress of cement paste with superplasticizer and its mechanism. *J. Southeast. Univ.* **2020**, *53*, 567–574.
6. Su, M.; Wang, Z.; Li, S.; Zhang, Y.; Liu, X. Evaluation of compatibility between comment and flash setting admixture for shotcrete. *J. Chin. Ceram. Soc.* **2023**, *51*, 1283–1292.
7. An, M.; Zhang, G.; Han, S. Research on the influence mechanism of accelerator main components on cement hydration. *J. Railw. Eng. Soc.* **2019**, *36*, 74–81.
8. Liu, X.; Xie, H.; Luo, Q.; Wang, Z.; Cui, S.; Guo, J.; Zhang, G. Study on regulation mechanism of triethanolamine to liquid alkali-free accelerator on accelerating-inhibiting of early hydration of cement. *Mater. Rep.* **2023**, *37*, 21100165-6.
9. Zeng, L.; Qiao, M.; Wang, W.; Ran, Q.; Hong, J. Effect of alkali-free accelerators on early age hydration of portland cement. *J. Build. Mater.* **2021**, *24*, 31–38.
0. Liu, Y.; Chi, Y.; Tian, W.; Hou, Y.; Zhang, J. Effect of different expanders on properties of cement-based grouting materials. *J. Build. Mater.* **2022**, *25*, 307–313.

Disclaimer/Publisher's Note: The statements, opinions and data contained in all publications are solely those of the individual author(s) and contributor(s) and not of MDPI and/or the editor(s). MDPI and/or the editor(s) disclaim responsibility for any injury to people or property resulting from any ideas, methods, instructions or products referred to in the content.

materials

MDPI

Article

A Study of the Influence of Thermoactivated Natural Zeolite on the Hydration of White Cement Mortars

Ventseslav Stoyanov [1,2], Vilma Petkova [3,*], Katerina Mihaylova [3] and Maya Shopska [4]

[1] Department of Technology and Construction Management, Faculty of Construction, University of Structural Engineering and Architecture "Lyuben Karavelov", 175 Suhodolska Str., 1373 Sofia, Bulgaria; vensy.stoyanov@vsu.bg

[2] Department of Safety Management and Prevention, Faculty of Fire Safety and Civil Protection, Academy of Ministry of Interior, 171 Pirotska Str., 1309 Sofia, Bulgaria

[3] Institute of Mineralogy and Crystallography "Acad. Ivan Kostov", Bulgarian Academy of Sciences, Acad. G. Bonchev Str., Block 107, 1113 Sofia, Bulgaria; kate_mih@imc.bas.bg

[4] Institute of Catalysis, Bulgarian Academy of Sciences, Acad. G. Bonchev Str., Bldg. 11, 1113 Sofia, Bulgaria; shopska@ic.bas.bg

* Correspondence: vpetkova@clmc.bas.bg

Abstract: One trend in the development of building materials is the partial or complete replacement of traditional materials that have a high carbon footprint with eco-friendly ecological raw materials and ingredients. In the present work, the influence of replacing cement with 10 wt% thermally activated natural zeolite on the structural and physical-mechanical characteristics of cured mortars based on white Portland cement and river sand was investigated. The phase compositions were determined by wavelength dispersive X-ray fluorescence (WD-XRF) analysis, X-ray powder diffraction (PXRD), diffuse reflectance infrared Fourier transformed spectroscopy (DRIFTS), and scanning electron microscopy (SEM), as well as thermogravimetric analysis simultaneously with differential scanning calorimetry (TG/DTG-DSC). The results show that the incorporation of zeolite increases the amount of pores accessible with mercury intrusion porosimetry by about 40%, but the measured strengths are also higher by over 13%. When these samples were aged in an aqueous environment from day 28 to day 120, the amount of pores decreased by about 10% and the compressive strength increased by nearly 15%, respectively. The microstructural analysis carried out proves that these results are due to hydration with a low content of crystal water and the realization of pozzolanic reactions that last over time. Replacing some of the white cement with thermally activated natural zeolite results in the formation of a greater variety of crystals, including new crystalline CSH and CSAH phases that allow better intergrowth and interlocking. The results of the investigations allow us to present a plausible reaction mechanism of pozzolanic reactions and of the formation of new crystal hydrate phases. This gives grounds to claim that the replacement of part of the cement with zeolite improves the corrosion resistance of the investigated building solutions against aggressive weathering.

Keywords: cement mortars; zeolite; river sand; cement hydration; pozzolanic activity; CSH and CSAH phases

check for updates

Citation: Stoyanov, V.; Petkova, V.; Mihaylova, K.; Shopska, M. A Study of the Influence of Thermoactivated Natural Zeolite on the Hydration of White Cement Mortars. *Materials* **2024**, *17*, 4798. https://doi.org/10.3390/ma17194798

Academic Editors: Mengjun Chen and Jiwen Bai

Received: 16 August 2024
Revised: 23 September 2024
Accepted: 25 September 2024
Published: 29 September 2024

Copyright: © 2024 by the authors. Licensee MDPI, Basel, Switzerland. This article is an open access article distributed under the terms and conditions of the Creative Commons Attribution (CC BY) license (https://creativecommons.org/licenses/by/4.0/).

1. Introduction

The increased rate of global urbanization in the past decades has led to the widespread implementation of cement-based materials in the construction sector [1]. Cement production, however, is associated with a very high environmental impact due to the amount of carbon dioxide (CO_2) released in the atmosphere during the manufacturing process (clinker production—limestone calcination), making it an unsustainable material in the long run and contributing greatly to climate change [2,3]. As such, in 2009, the Cement Technology Roadmap identified four levers for reducing emissions in the cement industry [4]: thermal and electric efficiency, use of alternative fuels, carbon capture and storage, and clinker substitution. Substitution of clinker with diverse supplementary cementitious materials (SCMs) is considered to be the most favorable among the identified levers due to its low economic and performance impacts on cement and concrete production [5].

The use of natural pozzolans (tuffs, volcanic ash, perlites, pumices, zeolites) as SCMs for modern cement and concrete production and their impact on the hardened product's properties have long since been investigated by different researchers [3,5–13]. Standardized methods are applied to assess their chemical and physical properties, such as loss on ignition, alkali content, fineness, increase in drying shrinkage, soundness, etc. [14]. The main advantage of SCMs substitution is the pozzolanic effect, which is associated with capability of providing amorphous silica that react with $Ca(OH)_2$ in the presence of water [10,12,15,16]. The pozzolanic activity includes two parameters, that is, the maximal amount of $Ca(OH)_2$ that a pozzolan can combine, and the rate at which such combination occurs [15,16]. Pozzolan substitution results in a small pozzolanic reaction (less hydration products) at the early stage. With an increase in age, the hydration of cementitious materials increases and the porosity of the mortars is reduced [16]. This significantly improves the strength, which is determined with respect to strength development by standard test procedures for evaluating the activity index of pozzolans [14,17].

Compared to volcanic ash, tuff, pumice, and other natural pozzolans, zeolite offers unique benefits as a supplementary cementitious material [7]. Zeolite addition has a multifaceted impact on cement pastes, mortar, and concrete. It lowers the heat generated during hydration, enhances water resistance, improves the balance between bending and compressive strength, increases the need for water and subsequent shrinkage, and raises the apparent viscosity of the mixture. The durability of zeolite containing cement mixtures is improved due to decreased amounts of C_3A- and CaO-containing hydration products with lower leachability, as well as reduced SO_3 and diffusion processes such as salt migration and efflorescence [15,16,18].

In the past, natural stone was one of the most commonly used building materials due to its durability and aesthetic appeal. It was used not only for construction purposes but also for creating rich ornaments and decorations on the facades of buildings. One approach to preserving architectural heritage is to create and exhibit replicas of the architectural elements placed on the facades of buildings. The requirements for materials for this use are to have good processability, high durability, weather resistance, and the possibility of being made in colors that will last over time. A potential choice is a mortar based on a hydraulic binder. To increase its resistance, increased amounts of cement, the addition of pozzolanic additive and the preparation of as dense a composition as possible are needed. The first is solved by using white Portland cement, the second by using a white pozzolanic additive of the metakaolin type (white powder obtained by calcination of kaolin clay), diatomaceous earth, rice husk ash, etc., and the third by a chemical additive based on polycarboxylates, which, however, does not change the coloring characteristics.

The potential for making decorative mortars based on blended binder, composed from white Portland cement and clinoptilolite, leads to interest in investigating the influence of zeolite in the process of hardening. The numerous benefits of this technology are due to the specific rheological behavior (high fluidity) of fresh mixes, which are characterized by the addition of large amounts of active and/or inert mineral additives, low water-to-binder ratio, and modified polycarboxylate-based water-reducing admixture [19–21].

In our previous works, we have studied the effects of zeolite addition in cement mortars containing high amounts of additives, along with investigations into the structure and thermal behavior of white cement containing river sand and marble powder [22–26].

The goal of the current work is to study the effect of the addition of natural Bulgarian clinoptilolite into the structure of white cement mortars during hydration and curing at 28 and 120 days, without the presence of any other additives. This effect is established by studying (i) the formation and development of the pore space in cement mortars, (ii) the macro- and microstructure, and (iii) the phase formation of new CSH and CSAH crystal hydrates. Samples containing 10% zeolite and different water-to-cement ratios were prepared so as to better study the process of phase formation.

The investigated parameters and their effects were studied with the following methods: wavelength dispersive X-ray fluorescence (WD-XRF) analysis, powder X-ray diffraction (PXRD), scanning electron microscopy (SEM), diffuse reflectance infrared Fourier transformed spectroscopy (DRIFTS), thermogravimetric analysis simultaneously with differential scanning calorimetry (TG/DTG-DSC), and physical-mechanical methods for obtaining the following properties: density after immersion, adsorption after immersion, compressive strength, and porosity.

2. Materials

The objects of research in the present work are cement mortars with different ratios of the solid components. In this research, white Portland cement CEM I 52.5 N was used, produced by Devnya Cement (Devnya, Bulgaria). The mineral composition, calculated by the Bogue method, was as follows (in wt%): C_3S—72.13; C_2S—15.28; C_3A—5.23; C_4AF—0.61. The river sand (clean, washed, and dried) that was used for the preparation of the mortars has a fineness modulus FM = 2.7 (EN 12620) and shape index—4.6% (EN 933-4), i.e., spheroid particles, over 85.0% SiO_2 content [27].

The zeolite addition was milled, (0–0.8 mm) natural clinoptilolite tuff, mined from Beli Plast deposit, Bulgaria. It contains about 80 wt% clinoptilolite and admixtures of montmorillonite, biotite, celadonite, low-cristobalite, calcite, quartz, and feldspars. The amount of clinoptilolite in the composition of the solutions is 10%. The limitation of 10% replacement of cement with clinoptilolite was necessary to avoid the dominance of the zeolite color and to avoid significant changes in the rheological behavior of the systems.

The zeolite (natural clinoptilolite) was thermally activated at 250 °C [7,23]. Thermally activated zeolites are classified in 3 categories [28]: (i) they preserve their skeletal structure but the zeolite water is dehydrated, leading to the opening of interlayer spaces and channels in the zeolite. Eventually, they can reabsorb water on cooling and restore their original state; (ii) substantial distortion in the skeletal structure while preserving the ability to rehydrate; (iii) breakdown of the T-O-T chains (where T can be a Si or Al atom) during the dehydration process while achieving a significant distortion in the topology of the zeolite skeletal structure and loss of the ability to rehydrate. It is assumed in the current study that most of the water will enter the skeletal structure upon hydration of the cementitious minerals following the thermal activation of zeolite up to 250 °C. This water will then be used for the formation of CSH/CSAH phases and ongoing hydration over time, thereby promoting the pozzolanic activity of zeolite. The present work aims to find evidence supporting this assumption in the findings of the analytical techniques applied.

To support the choice of materials, a short economic study was made on the current prices of some cement substitutes in the commercial network in Bulgaria. The data are presented in Table 1.

Table 1. Current prices of cement substitutes.

No	Type of Cement Replacement Material, Specification	Available	Price/t	Reference
1.	Clinoptilolite, 85% purity	Local	129 €	1 *
2.	Metakaolin	Local	3200 €	2 *
3.	Silica fume	Import	300 $	3 *
4.	Pumice	Local	7500 €	4 *

1 *—http://dprao.bg/images/%D0%94%D0%BE%D0%B3%D0%BE%D0%B2%D0%BE%D1%801.pdf (in Bulgarian) (accessed on 22 September 2024). 2 *—https://nmarket.bg/metakoalin (accessed on 22 September 2024). 3 *—https://www.globalsources.com/searchList/products?keyWord=silica+fume&pageNum=1 (accessed on 22 September 2024). 4 *—https://markita.net/perlit.html-0 (accessed on 22 September 2024).

The data in Table illustrate the feasibility of using an accessible, inexpensive, natural material with a high major component content such as natural clinoptilolite.

The experiments were carried out with two cement mortars (Table 2) following the mass ratio of 1:3:0.5 used in EN 196-1 to determine the compressive strength and, optionally, the flexural strength using prismatic samples with sizes 40 × 40 × 160 mm. The zeolite addition was always introduced into the mixtures together with distilled water. Immediately after the mixing procedure (according to EN 196-1 at 20 °C and 65% RH), the workability of the fresh mortar was evaluated using the standardized measurement of consistence [29]. The spreading diameter for mortars was measured by using a truncated cone, based on a flow table test (EN 1015-3) [30]. The results indicate that the addition of clinoptilolite-based zeolite reduces the spreading diameter from 111 ± 2 mm for Ms to 107 ± 3 mm Mz.

Table 2. Abbreviations and composition of mortars.

Mortar	Cement	Zeolite	Binder	Sand	Ratios (wt–wt)		
	wt Parts	wt Parts	wt Parts	wt Parts	Binder/Sand	Water–Binder	Water–Cement
Ms Ms28 * and Ms120	1.0	-	1.0	3.0	1:3	0.50	0.50
Mz Mz28 and Mz120	0.9	0.1	1.0	3.0	1:3	0.50	0.45

* Abbreviation meaning: M—mortar; s—sand; z—zeolite. The number in the notations Ms28, Ms120, Mz28 and Mz120 indicates the duration of sample curing in days.

After casting, the samples (6 prisms, 40 × 40 × 160 mm) were stored in the molds for 1 day in a moist atmosphere (>95% RH and 20 °C). Once demolded, the samples were kept under water (20 °C) until strength testing (28 and 120 days). The compressive strengths at 28 and 120 days of water curing were measured according to EN 196-1 [29].

3. Methods

Broken parts of samples with mass of 2.0 ± 0.3 mg were used to measure the porosity by the mercury intrusion porosimetry method (MIP) using Carlo Erba Porosimeter Mod. 1520 (Carlo Erba Strumentazione, Rodano (Milan), Italy), with the pressure range 0.10–150 MPa, corresponding to the pore size range 50–15,000 nm.

Wavelength dispersive X-ray fluorescence (WD-XRF) analysis was performed using spectrometer WD-XRF Super-mini 200 (Rigaku Corporation, Tokyo, Japan) (operating at 50 kV and 4 mA, 200 W X-ray tube with Pd-anode, 30 mm^2) under a helium atmosphere. Two different X-ray detectors were made use of: a gas flow proportional counter for light elements and a scintillation counter for heavy elements. Three analyzing crystals were utilized (according to the wavelength range): LIF 200 (for Ti-U), PET (for Al-Ti), and RX25 (for F-Mg). The samples were prepared as tablets with CERE-OX-BM-0002-1 powder. Rigaku's built-in software package "ZSX" ver. 7.67 was employed for the processing of the data.

The PXRD patterns were performed on an X-ray powder diffractometer D2 Phaser (Bruker AXS GmbH, Karlsruhe, Germany) using CuKα radiation (λ = 0.15418 nm) (operating at 30 kV, 10 mA) from 5 to 80° 2θ with a step of 0.05° (grinded sample with weight—1.0 ± 0.1 mg and particle sizes below 0.075 mm). Phase identification was carried out using various search-match software programs, as well as by using data from the Inorganic Crystal Structure Database (ICSD) [31].

Experiments were conducted to characterize the macro-, meso-, and microstructure of the investigated samples. The macrostructure was captured using a Nikon D3300 SLR digital camera with a Nikon AF-P 18–55 mm VR lens (Nikon Corporation, Tokyo, Japan), effective pixels—24.2 MP, processor—EXPEED 4, capture sensor—CMOS 23.5 × 15.6 mm, light sensitivity (ISO 100)—12,800 in 1 EV steps. The microstructure was observed with Philips PH, Model 515, regime of secondary electron emission. Following a 12 h drying process at 60 ± 5 °C, the fracture fragments of the samples, which had a roughly flat surfac measuring 10 × 10 mm, were covered with a thin layer of gold.

Additionally, DRIFTS was applied for the analysis of the samples. It was used in order to increase the sensitivity of the IR analysis, which, due to the measurement method required the use of 100% of the studied substance without any dilution. The samples were studied with a spectrometer Nicolet 6700 (Thermo Electron Corporation, Waltham MA, USA). A diffuse-reflectance accessory Collector II (Thermo Electron Corporation Waltham, MA, USA) was used. The spectra were recorded at a resolution of 4 (data spacing 1.928 cm^{-1}) and 100 scans.

Thermal studies (TG/DTG-DSC) were performed with a Setsys Evolution 2400 thermo analytical complex (THEMYS), SETARAM, Caluire-et-Cuire, France. A dynamic heating regime was selected in the temperature range from room temperature (RT) to 1300 °C with a heating rate of 10 °C min^{-1}. The mass of the samples for thermal characterization analysis was 18.0 ± 2.0 mg (mass resolution of 0.02 μg). The calorimetric measurements were performed with a B-type sensor with a temperature measurement range up to 1600 °C and a DSC rod with a resolution of 1.0 μW. The experiments were performed in a gas atmosphere of static air. Stabilized ceramic crucibles with a volume of 100 μL were used, respecting the requirement of filling with a low reaction layer to eliminate diffusion difficulties.

4. Results

4.1. Wavelength Dispersive X-ray Fluorescence Analysis

Table 3 presents the results of the semi-quantitative XRF measurements of the major component contents of the raw materials and the cement mortars.

Table 3. XRF analysis data of the main components of the initial raw materials and water-cured samples—Ms28, Ms120, Mz28, and Mz120.

Content of Components	White Cement	River Sand	Natural Zeolite	Sample Ms28	Sample Ms120	Sample Mz28	Sample Mz120
-	%	%	%	%	%	%	%
CaO	72.997	4.377	4.361	29.264	27.772	27.683	30.848
SiO_2	16.857	71.545	74.727	52.442	54.234	53.580	50.730
Al_2O_3	3.452	12.875	13.031	9.277	9.642	9.589	9.344
MgO	0.868	1.048	0.795	1.055	0.584	0.794	1.034
Na_2O	0.351	2.446	0.767	1.590	1.514	1.588	1.481
K_2O	0.671	5.073	4.881	3.343	3.419	3.783	3.632
Fe_2O_3	0.220	1.948	1.034	0.965	0.880	0.998	0.917
SO_3	4.312	0.100	0.023	1.560	1.581	1.539	1.569
P_2O_5	0.112	0.141	0.038	0.112	0.098	0.103	0.101
TiO_2	0.091	0.282	0.141	0.231	0.147	0.206	0.191

The results of the XRF analysis of the samples Ms28, Ms120, Mz28, and Mz120 present some trends in the major component oxide contents—CaO, SiO_2, Al_2O_3, Na_2O, K_2O, SO_3 etc. The data in Table 2 are the result of the cement mortars obtained by mixing white cement, river sand, and natural zeolite. The highest contents were SiO_2, 50.73–54.23%; CaO 27.68–30.84%; and Al_2O_3, 9.27–9.64%. The deviation from the average values for each of the major components is within approximately ±2%, which is evidence of compositional consistency. There is a greater increase in the amount of Al_2O_3, from 3.45% in the white cement to 9.46% average in the cement mortars. This result is related to the higher content of this component in river sand [32,33]. It is assumed that Al_2O_3 will make a significant contribution to the phase formation of CSAH hydrates in the hydration process.

The semi-quantitative results of the XRF analysis prove the presence of major oxides in the starting components used for the preparation of the mortars. The main prerequisites for their phase formation are expected to be the proportions between them, the influence of the water-to-cement ratio and the presence of zeolite, which will have an impact on the hydration process.

4.2. Physical-Mechanical Properties

The hydration process of cementitious materials is essential for the stability and strength of the resulting mortars. In their production, not only is the type of basic materials used essential but so are additives, inert fillers, and waste, which reduce the cost of their production but without compromising the quality of the final products. Therefore, the first analyses that provide information on the effectiveness of the technologies for obtaining building mortars are physical-mechanical studies.

The following physical-mechanical properties were measured: density after immersion, water adsorption after immersion, bending strength compressive strength, and pore volume at 28 days and 120 days. The measuring method and the average values of the properties are shown in Table 3. Due to the samples' varying density, the parameter "adsorption after immersion" is calculated in volume percentages.

From the data in Table 4, the high density of the Ms and Mz systems is reported. For all compositions, with increasing age, the densities remain almost unchanged, with changes within the margin of error. The replacement of 10% cement with zeolite reduces the parameter "density after immersion" due to air-entraining (increase in both the number and sizes of air bubbles). The addition of the zeolite leads to a reduction of the parameter "bending strength", which may be the result of air-entraining or the presence of unreacted soft zeolitic particles.

Table 4. Physical-mechanical properties of the samples.

Sample	Bulk Density after Immersion	Bending Strength	Adsorption after Immersion
	kg/m^3	N/mm^2 (MPa)	mm^3/cm^3
Ms	2126	7.84	173.8
Mz	2139	7.80	162.4

These values were determined according EN 1015-3:2001. Methods of test for mortar for masonry—Part 3: Determination of consistence of fresh mortar (by flow table).

In order to determine the "absorption after immersion" (Table 4), firstly, the samples are dried in an oven at 50 ± 5 °C for 3 days and their weight is measured. Then, they are immersed in water for 5 days, which ensures full water absorption (increase in mass was less than 0.5% of the heavier mass), and their weight is measured again. The amount of water permeated in the Mz system was greater by almost 150% compared to that of Ms. The reason for these results is the addition of clinoptilolite. The water absorption, measured at 28 days of curing, of both Ms and Mz samples is relatively large for this type of material, suggesting possibilities for obtaining a denser structure through a precise selection of fractions of inert/active fillers [34].

The formed structure of Mz samples is dense, which is determined when comparing the pure volume of the samples, recalculated from the measured value of the pore volume and density after immersion at 28 days of curing—21.1 mm^3/cm^3 (sample Ms); 30.0 mm^3/cm^3 (sample Mz) (Table 4). However, these samples have an open porosity, which allows for the penetration of water, causing a slow, continuous hydration of the cement grains. The high adsorption of the samples with natural zeolite and river sand can be explained by the high water absorption capacity of zeolite particles [35].

According to Table 4, the standard cement mortar Ms's 28-day compressive strength is similar to the factory's stated value. This suggests that the sand utilized is comparable to

EN 196-1, the CEN Standard sand. At 120 days, the pore volume drops by 6.8% and the newly formed hydrates fill the porous area, increasing the compressive strength by 7.6%.

Similarly, for samples Mz28 and Mz120, a 15.1% increase in the compressive strength was observed. The values of the measured parameters indicate the formation of a thin structure of hardened samples Mz, which are characterized by a 0.45 water-to-cement ratio.

The compressive strength of both samples Ms28 and Mz28 is very high and continues to grow over time. The use of zeolite as a partial binder substitute increases the 28-day (Mz28) compressive strength in comparison with the same parameter for the Ms28 sample with approximately 13.0% (Figure 1a). At 120 days of curing (samples Ms120 and Mz120) the difference between the compressive strengths is increased by 20.8%.

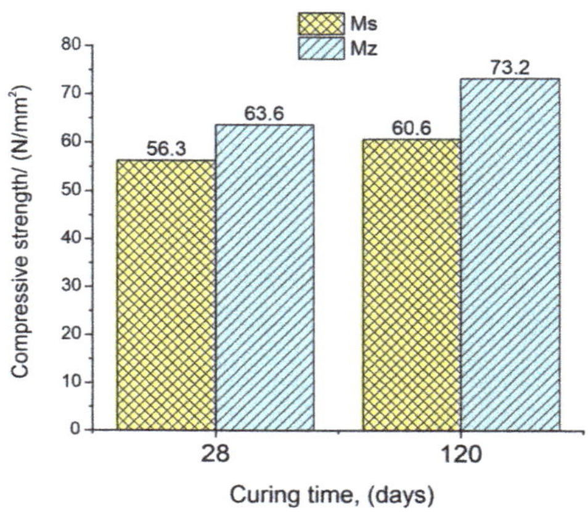

(a)

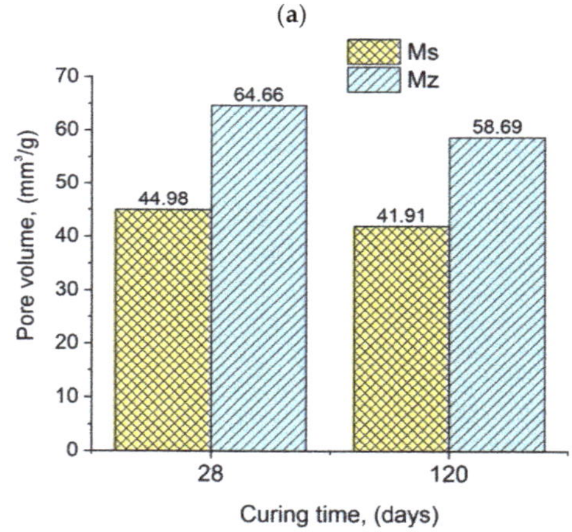

(b)

Figure 1. (**a**). Data presenting the compressive strength for samples Ms and Mz. (**b**). Data presenting the pore volume for samples Ms and Mz.

The results regarding the changes in pore volume have a different pattern compared to the "compressive strength" parameter. The pore volume in the series (Ms28–Ms120 and Mz28–Mz120) decreased by 6.8% for the Ms samples and similarly by 9.2% for the Mz samples (Figure 1b). This result is logical considering that in the course of hydration and deferred hydration, the pores are gradually filled with the crystallites of the CSH/CSAH phases. The difference in the pore volume results between the two series is also significant with the Ms28–Mz28 pair showing a 43.8% increase in pore volume and the Ms120–Mz120 pair showing a 40.0% increase. With the addition of 10% thermoactivated clinoptilolite, it can be assumed that the observed changes are due to the porous structure of the zeolite [36].

On one hand, the formation of a dense and robust structure is observed, but on the other hand, an increase in the pore volume is also noted, in which the role of clinoptilolite is considered as an opportunity to increase the pore space and growth potential of the CSH/CSAH phases.

The reported effects of the influence of natural clinoptilolite on the microstructure of the cement mortars can be confirmed by microscopic analysis—SEM.

4.3. Macro- and Microstructure of Mortars—Scanning Electron Microscopy (SEM)

The results of the macro- and microstructural analysis of the Ms and Mz samples are presented in Figures 2–5.

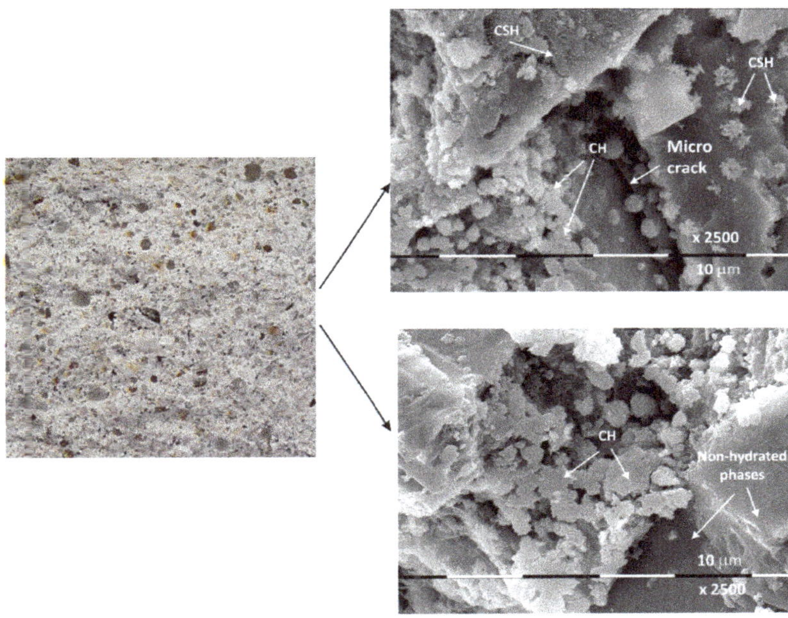

Figure 2. Macro- and micrographs of the surface structures of sample Ms at 28 days of water curing.

The macrostructure of the Ms-series samples with sand is characterized by single-grained particles visible to observation without magnification. Their shape is variable and irregular, and most are of different colors with shades between gray, dark gray, and yellow. The structure is well homogenized; however, characteristically, the air pores are easily visible, entrained during sample preparation and leaving empty circular cavities. It can be determined that the macrostructure is robust and dense, despite the multiple air pores. The sample does not crumble or spatter on contact.

Even at 28 days of curing, the micrographs in Figure 2 show stable and dense structures; as a result, there are no gaps in the structure that could allow new minerals to form. A fine-grained crystal aggregate with structural characteristics most likely below the limit of PXRD detection is formed by the CSH/CSAH gel. The micrographs also show regions where self-desiccation drying cracks are visible. On the surface of sample Ms28 are easily distinguishable areas of dense surface, probably unaffected by the hydration process. The observed effects are explained by water deficiency as a result of the type and ratio of the mortar components. Areas adjacent to these sites are also reported to be covered by relatively small flat formations and those that resemble the shape of a small rose flower. The main morphological characteristic of the sample is that two-dimensional flat crystals on the surface of the sample are predominant while other CSH/CSAH gel-specific formations are in limited areas and are small in size compared to the adjacent crystal formations. The plate crystals are characteristic of portlandite crystals, while those of the second type are characteristic of small crystal forms of the CSH phases. Similar results have been presented by other authors for building mortars with conventional compositions [13,37].

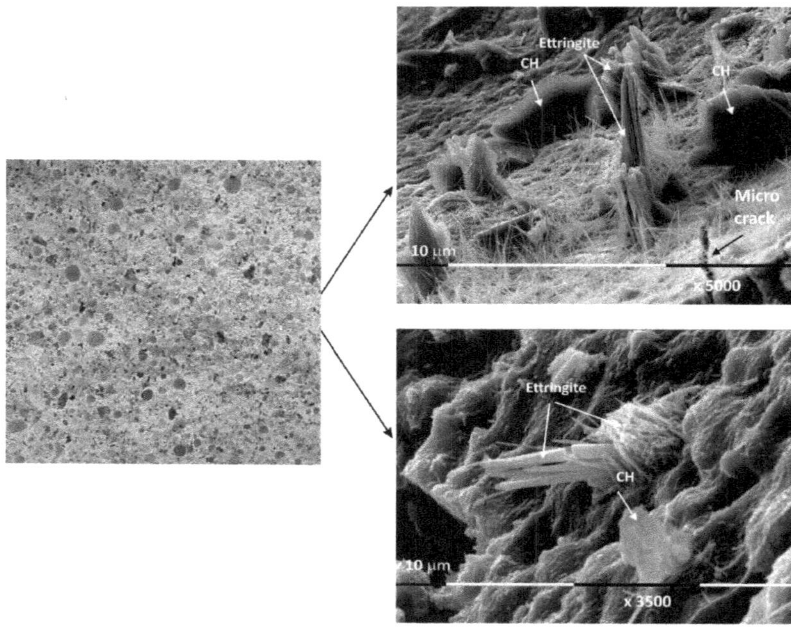

Figure 3. Macro- and micrographs of the surface structures of sample Ms at 120 days of water curing.

The micrographs of sample Ms120 clearly show long and fine crystallites covering the entire surface of the sample. This type of crystalline form is very characteristic of ettringite [38,39].

Although the surface of the sample is covered with hydration products, cracking is still visible in the foundation (Figure 3).

Macro images of the surface of the Mz series of samples show the same characteristic grain structure, with well-dispersed sand particles, which give the characteristic mélange structure of the two samples Mz28 and Mz120 (Figures 4 and 5). Sample Mz28 (Figure 4) exhibits larger-sized and more densely spaced air pores, which is consistent with the results of the pore volume measurement, which increases significantly (Figure 1). In sample Mz120 (Figure 5), the size of the air pores visibly decreases while the other characteristics are preserved. The macrostructure is again dense, strong, and crack-free. This result is also correlated with the pore volume measurement results, which are higher compared to the pore volume for the whole Ms series but lower compared to sample Mz28.

The microstructures of Mz28 and Mz120 differ from those of Ms28 and Ms120, with higher surface coverage of Mz samples with hydration products. No unhydrated zones are visible, and the crystallites are in larger volume and in greater variety.

Figure 4. Macro- and micrographs of the surface structures of sample Mz at 28 days of water curing.

Figure 5. Macro- and micrographs of the surface structures of sample Mz at 120 days of water curing.

Both two-dimensional plate-shaped crystallites and the characteristic needle-shaped crystals, the formation of druses, as well as a surface covered with a thin veil of honeycomb-like crystalline formations characteristic of tobermorite can be identified [40]. Cavities on the surface of the samples can be distinguished, but not micro-cracks, which is consistent with the results of the physical-mechanical measurements for compressive strength. The increase in the values of this parameter for Mz28 and Mz120 corresponds to the greater variety of crystallites formed during the hydration of the cement mortars. From the micrographs of the zeolite series samples, the addition of the crystallites into the basic framework of the cement mortar is evident [36]. In addition, coalescence of the flat crystallites into adjacent formations is noted. This implies that the compactness of the microstructure is improved, which is probably the result of the implementation of pozzolanic reactions, in the course of which additional calcium-silica crystal hydrates (CSH gel) are formed. Pozzolanic reactions can be carried out with fragments of the zeolite structure (based on amorphous SiO_2 and Al_2O_3) [10], in which secondary hydration between the portlandite and zeolite fragments is possible with the formation of CSH/CSAH phases, which is confirmed by the physical-mechanical and microscopic results.

In conclusion, due to the different cement-to-water ratio and empty space, these areas are filled with crystal hydrates of different morphology: plate crystals (portlandite), needle crystals (ettringite), and fine crystal aggregates (CSH/CSAH gels). They cover the surface of the samples with a fine veil of crystallites, the two-dimensional portlandite tiles being considerably less numerous. It is the relation of the portlandite crystallites that is the main difference in the morphology of the samples. In sample Ms28, they are most massively distributed and cover its surface, which is also represented in the SEM image (Figure 2). In the remaining samples (Figures 3–5), the flat portlandite formations are significantly fewer and are embedded in the CSH/CSAH network of crystals. These results can most likely be explained by the influence of clinoptilolite (Mz series), which absorbs water faster than cement, and for this reason, there is not enough water for it at the beginning of hydration. The absorbed moisture from the zeolite then participates in the formation of the new CSH/CSAH-type crystal hydrates as secondary hydration continues in the pores of the samples, compensating for the effects in the earlier stage of the hydration process.

In order to confirm the results of the morphological and physical-mechanical studies, X-ray powder diffraction studies were carried out on the phase composition of the cement mortars of the two series.

4.4. X-ray Phase Analysis

The PXRD analysis (Table 5 and Figure 6a–d) shows the presence of two groups of minerals in the studied samples: (i) relict minerals from the initial composition: belite, albite, anorthite, Mg-rich calcite, quartz, and dolomite; and (ii) newly formed minerals portlandite, yugawaralite, scolecite, ettringite, tobermorite 11A, and hibschite. The results of the complete analysis of the phase composition of the samples are presented in Table 4 and Figure 6a–d. The new phases are from CSH and CSAH gels. The formation of the CSAH phases is possible because of the presence of the cementitious minerals from the starting raw materials and the use of quartz sand as a filler, in the composition of which SiO_2 and Al_2O_3 are present (Table 2). Furthermore, its porous structure creates a basic framework that facilitates the formation of crystal hydrate phases (ettringite, tobermorite 11A, and scolecite) in the cavities and interlayer spaces into which water molecules can be inserted. Subsequently, they are used to carry out secondary hydration processes and grow new crystal hydrates. Two of the phases, yugawaralite and hibschite, are identified only in the Mz series samples. Most CSH are formed in both series because they contain quartz and aluminates imported from cement minerals and river sand.

Table 5. PXRD analysis results.

No	Description	Sample	Identified Phases
1.	Non-hydrated cement phases	Ms28, Ms120, Mz28, Mz120	Belite (C_2S), 49-1673—$2CaO{\cdot}SiO_2$
			Albite (C_3S), 11-0593—$(Na,Ca)Al(Si,Al)_3O_8$
			Anorthite (CAS_2), 41-1486—$CaO{\cdot}Al_2O_3{\cdot}2SiO_2$
			Quartz, 46-1045—SiO_2—3.34
2.	Initial component phases	Ms28, Ms120, Mz28, Mz120	Mg-rich Calcite, 47-1743—$CaCO_3$
3.	Newly formed phases: containing OH^-	Ms28, Ms120, Mz28, Mz120	Portlandite (CH), 44-1481—$Ca(OH)_2$
3.1.	containing $SO_4{}^{2-}$, OH^-, and crystal water H_2O	Ms28, Ms120, Mz28, Mz120	Ettringite, 41-1451—$Ca_6Al_2(SO_4)_3(OH)_{12}{\cdot}26H_2O$
		Ms28, Ms120, Mz28, Mz120	Monosulphoaluminate, 45-0158—$Ca_4Al_2SO_{10}{\cdot}12H_2O$
3.2.	hydroxyl silicates—CSH, formed from the main oxides CaO, SiO_2, OH^-, and/or crystal water H_2O	Ms28, Ms120, Mz28, Mz120	Hillebrandite, 42-0538—$Ca_6Si_3O_9(OH)_6$
		Ms28, Ms120, Mz28, Mz120	Tobermorite 11A, 45-1480—$Ca_5Si_6(O,OH)_{18}{\cdot}5H_2O$
3.3	hydroxyl silicates—CSAH, formed from the main oxides CaO, Al_2O_3, SiO_2, OH^-, and/or crystal water H_2O	Mz28, Mz120	Yugawaralite, 39-1372—$CaAl_2Si_6O_{16}{\cdot}4H_2O$
		Mz28, Mz120	Hibschite, 45-1447—$Ca_3Al_2(SiO_4)_{3-x}(OH)_{4x}$; (x = 0.2–1.5)
		Ms28, Ms120, Mz28, Mz120	Scolecite, 41-1355—$CaAl_2Si_3O_{10}{\cdot}3H_2O$

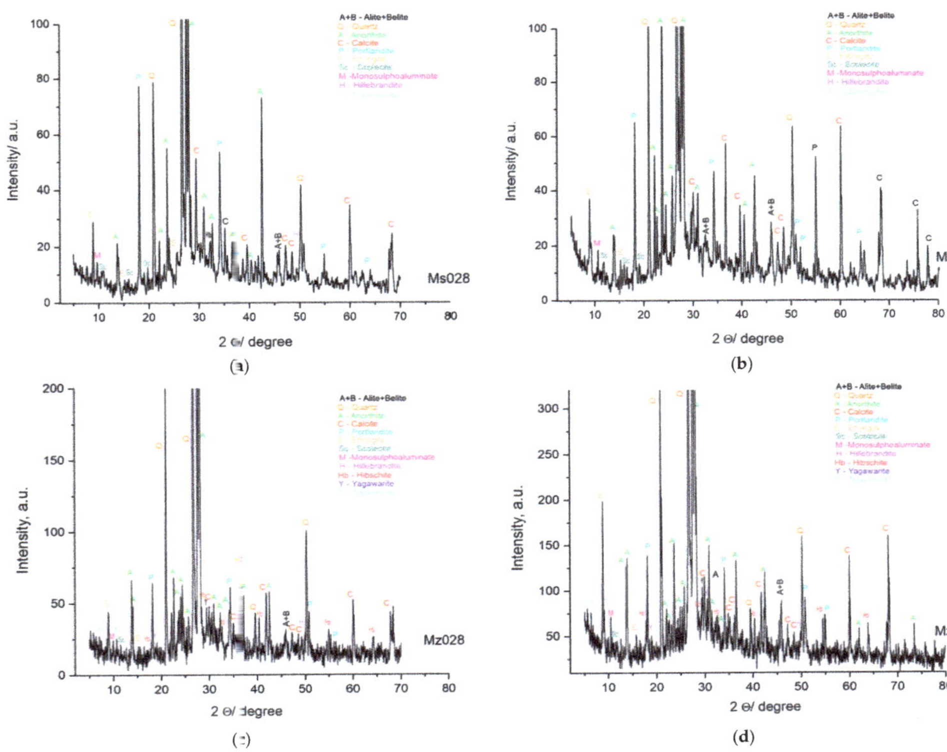

Figure 6. (**a**). PXRD pattern of sample Ms, water-cured for 28 days. (**b**). PXRD pattern of sample Ms water-cured for 120 days. (**c**). PXRD pattern of sample Mz, water-cured for 28 days. (**d**). PXRD pattern of sample Mz, water-cured for 120 days.

Inadequate water in the systems causes an incomplete hydration of the raw minerals which is linked to the identification of phases from the raw materials in the compositions of the samples.

The results of the powder PXRD analysis are in full correlation with the results obtained from the physical-mechanical analyses and the macro- and microstructure of the samples from both series. The hydration conditions and the composition of the materials are a prerequisite for the formation of CSH and CSAH phases. The introduction of clinoptilolite (part of zeolite) is involved in the distribution of the amount of water, and it can be assumed that, due to secondary hydration processes, water is in short supply. The PXRD results identify multiple new phases, but the intensity of the reflections is not well pronounced and it can be assumed that these phases have low crystallinity, consistent with the morphological images. Since the amount of water was predicted at the initial stage of sample preparation it can be argued that the results obtained are expected and their purpose is to assess the influence of the amount of natural zeolite, and in the subsequent stages of the studies, the amount of zeolite, as well as the water–cement ratio, will be refined.

4.5. *Diffuse Reflectance Infrared Fourier Transformed Spectroscopy (DRIFTS)*

IR spectroscopy is a powerful method for measuring organic and inorganic substances in the liquid or solid aggregate state. This method can be used to study cement composites allowing the identification of solids in minimum quantities and with fine dispersion [23]. In the present work, measurements were performed with diffuse reflectance infrared Fourier transformed spectroscopy (DRIFTS). The method is suitable for the study of substances with an amorphous structure where other structural methods are inapplicable, such as powder X-ray phase analysis. An advantage of DRIFTS is the possibility to directly measure spectra from powder samples with rough surfaces without prior preparation or as dispersions in IR transparent matrices such as KBr and KCl [41,42]. The collecting optics in the DRIFTS attachment is designed to gather as much of the diffuse reflected light as possible. DRIFTS is a suitable technique for the study of chemical bonds in a molecule, especially for determining the involvement of water molecules in the structure of substances. This makes the method particularly applicable for the characterization of cement mortars, especially for the distribution of structurally bound water in the composition of CSH/CSAH phases as a result of hydration of cement minerals involving natural clinoptilolite [43].

The results of the spectroscopic measurements using the DRIFTS technique are presented in Table 6 and Figure 7.

The application of the diffuse-reflectance methodology to the measurement of vibrations in molecules makes it possible to identify the vibrations in molecules and the bonds of individual atoms to the various functional groups and especially those to water. This characterization is important for the investigated cement mortars, since the amount of water used in the solutions is not only important in terms of the economic performance of the process but also relevant for the new phases formed, their diversity, and structural characteristics. In summarizing the results, groups of spectral bands characteristic of silicate, carbonate, sulfate, compounds with hydroxyl ions, and those containing crystallization water were identified. The main group of compounds corresponds to the spectra of the CSH and CSAH gel phases and accordingly combines the vibrations of the tetrahedral SiO_4 group, the pyroxene SiO_3 group, and the octahedral AlO_6 in combination with the water molecules. It is a characteristic feature of the studied system that phases containing Al-O-Si bonds are found both in the starting raw materials, e.g., natural clinoptilolite [22], and in the hydration products of cementitious minerals.

In confirmation of the XRD results, the combination of bands of the tetrahedral SiO_4^{4-} group (Si-O bond with bands at ν_4 566–576 cm^{-1} and ν_3 1190 cm^{-1}) is assigned to the newly formed CASH gel phases such as hibschite.

Table 6. DRIFTS spectroscopy results of samples Ms and Mz.

No	Description/ References	Bond	ν_1 (cm^{-1})	ν_2 (cm^{-1})	ν_3 (cm^{-1})	ν_4 (cm^{-1})	Samples
1.	AlO_6^{9-} [44–46]	Al-O	-	428–430	-	-	Ms
			-	414–424	856	-	Mz
2.	SiO_3^{2-} [44–46]	Si-O	-	468–472		781	Ms28
			-	470–472	1041–1053	790	Mz28
3.	SiO_4^{4-} [44–46]	Si-O	-	-	1189	566–576	Ms
					-	572–576	Mz
4.	SO_4^{2-} [44–46]	S-O	958–991	-	1155–1159	696–700 781	Ms
			979–991	-	1155	690–694 790–800	Mz
5.	CO_3^{2-} [45–47]	C=O	-	869	1411–1425 1425–1436 1484–1498 1538	-	Ms
			-	865	1409 1436–1438 1486–1488 1529–1554	-	Mz
			$\nu_1 + \nu_3$ 2524 2364–2622	-	-	$\nu_1 + \nu_4$ 1785–1793 1866–1872 1988–1990	Ms
			$\nu_1 + \nu_4$ 2524–2526 2588–2628	-	-	$\nu_1 + \nu_4$ 1785–1787 1873–1990	Mz
6.	SiO_4^{4+}-AlO_6^{9-} [48]	Si-O-Al	-	798–800	1022–1029 1278	522–528	Ms
			-	-	1029–1039 1276–1278	524–526	Mz
7.	SiO_2	Si-O	-	-	796–804	-	Ms
8.	O-H struct. (1) [49]	O-H	-	-	3592	-	Ms
			-	-	3590–3592	-	Mz
9.	$O\text{-}H^-$ cryst. (2) [49]	O-H	3411–3432	1616–1666	3201–3252	-	Ms
			3411–3419	1616–1662	3237–3251	-	Mz
10.	$O\text{-}H^-$ [44,49]	Ca-OH	-	-	3629–3631	-	Mz, Ms
11.	$O\text{-}H^-$ [50]	Al-OH	-	-	3737	-	Ms
			-	-	3735	-	Mz

O-H struct. (1)—O-H bond in structural OH^- anion [49]. O-H crystal. (2)—O-H bond belonging to crystal-bonded water molecules [49].

The pyroxene group SiO_3^{2-} (Si-O bond), with the most typical bands at ν_2 468–472 cm^{-1} and ν_3 1040–1053 cm^{-1}, is presented in CSH gel phases—hillebrandite, tobermorite-11A, and scolecite and in one new phase—yugawaralite.

Hibschite and yugawaralite are from the group of CASH gels and are formed only in the cement solution with the addition of natural clinoptilolite. They are characterized by Al-O-Si bonding, which is expressed by the bands at 1029–1039 cm^{-1} (ν_3 Si-O stretching vibration) and 522–528 cm^{-1} (ν_4 Al-O-Si bending vibration) for wairakite and yugawaralite [45].

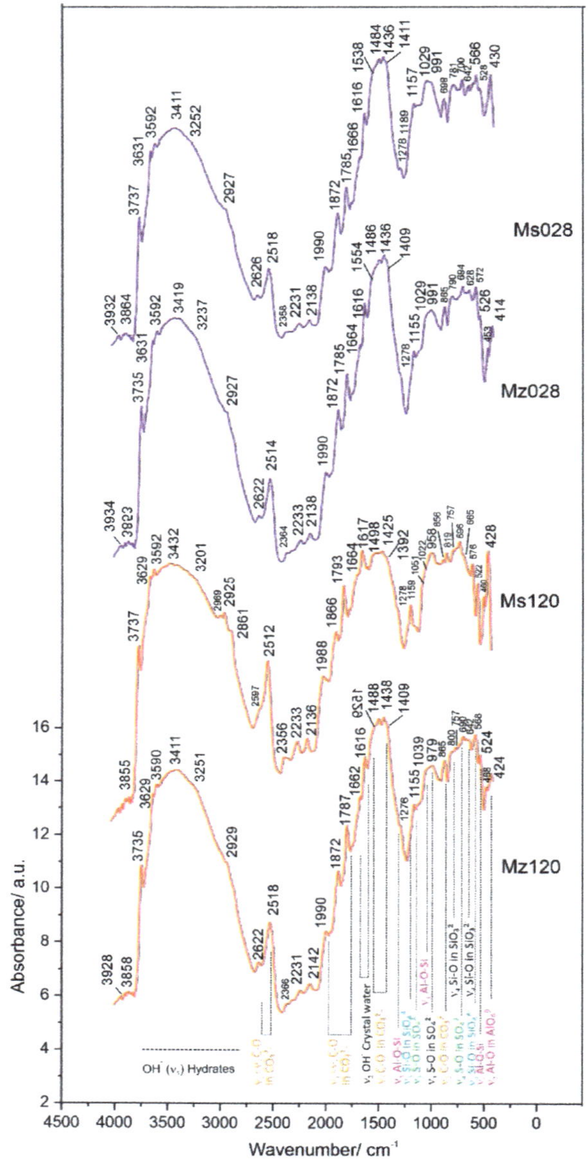

Figure 7. DRIFTS spectra of samples Ms28, Ms120, Mz28, and Mz120.

The octahedral AlO_6^{9-} groups (Al-O bond) from the raw tricalcium aluminate are distributed between the newly-formed monosulphoaluminate and ettringite. Their bands are situated at the spectral ranges 410–430 cm^{-1} and 800–950 cm^{-1}. The band at ν_3 856 cm^{-1} is typical for ettringite (Figure 7) [45]. The vibrational bands of the AlO_6^{9-}

groups combine with the bands of the sulphate group at ν_4 690–800 cm^{-1}, ν_3 1155 cm^{-1}, and ν_1 958–991 cm^{-1} and with that of the hydroxyl ion—ν_3 3590–3592 cm^{-1}.

A second group of bands includes the vibrations of the carbonate ion at ν_2 869 cm^{-1} and ν_3 1409–1554 cm^{-1}, which characterize the spectrum of calcite, a mineral that enters into the composition of white cement.

Using the DRIFTS method, the vibrational fluctuations of the Me-OH bonds are better expressed in the spectra. This is evidenced by the well-formed bands in the ν_3 region 3600–3750 cm^{-1}. In this particular system, this bond is realized both between Ca-OH at ν_3 3629–3631 cm^{-1} and between Al/Si-OH in the crystal hydrates of CSH and CSAH phases at ν_3 3737 cm^{-1}.

The composition of all crystal hydrate phases, formed in the process of hydration of the cement minerals, includes crystallization water. The vibrational bands of water are well expressed in the DRIFTS spectra and represent a broad and well-defined band with multiple insertion bands in the range 3411–3432 cm^{-1}. In the ν_2 region 1616–1666 cm^{-1}, a bending vibrational mode of crystal water is identified.

In conclusion, it can be summarized that the microstructure and properties of the cement mortars of the present study containing thermoactivated zeolite as an additive and cement replacement were characterized using a complex of analytical and physical methods. The results obtained allow us to evaluate the contribution of the additive to the modified properties of the solutions in the hydration process.

The DRIFTS spectra identify the vibrational modes of the functional groups that enter into the composition of the cement solution minerals, namely SiO_3^{2-}, SiO_4^{4-}, AlO_6^{9-}, SO_4^{2-}, CO_3^{2-}, and OH^-, as well as the cross vibrations between Al and Si ions across the oxygen bridges—Al-O-Si. The quantitative characteristics of the obtained spectra are presented in Table 6.

The role of clinoptilolite (part of zeolite) in the present study is explained by the following: (i) influence on the formation of pores in the structure, in which further secondary hydration can develop in the growth of crystal hydrate phases; (ii) participation in pozzolanic reactions, in which excess portlandite is absorbed and new CSH/CSAH phases are formed; (iii) preservation of the physical-mechanical performance of the building solutions, which provides a perspective for further development of the topic for practical applications.

4.6. Thermal Analysis TG/DTG-DSC

Thermogravimetric analysis, combined with derivative thermogravimetry and differential scanning calorimetry, is a powerful tool to complement the results of the analytical methods used. Highly sensitive modern instrumentation allows precise measurements of mass loss, heat effects, phase transitions, solid-phase synthesis, and other important characteristics of the samples, which reveal new data and provide new evidence for both the structure of the samples and their thermal behavior in the programmed heating regime. This also defines thermal analysis methods as very suitable both for the identification of structure-phase transformations and as an acid-free method for solid-phase synthesis [51,52]. In the present work, the simultaneous TG/DTG-DSC measurements were performed in an air-gas environment up to 1300 °C and using dynamic heating mode. Cement mortars are systems of inorganic composites mainly based on the oxides of calcium, silica, and aluminum. In these solutions, the chemical elements involved are usually in their higher oxidation state and are therefore not sensitive to oxygen from the air. This allows the experiments to be carried out at high temperatures up to 1200–1300 °C in a static air environment without the risk of additional oxidation reactions or syntheses between the main oxides as the results obtained are in response to the thermal decomposition of the constituent phases. This provides a rationale for using the complex of thermal methodologies to identify and, in this case, to complement the results of the other analytical methods and especially to characterize the process and products of hydration of the studied white cement solutions.

The results of the thermal measurements are presented in Table 7 and in Figure 8a–d. For convenience, Table 7 includes our own data on the thermal decomposition of white Portland cement (applied as a control sample to monitor changes in the solution), which was used to prepare the mortars [23,26]. The analysis of the results is presented in Figure 9a–d with complementary plots of the dynamics of the resulting mass losses in characteristic temperature intervals with thermal reactions.

Table 7. Thermal investigation results based on temperature at inflexion point ($T_{infl.}$) and mass loss (ML) of the raw material, white Portland cement, and samples Ms28, Ms120, Mz28, and Mz120.

Sample	1. TR *—30–200 °C		2. TR *—422–500 °C		3. TR *—500–730 °C		4. TR *—640–800 °C		ML^{Tot} **, (%)
	$T_{infl.}$, (°C)	ML, (%)	$T_{infl.}$, °C	ML, (%)	$T_{infl.}$, (°C)	ML (%)	$T_{infl.}$ (°C)	ML (%)	
Cement [26]	65.1 98.0	0.30 0.39	429.9	0.25	539.6	0.15	711.8	3.68	5.19
Ms28	29.8 108.5 177.1	0.91 1.01 0.52	465.3	0.70	569.6 625.1 682.8	1.46 1.90 1.00	742.5	3.33	11.44
Ms120	29.8 100.4 130.2 169.5	0.81 0.70 0.37 0.41	479.2	0.66	562.9	2.45	675.7 743.3	1.84 1.91	10.98
Mz28	55.3 98.92	0.31 0.93	458.9	0.75	553.8 592.6	1.40 2.43	719.3	2.89	10.18
Mz120	62.0 112.7 183.6	0.73 1.11 0.66	462.6	0.63	566.5 611.5 671.8	2.66 1.37 2.13	751.5	3.00	15.04

TR *—temperature range, (°C); ML^{Tot}**—Total mass losses, (%).

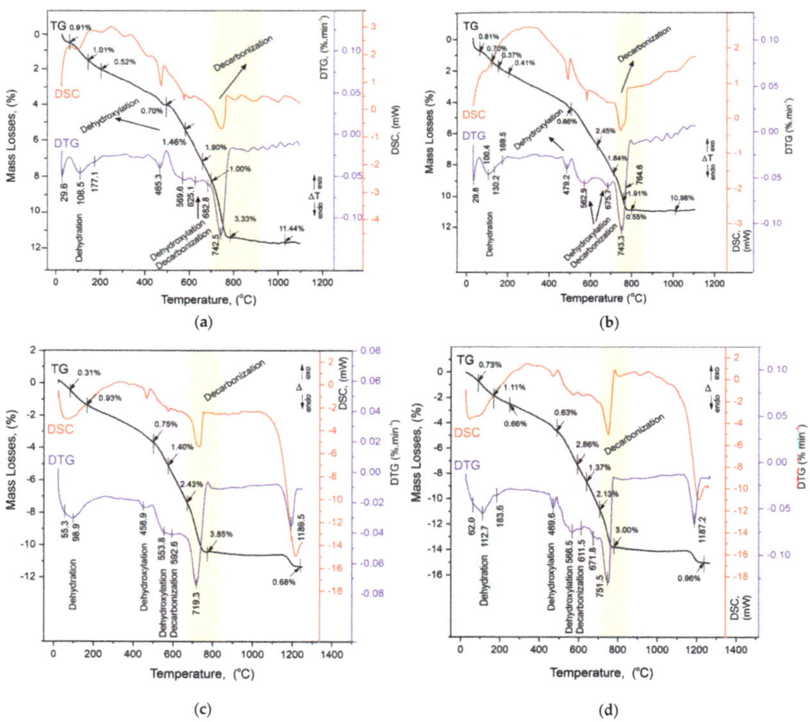

Figure 8. (**a**). TG/DTG-DSC curves of sample Ms28. (**b**). TG/DTG-DSC curves of sample Ms120. (**c**). TG/DTG-DSC curves of sample Mz28. (**d**). TG/DTG-DSC curves of sample Mz120.

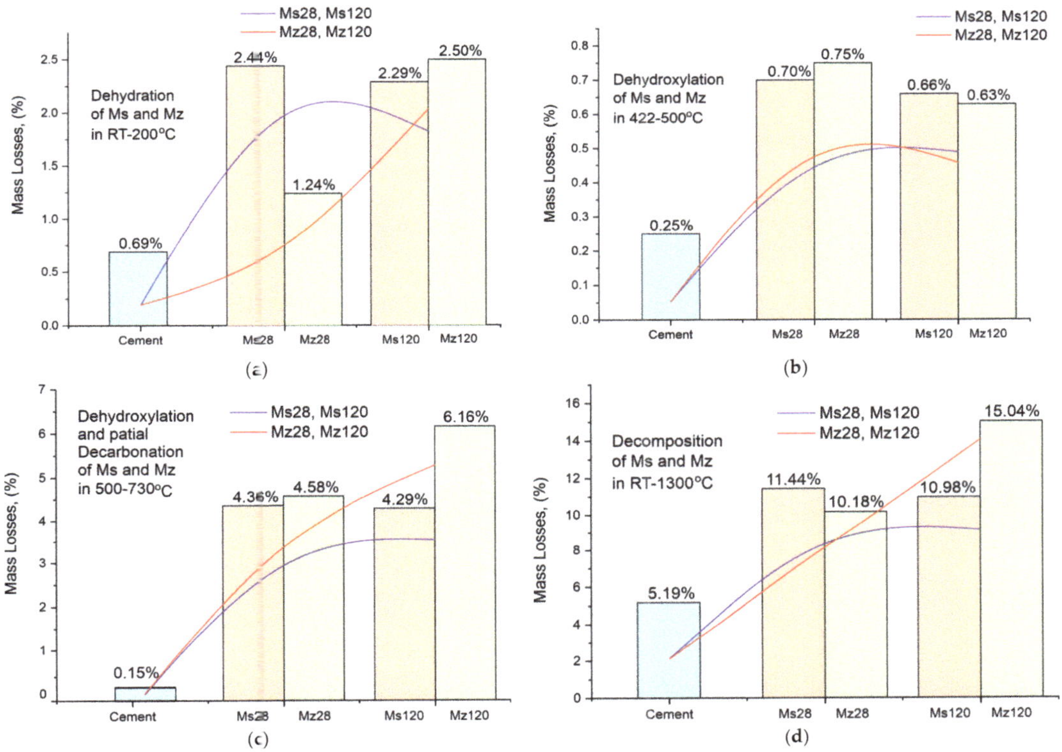

Figure 9. (**a**). Mass loss dynamics during dehydration of crystallization water in the RT–200 °C temperature range. (**b**). Mass loss dynamics during dehydroxylation of structurally bound water by $Ca(OH)_2$ in the temperature range 422–500 °C. (**c**). Mass loss dynamics during dehydroxylation and partial decarbonation of CSH/CSAH in the temperature range 500–730 °C. (**d**). Total mass loss dynamics in the temperature range RT–1300 °C.

The analysis of the results of the thermal experiments (Figure 8a–d) and the data from Table 7 allow us to claim that in the temperature interval RT–1300 °C, the recorded thermal reactions can be separated into four stages. In each of them, two, three (500–730 °C), or more (30–200 °C) mutually overlapping thermal reactions can be registered. The determination of the initial and final temperature and mass loss for each of them is performed using the derivative thermogravimetry (DTG curve) data, with the temperatures at their inflection points presented in Figure 8a–d and Table 7.

Based on the results of our previous studies [23,26], the thermal effects in the present study are also shown to be related to the following:

1. Temperature range—30–200 °C—Dehydration of physic sorption water and crystal water from crystal hydrates formed during the hydration stage. Their phase composition was identified by PXRD (Figure 6a–d, Table 5) and SEM (Figures 2–5) analyses and includes ettringite, tobermorite, yugawaralite, scolecite, and monosulphoaluminate. The diversity in the crystal hydrate phases explains the overlapping dehydration reactions. It can be noted that mass losses are low and do not exceed 2.50%, with the highest being observed in Mz120. Another characteristic feature is the gradual increase in dehydration temperatures due to densification of the structure, as evidenced by MIP (Figure 1b), SEM (Figures 2–5), and physical-mechanical measurements (Figure 1a, Table 4);

2. Temperature range—422–500 °C—It is characterized by a pronounced single thermal reaction occurring independently in the second temperature interval. It is also accompanied by low mass losses of 0.63% to 0.75% and a low-intensity endothermic effect. These mass losses are related to the dehydroxylation of $Ca(OH)_2$. The losses are low due to the low water–cement ratio and the additional influence of the thermoactivated zeolite, which absorbs some of the water. The portlandite in the samples is formed upon hydration of the unabsorbed portion of water to form CSH and CSAH crystal hydrates, as evidenced by PXRD (Figure 6a–d), SEM (Figures 2–5), and DRIFTS (Figure 7) results. There is a tendency to decrease the mass loss from dehydroxylation of $Ca(OH)_2$ in the compositions with zeolite, since its role is precisely to participate in pozzolanic reactions to eliminate hydroxyl ions.
3. Temperature range—500–730 °C—Dehydroxylation of CSH/CSAH, partial decarbonation. This temperature range is most closely related to the hydration of cement solutions and the influence of thermoactivated zeolite. A fraction of the water molecules bind to the calcium-silica/aluminum phases as crystallization water, while another fraction enters the compositions in the form of structurally bound water as OH ions. They form stronger bonds in the crystal lattice of the CSH/CSAH phases. Logically, the stronger bonds are broken at higher temperatures, which fall precisely in the third interval up to 730 °C. The thermal reactions are mutually overlapping, with mass losses ranging from 4.29% to 6.16%, and the effects are endothermic. Based on the PXRD results obtained (Figure 6a–d), it can be assumed that dehydroxylation of ettringite, hillebrandite, hibschite, and tobermorite takes place. The different forms of water molecules as crystallization or structurally bound OH ions were defined in the DRIFTS spectroscopy analyses (Figure 7, Table 6). The thermal experiments confirm these results by complementing the information with mass loss data and thermal decomposition temperatures.
4. Temperature range—640–800 °C—Decarbonation of $CaCO_3$. In the high-temperature region, thermal decomposition of a small amount of carbonate ions, mainly from calcite, is observed, as shown by PXRD (Figure 6a–d), SEM (Figures 2–5), and DRIFTS (Figure 7, Table 6). Mass losses range close to 3.00%, with a well-defined endothermic effect. It can be noted that the decomposition temperatures of carbonates are shifted towards the higher ones due to diffusion difficulties resulting from the formation of a more solid and dense structure.

In our previous studies [23,26], it was shown that along with the dehydroxylation of OH-ions, a partial decarbonation of thermally more unstable carbonate-containing phases takes place, whose thermal decomposition occurs at lower than usual temperatures, falling in the third interval.

For a clearer illustration of the effect of using thermally activated zeolite in building mortars, the results from the thermal studies are presented in the form of trend plots for the mass losses of the individual processes of dehydration of crystallization water (Figure 9a), dehydroxylation of structurally bound water by $Ca(OH)_2$ (Figure 9b), dehydroxylation and partial decarbonation of CSH/CSAH (Figure 9c), and total mass losses (Figure 9d). The data for the Ms series are in orange, for the Mz series in green, and for the white cement used for comparison in blue. The red and blue lines represent the increasing and decreasing trend of ML, respectively, for a given process. The mass loss data dynamics from crystallization water dehydration (Figure 9a) present a decreasing trend for the Ms series and an increasing trend for Mz, particularly well pronounced when comparing the ML data between Mz28—1.24% and Mz120—2.50%, which is the highest value. This means that water is retained when the thermally activated zeolite is used, and it is distributed as crystallization and structurally bound. The ML trends of the structurally bound water (Figure 9c) best illustrate the impact of using zeolite. Both series recorded relatively high MLs between 4.29% to 6.16%. The distinctly higher values are for the Mz series. This is the clearest evidence for the role of zeolite as a natural pozzolan and the possibilities for a secondary continuous hydration. Accordingly, this trend also applies to the total mass losses (Figure 9d), which increase by approximately 5% in the Mz series due to the increase in ML in the third stage, while they remain approximately the same 10–11% for the Ms series. The ML change trend from dehydroxylation of structurally bound water to $Ca(OH)_2$ is the least pronounced, but nevertheless, a decreasing tendency can be noted in the Mz series.

5. Discussion

According to the results from the complex of analytical methods—MIP, SEM, PXRD, and DRIFTS—the following reaction mechanism scheme of the samples' hydration have been defined:

$$2Ca_3SiO_5\ (C_3S) + 7H_2O \rightarrow Ca_3Si_2O_7{\cdot}4H_2O\ (\text{C-S-H gel}) + 3Ca(OH)_2\ (\text{fast}) \tag{1}$$

$$2Ca_2SiO_4\ (C_2S) + 5H_2O \rightarrow Ca_3Si_2O_7{\cdot}4H_2O\ (\text{C-S-H gel}) + Ca(OH)_2\ (\text{slow}) \tag{2}$$

Formation of ettringite:

$$Ca_3Al_2O_6\ (C_3A) + 3CaSO_4{\cdot}2H_2O + 26H_2O \rightarrow Ca_6Al_2(SO_4)_3(OH)_{12}{\cdot}26H_2O \tag{3}$$

Formation of hillebrandite (CSH):

$$Ca_2SiO_4\ (C_2S) + H_2O \rightarrow Ca_2SiO_3(OH)_2 \tag{4}$$

Formation of tobermorite 11A (CSH)—only in compositions with sand or zeolite:

$$2Ca_3SiO_5\ (C_3S) + 4SiO_2 + 6H_2O \rightarrow Ca_5Si_6O_{16}(OH)_2{\cdot}4H_2O\ (\text{C-S-H gel}) + Ca(OH)_2 \tag{5}$$

$$3Ca_2SiO_4\ (C_2S) + 3SiO_2 + 6H_2O \rightarrow Ca_5Si_6O_{16}(OH)_2{\cdot}4H_2O\ (\text{C-S-H gel}) + Ca(OH)_2 \tag{6}$$

Formation of hibschite (CSAH)—only in compositions with sand or zeolite

$$Ca_3Al_2O_6 + 2H_2O^- + 2SiO_2 \rightarrow Ca_3Al_2(SiO_4)_{3-x}(OH)_{4x},\ \text{where } x = 1 \tag{7}$$

Formation of scolecite (CSAH):

$$Ca_3Al_2O_6\ (C_3A) + 3SiO_2 + 5H_2O \rightarrow CaAl_2Si_3O_{10}{\cdot}3H_2O + 2Ca(OH)_2 \tag{8}$$

Formation of yugawaralite (CSAH):

$$Ca_3Al_2O_6\ (C_3A) + 6SiO_2 + 6H_2O \rightarrow CaAl_2Si_6O_{15}{\cdot}4H_2O + 2Ca(OH)_2 \tag{9}$$

A wider range of newly-formed hydrated phases is recorded during the phase composition identification in the current studies of mortars containing zeolite (clinoptilolite), in contrast with our results from earlier studies of the PXRD analysis of cement mortars without zeolite addition [24,26]. In addition to hillebrandite and scolecite, phases such tobermorite-11A, yugawaralite, and hibschite are formed in the presence of up to 10% clinoptilolite in the cement, even with less water present (Figure 6a–d, Table 4). Because of the implemented zeolite's high sorption capacity and its pozzolanic activity (resulting from the presence of active SiO_2 and Al_2O_3 from the zeolite addition), there is a higher variety of CSH and CSAH phases [11,34].

Under the impact of the zeolite additive, the solutions become more alkaline, which leads to the hydration of the minerals from the cement clinker. Reactions (10) and (11) [12] indicate that the production of the following anions facilitates the dissolution of the zeolite tuff in liquids with an alkaline reaction:

$$\equiv\text{Si–O–Si}\equiv + 8OH^- \rightarrow 2[SiO(OH)_3]^- + H_2O \tag{10}$$

$$\equiv\text{Si–O–Al}\equiv + 7OH^- \rightarrow [SiO(OH)_3]^- + [Al(OH)_4]^- \tag{11}$$

Pozzolanic reactions can occur in the presence of water when the zeolite's octahedral and tetrahedral lattice structure fragments and the cement's calcium dioxide are present. This gives rise to the growth of hydrated calcium aluminosilicate compounds (CSAH) and facilitates the creation of natural centers of crystallization, as exemplified in part by the following potential reactions (12) and (13) [12,24,53]:

Formation of ettringite with pozzolanic reaction:

$$6Ca^{2+} + 2[Al(OH)_4]^- + 4OH^- + 3SO_4{}^{2-} + 26H_2O \rightarrow Ca_6Al_2(SO_4)_3(OH)_{12}\cdot 26H_2O \quad (12)$$

Formation of hibschite with pozzolanic reaction:

$$Ca_3Al_2O_6 + [SiO(OH)_3]^- + OH^- + SiO_2 \rightarrow Ca_3Al_2(SiO_4)_{3-x}(OH)_{4x} + O^{2-}, \text{ where } x = 1 \quad (13)$$

The PXRD data and the DRIFTS identification of the newly formed crystal hydrate phases imply that there is a deficiency of bound water in their structure. The starting water-to-cement ratio and the zeolite additive's inclusion in the second series of cement mortar compositions serve as the foundation for this assertion. As noted by other writers, zeolite's distinct sorption characteristics aid in the development of a strong and dense structure [12,24].

The results obtained are also validated by scanning electron microscopy studies of the cement mortar morphology from the two series of samples.

6. Conclusions

In this study, an investigation was conducted on the changes in the microstructure of hardened mortars due to the replacement of 10 wt% of pure white cement with thermoactivated natural zeolite with high clinoptilolite content. Experiments carried out with plain sand and water–cement ratios complying with EN 197-1 show that the inclusion of zeolite increases the amount of pores accessible by mercury intrusion porosimetry by about 40%, but the measured strengths are also higher by more than 13%. When these samples were aged in an aqueous environment from day 28 to day 120, the amount of pores decreased by about 10% and the corresponding compressive strength increased by nearly 15%, i.e., the addition of thermally activated zeolite did not block the access of water to the cementitious minerals. Through microstructural studies, it was proven that new products such as ettringite, monosulphoaluminate, CSH gel—hillebrandite and tobermorite, and CSAH gel—yugawaralite, hibschite and scolecite are formed under delayed hydration. Replacing part of the white cement with thermally activated natural zeolite increases the density and strength of the structure as well as the amount and variety of new crystalline phases. This is a reason to claim that building solutions with the used zeolite content will have improved corrosion resistance against aggressive weathering.

Author Contributions: Conceptualization, V.P. and V.S.; methodology, V.S.; software, M.S.; validation, M.S.; formal analysis, V.P. and V.S.; investigation, V.P. and K.M.; resources, V.S.; data curation, K.M.; writing—original draft preparation, V.P.; writing—review and editing, K.M.; visualization, V.P.; supervision, V.P.; project administration, V.P. and K.M.; funding acquisition, V.P. All authors have read and agreed to the published version of the manuscript.

Funding: This work was supported by the Operational Program "Science and Education for Intelligent Growth", co-financed by the European Union through the European Structural and Investment Funds under grant BG05M2OP001-1.001-0008 of National Centre for Mechatronics and Clean Technology (V.P.). The authors gratefully acknowledge the Institute of Mineralogy and Crystallography Acad. I. Kostov, Bulgarian Academy of Sciences (K2-V.P., K.M.).

Institutional Review Board Statement: Not applicable.

Informed Consent Statement: Not applicable.

Data Availability Statement: The original contributions presented in the study are included in the article, further inquiries can be directed to the corresponding author.

Conflicts of Interest: The authors declare no conflicts of interest

References

1. Chuan, L.F. Innovative Cement Additives Quality Improvers in Sustainable Cement and Concrete. *Sains Malays.* **2015**, *44*, 1599–1607.
2. Barbhuiya, S.; Kanavaris, F.; Das, B.B.; Idrees, M. Decarbonising Cement and Concrete Production: Strategies, Challenges and Pathways for Sustainable Development. *J. Build. Eng.* **2024**, *86*, 108861. [CrossRef]
3. Dembovska, L.; Bajare, D.; Pundiene, I.; Vitola, L. Effect of Pozzolanic Additives on the Strength Development of High Performance Concrete. *Procedia Eng.* **2017**, *172*, 202–210. [CrossRef]
4. World Business Council for Sustainable Development. *Cement Technology Roadmap 2009: Carbon Emissions Reductions up to 2050*; World Business Council for Sustainable Development: Geneva, Switzerland; International Energy Agency: Paris, France, 2009.
5. Juenger, M.C.G.; Snellings, R.; Bernal, S.A. Supplementary Cementitious Materials: New Sources, Characterization, and Performance Insights. *Cem. Concr. Res.* **2019**, *122*, 257–273. [CrossRef]
6. Kapeluszna, E.; Szudek, W.; Wolka, P.; Zieliński, A. Implementation of Alternative Mineral Additives in Low-Emission Sustainable Cement Composites. *Materials* **2021**, *14*, 6423. [CrossRef]
7. Ahmadi, B.; Shekarchi, M. Use of Natural Zeolite as a Supplementary Cementitious Material. *Cem. Concr. Compos.* **2010**, *32*, 134–141. [CrossRef]
8. Snellings, R.; Suraneni, P.; Skibsted, J. Future and Emerging Supplementary Cementitious Materials. *Cem. Concr. Res.* **2023**, *171*, 107199. [CrossRef]
9. Alexa-Stratulat, S.-M.; Olteanu, I.; Toma, A.-M.; Pastia, C.; Banu, O.-M.; Corbu, O.-C.; Toma, I.-O. The Use of Natural Zeolites in Cement-Based Construction Materials—A State of the Art Review. *Coatings* **2023**, *14*, 18. [CrossRef]
10. Perraki, T.; Kontori, E.; Tsivilis, S.; Kakali, G. The Effect of Zeolite on the Properties and Hydration of Blended Cements. *Cem. Concr. Compos.* **2010**, *32*, 128–133. [CrossRef]
11. Perraki, T.; Kakali, G.; Kontori, E. Characterization and Pozzolanic Activity of Thermally Treated Zeolite. *J. Therm. Anal. Calorim.* **2005**, *82*, 109–113. [CrossRef]
12. Perraki, T.; Kakali, G.; Kontoleon, F. The Effect of Natural Zeolites on the Early Hydration of Portland Cement. *Microporous Mesoporous Mater.* **2003**, *61*, 205–212. [CrossRef]
13. Shekarchi, M.; Ahmadi, B.; Azarhomayun, F.; Shafei, B.; Kioumarsi, M. Natural Zeolite as a Supplementary Cementitious Material—A Holistic Review of Main Properties and Applications. *Constr. Build. Mater.* **2023**, *409*, 133766. [CrossRef]
14. *ASTM C311-07*; Standard Test Methods for Sampling and Testing Fly Ash or Natural Pozzolans for Use in Portland-Cement Concrete. ASTM: West Conshohocken, PA, USA, 2007.
15. Massazza, F. Pozzolana and Pozzolanic Cements. *Lea's Chem. Cem. Concr.* **1998**, *4*, 471–631.
16. Opoczky, L.; Tamas, F.D. Multicomponent Composite Cements. In *Advances in Cement Technology: Chemistry, Manufacture and Testing*; Ghosh, S.N., Ed.; CRC Press: New Delhi, India, 2002; pp. 559–594.
17. *ASTM C618-08a*; Standard Specification for Coal Fly Ash and Raw or Calcined Natural Pozzolan for Use in Concrete. ASTM: West Conshohocken, PA, USA, 2008.
18. Janotka, I.; Krajči, L.; Dzivák, M. Properties and Utilization of Zeolite-Blended Portland Cements. *Clays Clay Min.* **2003**, *51*, 616–624. [CrossRef]
19. Okamura, H.; Ouchi, M. Self-Compacting Concrete. *J. Adv. Concr. Technol.* **2003**, *1*, 5–15. [CrossRef]
20. Skarendahl, Å.; Billberg, P. *Report 35: Casting of Self Compacting Concrete-Final Report of RILEM TC 188-CSC*; RILEM Publications: Paris, France, 2006; Volume 35, ISBN 2-35158-001-X.
21. Concrete, S.-C. The European Guidelines for Self-Compacting Concrete. *BIBM* **2005**, *22*, 563.
22. Petkova, V.; Stoyanov, V.; Kostova, B.; Mihaylova, K. Effects of zeolite incorporation and inert fillers on the curing of cement mortars. *JCTM* **2024**, *59*, 313–322. [CrossRef]
23. Petkova, V.; Stoyanov, V.; Mihaylova, K.; Kostova, B. Impact of Pozzolanic and Inert Powders on the Microstructure and Thermal Chemistry of Cement Mortars. *Ceram. Int.* **2024**, *in press*. [CrossRef]
24. Petkova, V.; Stoyanov, V.; Pelovski, Y. TG–DTG–DTA in Studying White Self-Compacting Cement Mortars. *J. Therm. Anal. Calorim.* **2012**, *109*, 797–806. [CrossRef]
25. Stoyanov, V.; Kostova, B.; Petkova, V.; Pelovski, Y. Structure of White Cement Mortars with High Content of Marble Powder. *J. Therm. Anal. Calorim.* **2012**, *110*, 405–412. [CrossRef]
26. Petkova, V.; Stoyanov, V.; Kostova, B.; Kostov-Kytin, V.; Kalinkin, A.; Zvereva, I.; Tzvetanova, Y. Crystal-Chemical and Thermal Properties of Decorative Cement Composites. *Materials* **2021**, *14*, 4793. [CrossRef]
27. *BDS EN 12620:2002+A1:2008*; Aggregates for Concrete. Bulgarian Institute for Standardization: Sofia, Bulgaria, 2016.
28. Grifasi, N.; Ziantoni, B.; Fino, D.; Piumetti, M. Fundamental Properties and Sustainable Applications of the Natural Zeolite Clinoptilolite. *Environ. Sci. Pollut. Res.* **2024**, 1–36. [CrossRef]

29. *EN 196-1:2016;* Methods of Testing Cement—Part 1: Determination of Strength. Bulgarian Institute for Standardization: Sofia, Bulgaria, 2016.
30. *BDS EN 1015-3:2001/A2:2008;* Methods of Test for Mortar for Masonry—Part 3: Determination of Consistence of Fresh Mortar (by Flow Table). Bulgarian Institute for Standardization: Sofia, Bulgaria, 2008.
31. Gates-Rector, S.; Blanton, T. The Powder Diffraction File: A Quality Materials Characterization Database. *Powder Diffr.* **2019**, *34*, 352–360. [CrossRef]
32. Muliawan, A.; Sali, M.; Mustakyudin; Lutfi, M. XRD and XRF Characterization of White Sand from Sambera Village, East Kalimantan, Indonesia. *J. Phys. Conf. Ser.* **2019**, *1242*, 012029. [CrossRef]
33. Rafi, A.S.M.M.; Tasnim, U.F.; Rahman, M.S. Quantification and Qualification of Silica Sand Extracted from Padma River Sand. *IOP Conf. Ser. Mater. Sci. Eng.* **2018**, *438*, 012037. [CrossRef]
34. Burris, L.E.; Juenger, M.C.G. The Effect of Acid Treatment on the Reactivity of Natural Zeolites Used as Supplementary Cementitious Materials. *Cem. Concr. Res.* **2016**, *79*, 185–193. [CrossRef]
35. Wang, Y.; Guo, R.; Pan, T.; Fu, C.; Lin, R.; Ma, Q. Particle Size Effect of Pre-Wet Zeolites on Autogenous Shrinkage and Mechanical Properties of LECC. *Dev. Built Environ.* **2023**, *16*, 100290. [CrossRef]
36. Tuinukuafe, A.A.; Mills, M.M.; Walder, B.J.; Fritzsching, K.J.; Jové-Colón, C.F.; Bullard, J.W.; Lapeyre, J.; McEnroe, T.; Matteo, E.N.; Rimsza, J.M. Natural Carbonation of Portland Cement with Synthetic Zeolite Y as a Supplementary Cementitious Material. *Constr. Build. Mater.* **2024**, *425*, 136068. [CrossRef]
37. Zhu, D.; Wen, A.; Mu, D.; Tang, A.; Jiang, L.; Yang, W. Investigation into Compressive Property, Chloride Ion Permeability, and Pore Fractal Characteristics of the Cement Mortar Incorporated with Zeolite Powder. *Constr. Build. Mater.* **2024**, *411*, 134522. [CrossRef]
38. Ehwailat, K.I.A.; Ismail, M.A.M.; Ezreig, A.M.A. Ettringite Formation and Stabilization Methods of Sulfate-Bearing Soil: A State-of-the-Art Review. *Indian Geotech. J.* **2022**, *52*, 927–941. [CrossRef]
39. Pizoń, J.; Łaźniewska-Piekarczyk, B. Microstructure of CEM II/B-S Pastes Modified with Set Accelerating Admixtures. *Materials* **2021**, *14*, 6300. [CrossRef] [PubMed]
40. Schreiner, J.; Goetz-Neunhoeffer, F.; Neubauer, J.; Volkmann, S.; Bergold, S.; Webler, R.; Jansen, D. Advanced Rietveld Refinement and SEM Analysis of Tobermorite in Chemically Diverse Autoclaved Aerated Concrete. *Powder Diffr.* **2019**, *34*, 143–150. [CrossRef]
41. Larkin, P. Instrumentation and Sampling Methods. In *Infrared and Raman Spectroscopy;* Elsevier: Amsterdam, The Netherlands, 2011; pp. 27–54; ISBN 978-0-12-386984-5.
42. Khoshhesab, Z.M. Reflectance IR Spectroscopy. *Infrared Spectrosc. Mater. Sci. Eng. Technol.* **2012**, *11*, 233–244.
43. Król, M.; Minkiewicz, J.; Mozgawa, W. IR Spectroscopy Studies of Zeolites in Geopolymeric Materials Derived from Kaolinite. *J. Mol. Struct.* **2016**, *1126*, 200–206. [CrossRef]
44. Hughes, T.L.; Methven, C.M.; Jones, T.G.J.; Pelham, S.E.; Fletcher, P.; Hall, C. Determining Cement Composition by Fourier Transform Infrared Spectroscopy. *Adv. Cem. Based Mater.* **1995**, *2*, 91–104. [CrossRef]
45. Chukanov, N.V.; Vigasina, M.F. *Vibrational (Infrared and Raman) Spectra of Minerals and Related Compounds;* Springer Mineralogy; Springer International Publishing: Cham, Switzerland, 2020; ISBN 978-3-030-26802-2.
46. Chukanov, N.V.; Aksenov, S.M.; Pekov, I.V. Infrared Spectroscopy as a Tool for the Analysis of Framework Topology and Extra-Framework Components in Microporous Cancrinite- and Sodalite-Related Aluminosilicates. *Spectrochim. Acta Part A Mol. Biomol. Spectrosc.* **2023**, *287*, 121993. [CrossRef] [PubMed]
47. Stanienda, K.J. Carbonate Phases Rich in Magnesium in the Triassic Limestones of the Eastern Part of the Germanic Basin. *Carbonates Evaporites* **2016**, *31*, 387–405. [CrossRef]
48. Theodosoglou, E.; Koroneos, A.; Soldatos, T.; Zorba, T.; Paraskevopoulos, K.M. Comparative fourier transform infrared and x-ray powder diffraction analysis of naturally occurred k-feldspars. *Geosociety* **2017**, *43*, 2752. [CrossRef]
49. Chukanov, N.V.; Chervonnyi, A.D. *Infrared Spectroscopy of Minerals and Related Compounds;* Springer Mineralogy; Springer International Publishing: Cham, Switzerland, 2016; ISBN 978-3-319-25347-3.
50. Belskaya, O.B.; Danilova, I.G.; Kazakov, M.O.; Mironenko, R.M.; Lavrenov, A.V.; Likholobov, V.A. FTIR Spectroscopy of Adsorbed Probe Molecules for Analyzing the Surface Properties of Supported Pt (Pd) Catalysts. In *Infrared Spectroscopy-Materials Science, Engineering and Technology;* IntechOpen: London, UK, 2012; pp. 149–178.
51. Sharma, R.; Pei, J.; Miah, M.J.; Jang, J.G. Effect of Sillimanite Sand on the Mechanical Property and Thermal Resistance of Alkali-Activated Slag Mortar. *Constr. Build. Mater.* **2023**, *370*, 130654. [CrossRef]
52. Yalçınkaya, Ç.; Çopuroğlu, O. Hydration Heat, Strength and Microstructure Characteristics of UHPC Containing Blast Furnace Slag. *J. Build. Eng.* **2021**, *34*, 101915. [CrossRef]
53. Famy, C.; Brough, A.R.; Taylor, H.F.W. The C-S-H Gel of Portland Cement Mortars: Part I. The Interpretation of Energy-Dispersive X-ray Microanalyses from Scanning Electron Microscopy, with Some Observations on C-S-H, AFm and AFt Phase Compositions. *Cem. Concr. Res.* **2003**, *33*, 1389–1398. [CrossRef]

Disclaimer/Publisher's Note: The statements, opinions and data contained in all publications are solely those of the individual author(s) and contributor(s) and not of MDPI and/or the editor(s). MDPI and/or the editor(s) disclaim responsibility for any injury to people or property resulting from any ideas, methods, instructions or products referred to in the content.

materials

Article

Impact of Superplasticizers on the Performance of Low-Grade Limestone-Based Cement Mixes

Murugan Muthu [1,*], Boddapati Ganesh Kumar [2], Neven Ukrainczyk [3], Łukasz Sadowski [1] and Eddie Koenders [3]

1 Department of Materials Engineering, Wroclaw University of Science and Technology, 50-372 Wrocław, Poland; lukasz.sadowski@pwr.edu.pl
2 Larsen & Toubro Construction Research and Testing Center, Chennai 600 089, India; bgkk@lntecc.com
3 Institute of Construction and Building Materials, Technische Universität Darmstadt, 64287 Darmstadt, Germany; ukrainczyk@wib.tu-darmstadt.de (N.U.); koenders@wib.tu-darmstadt.de (E.K.)
* Correspondence: murugan.muthu@pwr.edu.pl; Tel.: +48-508-727-905

Abstract: Low-grade limestone (LGL) is not used to produce cement clinker, but this leftover material in cement quarries increases the water demand when used as a filler in concrete production. In this study, the effect of six commercial superplasticizers on the performance of cement mixes containing 35% LGL and 2% gypsum was investigated. The optimal doses of these superplasticizers were found in a range of different water/binder (w/b) ratios by conducting several Marsh cone and mini-slump tests. The addition of a superplasticizer with a higher active solid content produced a maximum cement flow, regardless of the w/b ratios. The LGL-based mortar samples admixed with this superplasticizer obtained a maximum compressive strength of about 36 MPa at the end of 28 days. SEM and XRD results showed the formation of a new calcium-rich mineral in their microstructure. These findings highlight the impact of the type and properties of superplasticizers on the performance of concrete mixes containing LGL as a supplementary cementitious material.

Keywords: low-grade limestone; cement; gypsum; superplasticizers; marsh cone test

check for updates

Citation: Muthu, M.; Kumar, B.G.; Ukrainczyk, N.; Sadowski, Ł.; Koenders, E. Impact of Superplasticizers on the Performance of Low-Grade Limestone-Based Cement Mixes. *Materials* **2024**, *17*, 2500. https://doi.org/10.3390/ma17112500

Academic Editors: Mengjun Chen and Jiwen Bai

Received: 30 April 2024
Revised: 20 May 2024
Accepted: 21 May 2024
Published: 22 May 2024

Copyright: © 2024 by the authors. Licensee MDPI, Basel, Switzerland. This article is an open access article distributed under the terms and conditions of the Creative Commons Attribution (CC BY) license (https://creativecommons.org/licenses/by/4.0/).

1 Introduction

Electricity and heat production, agriculture, forestry and transportation, industry, and buildings are the main economic sectors causing global anthropogenic greenhouse gas emissions [1]. The cement industry is one of the main contributors to industrial CO_2 emissions, accounting for approximately 8% of the global CO_2 emissions [2]. The use of industrial by-products, including fly ash and slag, in concrete mixes reduces CO_2 emission by up to 0.81 kg/kg of cement [3], but its availability is limited and cannot meet global demand [4]. The fly ash content is limited to 30% in most concrete mixes. The problem behind the use of high-volume fly ash in concrete mixes is the delay in setting and the slower rate of strength gain at the beginning of age [5]. Slag can be substituted for up to 70% clinker; however, its availability is inadequate [6]. Therefore, it is necessary to identify new sources of inorganic materials as partial cement replacements to protect the environment and sustainability.

Some non-reactive or weakly reactive powders, such as marble [7], granite [8], and limestone [9], showed promising contributions. Among these cement replacement materials, limestone powder shows great potential due to its very low embedded CO_2 emission, abundant reserve on Earth, and low cost [10]. Limestone reserves are abundant on Earth and up to 35% are recommended in the production of concrete mixes [11]. They are generally divided into high- and low-grade grades based on their CaO content [12]. Low-grade limestone (LGL) contains 38% CaO and is generally not considered in the production of cement clinker. This leftover material as a replacement for cement can greatly reduce cost and CO_2 emissions. In general, the addition of limestone accelerates the hydration of calcium silicates as a result of its nucleation effect and promotes the formation of calcium silicate hydrate (CSH) [13]. The nucleation of the CSH gel on limestone surfaces precipitates heterogeneously, but this precipitation facilitates the reduction in the volume of the open capillary pores and partially compensates for the dilution caused by the filler material [14]. The dissolution of limestone also releases calcium ions in the pore solution of the cement matrix, increasing the tendency to precipitate more CSH gel [10].

Gypsum plays a key role in cement mixes when limestone of any grade is used as a supplementary cementitious material. Gypsum determines the set time and the strength gain of concrete [15] and exists in many forms, including anhydrous, dihydrate, and hemihydrate gypsum, with different solubility rates. The amount of gypsum to be used in limestone-based cement mixes must be specified because it affects not only the setting time but also the strength development and expansion. The minimum gypsum content required to control the setting time is around 2%. Two main observations due to the additions of gypsum to the limestone-based cement mixes are (i) an increase in the degree of the hydration of tricalcium silicate (C_3S) due to the aluminate peak pushing beyond the silicate peak and (ii) an increase in the amount of ettringite crystals due to additional sulfate from the gypsum [16]. Furthermore, a suitable content of limestone and gypsum can have some positive influence on concrete properties, such as filler, nucleation, and chemical effects, as well as improving workability [17]. However, the optimal content of LGL–gypsum–cement blends still needs further study in concrete systems with a relatively low water/binder ratio and a high superplasticizer dose.

Limestone-based concrete mixes need a chemical superplasticizer due to the existing water scarcity problem in tropical countries with water shortages [18], further increasing the total cost of concrete and the environmental burden [19]. Superplasticizers, considered high-range water reducers, are often incorporated into such mixes to reduce water demand and thus achieve a higher solid content without eliminating consistency [20]. The addition of weakly reactive powders would result in the higher yield stress of fresh cement mixes and increased demand for plasticizers [21]. Kakali et al. [22] found that the setting time and consistency of cement mixes were reduced with increasing limestone additions to 35%. There is a significant reduction in the yield stress of cement mixes due to the addition of 15% limestone. These rheological characteristics of fresh concrete mixes are regulated by the fineness of the cement and the replacement levels [23]. The dose of superplasticizer depends on the type of cement, the shape, and the dimension of the cementitious materials, the water/binder ratio (w/b), the type of liquid admixture, the compatibility between cement and superplasticizer, as well as the temperature and humidity of the raw materials and the environment [24]. The compatibility and synergistic effect between the addition of LGL, gypsum, cement, and superplasticizer and the amount of water have very rarely been investigated.

This study aims to determine the optimal dose of superplasticizers based on polycarboxylate ether and sulfonated naphthalene formaldehyde required to obtain a maximum yield in cement mixes containing 35% LGL and 2% gypsum. The effects of the optimal doses of the superplasticizers on the various properties of LGL-based mortar samples were also examined by performing flow table, compressive strength, and shrinkage tests. The microstructure of these mortar samples at the end of 28 days was studied by conducting scanning electron microscopy (SEM) and X-ray diffraction (XRD) investigations. LGL is a leftover material in cement quarries, and its usage as a supplementary cementitious material requires more water, while the test findings of this study help to understand the impact of the dose, type, and properties of the superplasticizer on the performance of the cement mixes containing a higher volume of LGL and provide recommendations on the selection of superplasticizers that can produce maximum flow at lower doses.

2. Materials and Methods

2.1. Sample Preparation

Ordinary Portland cement of 53 grade according to IS 12269 [25] was used in the preparation of different mortar samples. Other raw materials were low-grade limestone

(LGL), gypsum, potable water, crushed granites derived from granite origin, and superplasticizers based on polycarboxylate ether (PCE) and sulfonated naphthalene formaldehyde (SNF). The SEM image in Figure 1 reveals the angular structure of the LGL sample. The raw material was mounted on a steel stub using a carbon adhesive and scanned with a JSM-7600-F SEM (JEOL, Tokyo, Japan) at a higher voltage to obtain information about the microstructure. The cementitious materials were obtained from a local cement manufacturer in India. The specific surface areas of LGL, gypsum, and cement reported by the manufacturer are 165, 140, and 310 m^2/kg. The samples of these raw materials were sieved to a size lower than 75 µm and scanned with a Bruker model X-ray diffraction at a rate of 0.02° 2θ/min for a 2θ range between 5 and 80°. The main XRD peaks illustrated in Figure 1 confirm the main presence of tricalcium silicate, tricalcium aluminate, and calcite in cement and LGL. These samples were pelletized on a circular metal disc and scanned with a Rigaku model X-ray fluorescence (XRF) to obtain information on the chemical composition. Table 1 lists the XRF results in which the CaO content of cement was calculated to be 1.6 times higher than that of LGL. Their loss of ignition was also found by heating them in a hot air oven at 1000 °C, and subsequent weight losses were calculated. The loss of ignition (LOI) of LGL was very high, indicating the main presence of organic species. Crushed granite sand conforming to Zone II of IS 383 [26] was used in the preparation of mortar samples. It had a specific gravity of 2.58 and a water absorption of 2.27. These aggregate properties were determined according to IS 2386 [27]. PCEs and SNFs according to IS 9103 [28] were obtained from three different chemical suppliers, Sika, Fosroc, and BASF, and were designated PCE1, PCE2, PCE3, SNF1, SNF2, and SNF3. Their pH and relative density were found to fall within the range of 6.37–8.31 and 1.06–1.31, while the solid content is illustrated in Figure 1. These physical properties were found according to IS 9103 [28]. The optimal doses of each superplasticizer in different w/b ratios of 0.35, 0.4, 0.45, and 0.5 were determined in fresh paste samples containing 63% cement, 35% LGL, and 2% gypsum. The optimum dose information obtained from the experiments on fresh paste samples was then adopted in the preparation of mortar samples to validate the impact of different superplasticizers on the performance of cement mixes containing a higher volume of LGL.

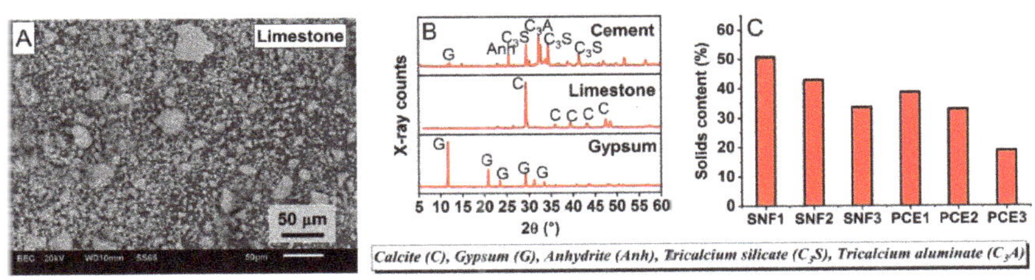

Figure 1. (**A**) SEM image of limestone, (**B**) XRD pattern of raw materials, and (**C**) solid content of different superplasticizers used in this study.

Table 1. Chemical composition of raw materials.

Sample (%)	CaO	SiO_2	Al_2O_3	Fe_2O_3	MgO	Na_2O	K_2O	SO_3	Cl	LOI
Cement	61.77	20.01	4.97	4.4	1.22	0.14	0.28	2.56	0.01	4.64
Limestone	39.27	15.77	3.37	0.43	1.56	0.07	0.17	0.24	-	39.12
Gypsum	29.81	3.34	1.35	0.49	1.33	-	-	43.85	0.01	19.82

Table 2 lists the details of the cement-based mortar mixture that was prepared in different w/b ratios and proportioned with the optimal doses of superplasticizers that resulted from the investigation of the fresh paste samples. The cementitious materials were mixed with crushed aggregates, water, and superplasticizers in a Hobart high-speed mixer for 3 min to cast samples of different sizes. Acrylic molds were used to prepare mortar samples that were demolded after 24 h of casting and stored in water to cure until the age of testing. Sample consolidation was performed using a vibrating table.

Table 2. Details of the cement-based mortar mixture.

Cement (g)	Limestone (g)	Gypsum (g)	Sand (g)
630	350	20	2500

2.2. *Isothermal Calorimetry and Vicat Apparatus*

Approximately 30 g of fresh cement paste was loaded into the test channels of an I-Cal 8000 Calmetrix high-precision isothermal calorimeter according to ASTM C1702 [29]. Heat developments in this sample were recorded for up to 7 days at 25 °C and 65% relative humidity (RH). The initial and final setting time of the fresh cement paste was measured according to IS 4031 [30]. About 300 g of cement was added to 72 g of water and quickly mixed before filling the Vicat apparatus sample mold according to IS 5513 [31]. A 1 mm square needle was allowed to penetrate this fresh paste every 10 min until the apparatus index scale read approximately 5 mm from the bottom of the mold. Then, the annular needle was replaced to measure the final setting time. This needle was released every 30 min until it made an impression on the sample. An average of three measurements was calculated.

2.3. *Mini Slump and Marsh Cone Tests*

Consistency was evaluated using the mini-slump cone apparatus [32] of dimensions: diameter 19 mm, bottom diameter 38 mm, and height 57 mm. The mold was placed firmly on a flat horizontal plastic sheet, filled with paste, and compacted with a spatula. When the mold was full, the top surface was leveled and excess paste was removed. The mold was vertically removed, ensuring minimal lateral disturbance, and to avoid sample disturbance, the slumped sample was left to harden for 24 h. The diameter of the hardened base was measured at five locations around the outline and the mean was used to calculate the area of the base. A metal cone was used according to EN 445 [33] with an 8 mm diameter bottom nozzle. Around 1000 mL of fresh cement paste was placed in the Marsh cone, while the bottom orifice of the tapered cone was kept closed. The orifice was then opened, and the fresh paste was allowed to flow into a 1000 mL capacity graduated cylindrical flask, which was kept below. The time it took 1000 mL of the cement paste to flow out of the Marsh cone was recorded as the efflux time of the paste. Figure 2 illustrates the details of the mini-slump and Marsh cones.

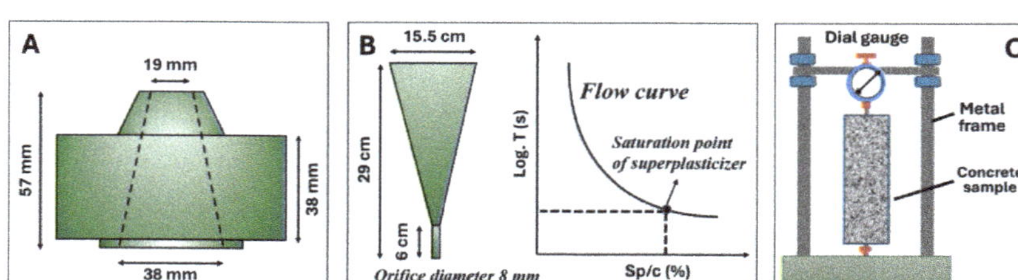

Figure 2. Details of the (**A**) mini-slump, (**B**) Marsh cone, and (**C**) shrinkage tests.

2.4. *Flow Table, Compressive Strength, and Shrinkage Tests*

The fresh mortar sample was filled into the truncated cone and placed in the center of the flow table apparatus. The cone was removed leaving the fresh sample, which was dropped continuously for 15 times. The mortar flow is the resulting increase in the average base diameter of the mortar mass, measured in at least four diameters at equivalently spaced intervals expressed as a percentage of the original base diameter. The mortar sample of dimensions 70 × 70 × 70 mm^3 was tested at the end of 28 days according to IS

516 [34] using a MATEST model servo-controlled compression test machine with a capacity of 3000 kN. The loading rate was maintained at 35 MPa/s. The load at failure divided by the cross-sectional area of the sample gives the compressive strength. Prismatic mortar samples of 25 × 25 × 285 mm^3 size were used to perform the shrinkage test at 25 °C and 65% RH according to ASTM C157 [35]. The change in sample length was recorded at frequent intervals until the end of 28 days using a length comparator frame supported with a 1 μm precision dial gauge. This frame was calibrated using a standard invar bar. The shrinkage strain was calculated by subtracting the initial reading from the dial gauge and the readings taken at the subsequent intervals of t and then divided by the length of the sample. In these tests, a mean of four replicates was calculated.

2.5. Characterization Studies

Small mortar fragments were collected from the cube samples tested under compression after 28 days. Care was taken to exclude the aggregates from the mortar pieces obtained. They were dried at room temperature for a day, powdered with mortar and pestle, sieved to a size of less than 75 μm, and finally scanned for a 2θ range of 5–80° using an XRD at a scanning rate of 0.02°/min. The mortar chunks obtained from the crushed samples were dried at room temperature for a day, mounted onto steel stubs using a carbon adhesive, gold-coated for 60 s, and analyzed at 20 kV current under secondary electron mode using the SEM.

3. Results and Discussion

3.1. Heat of Hydration and Setting Time

Figure 3 shows the isothermal calorimetry test results of the fresh paste samples containing 63% cement, 35% LGL, and 2% gypsum. These samples exhibited an exothermic reaction when water was added to them and exhibited the maximum amount of heat around 8 h after mixing. The heat release of these pastes was reduced with an increasing w/b ratio, indicating a slower increase in the concentration of calcium ions in the pore solution of these fresh samples at the beginning of age. LGL particles have little effect on the hydration of cement mixes [13]. Its nucleation effect accelerates the maximum hydration of C_3S and generates more hydration products at an early age. However, the dilution effect of the LGL particles affects the hydration of C_3S and reduces the formation of $Ca(OH)_2$ [36]. When the LGL and cement particles are mixed together, the water film governs the space between them and has a relatively significant effect on the rate of hydration of the cement during the post-peak hydration period [37]. The cement mixtures in this study include 63% cement, 35% LGL, and 2% gypsum. This raw cement was made up of 97% clinker and 3% gypsum according to the manufacturer. Therefore, the total gypsum content in the paste samples was calculated to be 3.9%. The average initial and final setting times for these samples were determined to be 160 and 310 min, while those for the plain cement paste were 170 and 295 min. Although the gypsum content in the plain cement and LGL-based mixtures was relatively higher, the initial cement setting still improved to 6% in the presence of a larger volume of LGL.

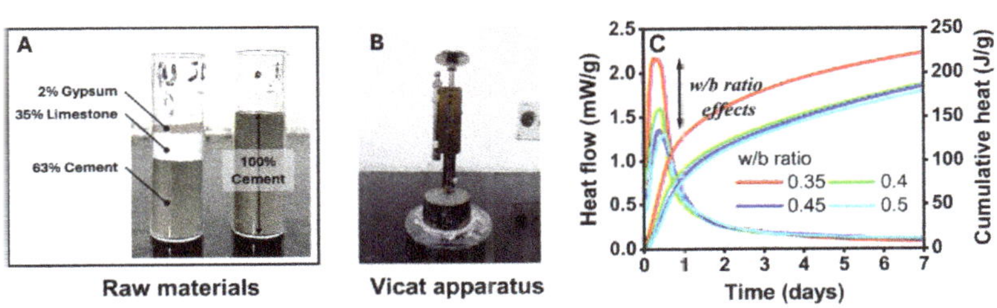

Figure 3. (A) Raw materials, (B) Vicat apparatus, and (C) isothermal calorimetry test results.

3.2. Mini-Slump Flow and Saturation Dose

Figures 4 and 5 show the results of the mini-slump and Marsh cone tests. The addition of SNF and PCE improved the slump flow of the paste mixes regardless of the w/b ratios used. They exhibited a mini-slump flow diameter of 200 mm when the dose of the superplasticizers was maintained above 1.5%. No slump flow was observed when the LGL-based cement pastes were made with w/b ratios lower than 0.4. They were sticky and stiff, and they needed a minimum dose of the superplasticizer of 0.5% to escape the test cone apparatus under gravity. The action of a superplasticizer is to prevent the flocculation of cement particles. The adsorption of SNFs leads to a decrease in the zeta potential and eventually causes (negative) charges on the cement particles. With the progress of hydration, the electrostatic charge decreases and the hydrating product flocculates [38]. The optimal amount of superplasticizer to be used in the design of the cement mix is determined by the flow curve. The efflux time in the Marsh cone decreases with an increase in the superplasticizer dosage. There is a saturation point of the superplasticizer dose beyond which there is no significant reduction in the efflux time. The results of the Marsh cone test showed that the efflux time of the fresh limestone-based cement pastes was reduced with an increase in the dose of SNF1, SNF2, and SNF3. The use of w/b ratios less than 0.4 resulted in a longer efflux time, but the fresh pastes containing low doses of such superplasticizers quickly drained out of the test apparatus under gravity at higher w/b ratios.

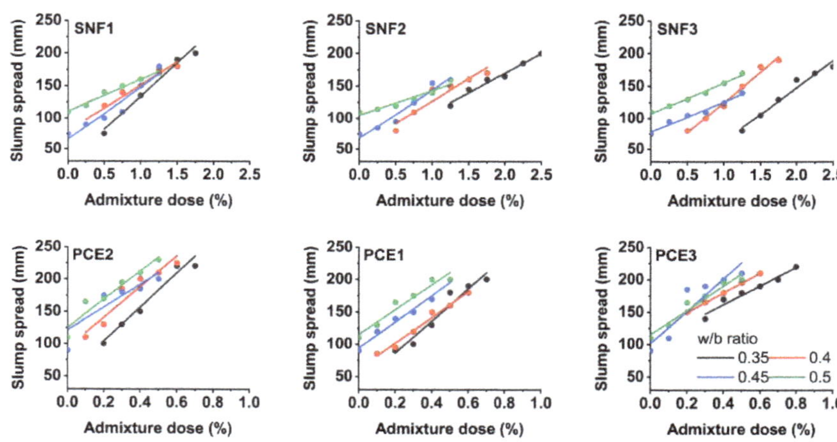

Figure 4. Results of the mini-slump tests.

The fresh limestone-based cement samples consumed less SNF1 to reach the saturation point in all the w/b ratios compared to those with SNF2 and SNF3. SNF1 has a higher solid content, which therefore influenced its saturation point in the limestone-based cement pastes. The active solid content of SNF1, SNF2, and SNF3 was 50.8%, 42.9%, and 33.8%, respectively. The efflux time of the limestone-based cement mixes was shorter when a minimum SNF dose of 1% was maintained, regardless of the w/b ratios used. No significant changes in the efflux time were observed when the fresh cement pastes contained doses of superplasticizer greater than 1%. PCE1, PCE2, and PCE3 are PCEs, and limestone-based cement pastes made with them also showed a rheological behavior like that occurring with SNFs. The use of PCEs in the limestone-based cement pastes resulted in a maximum slump flow diameter of 220 mm. At a 0.3 w/b ratio, the fresh limestone-based cement paste was able to escape the mini-slump cone apparatus when dosed with a minimum PCE dose of 0.2%. In general, SNFs work with the mechanism of lowering the zeta potential, leading to electrostatic repulsion. However, polymers with backbone and graft chains, such as PCE, cause the dispersion of cement grains by steric hindrance [39]. This phenomenon is related to the separation of superplasticizer molecules from each other because of bulky side chains. Steric hindrance is a more effective mechanism than electrostatic repulsion. The side chains, mainly polyethylene oxide, that extend on the surface of the cement particles migrate in water [40], and the cement particles are dispersed by the steric hindrance of the side chains [41]. In this study, the saturation points of PCE and SNF were determined using an analytical method proposed by da Silva et al. [42] and Gomes et al. [43]. The efflux time of the limestone-based cement paste was measured when the dose of the superplasticizer varied with respect to the cement content (Sp/c) and a graph illustrated in Figure 2 was plotted between the logarithm of time (T) and the percentage of the solid content of the superplasticizer. The saturation point of the superplasticizers (SPS) was then defined as the point within a 140° ± 10° interval. A descent exponential function shown in Equation (1) is used to define this graph between Log. T and Sp/c, where A_1, t_1, and y_0 are the constant parameters for each test curve [43]. From the function curve, it is possible to calculate its derivative and fit the curve to Equation (2) using data analysis and graphing software (e.g., OriginLab version 8.5), which automatically gives the coefficient values. When comparing the slope of the curve to −0.57, the value of 'x' was found, that is, the solid concentration of SP used per gram of cement at the saturation point.

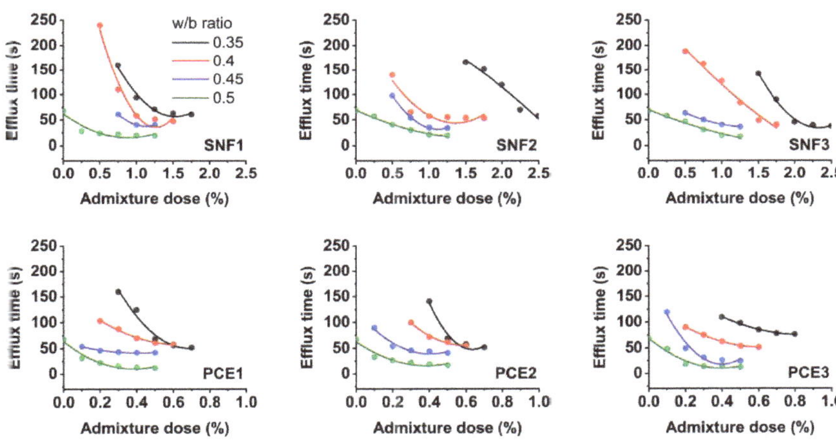

Figure 5. Results of the Marsh cone tests.

The optimal dose of SNFs and PCEs was found using the back-calculation technique and is shown in Figure 6. It was found that the SPS in the LGL-based cement pastes depended on the type of superplasticizer and the w/b ratios used. The optimal doses of both SNF and PCEs in the LGL-based cement pastes were found to decrease with an increase in the w/b ratios. When SNF3 was used in such pastes, its SPS in the w/b ratios of 0.35, 0.4, 0.45, and 0.5 was calculated to be 2.18, 1.63, 1.03, and 0.89%, respectively. The saturation point of the SNFs in the limestone-based cement pastes was almost 59% lower when the w/b ratio increased from 0.35 to 0.5. Similarly, to the plain cement mixes, the optimal doses of the SNFs in the limestone-based cement pastes were comparatively higher than the PCEs. The SPS in the w/b ratios of 0.35, 0.4, 0.45, and 0.5 was calculated to be 0.68, 0.54, 0.26, and 0.24%, respectively, when PCE1 admixture was used in the preparation of the limestone-based cement pastes. The dispersion of SNFs in cement mixes is caused by electrostatic repulsive forces, while both steric hindrance and electrostatic repulsion mechanisms govern the dispersion of PCEs in cement mixes. The optimal doses of these superplasticizers to be used in cement mixes depend on the content of active solids available in them. The degree of cement fluidity depends on the amount of superplasticizer adsorbed onto the surface of the cement particles. With increasing solid content, the amount of superplasticizer adsorbed on the cement particle increases. Both SNFs and PCEs are usually supplied as liquid formulations with an active solid content in the range of 30–40%. The behavior of superplasticizers is also a function of the structure and degree of polymerization. Side chains tend to extend from the adsorbed water-reducing admixture into the solution, and these side chains are anti-aggressive, and their steric hindrance significantly improves the fluidity of Portland limestone cement systems [44]. Increased fluidity decreases the efflux time and thus decreases the SPS values [45].

$$f(x) = A_1 e^{-\left(\frac{x}{t_1}\right)} + y_0 \quad (1)$$

$$\frac{dy}{dx} = -A_1 \frac{e^{-\left(\frac{x}{t_1}\right)}}{t_1} = -0.57 \quad (2)$$

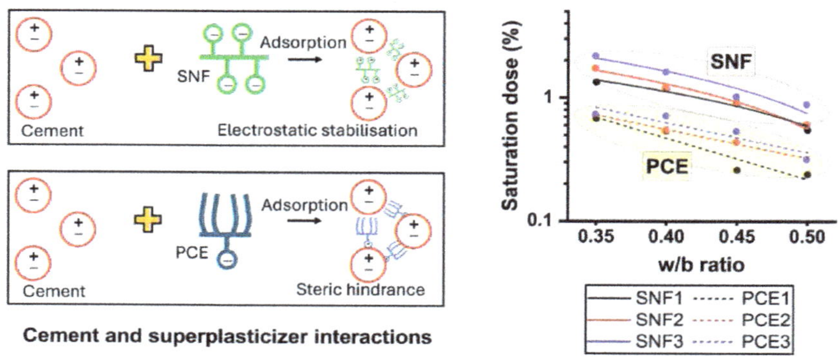

Figure 6. Saturation points of different superplasticizers obtained by conducting Marsh cone tests.

3.3. Mortar Performance

Figure 7 shows the flow table, compressive strength, and shrinkage test results of the mortar samples. The effect of the optimal doses of SNF and PCE on the flowability of fresh mortar mixes was determined at different w/b ratios. The fresh mortar samples were observed to be very sticky and stiff and did not flow in a 0.35 w/b ratio, but the samples made in other w/b ratios flowed in the fresh state. It was also observed that cement flow was reduced with a decrease in the w/b ratios regardless of the dose and type of the superplasticizers. The workability of fresh cement mixes rapidly decreases in a low w/b ratio. This effect is mainly due to the reduced distance between the cement particles, along with the constant consumption of free water through hydration [46]. The inclusion of a superplasticizer prevents (i) flocculation by adsorbing onto the surface of cement grains and (ii) the reduction in the entrapment of water in the flocculated structure, thus reducing the water demand to obtain the same fluidity in the cement matrix [47]. The flow diameter of the mortar samples was reduced up to three times when the w/b ratio was reduced from 0.5 to 0.35. There is a marginal decrease in the flowability of fresh mortar samples admixed with SNFs and PCEs when the active solid content in such superplasticizers is reduced. The addition of PCEs at lower doses was able to significantly improve the cement flow compared to SNFs. This beneficial effect is due to the dual working mechanisms of PCEs that include steric hindrance and electrostatic repulsion [48].

In this study, the compressive strength of the mortar samples tested after 28 days was reduced with increasing w/b ratios, regardless of the PCE and SNF used. However, the flowability and compressive strength of the mortar samples mixed with PCE were relatively higher than those containing SNF. The compressive strength of the mortar samples was reduced to almost 33% when the w/b ratio increased from 0.35 to 0.5. At a lower w/b ratio, the average compressive strength of the mortar samples admixed with SNF2 and PCE1 was found to be 34 and 36 MPa at the end of 28 days. There is no significant difference in the compressive strength of the mortar samples mixed with SNF and PCE when the active solid content of such superplasticizers is reduced. The shrinkage strain of these samples at the w/b ratios of 0.35 and 0.5 was measured over time. These mortar samples showed an increasing trend of shrinkage over time. At a lower w/b ratio, the shrinkage strain of the mortar samples admixed with SNF1 and PCE1 was calculated to be 0.029% and 0.019% at the end of 28 days. The addition of PCE reduced the mortar shrinkage by up to 34%. At lower w/b ratios, the use of PCEs marginally reduced the length change in the prismatic samples compared to those admixed with SNFs. However, this reduction in the mortar sample shrinkage due to SNF was relatively significant in the case of higher w/b ratios. The compressive strength of cement-based mixes decreases with increasing w/b ratio, and the content of raw cement is usually of minor influence, while its shrinkage and water absorption increase with the w/b ratio and cement content [49]. Sua-Iam and Makul [50] found a higher shrinkage in cement mixes containing a higher volume of rice husk ash, which absorbs more free water onto their surfaces while mixing. The use of PCE instead of SNF reduced this shrinkage, mainly because of their steric hindrance and electrostatic repulsion mechanisms.

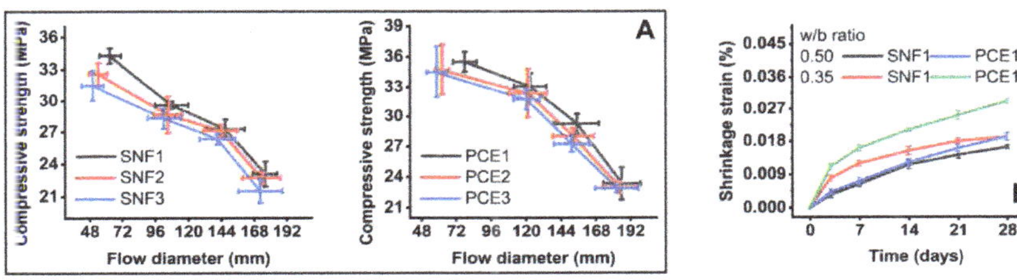

Figure 7. Results of the (A) flow table and compressive strength, and (B) shrinkage tests.

3.4. Microstructure

Figure 8 shows the SEM and XRD results. Unreacted LGL particles with rhombohedral structures were observed in the mortar samples admixed with PCE and SNF. Gypsum has an acicular structure and was not found in the sample microstructure as its amounts were relatively very low. The LGL particles improve the formation of the hydration rims of CSH surrounding C_3S particles because they increase the rate of the hydration of C_3S [51]. The increasing levels of LGL increased the formation of ettringite in the early ages [52]. The amount of ettringite then slowly decreased as the hydration proceeded. They did not observe any monosulfate [53]. To identify the crystalline phase and examine the crystal structure of specific phases existing in the mortar samples of this study, an XRD investigation was carried out on them. The major XRD peaks attributed to 9.1°, 10.7°, 13.1°, 20.7°, 21.8°, 26.5°, 27.8°, 29.4°, 34.1°, 39.3°, 42.5°, 48.5°, 50.2°, and 60.1° 2θ diffraction angle confirmed the availability of ettringite, gypsum, portlandite, quartz, calcite, C_3S, C_2S, and anorthite, respectively, in the mortar samples. The XRD method is only capable of identifying these crystalline reaction products and is unable to distinguish the CSH gel [54], which is because this major hydrate is poorly crystalline and amorphous. Anorthite could have formed because of the chemical reaction between calcium silicates and aluminate species in the mortar samples. The addition of LGL at the expense of gypsum can form what is known as carboaluminate instead of ettringite [55]. This often requires less water than in the case of gypsum [56].

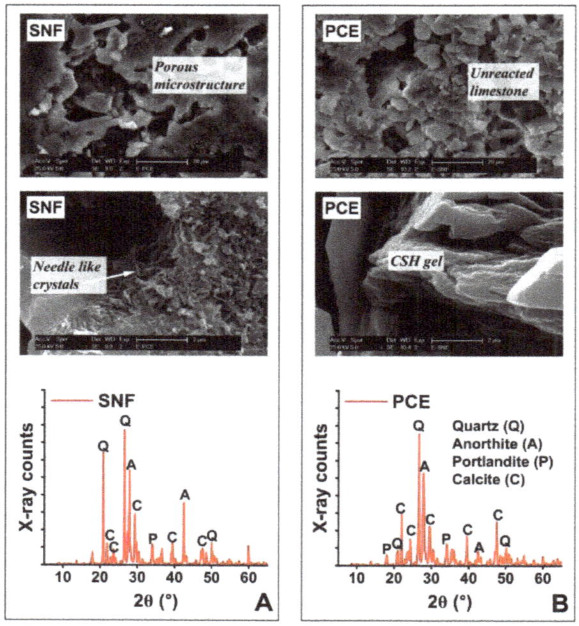

Figure 8. SEM and XRD results of the mortar samples admixed with (**A**) SNF and (**B**) PCE.

4. Conclusions

In this study, cement mixes containing a higher volume of LGL were demonstrated. The effect of the type and properties of superplasticizers on their performance was examined by performing multiple tests. The heat developments in these mixes decreased with an increasing w/b ratio, and their flow was found to be zero when the w/b ratios were less than 0.4. The fresh mixes were able to flow only when the superplasticizer dose was greater than 0.5% in the case of SNF and 0.2% in the case of PCE. The optimal doses of SNF and PCE in the LGL-based cement mixes were found to decrease with increasing w/b ratios. The optimal doses of these superplasticizers were found to depend greatly on the content of the active solids available in them. The addition of SNF improved the cement flow by electrostatic repulsive forces, while such improvements were caused by both steric hindrance and electrostatic repulsion mechanisms in the case of adding PCE polymers. The compressive strength of the LGL-based mixes mixed with PCE was found to be relatively higher, indicating a lower agglomeration of cement particles during mixing. Early-age shrinkage was also found to be relatively lower in these mixes. Anorthite mineral-like compounds were observed in the microstructure of such mixes according to the results of the SEM and XRD studies. LGL as a supplementary cementitious material in concrete mixes requires more superplasticizers, and the findings of this study suggest the use of PCE admixture containing a higher active solid content to produce maximum flow and obtain a higher compressive strength.

Author Contributions: Conceptualization, methodology, validation, formal analysis, data curation, and writing—original draft preparation, M.M.; investigation, B.G.K.; supervision and writing—review and editing, Ł.S., N.U. and E.K. All authors have read and agreed to the published version of the manuscript.

Funding: This research was funded by Narodowa Agencja Wymiany Akademickiej (NAWA), grant number BPN/ULM/2021/1/00120, and support from German Research Foundation (DFG) project number 451894070 as part of the DFG SPP 2005 program.

Institutional Review Board Statement: Not applicable.

Informed Consent Statement: Not applicable.

Data Availability Statement: The original contributions presented in the study are included in the article, further inquiries can be directed to the corresponding author.

Conflicts of Interest: The authors declare no conflicts of interest.

References

1. Benhelal, E.; Shamsaei, E.; Rashid, M.I. Challenges against CO_2 abatement strategies in cement industry: A review. *J. Environ. Sci.* **2021**, *104*, 84–101. [CrossRef] [PubMed]
2. Zhang, C.-Y.; Han, R.; Yu, B.; Wei, Y.-M. Accounting process-related CO_2 emissions from global cement production under Shared Socioeconomic Pathways. *J. Clean. Prod.* **2018**, *184*, 451–465. [CrossRef]
3. Lothenbach, B.; Scrivener, K.; Hooton, R.D. Supplementary cementitious materials. *Cem. Concr. Res.* **2011**, *41*, 1244–1256. [CrossRef]
4. Mocharla, I.R.; Selvam, R.; Govindaraj, V.; Muthu, M. Performance and life-cycle assessment of high-volume fly ash concrete mixes containing steel slag sand. *Constr. Build. Mater.* **2022**, *341*, 127814. [CrossRef]
5. Das, P.; Cheela, V.R.S.; Mistri, A.; Chakraborty, S.; Dubey, B.; Barai, S.V. Performance assessment and life cycle analysis of concrete containing ferrochrome slag and fly ash as replacement materials—A circular approach. *Constr. Build. Mater.* **2022**, *347*, 128609. [CrossRef]
6. Panesar, D.K. 3—Supplementary cementing materials. In *Developments in the Formulation and Reinforcement of Concrete*, 2nd ed.; Mindess, S., Ed.; Woodhead Publishing: Sawston, UK, 2019; pp. 55–85.
7. Ruiz-Sánchez, A.; Sánchez-Polo, M.; Rozalen, M. Waste marble dust: An interesting residue to produce cement. *Constr. Build. Mater.* **2019**, *224*, 99–108. [CrossRef]
8. Woźniak, Z.Z.; Chajec, A.; Sadowski, Ł. Effect of the Partial Replacement of Cement with Waste Granite Powder on the Properties of Fresh and Hardened Mortars for Masonry Applications. *Materials* **2022**, *15*, 9066. [CrossRef] [PubMed]
9. Dhandapani, Y.; Santhanam, M.; Kaladharan, G.; Ramanathan, S. Towards ternary binders involving limestone additions—A review. *Cem. Concr. Res.* **2021**, *143*, 106396. [CrossRef]
10. Wang, D.; Shi, C.; Farzadnia, N.; Shi, Z.; Jia, H.; Ou, Z. A review on use of limestone powder in cement-based materials: Mechanism, hydration and microstructures. *Constr. Build. Mater.* **2018**, *181*, 659–672. [CrossRef]
11. Lollini, F.; Redaelli, E.; Bertolini, L. Effects of portland cement replacement with limestone on the properties of hardened concrete. *Cem. Concr. Compos.* **2014**, *46*, 32–40. [CrossRef]
12. Panda, D.; Gotecha, S.; Roy, B. Marginal grade limestone resources upgradation: A challenge for indian cement industry. In Proceedings of the International Seminar on Mineral Processing Technology, Bhubaneswar, India, 19–21 February 2004.
13. Lothenbach, B.; Le Saout, G.; Gallucci, E.; Scrivener, K. Influence of limestone on the hydration of Portland cements. *Cem. Concr. Res.* **2008**, *38*, 848–860. [CrossRef]
14. Gupta, S.; Mohapatra, B.N.; Bansal, M. Development of Portland limestone cement in India using different composition of cement and marginal grade limestone: A sustainable approach. *J. Indian Chem. Soc.* **2022**, *99*, 100724. [CrossRef]
15. Gyabaah, G.; Miyazawa, S.; Nito, N. Effects of gypsum and limestone powder on fresh properties and compressive strength of concrete containing ground granulated blast furnace slag under different curing temperatures. *Constr. Mater.* **2022**, *2*, 114–126. [CrossRef]
16. Lushnikova, N.; Dvorkin, L. 25—Sustainability of gypsum products as a construction material. In *Sustainability of Construction Materials*, 2nd ed.; Khatib, J.M., Ed.; Woodhead Publishing: Sawston, UK, 2016; pp. 643–681.
17. Kim, J.; Na, S.; Zhang, W.; Sagawa, T.; Hama, Y. Effect of limestone powder and gypsum on the compressive strength mixture design of blast furnace slag blended cement mortar. *J. Adv. Concr. Technol.* **2017**, *15*, 67–80. [CrossRef]
18. Gupta, S.; Mohapatra, B.N.; Bansal, M. A review on development of Portland limestone cement: A step towards low carbon economy for Indian cement industry. *Curr. Res. Green Sustain. Chem.* **2020**, *3*, 100019. [CrossRef]
19. Nkinamubanzi, P.C.; Mantellato, S.; Flatt, R.J. 16—Superplasticizers in practice. In *Science and Technology of Concrete Admixtures*; Aïtcin, P.-C., Flatt, R.J., Eds.; Woodhead Publishing: Sawston, UK, 2016; pp. 353–377.
20. Meddah, M.S.; Lmbachiya, M.C.; Dhir, R.K. Potential use of binary and composite limestone cements in concrete production. *Constr. Build. Mater.* **2014**, *58*, 193–205. [CrossRef]
21. Sanjuán, M.Á.; Andrade, C. Reactive powder concrete: Durability and applications. *Appl. Sci.* **2021**, *11*, 5629. [CrossRef]
22. Kakali, G.; Tsivilis, S.; Aggeli, E.; Bati, M. Hydration products of C3A, C3S and Portland cement in the presence of $CaCO_3$. *Cem. Concr. Res.* **2000**, *30*, 1073–1077. [CrossRef]
23. Voglis, N.; Kakali, G.; Chaniotakis, E.; Tsivilis, S. Portland-limestone cements. Their properties and hydration compared to those of other composite cements. *Cem. Concr. Compos.* **2005**, *27*, 191–196.
24. De Schutter, G.; Ezzat, M.; Lesage, K.; Hoogenboom, R. Responsive superplasticizers for active rheology control of cementitious materials. *Cem. Concr. Res.* **2023**, *165*, 107084. [CrossRef]
25. *IS 12269*; Ordinary Portland Cement, 53 Grade—Specification. Bureau of Indian Standards: New Delhi, India, 2013; 10p.

26. *IS 383*; Coarse and Fine Aggregates for Concrete—Specification. Bureau of Indian Standards: New Delhi, India, 2016; 21p.
27. *IS 2386*; Methods of Test for Aggregates for Concrete—Specific Gravity, Density, Voids, Absorption and Bulking. Bureau of Indian Standards: New Delhi, India, 1963; p. 17.
28. *IS 9103*; Concrete Admixtures—Specifications. Bureau of Indian Standards: New Delhi, India, 2004; p. 17.
29. *ASTM C1702*; Standard Test Method for Measurement of Heat of Hydration of Hydraulic Cementitious Materials Using Isothermal Conduction Calorimetry. ASTM International: West Conshohocken, PA, USA, 2017; p. 9.
30. *IS 4031*; Methods of Physical Tests for Hydraulic Cement. Bureau of Indian Standards: New Delhi, India, 1988; p. 5.
31. *IS 5513*; Vicat Apparatus—Specification. Bureau of Indian Standards: New Delhi, India, 1996; p. 12.
32. Tan, Z.; Bernal, S.A.; Provis, J.L. Reproducible mini-slump test procedure for measuring the yield stress of cementitious pastes. *Mater. Struct.* **2017**, *50*, 235. [CrossRef] [PubMed]
33. *EN 445*; Grout for Prestressing Tendons—Test Methods. European Committee for Standardization: Brussels, Belgium, 2007; p. 15.
34. *IS 516-1*; Hardened Concrete—Methods of Test. Compressive Flexural Split Tensile Strength. Bureau of Indian Standards: New Delhi, India, 2021; p. 20.
35. *ASTM C157*; Standard Test Method for Length Change of Hardened Hydraulic-Cement Mortar and Concrete. ASTM International: West Conshohocken, PA, USA, 2017; p. 8.
36. Livesey, P. Strength characteristics of Portland-limestone cements. *Constr. Build. Mater.* **1991**, *5*, 147–150. [CrossRef]
37. Aïtcin, P.C. 1—The importance of the water–cement and water–binder ratios. In *Science and Technology of Concrete Admixtures*; Aïtcin, P.-C., Flatt, R.J., Eds.; Woodhead Publishing: Sawston, UK, 2016; pp. 3–13.
38. Hsu, K.-C.; Chiu, J.-J.; Chen, S.-D.; Tseng, Y.-C. Effect of addition time of a superplasticizer on cement adsorption and on concrete workability. *Cem. Concr. Compos.* **1999**, *21*, 425–430. [CrossRef]
39. Lei, L.; Hirata, T.; Plank, J. 40 years of PCE superplasticizers—History, current state-of-the-art and an outlook. *Cem. Concr. Res.* **2022**, *157*, 106826. [CrossRef]
40. Nair, N.; Mohammed Haneefa, K.; Santhanam, M.; Gettu, R. A study on fresh properties of limestone calcined clay blended cementitious systems. *Constr. Build. Mater.* **2020**, *254*, 119326. [CrossRef]
41. Hewlett, P.C.; Justnes, H.; Edmeades, R.M. 14—Cement and concrete admixtures. In *Lea's Chemistry of Cement and Concrete*, 5th ed.; Hewlett, P.C., Liska, M., Eds.; Butterworth-Heinemann: Oxford, UK, 2019; pp. 641–698.
42. da Silva, O.; Gomes, P.; Morais, K. Analytical method for determining the saturation point of superplasticizers in cement pastes using the Marsh cone. *Cerâmica* **2019**, *65*, 252–260. [CrossRef]
43. Gomes, P.C.; Gettu, R.; Agullo, L.; Bernad, C. Experimental optimization of high-strength self-compacting concrete. In Proceedings of the Second International Symposium on Self-compacting Concrete, Tokio, Japan, 23–25 October 2001; p. 377386.
44. Zhang, J.; Han, G.; Shen, D.; An, X.; Mendomo Meye, S. A new model to predict the optimal mix design of self-compacting concrete considering powder properties and superplasticizer type. *J. Mater. Res. Technol.* **2022**, *19*, 3980–3993. [CrossRef]
45. Schober, I.; Mader, U. Compatibility of polycarboxylate superplasticizers with cements and cementitious blends. In Proceedings of the SP-217, Seventh CANMET/ACI International Conference, Berlin, Germany, 20–23 October 2003.
46. Collepardi, M. Admixtures used to enhance placing characteristics of concrete. *Cem. Concr. Compos.* **1998**, *20*, 103–112. [CrossRef]
47. Bhandari, I.; Kumar, R.; Sofi, A.; Nighot, N.S. A systematic study on sustainable low carbon cement—Superplasticizer interaction: Fresh, mechanical, microstructural and durability characteristics. *Heliyon* **2023**, *9*, e19176. [CrossRef]
48. Ferrari, L.; Bernard, L.; Deschner, F.; Kaufmann, J.; Winnefeld, F.; Plank, J. Characterization of polycarboxylate-ether based superplasticizer on cement clinker surfaces. *J. Am. Ceram. Soc.* **2012**, *95*, 2189–2195. [CrossRef]
49. Kondraivendhan, B.; Bhattacharjee, B. Strength and w/c ratio relationship of cement based materials through pore features. *Mater. Charact.* **2016**, *122*, 124–129. [CrossRef]
50. Sua-Iam, G.; Makul, N. Effect of superplasticizer type and dosage on early-age shrinkage of portland cement and rice husk ash pastes. *Adv. Mater. Res.* **2012**, *450*, 407–412. [CrossRef]
51. Bentz, D.P. Modeling the influence of limestone filler on cement hydration using CEMHYD3D. *Cem. Concr. Compos.* **2006**, *28*, 124–129. [CrossRef]
52. Poppe, A.-M.; De Schutter, G. Cement hydration in the presence of high filler contents. *Cem. Concr. Res.* **2005**, *35*, 2290–2299. [CrossRef]
53. Garrault, S.; Finot, E.; Lesniewska, E.; Nonat, A. Study of C-S-H growth on C3S surface during its early hydration. *Mater. Struct.* **2005**, *38*, 435–442. [CrossRef]
54. Scrivener, K.; Snellings, R.; Lothenbach, B. *A Practical Guide to Microstructural Analysis of Cementitious Materials*; CRC Press: Boca Raton, FL, USA, 2016.
55. Darweesh, H.H.M.; Abou-El-Anwar, E.A.; Mekky, H.S. Addition of limestone at the expense of gypsum in Portland cement. *Int. Ceram. Rev.* **2018**, *67*, 18–27. [CrossRef]
56. Bonavetti, V.; Donza, H.; Menéndez, G.; Cabrera, O.; Irassar, E.F. Limestone filler cement in low w/c concrete: A rational use of energy. *Cem. Concr. Res.* **2003**, *33*, 865–871. [CrossRef]

Disclaimer/Publisher's Note: The statements, opinions and data contained in all publications are solely those of the individual author(s) and contributor(s) and not of MDPI and/or the editor(s). MDPI and/or the editor(s) disclaim responsibility for any injury to people or property resulting from any ideas, methods, instructions or products referred to in the content.

materials

Article

Mechanism of Rapid Curing Pile Formation on Shoal Foundation and Its Bearing Characteristic

Wei Li [1,2,3], Feng Liu [1], Yizhong Tan [4], Mengjun Chen [5,*], Yi Cai [2,*] and Jiayu Qian [1,3]

1 State Key Laboratory of Intelligent Construction and Healthy Operation and Maintenance of Deep Underground Engineering, China University of Mining and Technology, Xuzhou 221116, China; tbh259@cumt.edu.cn (W.L.); ly15938770068@163.com (F.L.); ts23030121a31@cumt.edu.cn (J.Q.)
2 Anhui Provincial Intelligent Underground Detection and Geoenvironmental Engineering Research Center, Anhui Jianzhu University, Hefei 230601, China
3 Yunlong Lake Laboratory of Deep Underground Science and Engineering, Xuzhou 221008, China
4 State Key Laboratory of Disaster Prevention and Mitigation of Explosion & Impact, Army Engineering University of PLA, Nanjing 210007, China; tanyizhong@163.com
5 College of Future Technology, Shandong University, Jinan 250012, China
* Correspondence: mjun@sdu.edu.cn (M.C.); caiyi@ahjzu.edu.cn (Y.C.)

Abstract: This study explores the application effect of the new non-isocyanate polyurethane curing agent on the rapid curing mechanism and bearing characteristics of piles in beach foundations. Through laboratory tests and field tests, the effects of the curing agent on the physical and mechanical properties of sand were systematically analyzed, including compressive strength, shear strength, and elastic modulus, and the effects of water content and cement–sand mass ratio on the properties of sand after curing were investigated. The results show that introducing a curing agent significantly improves the mechanical properties of sand, and the cohesion and internal friction angle increase exponentially with the sand mass ratio. In addition, the increase in water content leads to a decrease in the strength of solidified sand, and the microstructure analysis reveals the change in the bonding effect between the solidified gel and the sand particles. The field static load tests of single piles and pile groups verify the effectiveness of the rapid solidification pile in beach foundations and reveal the significant influence of pile length and pile diameter on the bearing capacity. This study provides a theoretical basis and technical support for the rapid solidification and reinforcement of tidal flat foundations and provides important guidance for related engineering applications.

Keywords: rapid curing; bearing characteristic; microscopic characteristic test; on-site testing

check for updates

Citation: Li, W.; Liu, F.; Tan, Y.; Chen, M.; Cai, Y.; Qian, J. Mechanism of Rapid Curing Pile Formation on Shoal Foundation and Its Bearing Characteristic. *Materials* **2024**, *17*, 2416. https://doi.org/10.3390/ma17102416

Academic Editor: Antonio Caggiano

Received: 7 April 2024
Revised: 12 May 2024
Accepted: 13 May 2024
Published: 17 May 2024

Copyright: © 2024 by the authors. Licensee MDPI, Basel, Switzerland. This article is an open access article distributed under the terms and conditions of the Creative Commons Attribution (CC BY) license (https://creativecommons.org/licenses/by/4.0/).

1. Introduction

Natural disasters like earthquakes, floods, and mudslides seriously threaten human society. Rapid response and effective emergency measures are essential to save lives and reduce property losses in the face of these disasters. The stability of foundations is the key factor to ensure the safety of buildings [1–3]. Especially when disasters occur, its importance is even more prominent. Traditional foundation reinforcement methods often take a long time, and it is challenging to meet the need for rapid reinforcement in emergencies. Therefore, developing and applying a new fast-curing agent will help to realize the rapid reinforcement of foundations [4–9]. This has become an urgent need in the engineering field.

A curing agent is a combination of chemical substances [10–13], including a hardener and liquid mixture, which is widely used to improve the engineering properties of soil [14–24], such as improving stability and shear strength and reducing settlement and deformation. Compared with the traditional foundation reinforcement method, the curing agent has the characteristics of rapid reaction, which can complete the curing in hours to days, significantly reducing construction time and costs [25–28]. In addition, the environmental friendliness and sustainability of curing agents are also important reasons for their popularity [29–32]. Curing agent treatment reduces the dependence on natural resources and environmental pollution and CO_2 emissions, which aligns with sustainable development.

The application of curing agents in environmental emergency treatment cannot be ignored [33–35]. In oil pollution accidents, curing agents can effectively control and reduce the diffusion of oil pollutants and protect the ecosystem from damage [31]. Inland pollution accidents and curing agents can quickly immobilize harmful substances and reduce their impact on the environment and human health. These applications demonstrate the vital value of curing agents in emergencies. Seyed Javad Ramezani et al. [36] used the soil stability of glass powder and silicon powder in bagasse ash-based geopolymer and used a large amount of SCBA and GP to develop a new environmentally friendly geological curing agent. Studies have shown that curing agents can effectively improve soil strength. Ammar Abdullah Saad Al-Dossary et al. [37] used the CCR and LABSA mixture as a UGB stabilizer in pavement engineering applications. Zhu Jianfeng et al. [38] studied the macro–micro investigation of using a ternary mixture of steel slag, fly ash, and calcium carbide residue to stabilize sludge as a roadbed filler. Studies have shown that this mixture can effectively improve the stability and mechanical properties of the filler. This study is of great significance to improve the sustainability of subgrade engineering. Lian Richeng et al. [39] studied the use of Cu (II) and Co (II) complex-modified ammonium polyphosphate as a co-curing agent to improve the fire safety and mechanical properties of epoxy-based architectural coatings. Xue Chen et al. [40] used the modified curing agent to treat the geological structure of loess. The results show that the modified curing material after adding CIM can effectively improve the engineering geological properties of loess foundations. Although the curing agent has shown great potential in foundation reinforcement and environmental emergency treatment [41–43], there is still a lack of research on its rapid solidification mechanism and bearing characteristics in tidal flat foundations. Traditional sand solidification materials have many limitations, such as poor permeability and low early strength, which make it challenging to meet the needs of rapid reinforcement [44]. This study used a new curing agent developed by the South China University of Technology to explore its application effect in beach foundations and its influence on the bearing capacity of single piles and pile groups.

In this study, the effects of the curing agent on sand's physical and mechanical properties were analyzed through laboratory tests, including compressive strength, shear strength, and elastic modulus. Through microscopic tests such as scanning electron microscopy, the microstructure changes of sand after curing were observed, and the bonding mechanism between the curing agent and sand particles was revealed. Then, through the static load test of a single pile and pile group, the bearing capacity of a fast-solidified pile was evaluated, and the influence of the slurry diffusion effect on the bearing capacity of the pile foundation was explored. Finally, this study will provide a theoretical basis and technical support for the rapid solidification and reinforcement of beach foundations and guidance for related engineering applications.

2. Curing Agent and Sample Preparation

As shown in Figure 1, firstly, a series of low-viscosity, small-molecule compounds containing epoxy functional groups were screened as raw materials, and low-viscosity trimethylolpropane triglycidyl ether [12,21] was used as a raw material to prepare a ternary cyclic carbonate material to form a cross-linked structure to improve the mechanical strength of the final product.

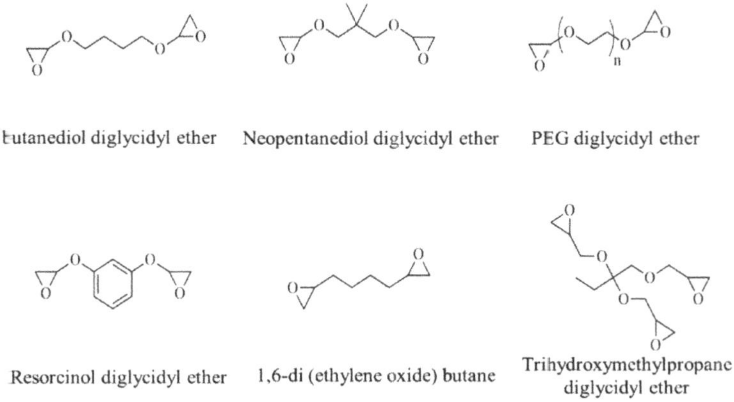

Figure 1. Structural formula of low-viscosity, small-molecule raw material containing epoxy group.

Based on the synthesized cyclic carbonates, as shown in Figure 2, a series of functional diamines or polyamines were selected as curing agents, such as ethylenediamine, diethylenetriamine, Mannich base polyamines, dopamine, etc., to adjust the structure and composition of polyurethane materials and obtain rapid infiltration and rapid solidification polyurethane materials with excellent performance.

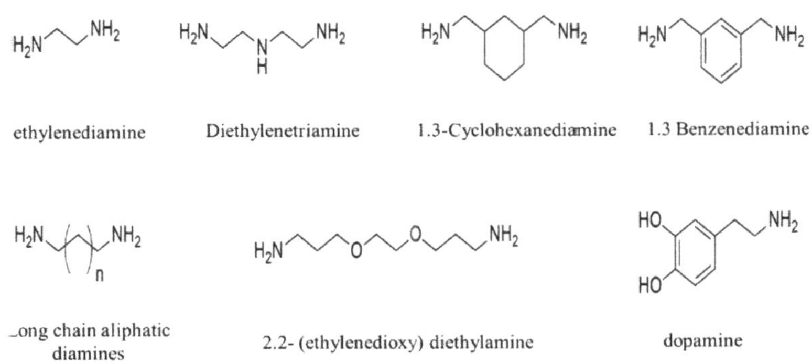

Figure 2. Functional curing agent.

Subsequently, the synthesized low-viscosity cyclic carbonate was subjected to a polyaddition reaction with a small-molecule diamine to form a non-isocyanate polyurethane. During the reaction, the cyclic carbonate group reacts with the amino group causing ring-opening polymerization to form the carbamate and hydroxyl groups, enhancing polyurethane's toughness and impact properties.

Subsequently, as shown in Figure 3, by introducing a low-viscosity, small-molecule glycidyl ether material containing an epoxy functional group, an epoxy–non-isocyanate polyurethane hybrid material with a double network structure is formed in the reaction with cyclic carbonates and amines to improve the mechanical properties of the material further and enhance its permeability in the sand.

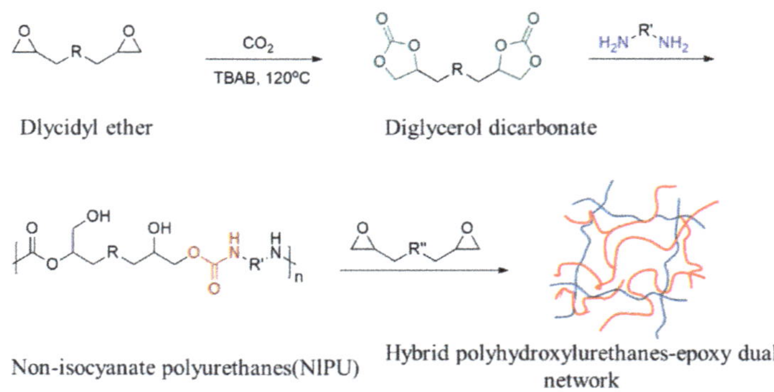

Figure 3. Diagram of the reaction of non-isocyanate polyurethane materials and epoxy–polyurethane materials.

Finally, using the above process, a non-isocyanate polyurethane curing agent with low viscosity, easy infiltration, and good mechanical properties was prepared. The curing agent also has environmental friendliness, which is suitable for the engineering requirements of rapid solidification and reinforcement of sand foundation.

The sample preparation process of this study is based on the combined application of a non-isocyanate polyurethane polymer curing agent and Daqingshan beach fine sand. Firstly, the beach sand in a specific area was selected as the source of test materials and dried. Subsequently, according to the predetermined moisture content requirements, the dried sand was mixed with water for 24 h to achieve a uniform moisture distribution. In the material ratio stage, the curing agent A and B components were accurately weighed according to the established mass ratio and quickly mixed to start the curing reaction. After preliminary stirring and standing, the mixture was poured into a pre-prepared mold, and the vibration method was used to ensure that the material was fully dense. To ensure that the surface of the sample was flat and defect-free, the surface of the material after perfusion was quickly flattened and smoothed and placed in a restricted expansion device for initial maintenance. Finally, after the specified curing time, the molded sample was obtained by demolding.

Two groups of experiments were designed for this study to systematically study the influence of water content and mortar mass ratio on the physical and mechanical properties of solidified sand. The first group of experiments focused on the change in water content, while the second group focused on the change in the mortar mass ratio. In each group of tests, the samples were numbered according to different treatment conditions to be effectively distinguished in subsequent analysis and discussion. Through this detailed sample preparation process, this study aims to explore the effect of curing agents on improving sand properties under different conditions and provide a scientific basis for related engineering applications.

(1) The effect of water content on the physical and mechanical properties of solidified sand under the same mass ratio of mortar was investigated:

According to the actual moisture content of 24.26%, the moisture content of the test sand was divided into five gradients: w = 0%, 5%, 10%, 15%, 20%, 24.26%, and the mass ratio of mortar was 20.56%, 33%. The total size of the sample prepared in the test is 1 diameter × height = 50 mm × 100 mm, see Table 1.

Table 1. Specimen test number with different water ratio.

Mass Ratio	Water Content					
	0%	**5%**	**10%**	**15%**	**20%**	**24.26%**
20.56%	X-1	X-2	X-3	X-4	X-5	X-6
33%	Y-1	Y-2	Y-3	Y-4	Y-5	Y-6

(2) Under the same water content, the influence of the mass ratio of mortar on the physical and mechanical properties of solidified sand was explored:

According to the mortar mass ratio of 5%, 10%, 15%, 20.56%, 25%, 33% (of which 20.56% and 33% correspond to the minimum void ratio and the ratio under the maximum void ratio, respectively), the moisture content was 24.26% of the real moisture content under the field condition, so the specimens were divided into six groups. A total of two sample sizes were prepared in the test: 1 diameter 50 mm, height 100 mm; 2 diameter 78.9 mm, height 100 mm; see Table 2.

Table 2. Specimen test number with different mortar ratio.

Specimen Size	Mortar Ratio					
	5%	**10%**	**15%**	**20.56%**	**25%**	**33%**
50 mm × 100 mm	Ad-1 Ad-2 Ad-3	Bd-1 Bd-2 Bd-3	Cd-1 Cd-2 Cd-3	Dd-1 Dd-2 Dd-3	Ed-1 Ed-2 Ed-3	Fd-1 Fd-2 Fd-3
79.8 mm × 100 mm	Gj-1 Gj-2 Gj-3 Gj-4	Hj-1 Hj-2 Hj-3 Hj-4	Ij-1 Ij-2 Ij-3 Ij-4	Jj-1 Jj-2 Jj-3 Jj-4	Kj-1 Kj-2 Kj-3 Kj-4	Lj-1 Lj-2 Lj-3 Lj-4

3. Physical and Mechanical Properties and Microscopic Characteristics of Solidified Sand

3.1. Compressive and Shear Properties

Using the ADS-500/HL-200 large-scale direct shear test system produced by WILLE Geotechnik in Rosdorf, Germany for underground structures shown in Figure 4, this study aims to evaluate the effect of curing agents on the properties of sand. The tests were carried out at different mass ratios of 5%, 10%, 15%, 20.56%, 25%, and 33%, of which 20.56% and 33% represent the minimum and maximum void ratios, respectively. The water content used in the test was 24.26%, which was based on the field measurement results. Under constant water content, the shear performance and the changing trend of samples with different mass ratios were studied to simulate the actual influence of solidified pile slurry diffusion on the mechanical properties of surrounding sand.

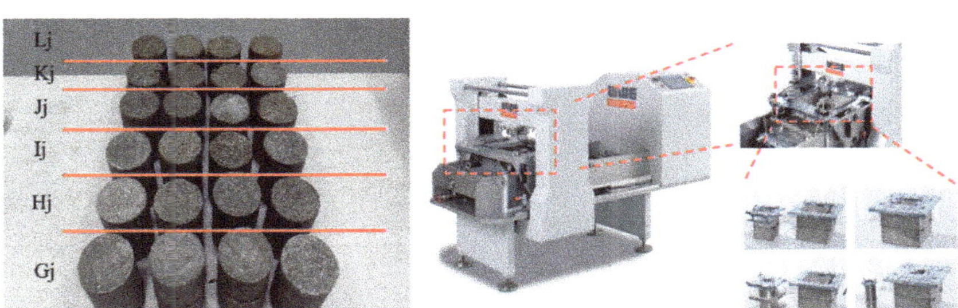

(**a**) Specimens (**b**) Large-scale direct shear apparatus

Figure 4. Straight shear test.

After the test, the relationship between the shear strength and the vertical pressure of the samples with different mass ratios under the same water content was obtained, as shown in Figure 5. For detailed data, refer to Table 3.

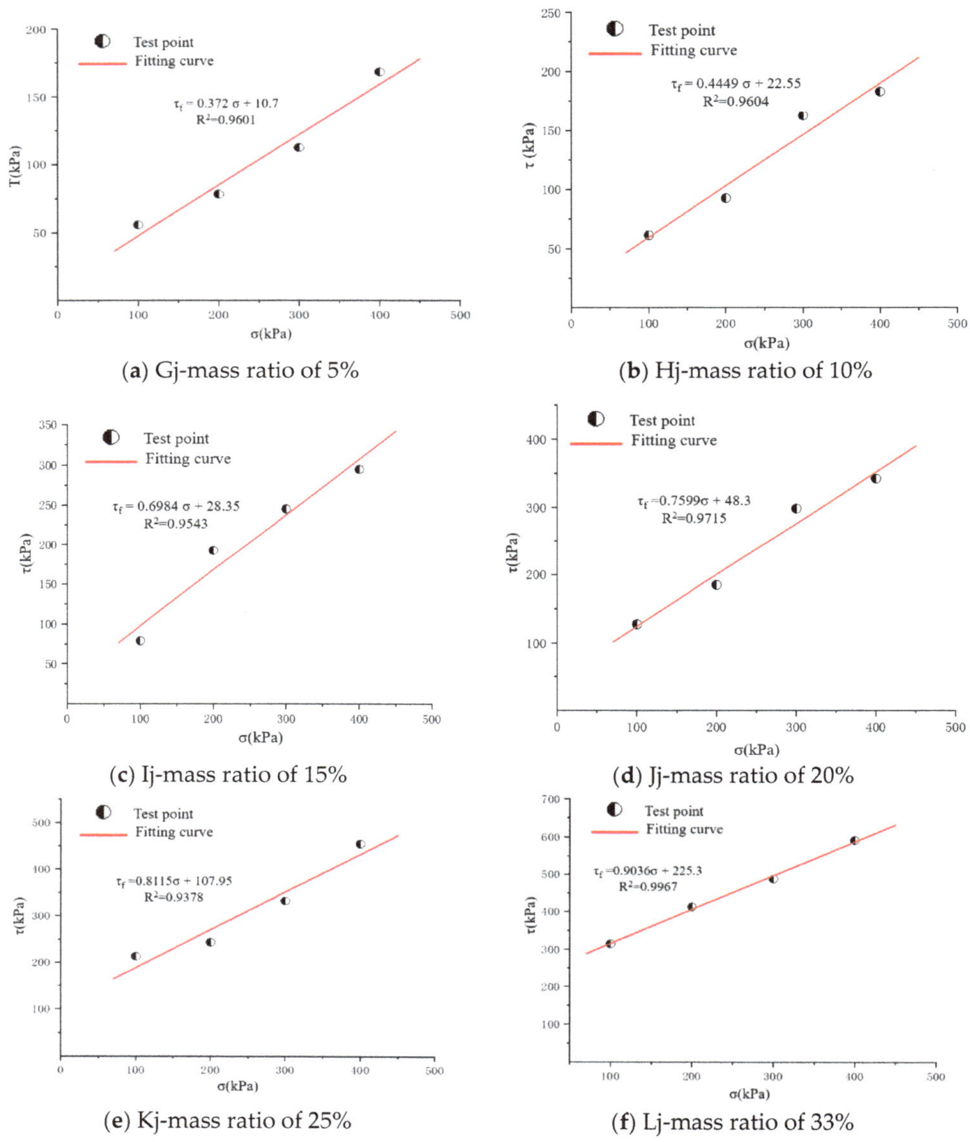

Figure 5. The fitting curves of shear stress (σ) and normal stress (τ).

Table 3. Uniaxial compression test results.

MB (%)	Sample	σ_p (MPa)	*E* (MPa)
5%	Ad-1	0.128	22.25
	Ad-2	0.126	21.11
	Ad-3	0.119	21.88
	Average value	0.124	21.74
10%	Bd-1	0.163	36.41
	Bd-2	0.167	36.55
	Bd-3	0.164	36.11
	Average value	0.165	36.35
15%	Cd-1	0.219	47.82
	Cd-2	0.213	47.98
	Cd-3	0.209	48.03
	Average value	0.214	47.94
20.56%	Dd-1	0.256	56.23
	Dd-2	0.251	55.98
	Dd-3	0.267	56.32
	Average value	0.258	56.18
25%	Ed-1	0.312	64.36
	Ed-2	0.292	64.18
	Ed-3	0.291	64.29
	Average value	0.298	64.27
33%	Fd-1	0.354	105.39
	Fd-2	0.352	105.18
	Fd-3	0.348	105.41
	Average value	0.351	105.32

The direct shear test results can be summarized, as shown in Table 4.

Table 4. Summary of direct shear test results.

Mortar Ratio (%)	Cohesion (kPa)	Internal Friction Angle (°)
5	10.70	20.40
10	16.25	23.40
15	28.10	36.10
20.56	48.30	37.23
25	107.95	39.06
33	225.30	42.10

According to the above data, the relationship equation between cohesion and the internal friction angle and mass ratio can be obtained. The fitting results are shown in Figure 6.

As shown in Figure 6, the cohesion of the solidified sand sample has an exponential line function relationship with the mass ratio of sand to rubber, and the internal friction angle has a quadratic function relationship with the mass ratio of sand to rubber.

As shown in Figure 7, the uniaxial compression test was carried out using the MTS816 electro-hydraulic servo rock mechanics test system produced by MTS System Company in the Eden Prairie, MN, USA. The sampling frequency was 10 Hz, and the pre-pressure was 0.5 kN. During the unconfined uniaxial compression test [14,26,29], Vaseline was applied to offset the possible errors in the test results due to friction forces at the interface between the faces of the specimen and the plates of the testing machine.

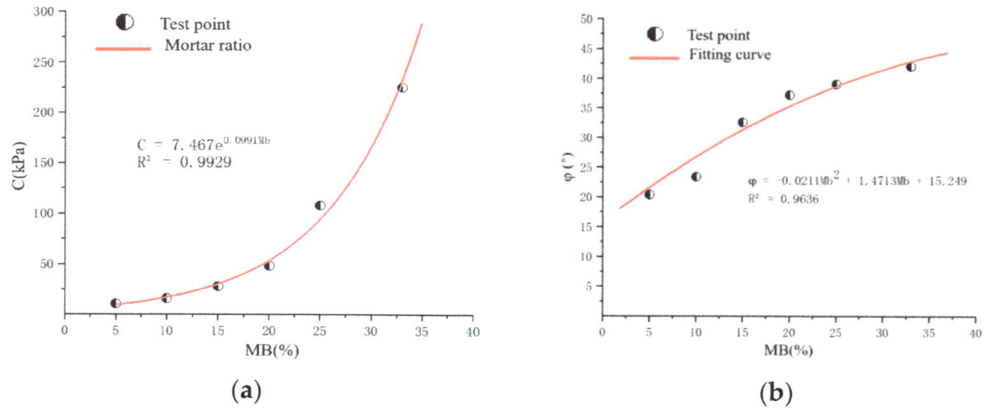

Figure 6. Fitting curves. (**a**) Fitting equation of the relationship between cohesion and mass ratio. (**b**) Fitting equation of the relationship between internal friction angle and mass ratio.

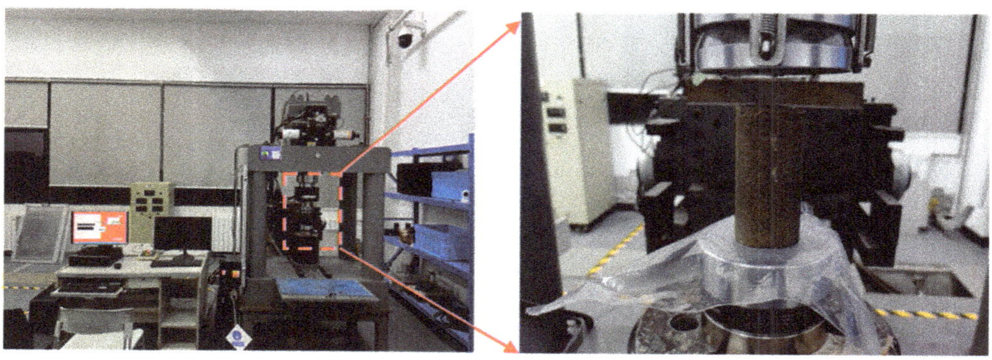

Figure 7. Uniaxial compression experiment.

The influence of water content on the physical and mechanical properties of solidified sand under the same mass ratio of mortar was explored. According to the actual moisture content of 24.26%, the moisture content of the test sand was divided into five gradients: w = 0%, 5%, 10%, 15%, 20%, 24.26%, and the mass ratio of mortar was 20.56%, 33%. The sample size had a diameter of 50 mm and a height of 100 mm; the results of the uniaxial compression test are shown in Table 5.

Table 5. Summary of test results.

No.	Compressive Strength (MPa)	No.	Compressive Strength (MPa)
X-1	15.203	Y-1	17.556
X-2	2.419	Y-2	3.011
X-3	1.612	Y-3	2.259
X-4	0.863	Y-4	1.056
X-5	0.67	Y-5	0.798
X-6	0.262	Y-6	0.353

Figure 8 shows the significant effect of water content on the strength of solidified sand specimens. Under the condition of a fixed mass ratio, the strength of the specimen decreased significantly with the increase in water content. In particular, when the specimen changed from a dry sand state to a water-bearing sand state. the strength decreased sharply. For example, when the sand–binder mass ratio was 20.56%, the strength of the specimen without water content was 15.203 MPa, while the strength decreased to 2.149 MPa when the water content was only 5%. Similarly, at a sand–binder mass ratio of 33%, the strength without water content was 17.556 MPa and decreased to 3.011 MPa when the water content was 5%. In addition, when the water content increased from 5% to 24.26%, the strength of the specimens with mass ratios of 20.56% and 33% decreased from 2.419 MPa and 3.011 MPa to 0.262 MPa and 0.353 MPa, respectively. These results highlight the important influence of water content on the strength of solidified sand and suggest that the formulation of the curing agent needs to be optimized to adapt to the environment of water-bearing sand.

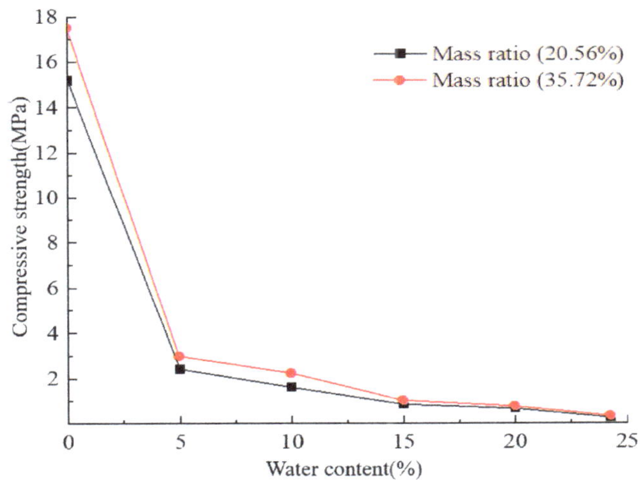

Figure 8. Effect of moisture content on compressive strength.

Under the condition of fixed water content, it was found that the increase in sand–binder mass ratio is positively correlated with the increase in specimen strength, indicating that an increase in curing agent content helps enhance the strength of the specimen. However, for two different sand mass ratios, its effect on the strength of the specimen is not significant, especially in the water-bearing sand; the change in the sand–binder mass ratio has a limited impact on the strength. The experimental data show that the specimens with higher sand–binder mass ratios always perform better with regard to strength under the same moisture content.

Figure 9 shows the effect of different water content on the failure mode of the solidified specimen at a 20.56% mortar mass ratio. Under the condition of low water content, the non-isocyanate polyurethane curing agent can better adhere to the sand particles, thereby enhancing the strength of the specimen and forming obvious shear bands during failure, showing 'X'-shaped or 'Y'-shaped cracks. With the increase in water content, the gel formed by the curing agent decreases, which leads to an increase in sand particle exposure, a decrease in compressive strength, and a change in failure mode into end bulging fracture. When the water content continues to increase, the supersaturated state leads to poor adhesion of the curing agent.

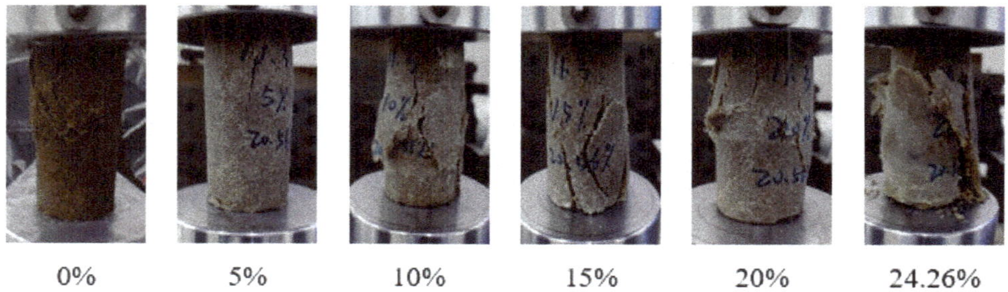

Figure 9. Specimen damage pattern.

With the loss of water, the compressive strength of the specimen was further weakened. Under continuous load, the internal structure of the specimen disintegrated, resulting in broken small particles accompanied by surface drainage. The failure mode of the specimen is directly related to the adhesion effect of the curing agent gel and the sand particles.

To evaluate the influence of the mass ratio of mortar on the physical and mechanical properties of solidified sand under constant water content, the specimens were divided into six groups with mortar mass ratios of 5%, 10%, 15%, 20.56%, 25%, and 33%, respectively, of which 20.56% and 33% correspond to the minimum and maximum void ratios. In the experiment, the water content of the actual working condition was 24.26%, and two specifications of the samples (diameter × height of 50 mm × 100 mm and 78.9 mm × 100 mm, respectively) were prepared. Each sample was uniquely numbered according to the working conditions. For detailed results, refer to Table 3.

The experimental data reveal that the elastic modulus of the sample increased with an increase in the mass ratio of the mortar, and the corresponding shear modulus could be calculated. As shown in Figure 10, an exponential growth relationship exists between elastic modulus and shear modulus and mass ratio. According to this relationship, the modulus value at any mass ratio can be predicted, or the mass ratio can be deduced from the known modulus. The results show that the increase in the concentration of the curing agent helped to improve the bonding performance of the sand, thereby enhancing its compressive and shear strength, and a corresponding mathematical model was established to describe this relationship. Detailed values are shown in Table 6.

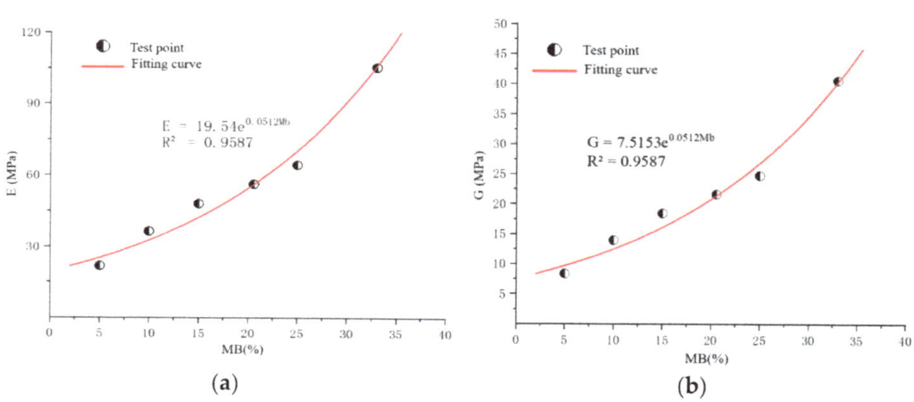

Figure 10. Fitting curves. (**a**) The relationship between mass ratio and elastic modulus. (**b**) Relationship between mass ratio of mortar and shear modulus.

Table 6. Elastic and shear modulus with different mass ratio.

Sample Property	MB (%) 5	MB (%) 10	MB (%) 15	MB (%) 20.56	MB (%) 25	MB (%) 33
E (MPa)	21.74	36.36	47.94	56.18	64.27	105.32
G (MPa)	8.36	13.98	18.44	21.61	24.72	40.51

3.2. Micro Characteristic Test

In this study, the microstructure of solidified sand particles was analyzed in detail by electron microscope scanning technology [27–30], with special attention given to the distribution of pores and cracks. The microstructure analysis of 12 samples was carried out under two different cement–sand mass ratios and six different water content conditions, aiming to reveal the influence of cement–sand mass ratio and water content on the microscopic characteristics of solidified sand, and further understand the formation mechanism of fast-solidified piles. The initial scanning used a magnification of 70 times to obtain the overall microstructure of the sample. Then, the key areas were observed by increasing the magnification, focusing on the microscopic morphology of holes and cracks. The test numbers for specimens with different water content and mass ratio are presented in Table 1.

Figure 11 shows that the gel formed after the reaction of the curing agent completely or partially encapsulates the sand particles, and the voids between the particles are filled. The filling effect of this gel promotes the mutual connection between sand particles, thus changing the transition of soil particles from a free state to a bonding state and effectively improving the overall strength of the material.

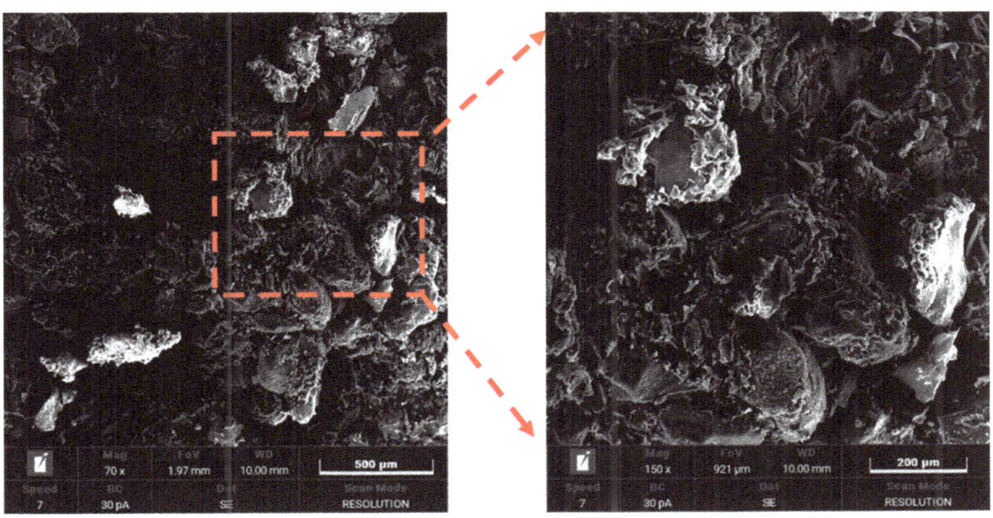

(**a**) Y-1 (×70) (**b**) Y-1 (×150)

Figure 11. Microstructure of sandy soil after curing.

It can be seen from Figure 12 that the pores existing in the solidified sand samples are divided into three types: ① intergranular pores formed by unfilled gels between sand particles; ② internal micropores formed inside the gel formed by the curing agent after curing; ③ tiny cracks formed between the gels during the adhesion process.

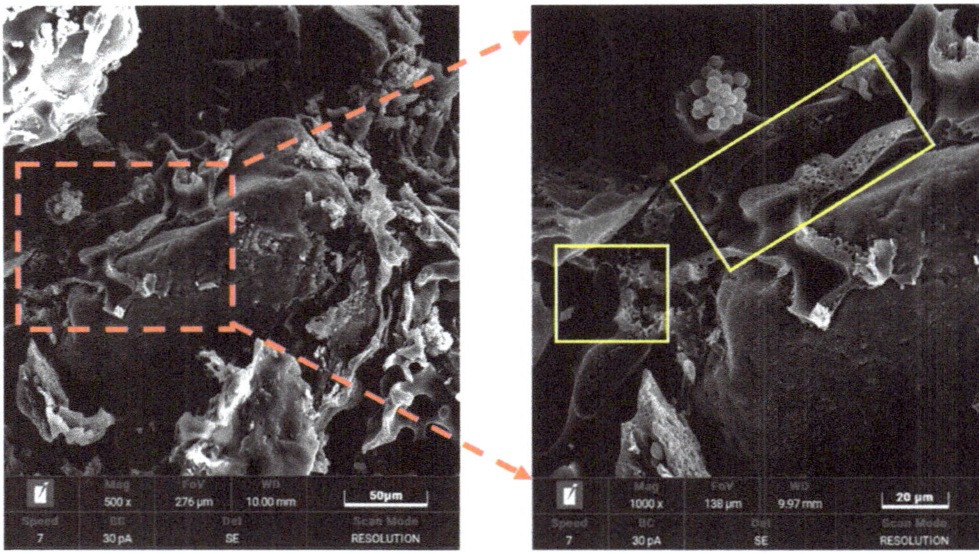

(**a**) Y-1 (×500) (**b**) Y-1 (×1000)

Figure 12. Type of microscopic pore.

Figure 13 is the microstructure image of sand-solidified samples with 70 times magnification under the condition of minimum and maximum water content with two kinds of sand–binder mass ratios:

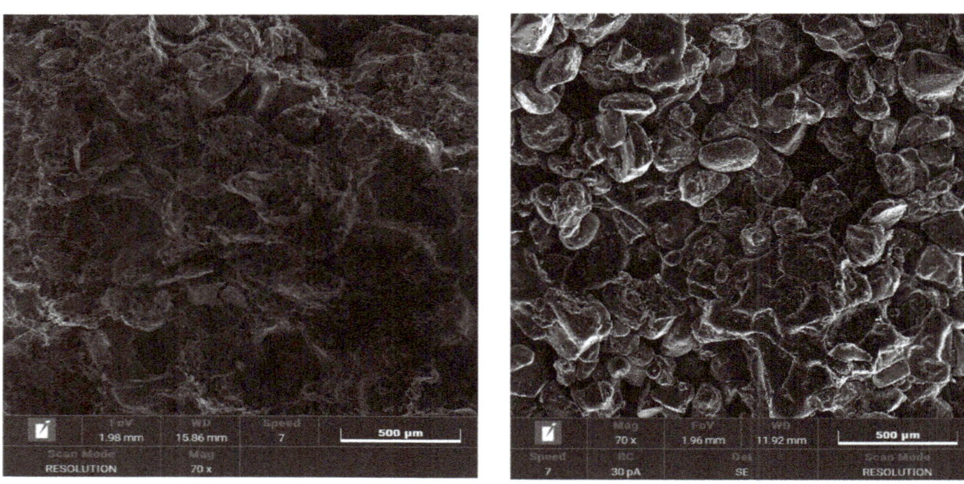

(**a**) X-1 (×70) (**b**) X-6 (×70)

Figure 13. *Cont.*

(**c**) Y-1 (×70) (**d**) Y-6 (×70)

Figure 13. Microstructure of specimens in different states.

Figure 13a,b shows that under the condition of a fixed mortar mass ratio, the increase in water content leads to a decrease in the number of gels formed by the curing agent, and more and more sand particles are observed. This indicates that in the mixing process of curing agent and sand, the increase in water content may lead to a loss in curing agent with water before the formation of gel, which reduces the effective adhesion of the sand particle surface, thus reducing its ability to withstand external loads. Further, by comparing Figure 13a,c, it is found that the number of gels increases with the increase in the mass ratio of mortar, which indicates that the increase in curing agent content helps to enhance the compressive strength of the specimen. However, when the mortar mass ratio reaches 35.72%, a supersaturation phenomenon occurs in the experiment, which affects the compaction effect of the specimen. This phenomenon leads to the loss of the gel before it forms an effective bond with the sand particles, thereby weakening the overall strength of the specimen.

The microstructure diagram shown in Figure 14a reveals the fracture of the solidified gel under the action of external force, exposing its internal micro-pores and obvious fracture surfaces. Figure 14b further shows that the detachment of the gel from the surface of the sand particles leads to the exposure of some sand particles, which weakens the condensation strength and promotes the formation of the fracture surface. The formation of cracks observed in Figure 14c,d further confirms the gel rupture under external force. These observations show that the insufficient bond strength between sand particles and the gel and the insufficient strength of the gel itself to resist external forces are the main reasons for the failure of the specimen at the micro level.

As shown in Figure 15a, with the increase in water content, the gel formed by the curing agent gradually changed from a continuous dense layer to a dispersed granular structure. This transformation leads to a decrease in the bonding area between the gel particles and the dispersion of the particles, which depends on the external thin-layer cementation film to maintain the structure. Once this layer of cementation film is broken, the internal particles will lead to a sharp decline in the overall structural strength due to insufficient contact and insufficient connection with the sand particles, which will eventually lead to the destruction of the gel.

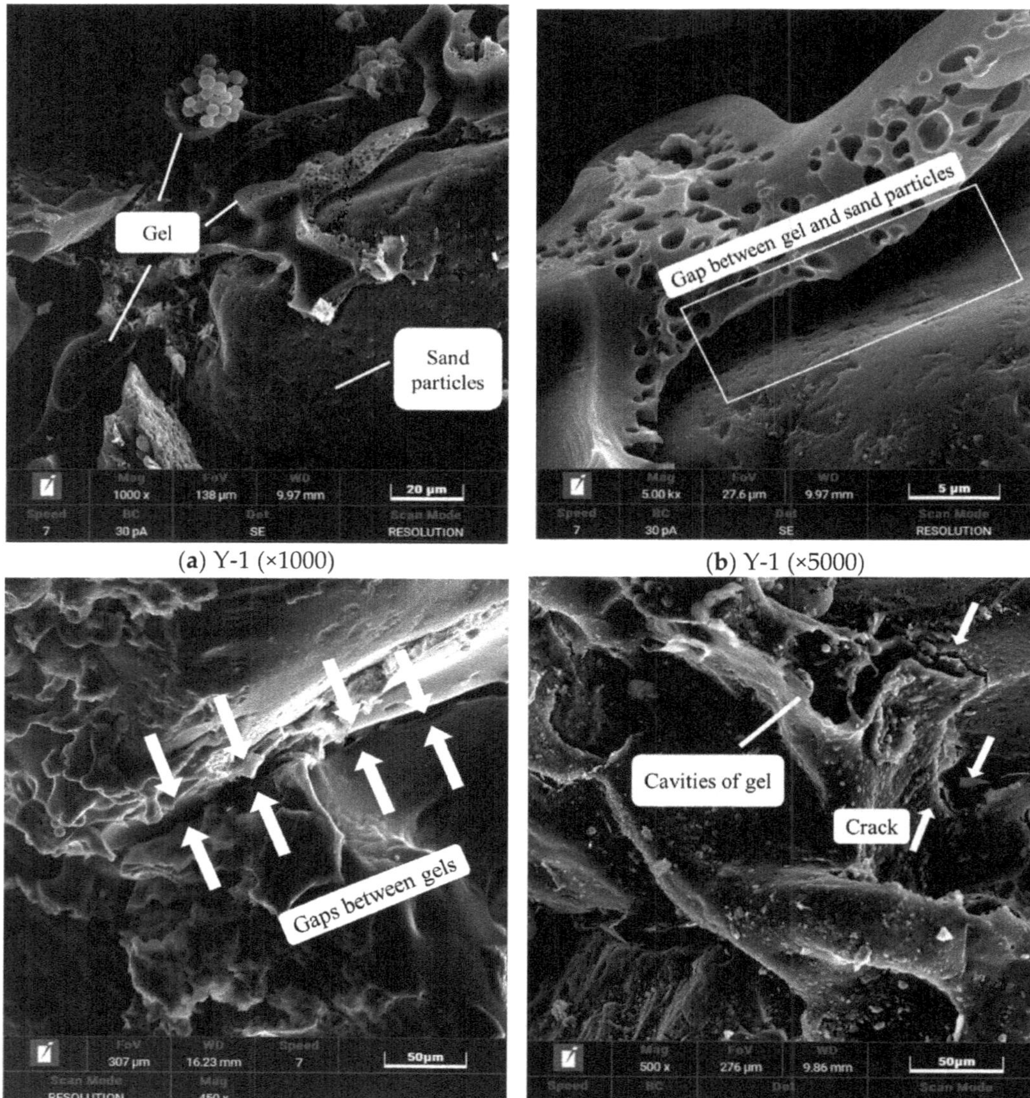

(**a**) Y-1 (×1000) (**b**) Y-1 (×5000)

(**c**) X-1 (×450) (**d**) Y-6 (×500)

Figure 14. The style of specimen damage.

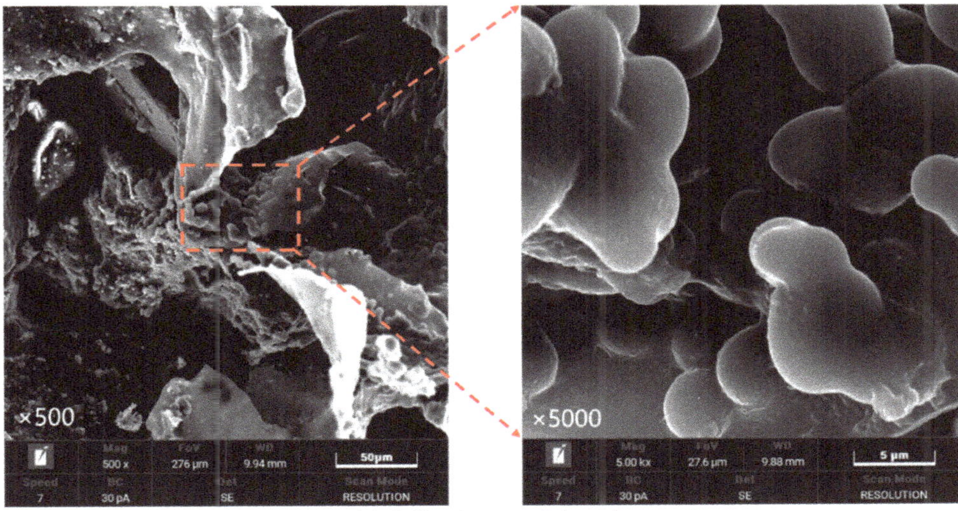

(**a**) Adhesive particle gel

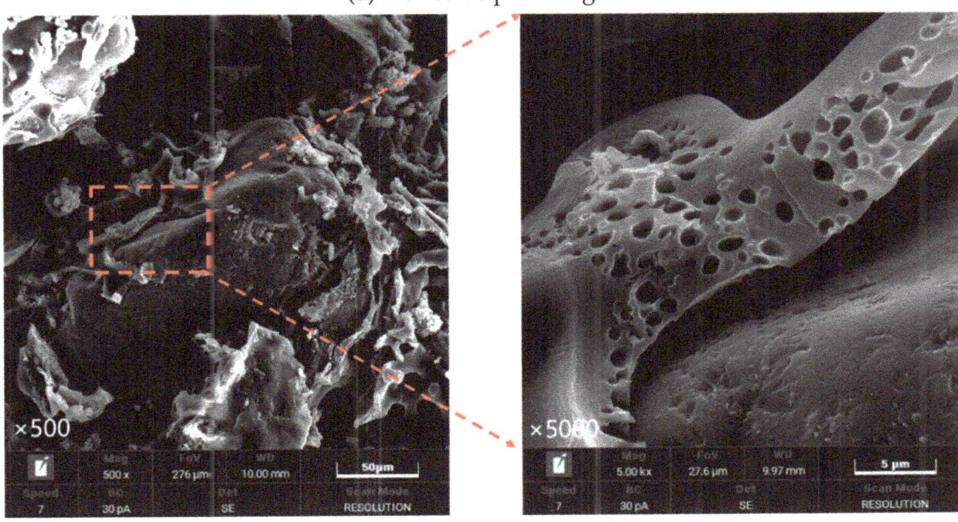

(**b**) Lamellar porous gel

Figure 15. Style of solids.

In summary, it can be seen from Figure 15b that the non-isocyanate polyurethane rapid curing agent used in this study forms a gel layer tightly wrapped with sand particles when solidifying dry, fine sand particles. It can be seen from Figure 15a that after curing in water-bearing sand, the formed gel layer structure presents a loose granular connection and is covered by a thin curing film.

4. Field Test of Rapid Curing Pile Foundation for a Tidal Flat Foundation

4.1. Single-Pile Static Load Tests

The design strategy employs small diameters for the piles and their boreholes, with diameters set at 100 mm, 200 mm, and 300 mm. The lengths of the piles are designed to be 1 m and 0.5 m. For each mixing of the piling material, approximately 9 kg of sand is used, and the pile is cast in several stages. Utilizing a novel curing material in this experiment the work condition design is based on a previous research framework, as detailed in Table 7 The loading approach incorporates a pile load-bearing platform and a reaction frame test arrangement, as illustrated in Figure 16.

Table 7. Design of working conditions for single pile.

Project	$P_{1\text{-}1}$	$P_{1\text{-}0.5}$	$P_{2\text{-}1}$	$P_{2\text{-}0.5}$	$P_{3\text{-}1}$	$P_{3\text{-}0.5}$
Pile diameter/m	0.1	0.1	0.2	0.2	0.3	0.3
Pile length/m	1	0.5	1	0.5	1	0.5

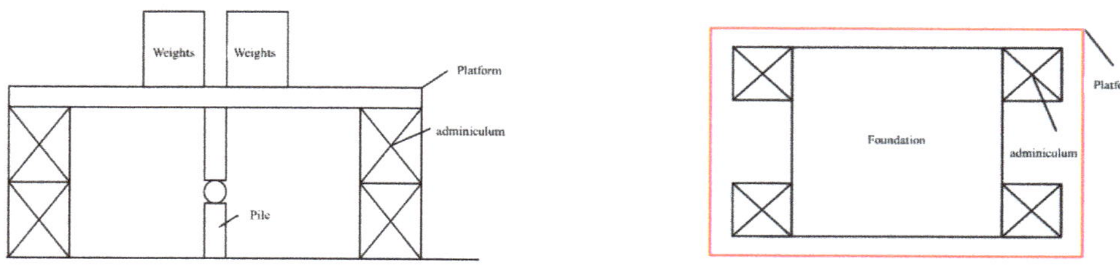

(**a**) Front view (**b**) Vertical view

Figure 16. The schematic diagram of the reaction frame of the static load test pile cap.

(1) Vertical static load tests of pile $P_{1\text{-}1}$ and pile $P_{1\text{-}0.5}$

The static load test results of both pile $P_{1\text{-}1}$ and pile $P_{1\text{-}0.5}$ are shown in Figure 17a in the form of a load–displacement curve. The data in the figure show that there is a linear relationship between the load and settlement displacement at the initial loading stage for both test piles.

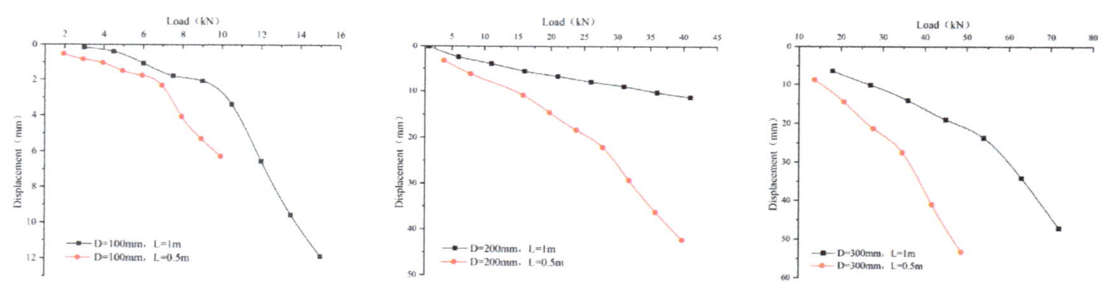

(**a**) load–displacement curve (D = 100 mm), (**b**) load–displacement curve (D = 200 mm), (**c**) load–displacement curve (D = 300 mm)

Figure 17. Load–displacement curve (D = 100, 200, 300 mm).

For pile $P_{1\text{-}1}$, the curve tends to flatten when the pile top load exceeds 10.5 kN, indicating a significant increase in pile top settlement. Specifically, when the load reaches 12 kN, the settlement reaches 7.37 mm. As the load continues to increase, the curve shows a significant change, with the load reaching 13.5 kN and the settlement sharply increasing to 9.53 mm, indicating a drastic change in the pile top load–displacement curve. Therefore, it can be determined that the ultimate bearing capacity of the $P_{1\text{-}1}$ pile is at least 10.5 kN.

However, the curve of pile $P_{1\text{-}0.5}$ tends to flatten when the load exceeds 7 kN, indicating a significant increase in pile top settlement. Specifically, when the load reaches 8 kN, the pile top settlement is 4.03 mm. With a further increase in load, the curve shows a notable change; when the load reaches 9 kN, the settlement sharply increases to 5.26 mm, indicating a drastic change in the pile top load–displacement curve. Therefore, it can be determined that the ultimate bearing capacity of the $P_{1\text{-}0.5}$ pile is at least 7 kN.

(2) Vertical static load tests of pile $P_{2\text{-}1}$ and pile $P_{2\text{-}0.5}$

Figure 17b presents the static load test results for the test piles with diameter of 0.2 m and the corresponding load–displacement curve.

Combining the above Figure 17b and load data, the pile $P_{2\text{-}1}$ shows a relatively flat curve change after the load exceeds 31 kN, indicating a significant increase in pile top settlement. Specifically, when the load increases to 36 kN, the pile top settlement reaches 17.25 mm. With a further increase in load, a significant change in the curve trend occurs; when the load reaches 31 kN, the curve sharply declines. The pile top settlement increases to 22.25 mm when the load reaches 41 kN. Based on these observations, the ultimate bearing capacity of the pile $P_{2\text{-}1}$ is not less than 31 kN.

Figure 17b also shows a linear relationship between the load and settlement displacement for the pile $P_{2\text{-}0.5}$ at the initial loading stage. When the load exceeds 28 kN, the curve becomes flatter, followed by a significant increase in pile top settlement. At a load of 32 kN, the settlement is 29.14 mm. As the load increases, a noticeable change in the curve occurs; when the load reaches 36 kN, the settlement sharply increases to 36.11 mm, indicating a drastic change in the pile top load–displacement curve. Therefore, the ultimate bearing capacity of the pile $P_{2\text{-}0.5}$ can be determined to be at least 23 kN.

(3) Vertical static load tests of pile $P_{3\text{-}1}$ and pile $P_{3\text{-}0.5}$

Figure 17c presents the static load test data of pile $P_{3\text{-}1}$ and pile $P_{3\text{-}0.5}$, as well as the corresponding load–displacement curve

The data in the figure show that there is a linear relationship between the load and settlement displacement of the pile $P_{3\text{-}1}$ at the initial loading stage. When the load exceeds 54 kN, the curve becomes flatter, followed by a significant increase in pile top settlement. At a load of 63 kN, the settlement is 34.00 mm. As the load further increases, a noticeable change in the curve trend occurs; when the load reaches 72 kN, the settlement sharply increases to 46.99 mm, indicating a drastic change in the pile top load–displacement curve. Therefore, the ultimate bearing capacity of the pile $P_{3\text{-}1}$ can be determined to be at least 54 kN.

The illustrated results reveal a linear relationship between the load and settlement displacement of the pile $P_{3\text{-}0.5}$ at the initial loading stage. As the load increases, the curve gradually flattens when it exceeds 35 kN, indicating significant settlement at the pile top. At a load of 42 kN, the settlement reaches 40.86 mm. The continued increase in load causes a noticeable change in the curve trend, especially when the load reaches 49 kN; the settlement sharply increases to 53.14 mm, indicating a severe turn in the pile top load–displacement curve. Therefore, the ultimate bearing capacity of the pile $P_{3\text{-}0.5}$ is determined to be no less than 35 kN.

The above analysis shows the bearing capacity of single piles under various conditions, as shown in Table 8. During the unconfined uniaxial compression test, Vaseline was applied at both ends of the sample to offset the possible errors in the test results due to friction forces at the interface between the faces of the specimen and the plates of the testing machine.

Table 8. Vertical bearing capacity of single pile.

Project	$P_{1\text{-}1}$	$P_{1\text{-}0.5}$	$P_{2\text{-}1}$	$P_{2\text{-}0.5}$	$P_{3\text{-}1}$	$P_{3\text{-}0.5}$
Pile diameter (mm)	100	100	200	200	300	300
Pile length (m)	1	0.5	1	0.5	1	0.5
Pile bearing capacity (kN)	10.5	7	31	28	54	35

(1) Effect of pile length on the vertical bearing capacity of a single pile.

The load–settlement curves of single piles when the pile diameter is 100 mm, 200 mm, and 300 mm, with pile lengths of 1 m and 0.5 m, respectively, are shown in Figures 17 and 18.

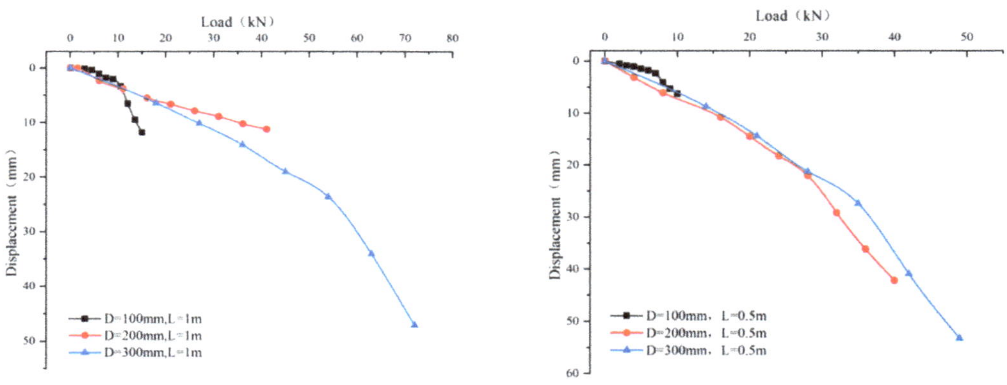

(**a**) L = 1 m (**b**) L = 0.5 m

Figure 18. Load–displacement curve.

As is revealed in the Figure 17:

① Studies have shown that an increase in pile diameter significantly enhances the bearing capacity of pile foundations.

Assuming a pile diameter of 100 mm, when the pile top settlement is 5 mm, the bearing capacity of a pile whose length is 0.5 m reaches 9 kN, while that of a pile whose length is 1 m reaches 11 kN. Assuming a pile diameter of 200 mm, when the pile top settlement is 15 mm, the bearing capacities increase to 20 kN (L = 0.5 m) and 35 kN (L = 1 m), respectively For a pile diameter of 300 mm, the bearing capacities increase to 40 kN and about 65 kN, respectively, when the pile top settlement is settled as 40 mm.

This phenomenon can be attributed to the increase in the contact area at the base of the pile, which increases the tip-bearing capacity of the pile. Additionally, longer piles exhibit greater load-bearing capacity as a longer pile length increases the contact area between the pile body and the surrounding soil, thereby increasing the pile-side friction resistance. In practical engineering, increasing the pile length to enhance the ultimate bearing capacity of a single pile has become a common practice due to the limitations on pile diameter.

② The inflection point of the load–displacement curve marks the ultimate bearing capacity of a single pile. The data show that, with an increase in pile length, the ultimate bearing capacity of a single pile correspondingly increases, and the settlement displacement at the pile top also increases with the increase in pile diameter. This is because pile side friction resistance exertion requires a relative displacement between the pile body and the surrounding sand soil. In the initial loading stage, the settlement of the pile foundation is small due to the low external load, resulting in the pile side friction resistance not being fully exerted.

In summary, increasing the pile length can effectively reduce the settlement of a single pile and enhance its ultimate bearing capacity, as a longer pile body increases the contact area with the surrounding soil, thereby increasing the pile side friction resistance and reducing the settlement under the same load. However, this improvement is not unlimited Under specific geological conditions, after the pile length is increased to a certain extent the pile top load will be fully supported by the pile side friction resistance. Once beyond this point, additional pile length will lead to excessive lateral friction resistance, causing excessive settlement, which may exceed the engineering tolerance limit for displacement Therefore, optimizing the pile length requires balancing, improving bearing capacity, and controlling settlement.

(2) The impact of pile diameter on the vertical bearing capacity of a single pile.

Load–settlement curves for single piles with 1 m and 0.5 m lengths and diameters of 100 mm, 200 mm, and 300 mm are shown in Figure 18.

As is revealed in the figures above:

① As the pile diameter increases, the inflection point of the load–settlement curve moves towards higher loads and smaller settlements, indicating that a larger pile diameter can bring about a higher ultimate bearing capacity. For piles with a length of 1 m, under a load of 10 kN, the settlements for piles with diameters of 100 mm, 200 mm, and 300 mm are approximately 3 mm,11 mm, and 25 mm, respectively, with corresponding ultimate bearing capacities of 15 kN, 41 kN, and 72 kN.

For piles with a length of 0.5 m, under a load of 15 kN, the settlements for piles with diameters of 200 mm, and 300 mm are approximately 22 mm and 24 mm, with corresponding ultimate bearing capacities of 40 kN and 49 kN, respectively.

② The data in the figure show that, for a fixed pile length, an increase in pile diameter significantly enhances the ultimate bearing capacity of a single pile. This phenomenon is attributed to an increase in pile diameter, resulting in a larger contact area between the pile body and the surrounding soil, thereby increasing the pile side friction and pile end resistance and reducing the settlement at the pile top. Specifically, for a pile length of 1 m, the piles with diameters of 100 mm, 200 mm, and 300 mm have pile–soil contact areas of 78.5 cm^2, 314 cm^2, and 706.5 cm^2, respectively. Under the same external load, a pile with a smaller diameter (D = 100 mm) experiences a greater vertical displacement than that of one with a larger diameter (D = 200 mm).

Expanding the pile diameter can enhance the maximum bearing capacity of a single pile and reduce its vertical displacement. This is mainly because the contact area between the pile tip and the soil below increases, thereby increasing the resistance at the pile tip. With the contact area between the pile body and the surrounding soil also expanding as the pile diameter increases, the lateral friction resistance increases. However, an increase in pile diameter also leads to higher costs.

4.2. Group Pile Static Load Tests

The group pile static load test selected two scenarios for comparative analysis. One scenario used a group of piles with a 200 mm thick cap at the bottom. To eliminate boundary effects, a square cap with a side length of 2.5 m was chosen, and the bearing plate used was a square with an area of 0.5 m^2 and a thickness of 20 mm. The other scenario involved piles without a bottom solidification, using only the upper cap for the experiment. Specific conditions can be found in Table 9 and Figure 19.

Table 9. Design of working conditions for group pile.

No.	Foundation Slab	Test Pile
S1#	Side length 2.5 m	-
S2#	Side length 2.5 m	Pile diameter 200 mm, Pile length 500 mm $\times 4$

(1) Analysis of test results for pile S1

After the experiment measurements were concluded, the pile S1 cap flat plate load results were obtained, and the load–displacement curve is illustrated in Figure 20a.

The on-site load–displacement curve shows that the vertical displacement increments at the pile top are small and uniform before a load level of 250 kN, making the curve gentle. Beyond this load, the increment in pile top displacement significantly increases, and the curve steeply declines. When the load increases to 300 kN, the displacement sharply rises, but there are no changes in the cap. As the load increases to 325 kN, the displacement further increases to 48.41 mm, and the cap plate begins to crack and sink. The slope of the curve after the inflection point is significantly steeper than before, indicating that the ultimate bearing capacity is 250 kN.

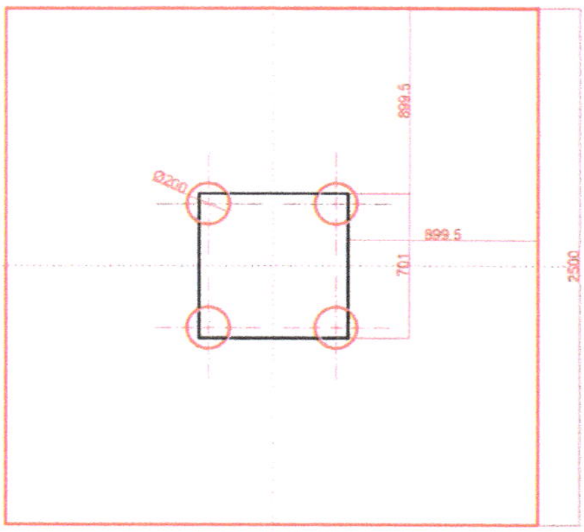

(**a**) Pouring position diagram

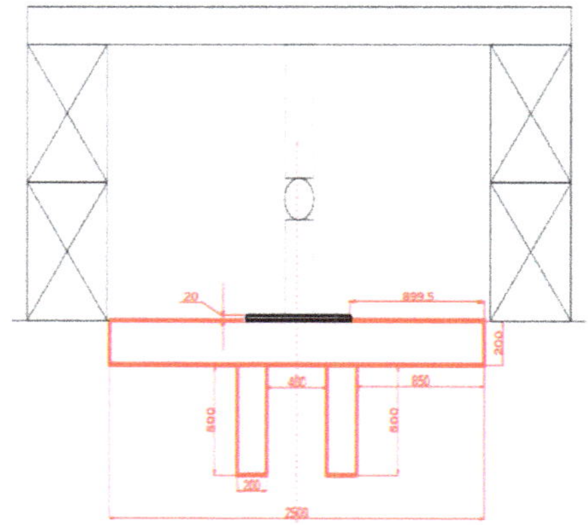

(**b**) Test loading diagram

Figure 19. Group pile casting design drawing.

(2) Analysis of test results for pile S2

S2 group pile plate load test results with load–displacement curves are shown in Figure 20b.

The on-site load–displacement curve analysis indicates that the vertical displacement growth at the pile top is slow and uniform before the load reaches 350 kN, presenting a smooth trend whose displacement reaches 40.81 mm.

However, when the load exceeds 350 kN, the increment in pile top displacement significantly increases, and the curve steeply declines. Further increasing the load to 400 kN causes the displacement to rise to 57.44 mm sharply. The slope of the curve after the inflection point is significantly steeper than before, indicating that the ultimate bearing capacity is located at the inflection point where the load is 350 kN.

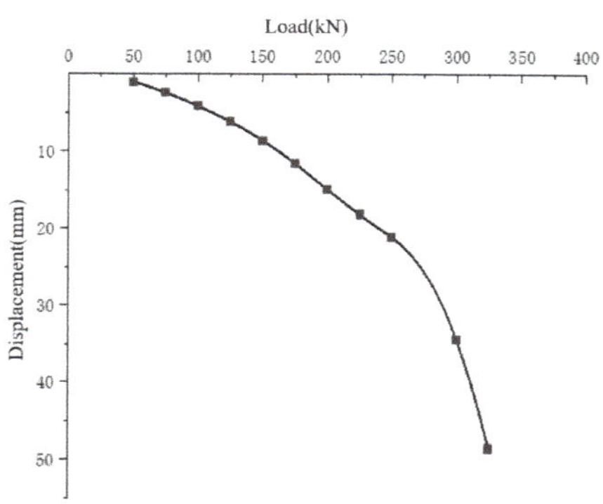

(**a**) Pile S1

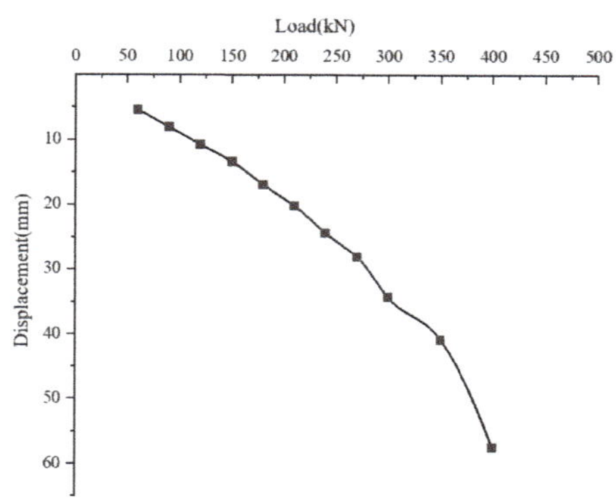

(**b**) Pile S2

Figure 20. Load displacement curve.

5. Conclusions

This study conducted a comprehensive investigation through a series of laboratory and field experiments to examine the impact of curing agents on the mechanical properties of sandy beach soils and elucidate the pile formation and bearing mechanisms of rapid-setting piles. The primary findings are summarized as follows:

(1) Adding a curing agent significantly improved the shear and compressive strength of the sandy soil. The experimental results indicate that with an increase in the mass ratio of glue to sand, both the cohesion and the angle of internal friction of the sandy soil samples exhibited a clear increasing trend, and exponential and quadratic functions can describe this growth relationship.

(2) The moisture content significantly impacts the mechanical properties of the cured sandy soil. Under the same mass ratio of glue to sand, an increase in moisture content leads to a decrease in the strength of the sandy soil samples. Moreover, the morphology and distribution of the gel formed by the curing agent after curing vary at different moisture contents, thereby affecting the microstructure and mechanical properties of the sandy soil.

(3) Field tests confirmed the viability and efficacy of rapid-curing piles in beach foundations. The ultimate load-bearing capacity of piles under various operational conditions was determined through static load tests on individual piles and plate load tests on pile groups. The impact of pile length and diameter on load-bearing capacity was thoroughly analyzed. Findings reveal that enhancing both the length and diameter of piles significantly boosts the ultimate bearing capacity of individual piles. However, this improvement is accompanied by increased settlement displacement at the pile head.

(4) The load-bearing mechanism of rapid-curing piles primarily relies on the diffusion and curing action of the curing agent slurry in the sandy soil around the pile. This process not only enhances the strength of the pile itself but also creates a certain range of influence around the pile, collectively bearing the upper load, thereby improving the overall load-bearing capacity of the pile foundation.

Author Contributions: Methodology, W.L., M.C. and J.Q.; Software, M.C. and J.Q.; Validation, F.L. and Y.C.; Formal analysis, W.L., M.C. and Y.C.; Data curation, F.L. and Y.T.; Writing—original draft, W.L.; Writing—review & editing, Y.T. and Y.C.; Visualization, J.Q.; Funding acquisition, W.L. and M.C. All authors have read and agreed to the published version of the manuscript.

Funding: This research was funded by Anhui Provincial Intelligent Underground Detection and Geoenvironmental Engineering Research Center (AHZT2023KF02), National Natural Science Foundation of China (Grant No. 52209151, 52109128), Basic research program project of Xuzhou (KC23045) and Yunlong Lake Laboratory of Deep Underground Science and Engineering Project (104023002).

Institutional Review Board Statement: Not applicable.

Informed Consent Statement: Not applicable.

Data Availability Statement: Data are contained within the article.

Acknowledgments: The authors would like to thank their colleagues of the Rock Mechanics research group at China University of Mining and Technology and Shandong University for the technical discussion and comments. In addition, the authors would like to express great appreciation to the reviewers for their valuable comments and suggestions that helped to improve the quality of the paper.

Conflicts of Interest: The authors declare that they have no known competing financial interests or personal relationships that could have appeared to influence the work reported in this paper.

References

1. Wan, J.H.; Zaoui, A. Insight into enhancing foundation stability with rubber-soil mixtures: A nanofriction study. *Comput. Geotech.* **2024**, *166*, 105971. [CrossRef]

2. Cui, Y.L.; Pan, F.R.; Zhang, B.B.; Wang, X.Q.; Diao, H.G. Laboratory test of waste mud treated by the flocculation-vacuum-curing integrated method. *Constr. Build. Mater.* **2022**, *328*, 127086. [CrossRef]
3. Bu, Y.; Ma, R.; Du, J.; Guo, S.; Liu, H.; Zhao, L. Utilization of metakaolin-based geopolymer as a mud-cake solidification agent to enhance the bonding strength of oil well cement-formation interface. *R. Soc. Open Sci.* **2020**, *7*, 191230. [CrossRef] [PubMed]
4. Liu, Y.; Chang, M.; Wang, Q.; Wang, Y.; Liu, J.; Cao, C.; Zheng, W.; Bao, Y.; Rocchi, I. Use of Sulfur-Free Lignin as a novel soil additive: A multi-scale experimental investigation. *Eng. Geol.* **2020**, *269*, 105551. [CrossRef]
5. An, X.; Zuo, D.; Wang, F.; Liang, C. Investigation on stabilization/solidification characteristics of lead-contaminated soil using innovative composite model of cement and soda residue. *Environ. Earth Sci.* **2022**, *81*, 508. [CrossRef]
6. Yan, K.; Shi, J.; Shi, K.; Wang, M.; Li, G.; Hong, Z. Effects of the chemical structure of curing agents on rheological properties and microstructure of WER emulsified asphalt. *Constr. Build. Mater.* **2022**, *347*, 128531.
7. Bonamigo Moreira, V.; Rintjema, J.; Bravo, F.; Kleij, A.W.; Franco, L.; Puiggalí, J.; Alemán, C.; Armelin, E. Novel Biobased Epoxy Thermosets and Coatings from Poly(limonene carbonate) Oxide and Synthetic Hardeners. *ACS Sustain. Chem. Eng.* **2022**, *10*, 2708–2719. [CrossRef] [PubMed]
8. Wei, W.; Sun, X.; Ye, W.; Zhang, B.; Fei, X.; Li, X.; Liu, X. Thermal latent curing agent for epoxy resins from neutralization of 2-methylimidazole with a phosphazene-containing polyfunctional carboxylic acid. *Polym. Adv. Technol.* **2020**, *31*, 1553–1561. [CrossRef]
9. Yao, D.; Qian, G.; Yao, J.; Liu, J.; Yu, X. Polymer Curing Agent in Ecological Protection Design Weak Rock Slope Engineering Application. *J. Perform. Constr. Facil.* **2020**, *34*, 4019115. [CrossRef]
10. Wazarkar, K.; Sabnis, A. Sustainable cardanol-based multifunctional carboxyl curing agents for epoxy coatings: Si–S synergism. *J. Coat. Technol. Res.* **2020**, *17*, 1217–1230. [CrossRef]
11. Liu, F.; Zhu, C.; Yang, K.; Ni, J.; Hai, J.; Gao, S. Effects of fly ash and slag content on the solidification of river-dredged sludge. *Mar. Georesour. Geotechnol.* **2019**, *39*, 1–9. [CrossRef]
12. Yang, B.; Mao, Y.; Zhang, Y.; Bian, G.; Zhang, L.; Wei, Y.; Jiang, Q.; Qiu, Y.; Liu, W. A novel liquid imidazole-copper (II) complex as a thermal latent curing agent for epoxy resins. *Polymer* **2019**, *178*, 121586. [CrossRef]
13. Ozgul, E.O.; Ozkul, M.H. Effects of epoxy, hardener, and diluent types on the hardened state properties of epoxy mortars. *Constr. Build. Mater.* **2018**, *187*, 360–370. [CrossRef]
14. Hu, Q.; Chen, G.; Sun, X.; Li, Y.; Liu, G. Effect of grouting on damage and fracture characteristics of fractured rocks under mode I loading. *Constr. Build. Mater.* **2024**, *418*, 135376. [CrossRef]
15. Yu, H.; Joshi, P.; Lau, C.; Ng, K. Novel application of sustainable coal-derived char in cement soil stabilization. *Constr. Build. Mater.* **2024**, *414*, 134960. [CrossRef]
16. He, X.; Xue, J.; Liao, M.; Wan, Y.; Liu, X.; Chen, Y.; Xue, Q. Strength and hygroscopic behavior of biopolymer-treated silty sand under remodeling and dry-wet cycles. *Constr. Build. Mater.* **2023**, *408*, 133642. [CrossRef]
17. Siddique, S.N.; Deng, J.; Mohamedelhassan, E. The Application of Laponite Nanoparticle to Lessen the Risks of Liquefaction: An Emerging Technique for Sand Improvement (A Review). *Soil Mech. Found. Eng.* **2023**, *60*, 149–157. [CrossRef]
18. Tran, T.Q.; Kim, Y.S.; Dang, L.C.; Do, T.M. A state-of-the-art review on the utilization of new green binders in the production of controlled low-strength materials. *Constr. Build. Mater.* **2023**, *393*, 132078. [CrossRef]
19. Zhao, G.; Zhu, Z.; Ren, G.; Wu, T.; Ju, P.; Ding, S.; Shi, M.; Fan, H. Utilization of recycled concrete powder in modification of the dispersive soil: A potential way to improve the engineering properties. *Constr. Build. Mater.* **2023**, *389*, 131626. [CrossRef]
20. Pi, Z.; Deng, C.; Pan, H.; Pei, K. Preliminary Results on Preparation and Performance of a Self-Emulsifying Waterborne Epoxy Curing Agent at Room Temperature. *Polymers* **2023**, *15*, 1673. [CrossRef]
21. Wang, Q.; Li, M.; Cai, G. Engineering mechanical properties and mechanism of carbonated solidified lead-cadmium contaminated clay with steel slag curing agent. *Constr. Build. Mater.* **2023**, *367*, 130261. [CrossRef]
22. Li, W.; Qin, J.; Yi, Y. Treating Pb-contaminated clay slurry by three curing agents. *Chemosphere* **2022**, *303*, 135011. [CrossRef] [PubMed]
23. Gholami, P.; Mardani, H.; Roghani-Mamaqani, H.; Salami-Kalajahi, M.; Easavinejad, H. Preparation of a hyperbranched hybrid curing agent for epoxidized novolac resin. *Fuller. Nanotub. Carbon Nanostruct.* **2021**, *29*, 793–802. [CrossRef]
24. Tan, X.; Zhang, J.; Guo, D.; Sun, G.; Zhou, Y.; Zhang, W.; Guan, Y. Preparation, characterization and repeated repair ability evaluation of asphalt-based crack sealant containing microencapsulated epoxy resin and curing agent. *Constr. Build. Mater.* **2020**, *256*, 119433. [CrossRef]
25. Zhang, Z.; Omine, K.; Li, C.; Shi, S.; Oye, F.S. Improvement effects of treating with calcined oyster shell and carbonized cow dung compost on clay with high water content. *Case Stud. Constr. Mater.* **2022**, *17*, e01654. [CrossRef]
26. Wang, F.H.; Zhao, B.; Zhang, F.; Gao, J.; Hao, H.T.; Zhang, S. A novel heavy metal chelating agent sixthio guanidine acid for in situ remediation of soils contaminated with multielements: Its synthesis, solidification, biodegradability, and leachability. *J. Soils Sediments* **2016**, *16*, 371–381. [CrossRef]
27. Zhang, Z.; Zhang, L.; Liu, H.; Yin, J. Effects of metakaolin and sodium silicate treatment on highwater content dredged clay for improved construction fill performance. *Constr. Build. Mater.* **2024**, *411*, 134196. [CrossRef]
28. Liu, S.; Zhan, J.; Wang, X. Influence of composition of curing agent and sand ratio of engineering excavated soil on mechanical properties of fluidized solidified soil. *Mater. Sci.-Pol.* **2023**, *41*, 57–67. [CrossRef]

29. Yu, X.; Lu, H.; Peng, J.; Ren, J.; Wang, Y.; Chen, J. Modified Lignin-Based Cement Solidifying Material for Improving Engineering Residual Soil. *Materials* **2023**, *16*, 7100. [CrossRef]
30. Lv, Y.; Liu, L.; Yang, P.; Xie, G.; Zhang, C.; Deng, S. Study on leaching and curing mechanism of heavy metals in magnesium coal based backfill materials. *Process Saf. Environ. Prot.* **2023**, *177*, 1393–1402. [CrossRef]
31. Shen, Y.; Li, B.; Wu, M.; Chen, X.; Guan, Y.; Wang, S.; Li, Y. Double skeleton network structure constructed by cellulose nanofibrils and graphene oxide as efficient oil gelling agent. *Cellulose* **2023**, *30*, 7763–7777. [CrossRef]
32. Kassa, A.; Sekine, R.; Dorji, T.; Pathak, G.K.; Hayano, K.; Yamauchi, H.; Mochizuki, Y. Insights into water absorption characteristics of various waste-based inorganic additives and their application for soil stabilization. *J. Clean. Prod.* **2024**, *446*, 141470. [CrossRef]
33. Safari, E.; Ansari, M.; Ghazban, F. Preliminary assessment of cement kiln dust in solidification and stabilization of mercury containing waste from a chlor-alkali unit. *J. Mater. Cycles Waste Manag.* **2017**, *19*, 406–412. [CrossRef]
34. Mrad, R.; Chehab, G. Mechanical and Microstructure Properties of Biochar-Based Mortar: An Internal Curing Agent for PCC. *Sustainability* **2019**, *11*, 2491. [CrossRef]
35. Wu, S.; Zhu, W.; Lv, Y.; Shu, S.; Han, T.; Wang, F.; Li, Y.; Liu, J. Quality control indexes and curing agent values for submerged poured solidifying-silt island; case study of the artificial island of Dalian Bay, China. *Constr. Build. Mater.* **2018**, *190*, 664–671. [CrossRef]
36. Ramezani, S.J.; Toufigh, M.M.; Toufigh, V. Utilization of Glass Powder and Silica Fume in Sugarcane Bagasse Ash-Based Geopolymer for Soil Stabilization. *J. Mater. Civ. Eng.* **2023**, *35*, 4023042. [CrossRef]
37. Al-Dossary, A.A.S.; Awed, A.M.; Gabr, A.R.; Fattah, M.Y.; El-Badawy, S.M. Performance enhancement of road base material using calcium carbide residue and sulfonic acid dilution as a geopolymer stabilizer. *Constr. Build. Mater.* **2023**, *364*, 129959. [CrossRef]
38. Zhu, J.F.; Wang, Z.Q.; Tao, Y.L.; Ju, L.Y.; Yang, H. Macro–micro investigation on stabilization sludge as subgrade filler by the ternary blending of steel slag and fly ash and calcium carbide residue. *J. Clean. Prod.* **2024**, *447*, 141496. [CrossRef]
39. Lian, R.; Ou, M.; Guan, H.; Cui, J.; Zhao, Z.; Liu, L.; Chen, X.; Jiao, C. Cu(II) and Co(II) complexes decorated ammonium polyphosphate as co-curing agents on improving fire safety and mechanical properties of epoxy-based building coatings. *Constr. Build. Mater.* **2023**, *389*, 131786. [CrossRef]
40. Xue, C.; Wang, X.; Lian, B.; Luo, L.; Liu, K. Research on the mechanism of composite improvement of loess based on quantitative analysis of microstructure and mechanical strength. *Constr. Build. Mater.* **2023**, *379*, 131215. [CrossRef]
41. Yang, S.; Yang, Z.; Chen, K.; Zhang, L.; Chu, J. Using case study on the performance of rural cement stabilizing construction waste recycling road base. *Constr. Build. Mater.* **2023**, *405*, 133351. [CrossRef]
42. Zhang, X.; Fang, X.; Hu, F.; Chen, C.; Shen, C. Freeze–Thaw Cycle Characteristics of Solidified Sludge with Composite Rapid Soil Stabilizer. *J. Mater. Civ. Eng.* **2023**, *35*, 04023429. [CrossRef]
43. Du, W.; Liu, B.; Zuo, D.; Wu, M.; Li, H.; Ba, M.; Liu, J.; Lin, R.; Liu, Q. Effect of microcapsules on the self-repairing ability of limestone calcined clay cement (LC3) mortar at different temperatures. *Constr. Build. Mater.* **2023**, *400*, 132718. [CrossRef]
44. Weng, Z.Y.; Yu, J.; Deng, Y.F.; Cai, Y.Y.; Wang, L.N. Mechanical behavior and strengthening mechanism of red clay solidified by xanthan gum biopolymer. *J. Cent. South Univ.* **2023**, *30*, 1948–1963. [CrossRef]

Disclaimer/Publisher's Note: The statements, opinions and data contained in all publications are solely those of the individual author(s) and contributor(s) and not of MDPI and/or the editor(s). MDPI and/or the editor(s) disclaim responsibility for any injury to people or property resulting from any ideas, methods, instructions or products referred to in the content.

materials

MDPI

Article

Study on Static Mechanical Properties and Numerical Simulation of Coral Aggregate Seawater Shotcrete with Reasonable Mix Proportion

Yuxuan Peng [1], Liyuan Yu [1,2,*], Wei Li [1,3], Tao Zhang [1], Linjian Ma [2], Dongyang Wu [1], Changan Wu [1] and Linjie Zhou [1]

[1] State Key Laboratory of Intelligent Construction and Healthy Operation and Maintenance of Deep Underground Engineering, China University of Mining and Technology, Xuzhou 221116, China; yxpeng134885@163.com (Y.P.); tbh259@cumt.edu.cn (W.L.); ts17030057a3tm@cumt.edu.cn (T.Z.); 15651352723@163.com (D.W.); ts22030236p31@cumt.edu.cn (C.W.); 18168215683@163.com (L.Z.)

[2] State Key Laboratory of Explosion Shock Prevention and Mitigation, Army Engineering University of PLA, Nanjing 210007, China; patton.4400@163.com

[3] Yunlong Lake Laboratory of Deep Underground Science and Engineering, Xuzhou 221008, China

* Correspondence: yuliyuancumt@163.com

Abstract: This study aims to explore the static mechanical characteristics of coral aggregate seawater shotcrete (CASS) using an appropriate mix proportion. The orthogonal experiments consisting of four-factor and three-level were conducted to explore an optimal mix proportion of CASS. On a macro-scale, quasi-static compression and splitting tests of CASS with optimal mix proportion at various curing ages employed a combination of acoustic emission (AE) and digital image correlation (DIC) techniques were carried out using an electro-hydraulic servo-controlled test machine. A comparative analysis of static mechanical properties at different curing ages was conducted between the CASS and ordinary aggregate seawater shotcrete (OASS). On a micro-scale, the numerical specimens based on particle flow code (PFC) were subjected to multi-level microcracks division for quantitive analysis of the failure mechanism of specimens. The results show that the optimal mix proportion of CASS consists of 700 kg/m^3 of cementitious materials content, a water–binder ratio of 0.45, a sand ratio of 60%, and a dosage of 8% for the accelerator amount. The tensile failure is the primary failure mechanism under uniaxial compression and Brazilian splitting, and the specimens will be closer to the brittle material with increased curing age. The Brazilian splitting failure caused by the arc-shaped main crack initiates from the loading points and propagates along the loading line to the center. Compared with OASS, the CASS has an approximately equal early and low later strength mainly because of the minerals' filling or unfilling effect on coral pores. The rate of increase in CASS is swifter during the initial strength phase and decelerates during the subsequent stages of strength development. The failure in CASS is experienced primarily within the cement mortar and bonding surface between the cement mortar and aggregate.

Keywords: coral aggregate seawater shotcrete; particle flow code; mix proportion; static mechanical properties; orthogonal experiment

check for updates

Citation: Peng, Y.; Yu, L.; Li, W.; Zhang, T.; Ma, L.; Wu, D.; Wu, C.; Zhou, L. Study on Static Mechanical Properties and Numerical Simulation of Coral Aggregate Seawater Shotcrete with Reasonable Mix Proportion. *Materials* **2024**, *17*, 2353. https://doi.org/10.3390/ma17102353

Academic Editor: Silvina Cerveny

Received: 23 March 2024
Revised: 24 April 2024
Accepted: 13 May 2024
Published: 15 May 2024

Copyright: © 2024 by the authors. Licensee MDPI, Basel, Switzerland. This article is an open access article distributed under the terms and conditions of the Creative Commons Attribution (CC BY) license (https://creativecommons.org/licenses/by/4.0/).

1. Introduction

Owing to the ongoing advancement of islands and reefs in proximity to the mainland, incorporating coral debris and coral sand into construction materials for infrastructure such as roads, docks, slope protection, and buildings has emerged as the predominant selection for island reef projects. This preference is attributed to its cost-effectiveness, durability, and workability characteristics [1–7]. Specifically, coral serves as a natural lightweight aggregate, displaying a comparatively elevated water-absorption rate and possessing traits for both water absorption and release when contrasted with standard coarse aggregates made from crushed stone [8]. The surface roughness of coral aggregates surpasses that of traditional lightweight aggregates, resulting in an increased frictional interaction between the aggregate and cement paste. This, in turn, strengthens the interfacial bond between the cement paste and matrix [9,10]. Moreover, salt compounds like chloride ions and sulfate ions present in coral contribute to the initial strength advancement of concrete [11,12]. However, shotcrete serves as an essential means and method for structural support during the initial phases of construction [13], and it needs such superior early strength. Exploring the static mechanical characteristics of CASS with a reasonable mix proportion is essential to alleviate pressure on the supply of raw materials for the initial support undertaking of island reef shotcrete projects.

It is worth noting that there are no universally applicable mix proportion design criteria specifically tailored for coral aggregate concrete (CAC). Earlier studies have indicated that various factors, such as the cementitious materials content, the water–binder ratio, and the sand ratio, influence the workability and mechanical characteristics of CAC [14,15]. Moreover, the accelerator amount is a crucial parameter that necessitates consideration when applying CAC as shotcrete [16,17]. Nevertheless, employing the conventional method of single-factor control to ascertain the impacts of all parameters on the optimal mix proportion design can be both time-consuming and challenging. Orthogonal experiment is a commonly used method for multi-factor experiments and provides an excellent solution to the challenges linked with the traditional single-factor control approach [18–20]. Based on the orthogonality, only a handful of representative experiments are necessary to find the optimal mix proportion.

On the one hand, machinery and laborers must be capable of sustaining drive progression before the shotcrete attains maximum strength. However, the existing experimental data concerning the time-dependent material properties of shotcrete is somewhat limited [21,22], with many of the data sets being outdated. On the other hand, coral aggregates exhibit variations in morphology and porosity when compared to typical natural and lightweight aggregates. This disparity results in a significant structural and performance distinction between CASS and OASS [23]. Hence, there is a need to examine the static mechanical characteristics of CASS at various curing ages and conduct a comparative analysis with OASS to verify the validity of CASS mix proportion [24].

Meanwhile, to address the limitations of laboratory tests that fail to capture the complete deformation and damage process of structures in real time, the remarkable advancements in computer technology have facilitated the growing adoption of numerical simulations for investigating the static mechanical properties of concrete [25]. Concrete is a composite material with heterogeneous phases, including both coarse and fine aggregates, water, cement, and additional constituent elements [26]. It is noteworthy to understand that the meso-modeling approach posits concrete as a composite material with three phases: aggregate, interfacial transition zone, and cement mortar components. This methodology has gained substantial application and has been extensively developed in various research studies [27–30]. Meso-modeling offers valuable insights into the macroscopic behavior and performance of materials. In contrast to the meso-modeling approach, the discrete element method (DEM) holds distinct advantages for more accurately reproducing grain shapes [31–33] and their interactions [34–37]. The software particle flow code (PFC 6.0) based on the discrete element method has gained significant popularity within geo-materials due to its properties similar to the fundamental assumptions and construction principles of geo-materials [38–40]. Among them, Haeri and Sarfarazi utilized the particle flow code in two dimensions (PFC2D) to investigate the damage mechanism of concrete under tensile failure and suggested that a modified tension test can be a proper test for the determination of the tensile strength of concrete in absence of direct test [41]; Lian et al. presented a numerical model utilizing the PFC2D to estimate the mechanical characteristics of porous concrete [42]; Song et al. elucidated the mechanical response of concrete subjected to multi-level cyclic loading and unloading based on particle flow code in three dimensions (PFC3D) [38]. Nevertheless, most prior investigations had focused on the macro-scale failure mode of the specimen without delving into the micro-scale failure mechanisms at a finer scale.

Various models have been employed to simulate aggregates in concrete materials with the growing adoption of numerical simulations. These include 2D circular models [43], 2D random polygon models, 3D spherical models [44], 3D ellipsoid models [45], 3D random convex polyhedron models [46,47], as well as non-convex polyhedron models [48]. However, these studies have simplified the coarse aggregate by representing it as clusters of particles resulting from overlapping a limited number of individual particles. Unfortunately, this approach fails to reproduce the influence of the rough porousness characteristic of coral aggregate on the mechanical properties of specimens. Moreover, the densification effect resulting from filling coral aggregate pores with small mineral particles has yet to be involved.

This study conducted four-factor and three-level orthogonal experiments to explore the optimal mix proportion of CASS. First, the AE technique was used to analyze the compressive failure mechanism and damage phenomenon of CASS with optimal mix proportion. The digital image correlation (DIC) technique was used to analyze the splitting failure mechanism and deformation characteristics of CASS with optimal mix proportion. The static mechanical properties of CASS and OASS at different curing ages were compared to verify the validity of the CASS mix proportion. The minerals' filling or unfilling effect on coral pores was systematically analyzed. After that, a novel three-dimensional numerical model based on PFC was proposed to investigate the static mechanical properties and failure mechanism of CASS. Multi-level division and quantitative analysis of microcracks generated between various mineral particles calibrated with different mechanical parameters were carried out. Finally, the failure mechanism of CASS was quantitatively analyzed with the results of numerical simulation and experimental microstructure observation

2. Materials and Experiment Procedure

2.1. Raw Materials and Mix Proportion

Both coral debris and coral sand, serving as coarse and fine aggregates, were directly obtained from the South China Sea islands. Different from natural quartz sand or mineral rocks originating from physical or chemical processes, coral debris and coral sand predominantly constitute the remains of hermatypic polypary corals and shells. These materials mainly arise as biologically derived sediments. Coral debris and coral sand share an identical chemical composition, consisting predominantly of 62.2% calcium carbonate, along with iron, magnesium, and silicon ions (Figure 1a). Microscopic examination of the coral surface, as depicted in Figure 1b, reveals a visual rough and porous texture. This qualitative assessment is indicative of the coral's natural structure, which differs significantly from that of conventional natural aggregates such as those found in river beds, which results in its diminished physical and mechanical properties. However, coral sand has a relatively smooth surface due to its smaller particle size and significant weathering. In order to ensure optimal fluidity and sprayability of CASS, the particle size of coral debris is controlled within the range of 5–10 mm. Figure 2 depicts the distribution of grain sizes in coral sand, exhibiting a fineness modulus of 2.88. The fundamental physical characteristics of both coarse and fine aggregates, such as bulk and apparent densities, porosity, water absorption, cylindrical compressive strength, and saturated surface dry moisture content, have been examined in accordance with the Chinese standards GB/T 14684-2011 [49]. The corresponding test outcomes are available in both Tables 1 and 2.

Table 1. Physical properties of coral debris.

Bulk Density (kg/m^3)	Apparent Density (kg/m^3)	Water Absorption (%)	Porosity (%)	Cylindrical Compressive Strength (MPa)
894	1973	12.52	48.97	2.69

Table 2. Physical properties of coral sand.

Fineness Modulus	Bulk Density (kg/m^3)	Apparent Density (kg/m^3)	The Saturated Surface Dry Moisture Content (%)
2.88	1138	2751	1.96

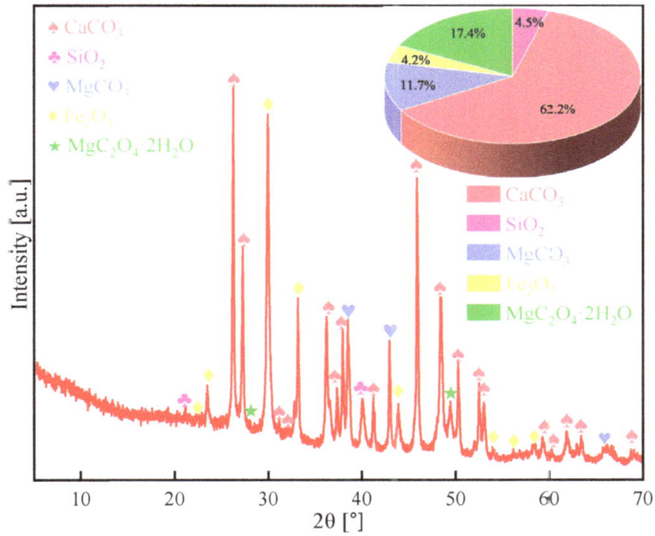

(**a**) X-ray diffraction

(**b**) Rod/blocky-shaped coral debris

Figure 1. Microstructure and mineral composition of coral in its natural state.

As shown in Figure 3a, all the raw materials for the preparation of CASS are presented. Among these components, the cement used is 42.5 ordinary Portland cement (P.O.42.5) from Xuzhou Zhonglian Cement Co., Ltd. (Xuzhou, China). Silica fume and water-reducing agents consist of ultra-fine wollastonite powder and a high-performance water-reducing agent with weak alkalinity, provided by Shanghai Chenqi Chemical Technology Co., Ltd. (Shanghai, China). The alkali-free liquid accelerator is sourced from Laiyang Keyu Construction Admixture Factory (Laiyang, China). Additionally, artificial seawater was prepared following the American ASTM D1141-2003 standard [50], and its chemical composition is detailed in Table 3. In this study, all chemicals used for artificial seawater preparation were obtained from Nanjing Reagent Factory with a purity of analytical grade.

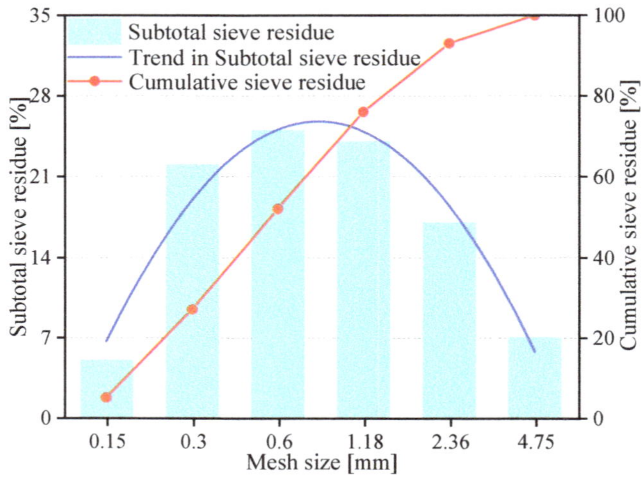

Figure 2. Coral sand particle grading curve.

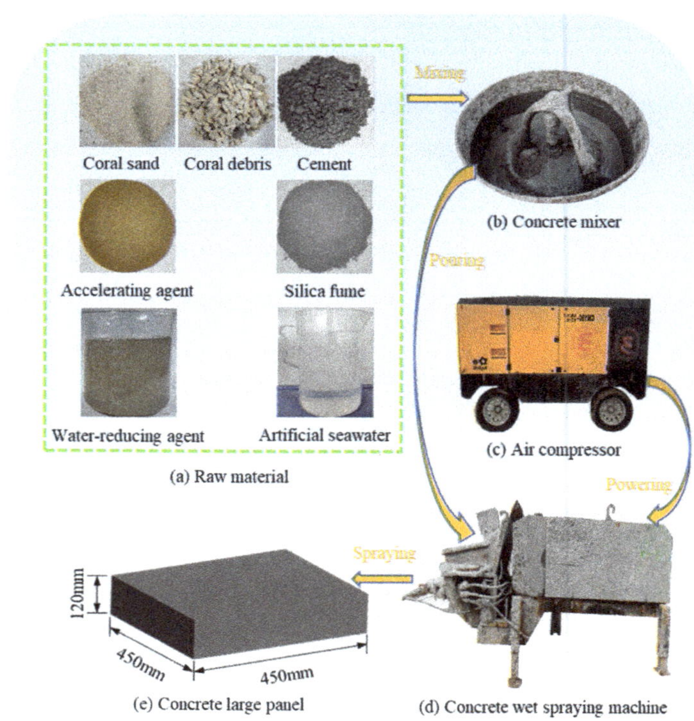

Figure 3. Schematic of the large-panel specimen-making process.

Table 3. Chemical composition of artificial seawater.

NaCl (kg/m^3)	$MgCl{\cdot}6H_2O$ (kg/m^3)	Na_2SO_4 (kg/m^3)	$CaCl_2$ (kg/m^3)	KCl (kg/m^3)
24.5	11.1	4.1	1.2	0.7

In this study, the mixed proportions of the coral aggregate seawater shotcrete (CASS) were designed following the guidelines of the national standards JGJ51-2002 [51] and JGJ/T 372-2016 [52]. These standards are equivalent to and have been aligned with the principles of the European Standard (EN) 12620:2012 [53] for aggregates for concrete and the American Concrete Institute (ACI) Guide for Selecting Proportions for Normal, Heavyweight, and Mass Concrete (ACI 211.1R-19), respectively. This alignment ensures that our findings are applicable within the national context and relevant to the broader international community. However, owing to the notable distinction between coral aggregate and conventional aggregate, a set of compressive strength tests focusing on four factors, cementitious material content, water–binder ratio, sand ratio, and accelerator quantity, was conducted. Through extensive mix proportion trials, it was revealed that specimens cured for 28 days exhibited relatively higher strength with a cementitious material content of 700 kg/m^3, a water–binder ratio of 0.45, a sand ratio of 50%, and an accelerator amount of 6%. Building upon this information, an orthogonal experiment employing a four-factor and three-level design (refer to Table 4) was executed to ascertain the optimal mix ratio for CASS. The experiment comprised nine mix proportions, detailed in Table 5.

Table 4. Orthogonal test table.

Mix	Cementitious Material Content (kg/m^3)	Water–Binder Ratio	Sand Ratio (%)	Accelerator Amount (%)
Mix. 1	600	0.4	40	4
Mix. 2	600	0.45	50	6
Mix. 3	600	0.5	60	8
Mix. 4	700	0.4	50	8
Mix. 5	700	0.45	60	4
Mix. 6	700	0.5	40	6
Mix. 7	800	0.4	60	6
Mix. 8	800	0.45	40	8
Mix. 9	800	0.5	50	4

Table 5. Mix proportion of CASS.

Mix	Cementitious Material Content (kg/m^3)	Cement (kg/m^3)	Seawater (kg/m^3)	Coral Sand (kg/m^3)	Coral Debris (kg/m^3)	Water Reducer (kg/m^3)	Accelerating Agent (kg/m^3)
Mix. 1	600	552	240	541	812	12	24
Mix. 2	600	552	270	655	655	13.5	36
Mix. 3	600	552	300	760	506	15	48
Mix. 4	700	644	280	590	590	14	56
Mix. 5	700	644	315	702	468	15.7	28
Mix. 6	700	644	350	448	672	17.5	42
Mix. 7	800	736	320	627	418	16	48
Mix. 8	800	736	360	395	395	18	64
Mix. 9	800	736	400	489	489	20	32

2.2. Specimen Preparation and Basic Physical Properties

The sequence of cement, cementitious material, coral sand, coral debris, water reducer, and seawater was employed while stirring raw materials using a concrete mixer with a rotation speed of 300 revolutions per minute. To achieve consistent mixing, half of the seawater was initially added to the mixture and stirred for 60 s, followed by the addition of the remaining half and subsequent mixing for 120 s. As shown in Figure 3, the wet spraying method was used in this study. The wet-mixed concrete was then prepared for spraying by adjusting the air compressor's pressure to 0.5 MPa, which was used to propel the mixture to the nozzle of the concrete wet-spraying machine and mixed with the accelerator. Lastly, the specimen preparation was completed by spraying the concrete into a 450 mm × 450 mm × 120 mm size mold with an angle of 75° to the ground by opening the nozzle valve. In addition, as shown in Table 6, the slump and rebound rate tests were carried out during specimen preparation. The CASS specimens were demoulded after one day and placed in a curing room with a constant temperature of 20 °C and a relative humidity of 95% for 28 days. The large-panel specimens made by spraying needed to be cored, cut, and polished to gain standard specimens for uniaxial compression tests (UCS) and Brazilian splitting tests (ST).

Table 6. The slump and rebound rate of CASS.

Parameter	Mix. 1	Mix. 2	Mix. 3	Mix. 4	Mix. 5	Mix. 6	Mix. 7	Mix. 8	Mix. 9
Slump (mm)	90	105	125	120	135	165	125	155	190
Rebound rate (%)	16.99	11.7	12.92	11.72	7.04	8.22	14.61	9.67	14.97

2.3. Quasi-Static Tests

A series of orthogonal experiments, including the uniaxial compression and Brazilian splitting with a loading rate of 0.3 mm/min and 0.05 mm/min, respectively, were conducted on CASS specimens with different mix proportions and curing ages using the DNS 100 electronic universal testing machine at the China University of Mining and Technology. Simultaneously, vaseline was administered at both ends of the specimens to alleviate the impacts of end friction and stress concentration before the application of the uniaxial compression load. Each specimen's peak compressive strength and tensile strength were recorded and analyzed during the tests to obtain the optimal mix proportion of CASS. In order to verify the validity of the optimal mix proportion and quantify the effect of aggregate type on the macro-mechanical parameters of concrete at various curing ages, the optimal mix proportion of CASS was selected, and the ordinary aggregate seawater shotcrete (OASS) specimens were made with ordinary aggregate instead of coral aggregate.

During the Brazilian splitting tests, the tensile strength σ_t can be calculated as follows [54]:

$$\sigma_t = \frac{2P_{max}}{\pi DB} \tag{1}$$

where P_{max} denotes the applied load maximum, D denotes the diameter of the test specimen, and B denotes the thickness of the test specimen.

In order to clarify the fracture failure mechanism and damage phenomenon of concrete with an optimal mix proportion, a Micro-II AE technique monitoring system developed by American Physical Acoustics Company (PAC) was used to record the changes in AE characteristic signals induced by microcrack development under uniaxial compression, such as counting, energy, and frequency. To precisely capture the AE signals produced by the upper and lower ends of the specimens, the receiving sensor was affixed at the midpoint of each specimen. In the AE monitoring system shown in Figure 4a, the elastic wave emitted by the signal source propagates to the surface of the specimens, causing the surface displacement of the AE sensor and converting the mechanical vibration into electrical signals. It is essential to highlight that, for efficient filtering of environmental noise and enhanced monitoring of cracking information quality, the threshold value was established at 45 dB. To account for the impact of mechanical noise and instrument sensitivity, the acquisition frequency for AE signals was chosen to be 3 MHz. In the Brazilian splitting tests, the duration from crack initiation to propagation and penetration until the specimen failure is brief. Particularly, the period from crack penetration to specimen failure is nearly instantaneous. Therefore, the AE characteristic signal induced by microcrack development in Brazilian splitting tests cannot explain the failure mechanism obviously. However, DIC is a non-contact visual processing method for measuring surface deformation of materials widely used in research related to crack propagation [55,56]. Specifically, DIC enables the observation of non-uniform changes in the macroscopic strain field due to the cumulative expansion of microcracks. Its basic principle involves using an initial reference image as a baseline. The target research area is divided into a network, and the motion of segmented subregions is treated as rigid transformations. Through a predefined matching algorithm, specific subsets of position changes before and after surface deformation are identified. This process allows for calculating displacement fields and the evolution of strain fields on the observed object's surface. The translation, rotation, and shear transformations of each pixel's positions before and after motion are calculated using expressions (2)–(4) [57].

$$\varepsilon_x = \frac{\partial u}{\partial x} + \frac{1}{2}[(\frac{\partial u}{\partial x})^2 + (\frac{\partial v}{\partial x})^2] \tag{2}$$

$$\varepsilon_y = \frac{\partial v}{\partial y} + \frac{1}{2}[(\frac{\partial u}{\partial y})^2 + (\frac{\partial v}{\partial y})^2] \tag{3}$$

$$\gamma_{xy} = \frac{1}{2}(\frac{\partial u}{\partial y} + \frac{\partial v}{\partial x} + \frac{\partial u}{\partial x}\frac{\partial u}{\partial y} + \frac{\partial v}{\partial x}\frac{\partial v}{\partial y}) \tag{4}$$

where ε_x, ε_y, and γ_{xy} represent distinct strain components, and u and v denote displacements in the x and y directions, respectively.

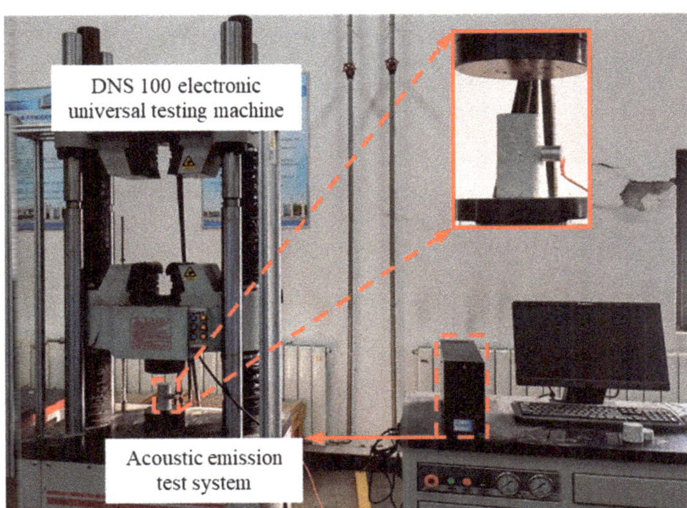

(**a**) Digital acoustic emission (AE techniques).

Figure 4. *Cont.*

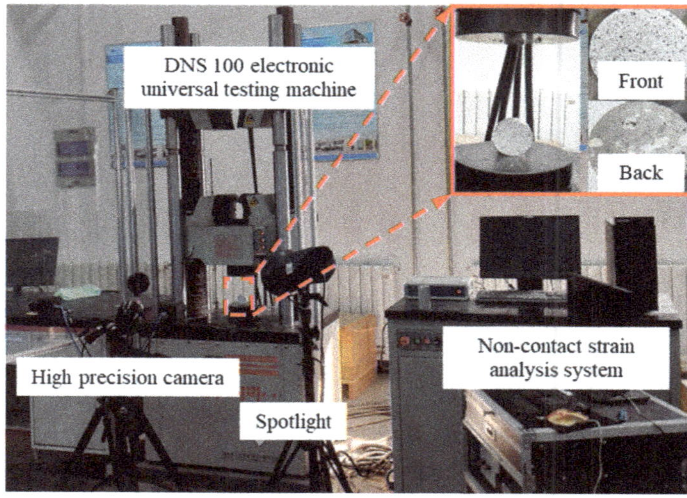

(**b**) Digital image correlation (DIC)

Figure 4. Monitoring system.

The DIC depends on the high-contrast identifiable optical characteristics attached to the surface. As the attachment point deforms, the identifiable optical characteristics will move. Therefore, a thin and uniform white background was sprayed on the surface of CASS specimens after cleaning the impurities on the surface of CASS specimens. Then, the black non-repeating, random, and isotropic speckles were scattered on the front surface of CASS disc specimens, as shown in the specimen magnification diagram of Figure 4b. During the experiment loading, image acquisition was conducted at a constant rate of 1 frame per second (fps) with a resolution of 2048 × 2048 pixels.

3. Experiment Results and Discussion

3.1. *The Optimal Mix Proportion of CASS*

The stress–strain and stress–time curves for CASS, exhibiting various mix proportions at curing ages of 3 d, 7 d, and 28 d under uniaxial compression and Brazilian splitting tests, are illustrated in Figure 5. A visual inspection of the curves reveals a distinct trend in the mechanical behavior of CASS across different curing stages. Notably, the stress–strain curves exhibit a characteristic nonlinearity, indicative of the material's ductile behavior at early stages, which transitions to a more brittle response as the curing age increases. This shift towards brittleness is evidenced by the steeper slope in the post-peak regime of the stress–strain curves for the 28-day curing age, suggesting a reduction in the material's capacity for plastic deformation. The stress–time curves from the Brazilian splitting tests further substantiate this observation, with a more rapid decline in load-bearing capacity observed in the specimens with higher curing ages, highlighting an increased susceptibility to tensile failure. Observations of the peak compressive/tensile stress for CASS specimens with nine different mix proportions at 3 d, 7 d, and 28 d curing ages are presented in Table 7, based on Figure 5. It can be seen that strength values generally increase with the curing age, reflecting the improved bond strength and material cohesion over time. However, the increase in strength is more pronounced at earlier curing ages, with a subsequent tapering off at 28 days, indicating a maturation in the material's strength.

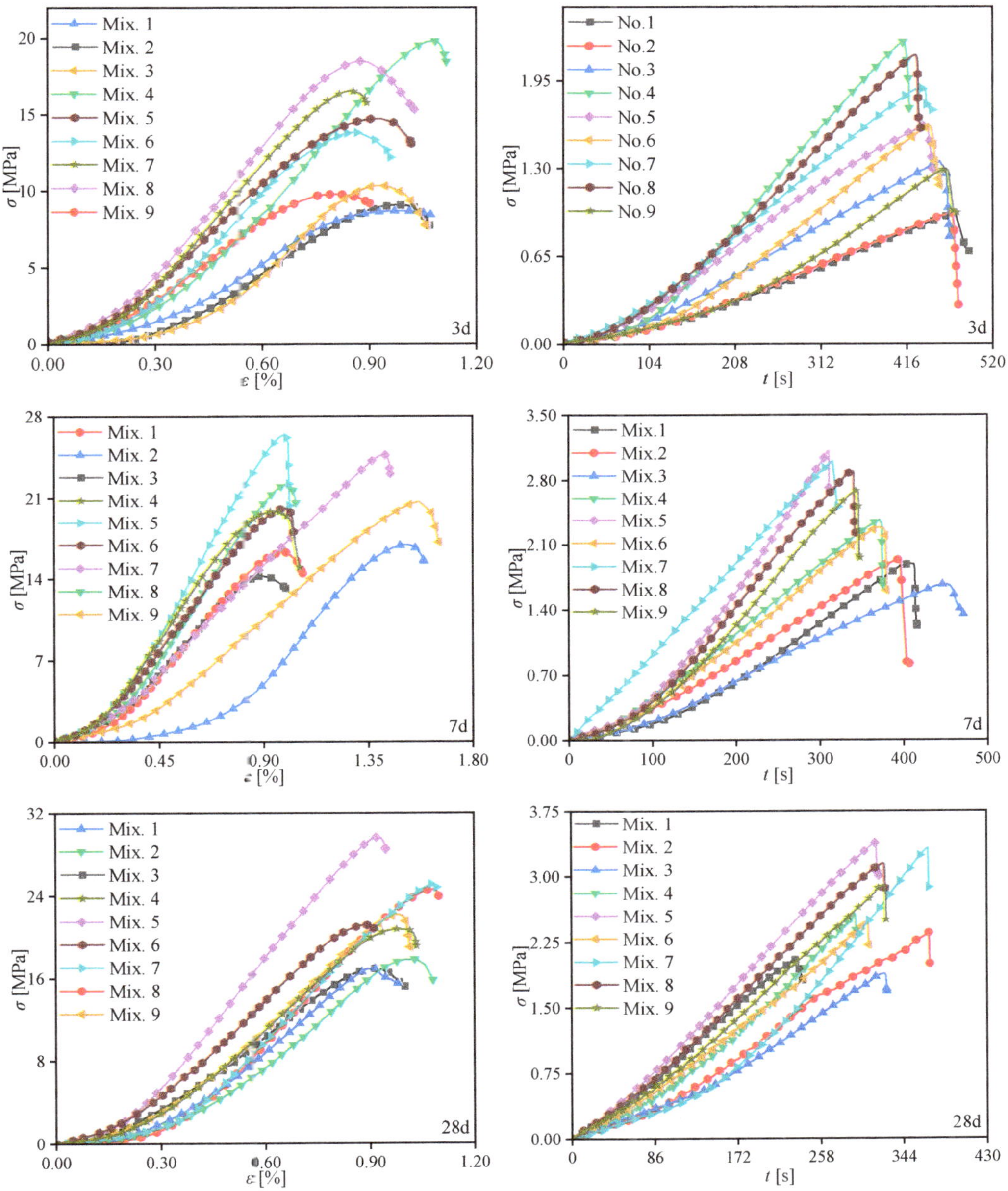

(a) Stress–strain curves

(b) Stress–time curves

Figure 5. Stress–strain and stress–time curves of CASS with various mix proportions at 3 d, 7 d, and 28 d curing age under uniaxial compression and Brazilian splitting tests.

Table 7. Peak compressive stress (CS) and tensile stress (TS) table.

	Mix	Curing Age		
		3 d	**7 d**	**28 d**
CS (MPa)	Mix. 1	8.70	16.28	16.97
	Mix. 2	9.06	16.92	17.83
	Mix. 3	10.35	14.23	16.91
	Mix. 4	19.84	19.86	20.75
	Mix. 5	14.73	26.44	29.63
	Mix. 6	13.84	20.10	21.17
	Mix. 7	16.53	24.72	25.11
	Mix. 8	18.50	22.21	24.59
	Mix. 9	9.79	20.69	22.19
TS (MPa)	Mix. 1	0.96	1.89	2.05
	Mix. 2	0.97	1.94	2.36
	Mix. 3	1.35	1.67	1.88
	Mix. 4	2.24	2.36	2.58
	Mix. 5	1.63	3.12	3.38
	Mix. 6	1.61	2.29	2.49
	Mix. 7	1.90	3.01	3.32
	Mix. 8	2.14	2.91	3.15
	Mix. 9	1.29	2.69	2.90

To comprehensively explore the impact of four factors in orthogonal experiments—cementitious material content, water–binder ratio, sand ratio, and accelerator amount—on the compressive and tensile strength of CASS specimens, a range analysis using the data from Table 7 was conducted. Table 8 provides the results of the range analysis, where the R-value indicates the extent of variation in test indicators with changing influencing factors. Essentially, the R-value serves as an indicator for determining primary and secondary relationships among these factors. Notably, in Table 8, when assessing the impact of factors on compressive and tensile strength at curing ages of 3 d, 7 d, and 28 d, the influence of the accelerator amount on both strength parameters gradually diminishes with increasing curing age. For compressive strength, the cementitious material content and the water–binder ratio are the primary factors, with decreasing influence observed with the accelerator amount as the curing age increases. This trend underscores the importance of an appropriate balance between these components for achieving optimal strength. Similar trends are observed for tensile strength, with the sand ratio also emerging as a significant factor, particularly at 7 and 28 days of curing. These findings are instrumental in guiding the mix design process for CASS, emphasizing the need for a multifactorial approach to optimize the material's static mechanical properties.

The variation in both compressive and tensile strength of the coral aggregate seawater shotcrete (CASS) specimens is illustrated in Figure 6, with respect to different curing ages and mix proportions. An increase in the content of cementitious material from 600 kg/m^3 to 700 kg/m^3 corresponded to a significant enhancement in compressive strength, amounting to 6.7 MPa, 6.3 MPa, and 11.7 MPa, and in tensile strength by 0.7 MPa, 0.8 MPa, and 0.7 MPa, for the curing ages of 3 d, 7 d, and 28 d, respectively. However, a further increase in the cementitious material content from 700 kg/m^3 to 800 kg/m^3 led to a decrease in compressive strength at the same curing ages by −1.2 MPa, 0.4 MPa, and 0.1 MPa, respectively, while the tensile strength exhibited an increment of 0 MPa, 0.3 MPa, and 0.3 MPa. These findings indicate that there exists an optimal threshold for the cementitious content, beyond which additional increments do not yield a proportionate enhancement in the concrete's strength.

Table 8. Range table of influence factors of compressive strength (CS) and tensile strength (TS).

	Curing Age		Cementitious Material Content	Water–Binder Ratio	Sand Ratio	Accelerator Amount
CS	3 d	K_1	9.4	15.0	13.7	11.1
		K_2	16.1	14.1	12.9	13.1
		K_3	14.9	11.3	13.9	16.2
		R	6.77	3.70	0.97	5.16
	7 d	K_1	15.8	20.3	19.5	21.1
		K_2	22.1	21.9	19.2	20.6
		K_3	22.5	18.3	21.8	18.8
		R	6.73	3.52	2.64	2.37
	28 d	K_1	17.2	20.9	20.9	22.9
		K_2	23.9	24.0	20.3	21.4
		K_3	24.0	20.1	23.9	20.8
		R	6.73	3.93	3.63	2.18
TS	3 d	K_1	1.1	1.7	1.6	1.3
		K_2	1.8	1.6	1.5	1.5
		K_3	1.8	1.4	1.6	1.9
		R	0.73	0.28	0.12	0.62
	7 d	K_1	1.8	2.4	2.4	2.6
		K_2	2.6	2.7	2.3	2.4
		K_3	2.9	2.2	2.6	2.3
		R	1.03	0.44	0.27	0.25
	28 d	K_1	2.1	2.7	2.6	2.8
		K_2	2.8	3.0	2.6	2.7
		K_3	3.1	2.4	2.9	2.5
		R	1.03	0.54	0.30	0.24

Note: K_j denotes the average value of compressive strength at the level of each influence factor j; R denotes the K-value range for each influencing factor.

Figure 6 reveals that increasing the water–binder ratio from 0.4 to 0.45 decreased compressive and tensile strength at 3 d curing age by 6%, 24.7%, 5.9%, and 17.6%. For specimens cured for 7 d and 28 d, the compressive and tensile strength apex was attained at a water–binder ratio of 0.45, with a subsequent decline observed as the ratio was adjusted to 0.4 and 0.5. Specifically, at a 7 d curing stage, a reduction in compressive and tensile strength of 7.3%, 16.4%, 11.1%, and 18.5% was recorded. This trend continued at a 28 d curing stage, with 12.9%, 16.3%, 10%, and 20% noted decreases. These results indicate that, after reaching a certain curing age, strength initially increases with an increased water–binder ratio but eventually decreases.

For the change rule of strength with sand ratio, compressive and tensile strength remains relatively stable at lower sand ratios of 40% and 50%. However, a 60% sand ratio increase significantly enhanced compressive and tensile strengths by approximately 10% at both the 7 d and 28 d curing stages. This improvement is attributed to the higher sand ratio, which fosters a more homogeneous and densified concrete microstructure, an effect that is less pronounced at the lower sand ratios.

Contrary to the water–binder ratio, the accelerator amount enhances early strength. It shows a positive correlation between compressive/tensile strength at 3 d curing age and the accelerator amount. Specifically, 6% and 8% increase results in a respective 18%, 45.9%, 15.4%, and 30.8% augmentation in compressive and tensile strength. However, at 7 d and 28 d curing ages, there is a negative correlation, with compressive and tensile strength decreasing by 2.4%, 10.9%, 7.7%, and 11.5% at 7 d and 6.6%, 9.2%, 3.6%, and 10.7% at 28 d, respectively. This suggests that a high accelerator amount reduces compressive strength after a specific curing period.

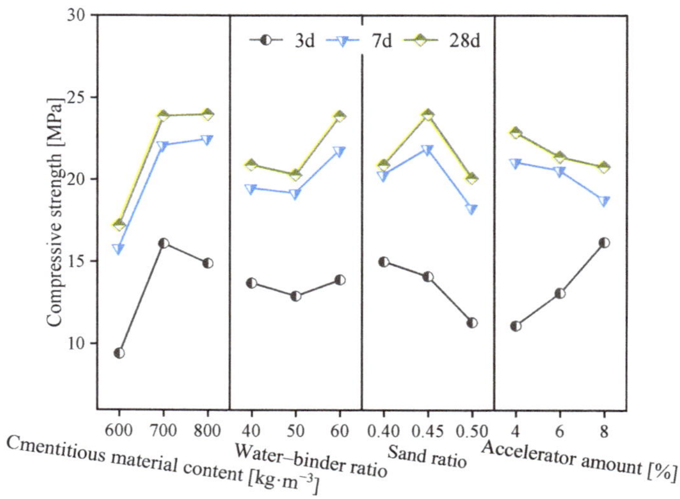

(**a**) Compressive strength

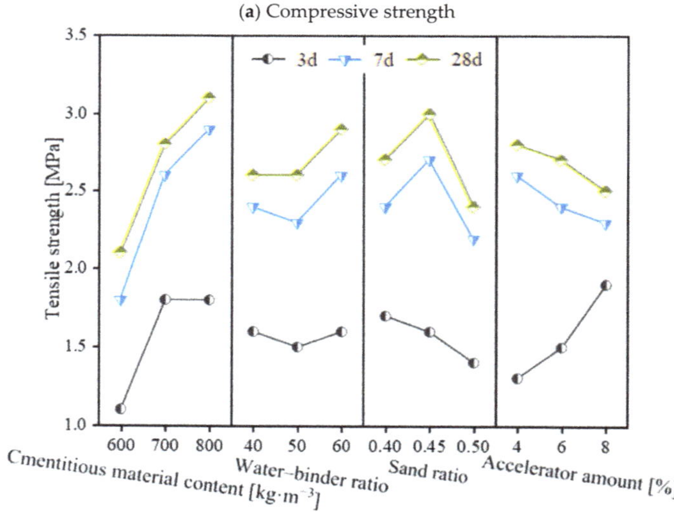

(**b**) Tensile strength

Figure 6. The relationship between the compressive/tensile strength of CASS and the variation in cementitious material content, water–binder ratio, sand ratio, and accelerator amount at different curing ages.

In summary, the CASS mix proportions exert a similar influence on the tensile/compressive strength of specimens. Considering compressive and tensile strength across all curing ages, the most effective mix proportion comprises 700 kg/m^3 of cementitious materials content, a water–binder ratio of 0.45, a 60% sand ratio, and an 8% dosage for the accelerator amount. Subsequently, an analysis of the static mechanical properties of specimens with this optimal mix proportion was conducted.

3.2. *Strength and Failure Behavior under Uniaxial Compression*

When combining the concurrently measured outcomes from the DNS load transducer and AE sensor affixed to the specimens, Figure 7 portrays the nonlinear stress–strain relationships and axial load AE count curves for CASS with optimal mix proportions under uniaxial compression at various curing ages. As illustrated in Figure 7a–c, continuous weak AE signals signifying the initiation of microcracks were identified during pre-peak stages. The cumulative count gradually increased, while the instantaneous count remained relatively low in this period. However, as macrocracks began to form, a sudden surge in AE counts occurred around the axial load peak, leading to a rapid rise in cumulative counts within a short duration. Additionally, the more pronounced phenomenon with the advancement of curing age indicates the increasing brittleness of CASS specimens.

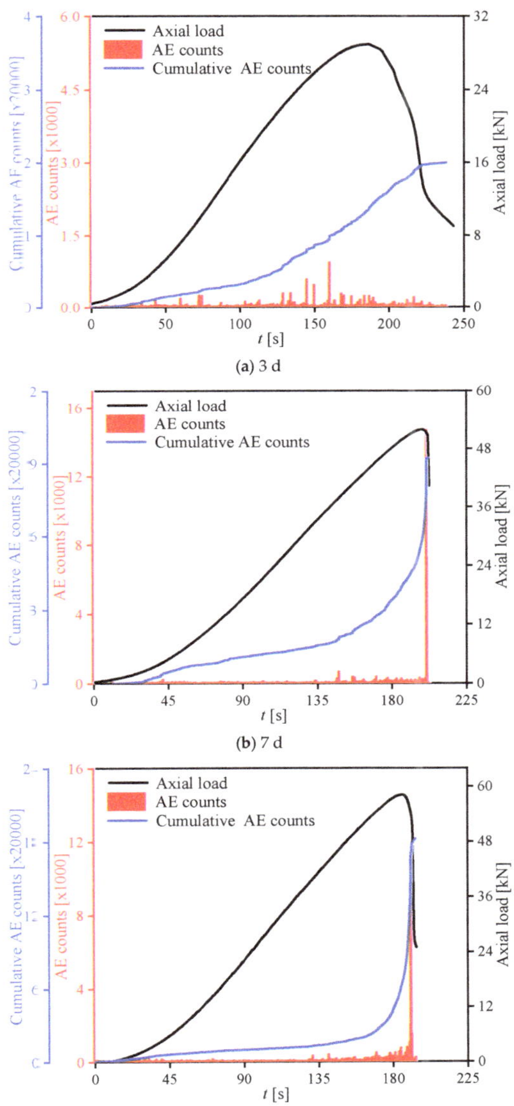

Figure 7. Axial load AE count curves of CASS at various curing ages.

The complete compressive stress–strain curves of CASS at different curing ages can be categorized into four stages: consolidation, elastic, plastic, and fracture. The consolidation stage highlights the porous and loose characteristics of the coral concrete microstructure, with the curve exhibiting an initial concave rise due to compaction of the pore structure of coral aggregate and voids within the concrete matrix under increasing loading stress. Subsequent stages—elastic, plastic, and fracture—are akin to the characteristics of brittle materials like rock, attributed to the relatively low compressive strength and brittle nature of coral itself.

Independent of what kind of micro-fracture forms in brittle materials, it is accompanied by the release of strain energy stored in brittle materials and propagated in the form of elastic waves at the moment of its occurrence, which is AE. Different micro-fracture behaviors correspond to different AE information characteristics. Therefore, this study obtained the tensile–shear properties of brittle materials by judging the difference of AE information, discussed the evolution process and law of crack development induced by tensile stress and shear stress at the meso-level, and further explained the internal tensile–shear failure mechanism of materials.

Studies in this domain have revealed that micro-fracture AE signals' RA value (rise time/amplitude) and AF value (ring count/duration time, average frequency) can serve as indicators of brittle material crack tensile or shear properties, facilitating further classification of micro-fracture forms [58]. The characteristic parameters of AE signals are visually represented in Figure 8. Generally, a low RA value and high average frequency in the AE signal suggest micro-fractures induced by tensile stress surpassing the cementation's tensile strength, indicating a tensile crack. Conversely, a high RA value and low average frequency indicate micro-fractures caused by shear stress exceeding the cementation's shear strength, signifying a shear crack. The determination of the relative RA value and AF value ratio is crucial for understanding the cause of microcrack initiation. Nevertheless, in current research, there is no clearly defined ratio between RA value and average frequency as a criterion for distinguishing tensile and shear cracks.

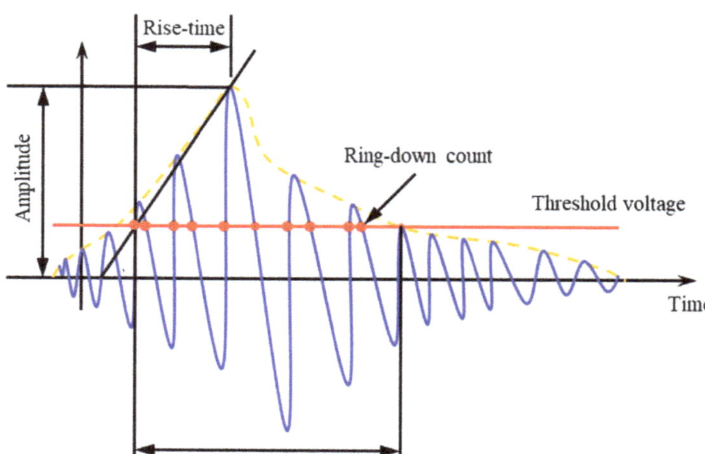

Figure 8. Schematic figure of the characteristic parameter definition of the acoustic emission signal.

Drawing on the concept that the ratio of RA value to AF value during tensile–shear crack initiation falls within a relatively stable interval, K-means clustering analysis, employing a minimization criterion, was utilized for statistical classification of AE data. This approach deepened exploration into the concealed micro-fracture formation mechanism in CASS specimens. Figure 9 illustrates the cluster analysis outcomes of acoustic emission AF-RA values for CASS specimens with 3 d, 7 d, and 28 d curing ages.

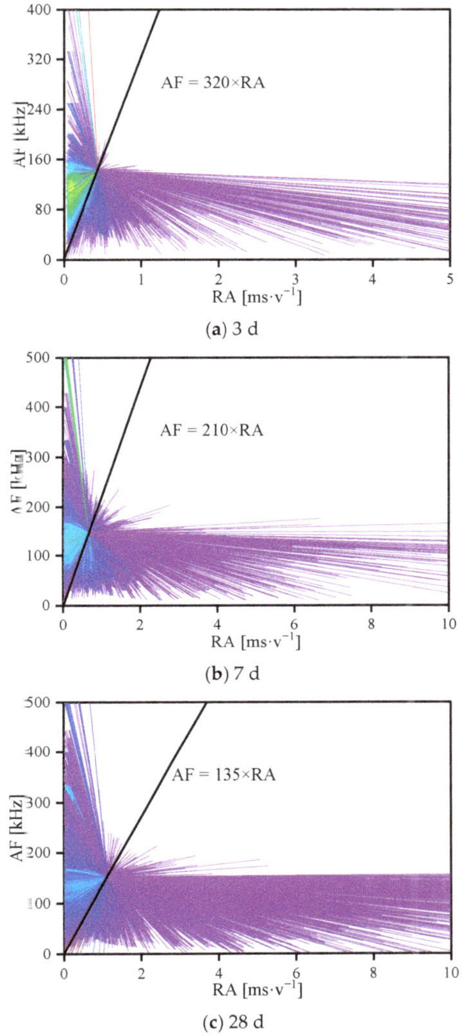

Figure 9. The cluster analysis results of acoustic emission RA-AF values of CASS at various curing ages.

As displayed in Figure 9, the dividing boundary between the final iterative convergence particle and the coordinate origin in the K-means clustering analysis serves as the demarcation line distinguishing the tensile crack and shear crack clusters. Points above the oblique line in the AE data denote occurrences of tensile micro-fractures, while points below signify shear micro-fractures. The cluster analysis results reveal that AE signals with higher average frequency and lower RA value primarily manifest in the initial loading stage. Subsequently, as the load intensifies, lower AF value and RA value gradually increase, paralleled by a rise in shear cracks. Typically, shear crack formation ensues after the initiation, propagation, and evolution of tensile cracks, leading to significant damage to the internal structure of concrete specimens, compromising their integrity and eventual failure. In comparison to specimens aged 3 d, those aged 7 d and 28 d exhibit increased occurrences of tensile cracks in the early loading stages. As tensile cracks accumulate, shear cracks proliferate rapidly, culminating in the specimens' instability and failure. This underscores that tensile failure constitutes the primary mechanism behind the ultimate instability of concrete specimens. As curing age increases, CASS specimens tend towards a more brittle material nature, and the severity of brittle and shear failure intensifies upon subjecting the specimens to higher loads.

3.3. Strength and Failure Behavior under Splitting Tensile

Determining tensile strength traditionally involves a direct uniaxial tensile test. However, the Brazilian splitting tensile test, an indirect method outlined in the ASTM standard [59], presents notable advantages in terms of practicality, simplicity, and cost-effectiveness. This test gains significance when engineers encounter intricate stress fields, combining compressive and tensile stresses in material mechanic design. Accurately representing field conditions necessitates considering tensile strength in the presence of compressive stresses. The splitting tensile strength test emerges as a straightforward method for simulating compression-induced stress fields.

Besides its practicality, the splitting tensile strength test is commonly employed to estimate compressive strength. Birid [60] established a correlation between compressive strength and splitting tensile strength test results. Incorporating parameter adjustments based on related research, the equation was adapted to predict CASS tensile strength by compressive strength. This modification demonstrated comparable accuracy in predicting tensile strength:

$$\frac{UCS}{ST} = 6.3\frac{\pi}{2}(\frac{H}{D})^{0.2} \tag{5}$$

where H is the height, and D is the diameter of the specimen for the STS test.

The evolution of the major principal strain nephograms of the specimens can be seen in Figure 10. At the beginning of loading, the pore structure of coral aggregate and the voids inside the concrete matrix were relatively uniformly distributed in the plane of the disc resulting in a relatively uniform strain distribution. When the load reached peak pressure, a strain concentration zone appeared along the loading diameter, with a strain of about 2.6%. As the loading continues, the strain concentration zone expands. Correspondingly, the cracks extend from both ends to the center until the specimen loses its load-bearing capacity. It is noteworthy that the major principal strain of specimen in 28 d curing age reached about 14%, which was higher than that of 5% in 3 d and 7% in 7 d. This is due to the increasingly obvious brittle properties of CASS with the increasing curing age. As a whole, the Brazilian splitting failure is caused by the main crack that initiates from the ends and propagates along the loading line, and the main crack is arc-shaped.

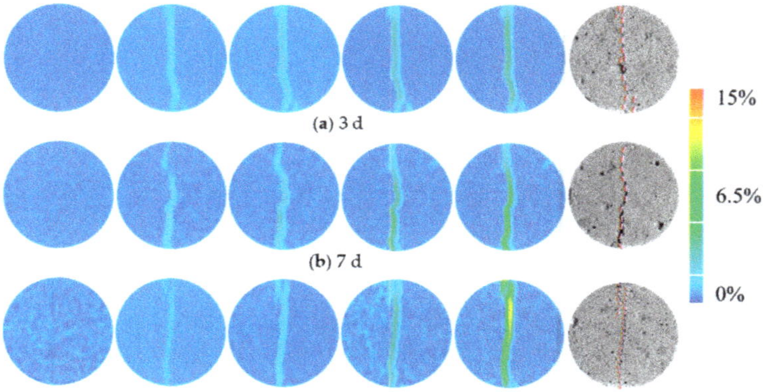

Figure 10. Failure pattern and major principal strain nephograms of CASS specimens at various curing ages under Brazilian splitting tests.

3.4. Comparative Analysis of Static Mechanical Properties

To delve deeper into the static mechanical properties of CASS and verify the validity of mix proportion, this investigation conducted a comparative analysis between OASS and CASS. Both were subjected to identical specimen preparation methods, curing conditions, and mix proportions. Illustrated in Figure 11 is the nonlinear stress–strain relationship of OASS and CASS at various curing ages. Notably, CASS exhibited a swifter increase in early strength compared to conventional shotcrete, followed by a more gradual progression in later strength. Specifically, the strength of coral concrete surged by 40% and 44% from 3 d to 7 d concerning the 28 d strength. The subsequent development of the remaining 10% of ultimate curing strength spanned three weeks. Nevertheless, the later strength of CASS proved to be considerably lower than that of OASS.

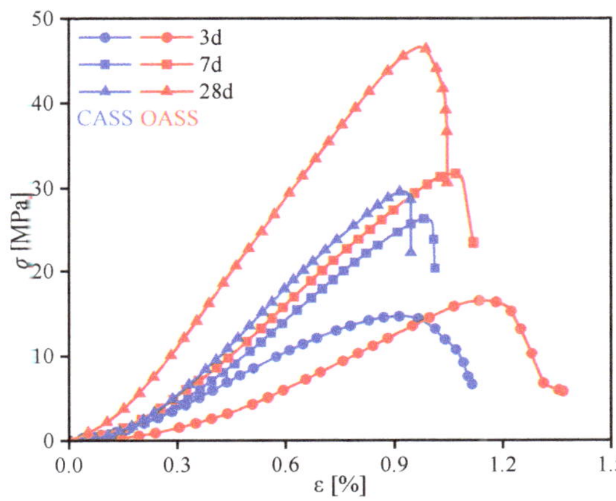

(**a**) Compressive strength

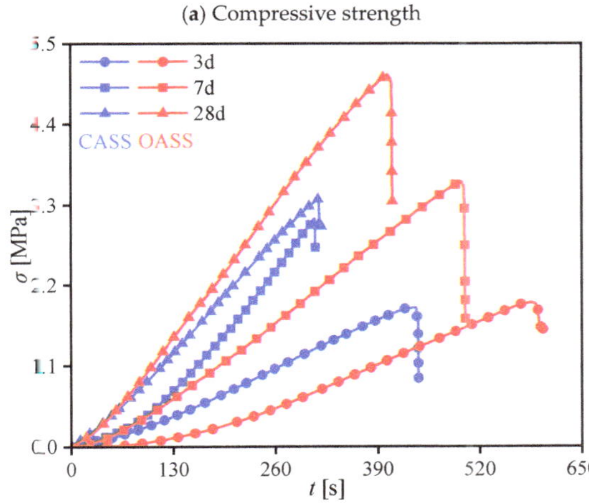

(**b**) Tensile strength.

Figure 11. Comparison of strength at various curing ages between ordinary shotcrete and CASS.

On one side, the porous microstructure inherent in coral debris serves as a water reservoir, absorbing and retaining a specific quantity of water from the concrete slurry. This reservoir releases water during the hydration and hardening process. Conversely, the infusion of small-particle minerals in CASS into coral pores enhances the embedding of cementitious material and aggregate, as illustrated in the blue box in Figure 12. This dual mechanism not only heightens specimen compactness but also elevates early strength and elastic modulus. Nonetheless, the presence of unfilled pores (highlighted in the red box in Figure 12) emerges as water evaporates, causing dispersion of energy and deformation in specimens. This, in turn, diminishes the material's strength and elastic modulus in the later stages. In summary, in comparison to OASS, the heightened early strength and elastic modulus in CASS result partly from the mineral-filling effect on coral pores. Simultaneously, the unfilled pores contribute to the reduced strength and elastic modulus in the later stages.

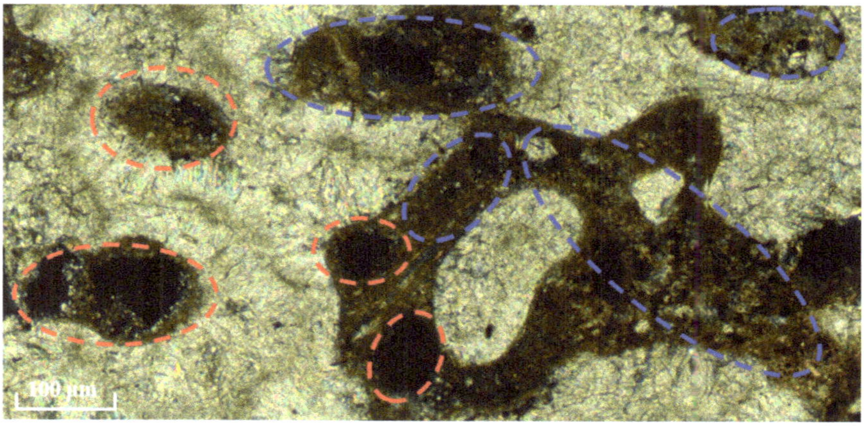

(**a**) Uniaxial compression

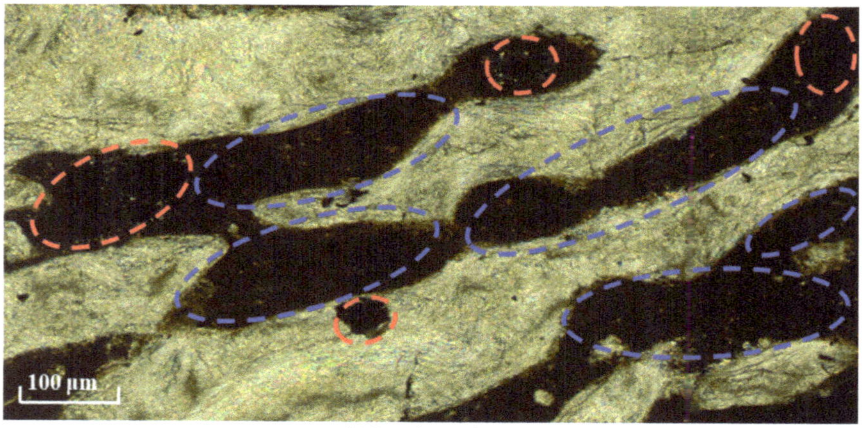

(**b**) Brazilian splitting

Figure 12. Microscopic enlarged figure of fracture surface after the failure of the laboratory test specimen, in which filling of small particle minerals and pore are identified by the blue dotted frame and red dotted frame, respectively.

4. Numerical Simulation

The preceding study conducted quasi-static compression and splitting tests on CASS, briefly discussing the static mechanical properties coupled with DIC and AE techniques Nevertheless, although laboratory tests present a dependable approach for investigating the macroscopic static mechanical behavior of CASS, the existing constraints of monitoring instrumentation impose significant challenges in comprehensively monitoring the micro-morphology and complete deformation damage process of the structural body at the micro-scale. As a result, a mesoscopic model in three dimensions based on PFC was developed for CASS, taking into account the arbitrary shapes, sizes, and distributions of aggregates. Verification of the model involved comparing the outcomes of quasi-static compression and splitting tests on cylindrical/disc specimens through both experimental and numerical analyses. The microcrack behavior of CASS was quantitatively analyzed at the micro-scale.

4.1. Modeling Process

The parallel bond model (PBM) was employed as the contact model for particles in the simulation of CASS in this study as the first step of constructing the numerical model. The PBM implemented in this study incorporates linear elastic components and bonded parts at the contact interface, offering two distinct interfacial behaviors (refer to Figure 13a,b) [61,62]: (i) A minuscule, linearly elastic interface designed to transmit forces without tension and display frictional characteristics. This interface functions based on identical mechanical principles as the linear model, allowing relative rotation without resistance, with shear forces governed by a Coulomb limit. (ii) A finite-sized, linearly elastic, and bonded interface that can transfer both forces and moments. In cases where the interface is bonded, it resists the relative rotation of the particles on either side of the contact. However, the parallel bonding may fracture if the tensile strength and shear stress exceed the bonding material's strength. The rupture of the parallel bond results in the loss of bonding material, accompanied by the dissipation of associated forces, moments, and stiffness.

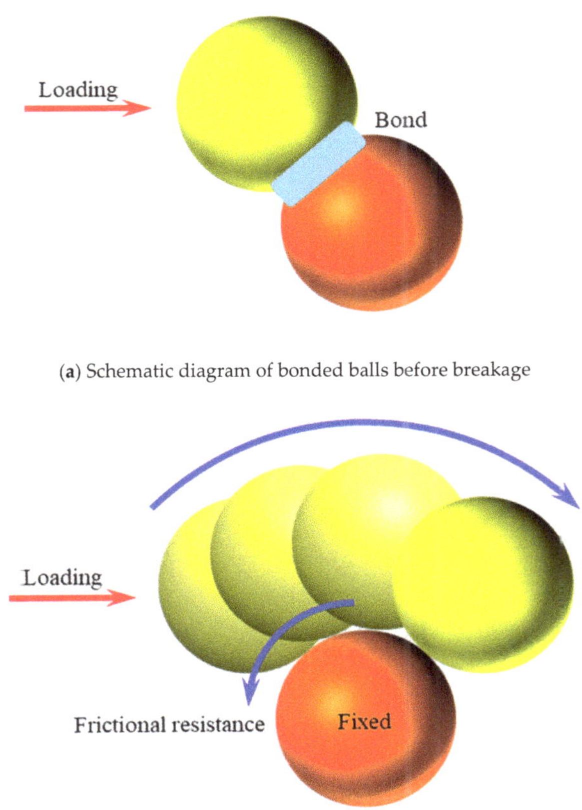

(**a**) Schematic diagram of bonded balls before breakage

(**b**) Displacement process of balls after bond breakage

Figure 13. Structural and mechanical behavior of the PBM.

Considering the porous characteristics of both concrete and coral aggregates and aiming to represent the enhanced compactness of specimens by incorporating small particle minerals, this study separated silica fume from the cement mortar phase system during the modeling process. Then, the CASS was treated as a four-phase material comprising cement mortar, silica fume, coral debris, and the interfacial transition zone. Within this study, a discrete element model was constructed to represent the mixed materials by generating two types of units: balls and clusters. The ball units were employed to characterize the shape of the smallest constituent unit of each material phase, while the cluster units were employed to characterize the coral debris component.

Figure 14 shows the modeling process of the PFC as follows:

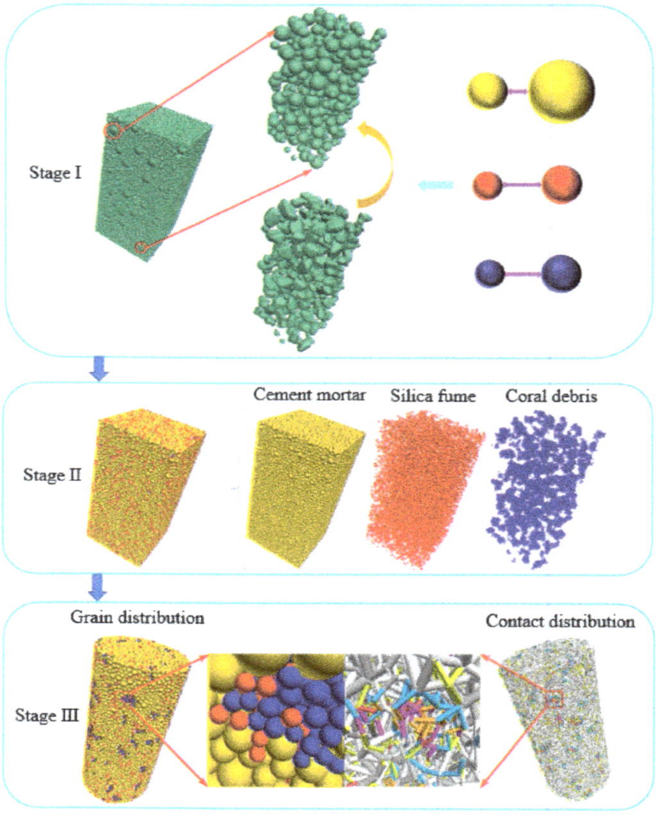

Figure 14. The figure of the modeling process.

(1) Stage I: To reproduce laboratory findings, we selected, categorized, and 3D-scanned corals used for mixing in PFC. Initially, a concrete specimen model with only spherical particles was created based on the established gradation. Subsequently, larger particles were randomly replaced with coral debris shapes based on volume equivalence. This process culminated in a realistic concrete structure model, which was preloaded with isotropic stress to simulate initial conditions.

(2) Stage II: Mineral components were divided according to the concrete structure model, CASS mix proportions, and grading curves. Red particles, sized between 0.45 and 0.6 mm, symbolized silica fume, while yellow particles of 0.6 to 1 mm diameter represented cement mortar. The coral debris in the model was filled with blue particles

of 0.45 to 0.6 mm. The model also incorporated the random distribution of red silica fume particles within coral clusters to enhance specimen compactness, as detailed in the enlarged view of Figure 14 (Stage III).

(3) Stage III: Models were constructed with dimensions matching laboratory specimens (Φ50 × 100 mm and Φ50 × 25 mm) by refining the Stage II model. Contact between different particles was accounted for, assigning different values. Figure 14 (Stage III) shows the contact distribution, color-coded to indicate six distinct contact types: cement mortar to cement mortar (F-F), silica fume to silica fume (S-S), coral debris to coral debris (C-C), cement mortar to coral debris (F-C), cement mortar to silica fume (F-S), and coral debris to silica fume (C-S). The micro-parameter assignment endowed the numerical specimens with defined bearing strength, finalizing the CASS model building.

4.2. Calibration of Micro-Parameters

Only the specimen with optimal mix proportion at 28 d curing age was subjected to numerical analysis in this investigation to mitigate the intricacy of the task and guarantee the practical implications of the numerical analysis computations. Currently, the "trial-and-error" method is prevalently implemented in the micro-parameter calibration of discrete element simulation specimens, and it has exhibited good outcomes [63–65]. The micro-parameters of the specimens calibrating results are shown in Table 9. A comparison of the specimens' uniaxial compression and Brazilian splitting test results with the simulation findings presented in Figure 15 reveals that the stress–strain simulation curves highly agreed with the laboratory test curves. Particularly, the numerical simulation and laboratory test values of some key macroscopic mechanical parameters, including the specimens' uniaxial compressive strength, splitting tensile strength, and elastic modulus, were approximately equal, indicating that the calibrated micro-parameters were reasonable.

Table 9. Micro-parameters of numerical model.

Microparameters	F-F	S-S	C-C	F-S	F-C	C-S
Tensile strength (MPa)	32.76	32.76	18.72	32.76	18.72	18.72
Cohesion strength (MPa)	48	48	28.8	48	28.8	28.8
Bonding activation gap (mm)	0.01	0.01	0.01	0.01	0.01	0.01
Elastic modulus (GPa)	8.5	8.5	21.25	8.5	14.45	14.45
Stiffness ratio	1.3	1.3	1.3	1.3	1.3	1.3
Friction angle (°)	13	13	13	13	13	13

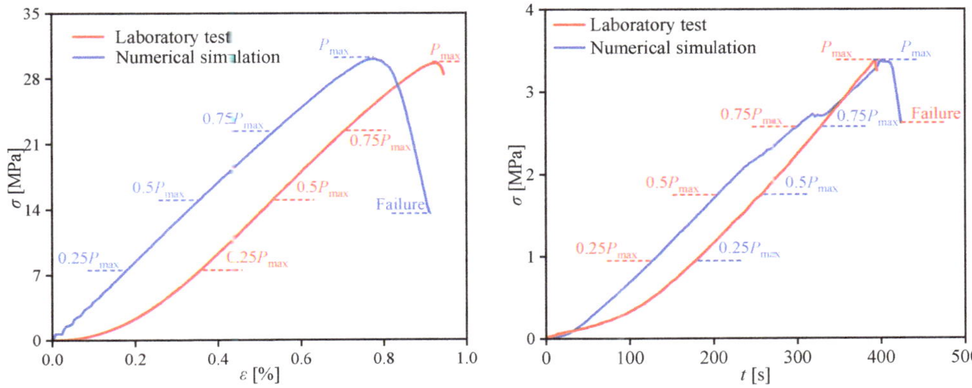

(a) Comparison of stress–strain (UC)/stress–time (ST) curves obtained by laboratory test and numerical simulation

Figure 15. *Cont.*

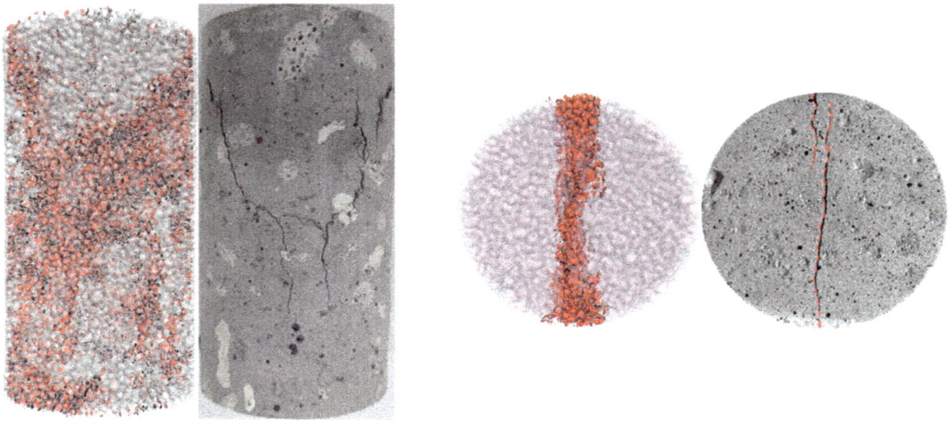

(**b**) Comparison of failure pattern

Figure 15. Comparison of numerical results based on PFC and experimental results in uniaxial compression (UC) and Brazilian splitting tests (ST).

4.3. *Simulated Results and Discussion*

In the model, two scale failure modes were simulated. First, a micro-scale crack was generated when a contact fracture occurred between two adjacent basic elements. According to fracture mechanics, the generated micro-scale cracks were divided into tensile cracks (TC) and shear cracks (SC). All symbolic representations of crack types and their percentage are listed in Table 10. With the increasing number of cracks, macro-scale fractures formed.

Table 10. All symbolic representation of crack types and their percentage.

	Crack Types	Symbol	Proportion Symbol
Tensile crack (Tc)	Cement mortar–Silica fume	Tfs	P_{Tfs}
	Cement mortar–Cement mortar	Tff	P_{Tff}
	Cement mortar–Coral debris	Tfc	P_{Tfc}
	Silica fume–Silica fume	Tss	P_{Tss}
	Coral debris–Silica fume	Tcs	P_{Tcs}
	Coral debris–Coral debris	Tcc	P_{Tcc}
Shear crack (Sc)	Cement mortar–Silica fume	Sfs	P_{Sfs}
	Cement mortar–Cement mortar	Sff	P_{Sff}
	Cement mortar–Coral debris	Sfc	P_{Sfc}
	Silica fume–Silica fume	Sss	P_{Sss}
	Coral debris–Silica fume	Scs	P_{Scs}
	Coral debris–Coral debris	Scc	P_{Scc}

To facilitate subsequent analysis, we selected five representative moments throughout the loading process: $0.25P_{\mathrm{max}}$, $0.5P_{\mathrm{max}}$, $0.75P_{\mathrm{max}}$, P_{max}, and failure moment, where P_{max} is the peak load. According to the analysis of Figures 16 and 17, the loading process of uniaxial compression and Brazilian splitting can be divided into the following stages:

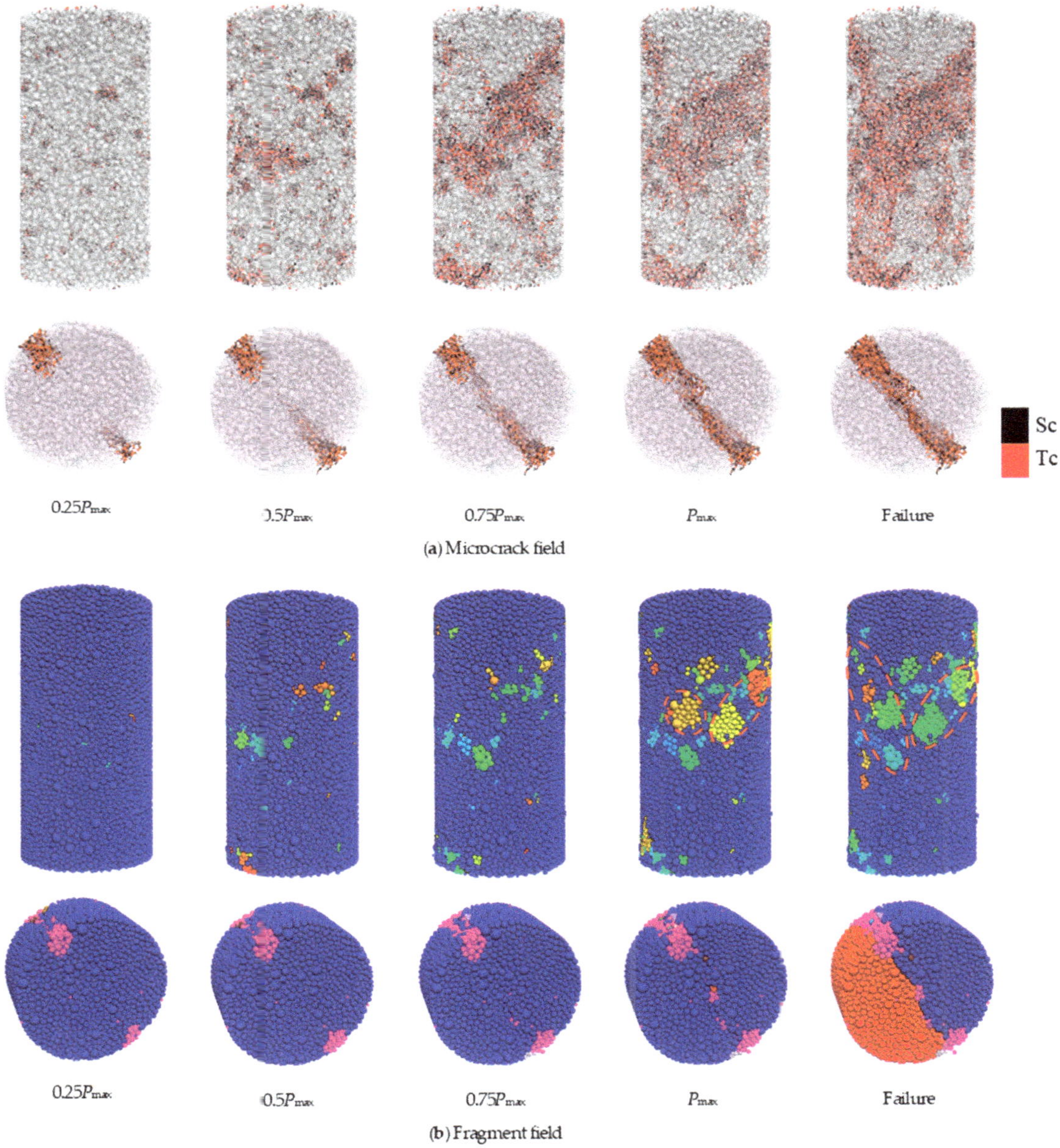

Figure 16. Numerical static damage accumulation process in uniaxial compression and Brazilian splitting tests.

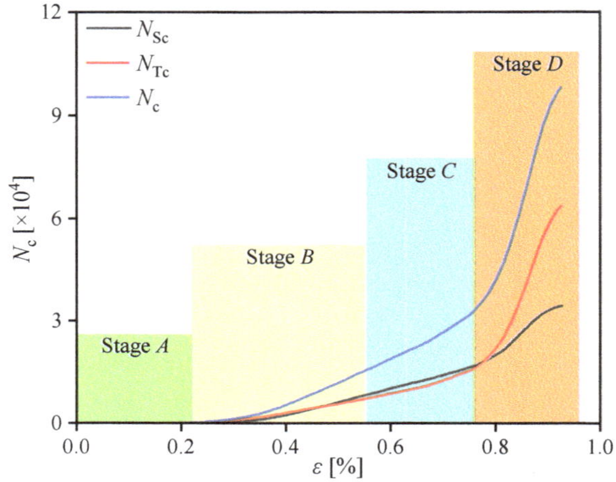

(**a**) Uniaxial compression

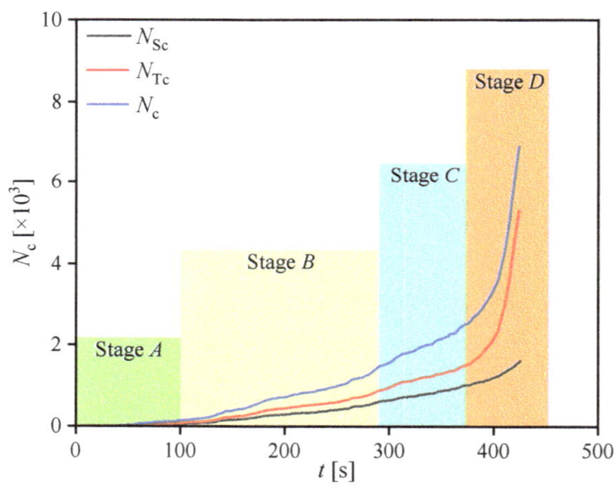

(**b**) Brazilian splitting

Figure 17. Variations in the number of cracks.

Uniaxial compression:

(1) Stage A: With the load increasing from 0 to $0.25P_{max}$, exceeding the contact parameter, cracks and fragments emerge. During this stage, the integrity of the numerical specimen is comparatively superior;

(2) Stage B: In this stage, axial load increases from $0.25P_{max}$ to $0.5P_{max}$, and a small number of cracks and damage are observed within the numerical specimen, along with the sporadic appearance of fragments. However, the number of cracks and fragments retains a low level;

(3) Stage C: As the axial load increased from $0.5P_{max}$ to $0.75P_{max}$, the number of cracks inside the specimen further increased, the cracks in the numerical specimen began to hook up with each other and penetrate through, and the damage inside the model further accumulates;

(4) Stage D: With the axial load increased from $0.75P_{max}$ to P_{max}, the number of cracks increased rapidly, and the large fragment field started to appear along the direction of the main crack extension, as shown by the red box in Figure 16b;

(5) Failure: The specimen transitioned into the macroscopic rupture phase, characterized by a steep increase in cracks and fragments. A large fragment field marked by red boxes occurred in the area of crack penetration;

Brazilian splitting:

(1) Stage A: With the load increasing from 0 to $0.25P_{max}$, the specimen began to be subjected to an external load. Stress concentration and fragment field began to form around the upper and lower loading points. Due to the low-stress concentration, only a small number of cracks and fragments occur;

(2) Stage B: The stress concentration around the loading points gradually increased with the load increasing from $0.25P_{max}$ to $0.5P_{max}$, resulting in the initiation of fresh cracks and the propagation of original cracks. Then, with the slow growth of the number of cracks and fragments, the high-stress concentration region inside the specimen gradually propagated from the loading points to the center;

(3) Stage C: As the load increased from $0.5P_{max}$ to $0.75P_{max}$, the crack propagation path and fragment field began propagating to the center of the specimens, forming the main crack path and fragment field.

(4) Stage D: When the load increases from $0.75P_{max}$ to P_{max}, the load on the specimens reaches the maximum value. The relatively large number of cracks leads to significant particle displacement around the loading points, and the main crack gradually propagates to the specimen's center. The specimen was on the threshold entry to the splitting failure stage, and the number of cracks and fragments increased relatively rapidly.

(5) Failure: Before the specimen was destroyed, the crack propagation rate and the number of cracks increased rapidly. At the moment of failure, the specimen was divided into two large fragments by the main crack propagating along the connection line between the upper and lower loading points.

A multi-level characterization of cracks was developed in a static mechanical simulation based on PFC. Quantitative analysis was conducted on the cracks observed in the broken numerical specimen. Figure 18 provided an example of uniaxial compression where crack formations within a numerical model were divided into two levels. Figure 18a shows all cracks within the numerical specimen. Figure 18b further divided the cracks into tensile and shear, labeled as first-level cracks. Then, Figure 18c presented a further division of cracks into tensile/shear between various minerals and tensile/shear occurring within the same minerals, labeled as second-level cracks.

The quantities of various cracks presented in both uniaxial compression and Brazilian splitting were counted, as detailed in Figure 19. During the first-level cracks, the proportions of tensile/shear cracks to the total number of cracks in uniaxial compression and Brazilian splitting were 64.7%/35.3% and 76.7%/23.3%, which suggests that tensile failure was the main failure mechanism in uniaxial compression and Brazilian splitting. In second-level cracks of cylindrical specimens, the sum of P_{Tfs}, P_{Tff}, P_{Tfc}, P_{Tcs}, P_{Sfs}, P_{Sff}, P_{Sfc}, and P_{Scs} is 80.9%. Identically, the sum in the disc specimen is 87.1%. That is because the CASS primarily experiences failure within the cement mortar and bonding surface between the cement mortar and aggregate (coral debris). Of particular note, in cylindrical specimens, the respective values of P_{Tcc} and P_{Scc} are 9.5% and 7.5%. The values of P_{Tcc} and P_{Scc} in the disc are 7% and 2.2%, which are not low. This can be attributed to the relatively weak physical and mechanical properties of coral debris in relation to other aggregates, which leads to a certain number of tensile and shear fractures of the coral debris upon the failure of concrete specimens. However, silica fume distributed between large-sized particles is a filling material with a relatively small particle size to improve the compactness of the specimen, which leads to little contact within silica fume and is also the reason why the number of tensile and shear cracks within silica fume is the least.

Figure 18. Multi-level crack division.

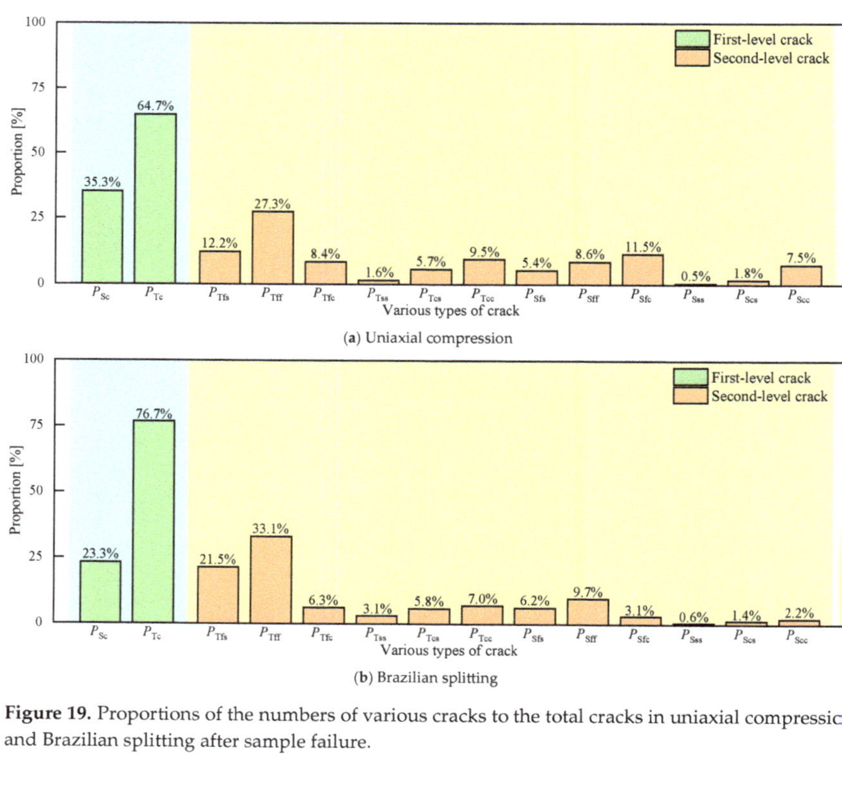

Figure 19. Proportions of the numbers of various cracks to the total cracks in uniaxial compression and Brazilian splitting after sample failure.

Figure 20 shows the optical microscopic observations of the microstructure in a real CASS specimen after loading. As can be seen, along the macro fracture path, the number of cracks within the cement mortar and bonding surface between the cement mortar and aggregate (identified by a blue dotted line) is much larger than that of cracks within other mineral components (identified by red dotted line), which is consistent with the numerical results. This agreement verifies the reliability of the model.

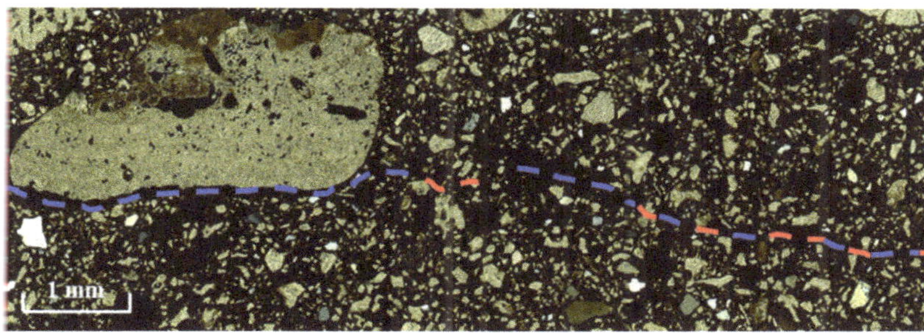

(**a**) Uniaxial compression

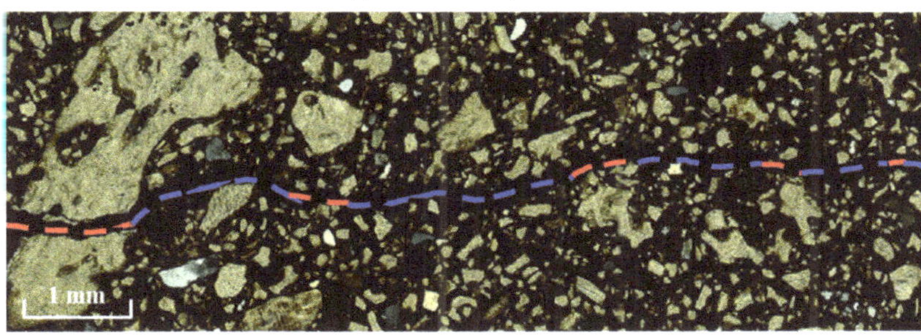

(**b**) Brazilian splitting

Figure 20. Experimental observation results of the microstructure of the real CASS specimen after failure, in which cracks within the cement mortar and bonding surface between the cement mortar and aggregate and cracks within other mineral components are identified by the blue dotted line and red dotted line, respectively.

5. Conclusions

This study investigated the static mechanical properties of CASS. The orthogonal experiments, which consisted of four-factor and three-level, were employed to explore the optimal mix proportion of CASS. On a macro-scale, uniaxial compression with the AE technique and splitting tests with the DIC technique were conducted on CASS at different curing ages using an electro-hydraulic servo-controlled test machine. The OASS was introduced to validate the effectiveness of the mix proportions for CASS by conducting macro-mechanical tests on two types of samples with identical mix proportions but differing in aggregate types. Meanwhile, on a micro-scale, the microcracks of numerical specimens were multi-level divided, and the behavior of microcracks was quantitatively analyzed. The following main conclusions can be drawn:

(1) The optimal mix proportion of CASS consists of 700 kg/m^3 of cementitious materials content, a water–binder ratio of 0.45, a sand ratio of 60%, and a dosage of 8% for the accelerator amount.

(2) Tensile failure is the primary failure mechanism of uniaxial compression and Brazilian splitting. Among them, the main failure form of the Brazilian split is the two ends

crack initiation and spread to the central. Meanwhile, the specimens of CASS exhibit an increased brittleness with longer curing age.

(3) Compared to OASS, the CASS with an optimal mix proportion has approximately equal early strength but low later strength. The early strength of CASS increases rapidly, but the later strength increases slowly. However, the strength of OASS increases evenly. The filling and water bag effect on coral pores makes a high early strength of specimens, but the unfilled pores in the specimens are also the reason for the low later strength.

(4) A novel numerical three-dimensional model based on PFC was proposed to simulate the static mechanical properties of CASS. The multi-level division and quantitative description of cracks are realized. The failure in CASS under uniaxial compression and Brazilian splitting tests is primarily experienced within the cement mortar and bonding surface between the cement mortar and aggregate (coral debris).

In conclusion, the study of coral aggregate seawater shotcrete (CASS) has revealed promising properties for its application in construction. The material's early strength development and its environmental benefits, stemming from the use of coral as an aggregate, make it a sustainable option for construction in coastal and marine environments. However, consideration must be given to its performance at later stages of curing, which, while showing a slower increase in strength, still meets the requirements for many construction applications. Combined with understanding its static mechanical properties and failure mechanisms, the optimal mix proportion determined in this study provides a foundation for the potential use of CASS in structural support and other construction elements. Future research should focus on long-term performance and durability testing to fully assess its viability in construction practices.

Author Contributions: Y.P. contributed to the original writing of the manuscript. L.Y. contributed to searching and sorting the references. W.L. and T.Z. contributed to reviewing and editing the manuscript and funding acquisition. L.M. and D.W. contributed to the preparation of data and figures. C.W. and L.Z. contributed to supervision and funding acquisition. All authors have read and agreed to the published version of the manuscript.

Funding: The research presented in this paper was carried out under the financial support of the National Natural Science Foundation of China (Grant Nos. 52179118, 52209151), the Basic Research Program Project of Xu Zhou (KC23045), the Yunlong Lake Laboratory of Deep Underground Science and Engineering Project (104023002) and the Graduate Innovation Program of China University of Mining and Technology (2024WLKXJ209).

Institutional Review Board Statement: Not applicable.

Informed Consent Statement: Not applicable.

Data Availability Statement: Data will be made available on request.

Acknowledgments: The authors would like to thank their colleagues in the Rock Mechanics research group at the China University of Mining and Technology and Army Engineering University of PLA for technical discussion and comments.

Conflicts of Interest: The authors declare no conflict of interest.

References

1. Howdyshell, P.A. *The Use of Coral as an Aggregate for Portland Cement Concrete Structures*; DTIC Document; Construction Engineering Research Laboratory: Champaign, IL, USA, 1974.
2. Vines, F.R. Experience with use of coral detritus as concrete as concrete aggregate in Western Samoa. *Aust. Road Res.* **1982**, *12*, 17–28.
3. Ehlert, R.A. Coral concrete at Bikini Atoll. *Concr. Int.* **1991**, *13*, 19–24.
4. Kaushik, S.; Islam, S. Suitability of seawater for mixing structural concrete exposed to a marine environment. *Cem. Concr. Compos.* **1995**, *17*, 177–185. [CrossRef]
5. Zentar, R.; Dubois, V.; Abriak, N.E.; Ballivy, G. Mechanical behaviour and environmental impacts of a test road built with marine dredged sediments. *Resour. Conserv. Recycl.* **2008**, *52*, 947–954. [CrossRef]

6. Dubois, V.; Abriak, N.E.; Zentar, R.; Ballivy, G. The use of marine sediments as a pavement base material. *Waste Manag.* **2009**, *29*, 774–782. [CrossRef] [PubMed]
7. Limeira, J.; Etxeberria, M.; Agulló, L.; Molina, D. Mechanical and durability properties of concrete made with dredged marine sand. *Constr. Build. Mater.* **2011**, *25*, 4165–4174. [CrossRef]
8. Bayrak, B.; Çelebi, O.; Öz, A.; Ustabas, I.; Kaplan, G.; Aydın, A.C. Effect of aluminosilicate precursors and curing regime on physico-mechanical durability and microstructural characteristics of coral geopolymers (Cor-Geo): Cleaner production for coral islands. *Constr. Build. Mater.* **2023**, *407*, 133596. [CrossRef]
9. Tenza-Abril, A.J.; Benavente, D.; Pla, C.; Baeza-Brotons, F.; Valdes-Abellan, J.; Solak, A.M. Statistical and experimental study for determining the influence of the segregation phenomenon on physical and mechanical properties of lightweight concrete. *Constr. Build. Mater.* **2020**, *238*, 117642. [CrossRef]
10. Wang, Y.Y.; Huang, J.J.; Wang, D.J.; Liu, Y.F.; Zhao, Z.J.; Liu, J.P. Experimental study on hygrothermal characteristics of coral sand aggregate concrete and aerated concrete under different humidity and temperature conditions. *Constr. Build. Mater.* **2020**, *230*, 117034. [CrossRef]
11. Younis, A.; Ebeada, U.; Suraneni, P.; Nanni, A. Short-term flexural performance of seawater-mixed recycled-aggregate GFRP-reinforced concrete beams. *Compos. Struct.* **2020**, *236*, 111860. [CrossRef]
12. Korichi, B.; Zazi, N.; Delbrel, S.; Ngo, K.; Chopart, J.P. Microstructural, morphological characterization and corrosion behavior of sand cast AlSi10Cu(Fe) alloy in chloride solution. *Chem. Pap.* **2022**, *76*, 2947–2967. [CrossRef]
13. Arumugam, R.A.; Ramamurthy, K. Study of compressive strength characteristics of coral aggregate concrete. *Mag. Concr. Res.* **1996**, *48*, 141–148. [CrossRef]
14. Tan, Y.S.; Yu, H.F.; Mi, R.J.; Zhang, Y. Compressive strength evaluation of coral aggregate seawater concrete (CAC) by non-destructive techniques. *Eng. Struct.* **2018**, *176*, 293–302. [CrossRef]
15. Castagnetti, C.; Rossi, P.; Righi, S.; Cattini, S.; Simonini, R.; Rovati, L.; Capra, A. Potentialities of the combined use of underwater fluorescence imagery and photogrammetry for the detection of fine-scale changes in marine bioconstructors. *Front. Mar. Sci.* **2024**, *10*, 1305807. [CrossRef]
16. Salvador, R.P.; Cavalaro, S.H.P.; Cincotto, M.A.; Figueiredo, A.D. Parameters controlling early age hydration of cement pastes containing accelerators for shotcrete. *Cement. Concr. Res.* **2016**, *89*, 230–248. [CrossRef]
17. Steindl, F.R.; Mittermayr, F.; Sakoparnig, M.; Juhart, J.; Briendl, L.; Lindlar, B.; Ukrainczyk, N.; Dietzel, M.; Kusterle, W.; Galan, I. On the porosity of low-clinker shotcrete and accelerated pastes. *Constr. Build. Mater.* **2023**, *368*, 130461. [CrossRef]
18. Freddi, A.; Salmon, M. Introduction to the Taguchi Method. In *Design Principles and Methodologies. Springer Tracts in Mechanical Engineering*; Springer: Cham, Switzerland, 2019. [CrossRef]
19. Berger, P.D.; Maure, R.E.; Celli, G.B. Introduction to Taguchi methods. In *Experimental Design*; Springer: Cham, Switzerland, 2018.
20. Sharifi, E.; Sadjadi, S.J.; Aliha, M.R.M.; Moniri, A. Optimization of high-strength self-consolidating concrete mix design using an improved Taguchi optimization method. *Constr. Build. Mater.* **2020**, *236*, 117547. [CrossRef]
21. Neuner, M.; Cordes, T.; Drexel, M.; Hofstetter, G. Time-Dependent Material Properties of Shotcrete: Experimental and Numerical Study. *Materials* **2017**, *10*, 1067. [CrossRef] [PubMed]
22. Hammera, A.L.; Thewesa, M.; Galler, R. Time-dependent material behaviour of shotcrete-New empirical model for the strength development and basic experimental investigations. *Tunn. Undergr. Space Technol.* **2020**, *99*, 103238. [CrossRef]
23. Lyu, B.C.; Wang, A.G.; Zhang, Z.H.; Liu, K.W.; Xu, H.Y.; Shi, L.; Sun, D.S. Coral aggregate concrete: Numerical description of physical, chemical and morphological properties of coral aggregate. *Cem. Concr. Compos.* **2019**, *100*, 25–34. [CrossRef]
24. Mohajerani, A.; Rodrigues, D.; Ricciuti, C.; Wilson, C. Early-age strength measurement of shotcrete. *J. Mater.* **2015**, *2015*, 470160. [CrossRef]
25. Lee, M.J.; Park, G.K. Investigation of constitutive models of HPFRCC subjected to static and dynamic loadings. *Compos. Struct.* **2023**, *324*, 117525. [CrossRef]
26. Verma, V.; Kumar, U.; Ghosh, S.; Gurnani, L.; Mukhopadhyay, A. Developing intragranular zirconia-reinforced alumina possessing vastly improved mechanical and tribological properties. *J. Am Ceram. Soc.* **2024**, *107*, 760–775. [CrossRef]
27. Mazzucco, G.; Majorana, C.E.; Salomoni, V.A. Numerical simulation of polypropylene fibres in concrete materials under fire conditions. *Comput. Struct.* **2015**, *154*, 17–28. [CrossRef]
28. Mukhtara, F.; El-Tohfa, A. A review on fracture propagation in concrete: Models, methods, and benchmark tests. *Eng. Fract. Mech.* **2023**, *281*, 109100. [CrossRef]
29. Tomporowski, D.; Nitka, M.; Tejchman, J. Application of the 3D DEM in the modelling of fractures in pre-flawed marble specimens during uniaxial compression. *Eng. Fract. Mech.* **2023**, *277*, 108978. [CrossRef]
30. Karam, M.S.; Nakamura, H.; Yamamoto, Y.; Tahir, M.; Hameed, R. Mesoscopic evaluation of the bond behavior of concrete with deformed rebar subjected to passive confinement employing 3D discrete model. *Eng. Fract. Mech.* **2024**, *295*, 109790. [CrossRef]
31. Engelke, L.; Brendel, L.; Wolf, D.E. Microstructure evolution during sintering: Discrete element method approach. *J. Am. Ceram. Soc.* **2023**, *106*, 5022–5032. [CrossRef]
32. Mollon, G.; Zhao, J. 3D generation of realistic granular samples based on random fields theory and Fourier shape descriptors. *Comput. Methods Appl. Mech. Eng.* **2014**, *279*, 46–65. [CrossRef]
33. Invernizzi, S.; Lacidogna, G.; Carpinteri, A. Particle-based numerical modeling of AE statistics in disordered materials. *Meccanica* **2013**, *48*, 211–220. [CrossRef]

34. Potyondy, D.O.; Cundall, P.A. A bonded-particle model for rock. *Int. J. Rock Mech. Min. Sci.* **2004**, *41*, 1329–1364. [CrossRef]
35. Stahl, M.; Konietzky, H. Discrete element simulation of ballast and gravel under special consideration of grain-shape, grain-size and relative density. *Granul. Matter* **2011**, *13*, 417–428. [CrossRef]
36. Shang, J.; Zhao, Z.; Hu, J.; Handley, K. 3D Particle-based DEM investigation into the shear behaviour of incipient rock joints with various geometries of rock bridges. *Rock Mech. Rock Eng.* **2018**, *51*, 3563–3584. [CrossRef]
37. Shang, J.; Yokota, Y.; Zhao, Z.; Dang, W. DEM simulation of mortar-bolt interface behaviour subjected to shearing. *Constr. Build. Mater.* **2018**, *185*, 120–137. [CrossRef]
38. Song, Z.Y.; Konietzky, H.; Herbst, M. Three-dimensional particle model based numerical simulation on multi-level compressive cyclic loading of concrete. *Constr. Build. Mater.* **2019**, *225*, 661–677. [CrossRef]
39. Asadi, M.S.; Rasouli, V.; Barla, G. A Laboratory Shear Cell Used for Simulation of Shear Strength and Asperity Degradation of Rough Rock Fractures. *Rock Mech. Rock Eng.* **2013**, *46*, 683–699. [CrossRef]
40. Li, X.B.; Zou, Y.; Zhou, Z.L. Numerical Simulation of the Rock SHPB Test with a Special Shape Striker Based on the Discrete Element Method. *Rock Mech. Rock Eng.* **2014**, *47*, 1693–1709. [CrossRef]
41. Haeri, H.; Sarfarazi, V. Numerical simulation of tensile failure of concrete using Particle Flow Code (PFC). *Comput. Concr.* **2016**, *18*, 39–51. [CrossRef]
42. Lian, C.Q.; Yan, Z.G.; Beecham, S. Numerical simulation of the mechanical behaviour of porous concrete. *Eng. Comput.* **2011**, *28*, 984–1002. [CrossRef]
43. Saksala, T. Numerical modeling of concrete fracture processes under dynamic loading: Meso-mechanical approach based on embedded discontinuity finite elements. *Eng. Fract. Mech.* **2018**, *201*, 282–297. [CrossRef]
44. Potapov, S.; Masurel, A.; Marin, P.; Daudeville, L. Mixed DEM/FEM modeling of advanced damage in reinforced concrete structures. *J. Eng. Mech.* **2016**, *143*, 04016110. [CrossRef]
45. Fang, Q.; Zhang, J.H.; Zhang, Y.D.; Gong, Z.M.; Chen, L.; Liu, J.C. 3D numerical investigation of cement mortar with microscopic defects at high strain rates. *J. Mater. Civ. Eng.* **2016**, *28*, 04015155. [CrossRef]
46. Dai, L.Z.; Long, D.X.; Wang, L. Meso-scale modeling of concrete cracking induced by 3D corrosion expansion of helical strands. *Comput. Struct.* **2021**, *254*, 106615. [CrossRef]
47. Ma, H.Y.; Wu, Z.Y.; Yu, H.F.; Zhang, J.H.; Yue, C.J. Experimental and three-dimensional mesoscopic investigation of coral aggregate concrete under dynamic splitting-tensile loading. *Mater. Struct.* **2020**, *53*, 12. [CrossRef]
48. Jia, M.K.; Xu, W.X.; Zhu, Z.G. Numerical study on the excluded volumes of realistic 3D non convex particles. *Powder Technol.* **2019**, *349*, 52–58. [CrossRef]
49. *GB/T 14684-2011*; Technical Specification for Lightweight Aggregate Concrete. Chinese National Standard: Beijing, China, 2011.
50. *ASTM D1141-2003*; Standard Specification for Chemical Requirements for Utility Water Used in the Production of Hydraulic Cement. ASTM International: West Conshohocken, PA, USA, 2003.
51. *JGJ 51-2002*; Technical Specification for Lightweight Aggregate Concrete. China Architecture & Building Press: Beijing, China, 2002.
52. *JGJ/T 372-2016*; Technical Specification for Application of Shotcrete. China Architecture & Building Press: Beijing, China, 2016.
53. *EN 12620:2012*; Aggregates and Aggregate Preparation for Testing. Standard, European Committee for Standardization: Brussels, Belgium, 2012.
54. Khanlari, G.R.; Heidari, M.; Sepahigero, A.A.; Fereidooni, D. Quantification of strength anisotropy of metamorphic rocks of the Hamedan province, Iran, as determined from cylindrical punch, point load and Brazilian tests. *Eng. Geol.* **2014**, *169*, 80–90. [CrossRef]
55. Thériault, F.; Noël, M.; Sanchez, L. Simplified approach for quantitative inspections of concrete structures using digital image correlation. *Eng. Struct.* **2022**, *252*, 113725. [CrossRef]
56. Yang, L.Y.; Xie, H.Z.; Zhang, D.B.; Zhang, F.; Lin, C.Y.; Fang, S.Z. Acoustic emission characteristics and crack resistance of basalt fiber reinforced concrete under tensile load. *Constr. Build. Mater.* **2021**, *312*, 125442. [CrossRef]
57. Nie, Y.J.; Su, H.J.; Yu, L.Y.; Feng, Y.J.; Wang, W.B. Bonding fracture and deformation behaviors of sandstone-concrete interface subjected to different temperatures under three-point bending. *Int. J. Geomech.* **2023**, *23*, 04023020. [CrossRef]
58. Deresse, N.E.; VanSteen, C.; Soete, J.; Sarem, M.; Vanhulst, J.; Wevers, M.; François, S. Fracture mode analysis of cementitious mortars by simultaneous application of 4D-XCT and acoustic emission technique. *Constr. Build. Mater.* **2024**, *419*, 135486. [CrossRef]
59. *ASTM 3967-16*; Standard Test Method for Splitting Tensile Strength of Intact Rock Core Specimens. Annual Book of ASTM Standards: West Conshohocken, PA, USA, 2016.
60. Birid, K.C. An Equation to Evaluate the Unconfined Compressive Strength of Rock from Splitting Tensile Strength Test Results. *Geotech. Geol. Eng.* **2016**, *34*, 391–401. [CrossRef]
61. Quan, J.S.; Rong, G.; Xu, L.D.; Chen, Z.H. A three-dimensional grain-based model for studying the microscopic fracture behavior of granite. *Comput. Geotech.* **2023**, *159*, 105427. [CrossRef]
62. Itasca Consulting Group Inc. *PFC3D (3 Dimensional Particle Flow Code)*, version 6.0; Itasca Consulting Group Inc.: Minneapolis, MN, USA, 2020.

63. Peng, Y.X.; Zhang, T.; Yu, L.Y.; Gao, J.L.Y.A.; Tian, W.L. Numerical investigation on the effect of intergranular contact bonding strength on the mechanical properties of granite using PFC3D-GBM. *Int. J. Numer. Anal. Methods Geomech.* **2023**, *47*, 694–716. [CrossRef]
64. Rasmussen, L.L.; Min, K.B. Developments to the Bonded Block Modeling technique for Discrete Element simulation of transversely isotropic rocks. *Int. J. Rock Mech. Min. Sci.* **2023**, *170*, 105518. [CrossRef]
65. Xu, Y.; Dai, F.; Xu, N.W.; Zhao, T. Numerical investigation of dynamic rock fracture toughness determination using a semi-circular bend specimen in split Hopkinson pressure bar testing. *Rock Mech. Rock Eng.* **2016**, *49*, 731–745. [CrossRef]

Disclaimer/Publisher's Note: The statements, opinions and data contained in all publications are solely those of the individual author(s) and contributor(s) and not of MDPI and/or the editor(s). MDPI and/or the editor(s) disclaim responsibility for any injury to people or property resulting from any ideas, methods, instructions or products referred to in the content.

materials

MDPI

Article

The Influence of the Addition of Basalt Powder on the Properties of Foamed Geopolymers

Michał Łach [1], Barbara Kozub [1], Sebastian Bednarz [1], Agnieszka Bąk [1], Mykola Melnychuk [2] and Adam Masłoń [3,*]

[1] Faculty of Material Engineering and Physics, Chair of Material Engineering and Physics, Cracow University of Technology, Jana Pawła II 37, 31-864 Cracow, Poland; michal.lach@pk.edu.pl (M.Ł.)
[2] Department of Materials Science, Lutsk National Technical University, Lvivska 75, 43000 Lutsk, Ukraine
[3] Department of Environmental Engineering and Chemistry, Rzeszow University of Technology, Powstańców Warszawy 6, 35-959 Rzeszów, Poland
* Correspondence: amaslon@prz.edu.pl

Abstract: Geopolymers are binder materials that are produced by a chemical reaction between silica or aluminum compounds with an alkaline activating solution. Foamed geopolymer materials are increasingly being cited as a viable alternative to popular organic insulation materials. Since the foaming process of geopolymers is difficult to control, and any achievements in improving the performance of such materials are extremely beneficial, this paper presents the effect of the addition of basalt powder on the properties of foamed geopolymers. This paper presents the results of physicochemical studies of fly ash and basalt, as well as mechanical properties, thermal properties, and structure analysis of the finished foams. The scope of the tests included density tests, compressive strength tests, tests of the thermal conductivity coefficient using a plating apparatus, as well as microstructure tests through observations using light and scanning microscopy. Ground basalt was introduced in amounts ranging from 0 to 20% by mass. It was observed that the addition of basalt powder contributes to a reduction in and spheroidization of pores, which directly affect the density and pore morphology of the materials tested. The highest density of 357.3 kg/m^3 was characterized by samples with a 5 wt.% basalt powder addition. Their density was 14% higher than the reference sample without basalt powder addition. Samples with 20 wt.% basalt addition had the lowest density, and the density averaged 307.4 kg/m^3. Additionally, for the sample containing 5 wt.% basalt powder, the compressive strength exceeded 1.4 MPa, and the thermal conductivity coefficient was 0.1108 W/m $\times$ K. The effect of basalt powder in geopolymer foams can vary depending on many factors, such as its chemical composition, grain size, content, and physical properties. The addition of basalt above 10% causes a decrease in the significant properties of the geopolymer.

Keywords: alkali-activated materials; foamed geopolymers; basalt powder; waste materials; insulating materials

check for updates

Citation: Łach, M.; Kozub, B.; Bednarz, S.; Bąk, A.; Melnychuk, M.; Masłoń, A. The Influence of the Addition of Basalt Powder on the Properties of Foamed Geopolymers. *Materials* **2024**, *17*, 2336. https://doi.org/10.3390/ma17102336

Academic Editor: Mengjun Chen

Received: 19 March 2024
Revised: 9 May 2024
Accepted: 11 May 2024
Published: 14 May 2024

Copyright: © 2024 by the authors. Licensee MDPI, Basel, Switzerland. This article is an open access article distributed under the terms and conditions of the Creative Commons Attribution (CC BY) license (https://creativecommons.org/licenses/by/4.0/).

1. Introduction

Geopolymers are materials of increasing interest to the scientific community and the construction industry. They have been studied for several decades [1–3]; however, many aspects related to improving their properties remain undiscovered. Geopolymer materials are a very interesting and attractive material; however, comparing their potential 20 years ago, it must be stated that the situation regarding the feasibility of their implementation has changed significantly. More and more often, scientists present critical comments regarding geopolymerization technology. This is related to certain limitations such as difficulties in eliminating efflorescence and the fact that this technology is very sensitive to changes in raw material prices, and in recent years, up to 300% increases in the price of sodium hydroxide have been observed. Most research, publications, and first implementations have been carried out for geopolymers produced based on fly ash and slag. It should be borne in mind that these raw materials are no longer as available as they were in the 1980s, 1990s, and at the beginning of the 21st century. Many steel mills are closed in Europe and production has been moved to Asia. The situation is similar for coal combustion and fly ash. The current policy of many countries is to abandon coal burning, which results in smaller amounts of available fly ash.

Therefore, advanced research and the search for alternative sources of waste raw materials are of great importance for the further development of geopolymers.

Geopolymer foams are a special type of porous material that is produced by a chemical reaction between silica or aluminum materials and an alkaline activating solution [1]. This process leads to the formation of a three-dimensional polymer network, which provides the structure of the material [4]. Geopolymer foams are used in a variety of construction applications, including as insulation materials, structural materials, and civil engineering [5]. Geopolymer foams are typically lightweight, which makes them attractive for lightweight applications such as thermal insulation and lightweight structural components. Despite their low density, geopolymer foams have good mechanical strength. Thanks to their porous structure, geopolymer foams have good insulating capacity. They are often resistant to many chemicals [6–11]. Due to their chemical composition and structure, geopolymer foams can exhibit good heat resistance. Many geopolymer foams are made from natural raw materials, making them more environmentally friendly than some traditional building materials [6].

Despite the continuous development of these materials and the numerous scientific studies conducted in the area of the effect of ceramic additives on their properties, there is still much to be discovered to make their implementation more feasible. Continuous efforts should be made to develop compositions with the least possible environmental impact and ease of large-scale application. It is known that the most commonly described raw materials thus far, such as fly ash and blast furnace slag in many countries, are already scarcely available, and other alternative waste resources should be sought. All over the world, due to environmental policies, coal combustion is being abandoned, and heavy industry generates slags, which are largely used in cement plants. However, it should be remembered that the mining industry still generates quite a lot of waste raw materials from the extraction and processing of rocks. One such example is basalt powder [12–14].

Basalt powder is a natural product extracted from basalt volcanic rocks. It has many properties that make it a popular additive in many fields, such as agriculture, horticulture, construction, and industry. The chemical composition of basalt powder is as follows: (SiO_2) 46.6%, aluminum oxide (Al_2O_3) 14.3%, iron oxide (Fe_2O_3) 11.4%, calcium oxide (CaO) 9.21%, magnesium oxide (MgO) 7.90%, sodium oxide (Na_2O) 3.10%, and titanium oxide (TiO_2) 1.95%. In addition, potassium oxide (K_2O) 0.823%, phosphorus oxide (P_2O_5) 0.48%, and manganese oxide (Mn_2O_3) 0.266% are present in amounts of less than one percent [15,16].

The powder in its composition also contains micronutrients, including iron, magnesium, manganese, zinc, boron, and silicon. Due to its calcium carbonate content, it is widely used in horticulture. Nevertheless, the main reason for its use is to balance the pH of soils. Another feature of this natural product is water absorption. This factor can be considered negatively or positively depending on the use of basalt powder. In agriculture and horticulture in the broadest sense, this ability is considered as a favorable aspect for growing plants and vegetables, since it facilitates the plants' access to water. When used as a material for concrete or geopolymers, this property can be problematic due to the risk of having to use larger amounts of liquid activating solutions [17–19].

Due to its chemical properties, it is increasingly noted that basalt powder can be used to produce geopolymers or also to form an alkaline solution, the so-called alkaline activator, due to the presence of calcium carbonate, which acts as a catalyst during the geopolymer formation process. However, focusing attention on its use in geopolymer formation and its effect on strength, as well as mechanical properties, it is important to note its porous structure. The porosity of the structure affects absorptivity and permeability, as well as mechanical strength. The use of basalt powder is also ecologically advantageous because, as a natural product, it is not harmful to the environment [20,21].

The potential applications of foamed geopolymers based on fly ash and basalt powder are wide and cover many areas of construction. Therefore, they are one of the more interesting materials to look at in the context of modern and sustainable construction [22,23].

Despite the interesting properties of basalt and the existence of a large amount of waste basalt material, no attempt has been made thus far to use it as a powdered material to improve the performance of geopolymers. Basalt fibers are of greatest interest as a reinforcing material for various types of composites. The Scopus database registers as many as 237 articles from 2004 to 2024 on the introduction of basalt fibers into the geopolymer matrix, while only 28 articles deal with the introduction of basalt in powdered form. Figures 1 and 2 below show an analysis of publications on this topic (according to the Scopus database). The number of articles regarding 2024 is incomplete because only 2 months of this year were covered by the analysis. Examples of the use of basalt fibers in geopolymer composites as reinforcement are widely reported in the literature [24–27]. However, due to its chemical composition, basalt in powdered form can also be used as an additive to improve the performance of foamed geopolymers.

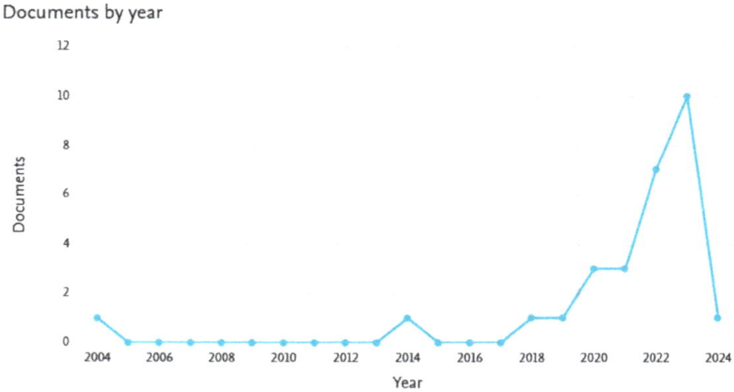

Figure 1. Analysis of the number of publications registered in the Scopus database on the introduction of basalt materials in powder form (crushed basalt) into geopolymer composites.

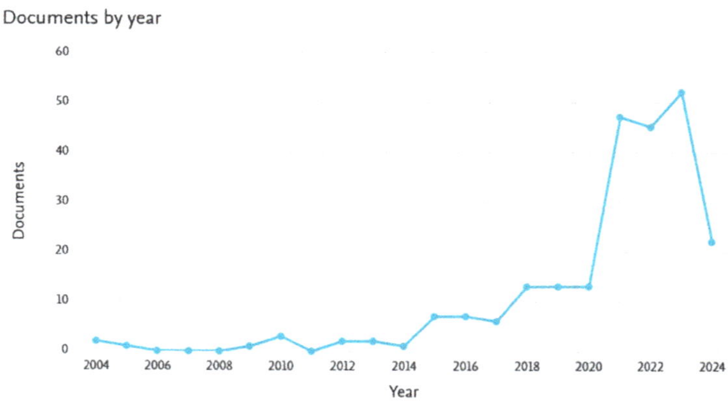

Figure 2. Analysis of the number of publications registered in the Scopus database on the introduction of basalt materials (mainly fibers) into geopolymer composites.

As analysis in the SCOPUS database showed, the addition of powdered basalt or basalt fibers to foamed geopolymers was described in only four articles (search criteria words: basalt AND powder AND geopolymer AND foam) [28–31], of which only one was about shredded material introduced as an additive to foamed geopolymers. A careful analysis using various keywords found a few more scientific papers, such as [32,33]. The addition of basalt powder to geopolymers or cement mortars was also presented in articles by other authors [34–37]. The authors of these works confirmed the validity of using basalt powder for the production of cement mortars or geopolymers [38,39]. It has also been confirmed experimentally that basalt powder has a positive effect on the consistency of fresh cement composites and the strength of the cured composite [40]. As for geopolymers, it has been possible to successfully synthesize geopolymers from basalt by activation with sodium hydroxide solutions [35]. In that study, XRD analysis of various minerals found in basalt showed that basalt moderately reacted and dissolved with sodium hydroxide. Consequently, particles of the residue were placed as fillers in geopolymer matrices. The geopolymerization reactions occurred on the basalt surface, and the unreacted basalt particles play a supporting role in the geopolymer properties.

Since the number of scientific articles related to the introduction of powdered basalt into foamed geopolymers is small, and there is an identified knowledge gap in this area, it was decided to conduct a study involving the introduction of basalt powder additives into geopolymer paste in amounts ranging from 0 to 20% by mass, and then subject such compositions to foaming. This article presents the results of this research. The purpose of the study was to demonstrate the effect that different additions of basalt powder have on the properties of foamed fly ash-based geopolymers. The innovation of the research is mainly the introduction of a basalt additive into the composition of foamed geopolymers and the determination of the effect of this additive on density, thermal conductivity, compressive and tensile strength, and microstructure. As the analysis of the literature shows, the described research is innovative and very relevant to the possibility of implementing such materials. Analysis of the literature showed that the topic of basalt addition to geopolymer composites became particularly attractive from 2019 to 2020, and since then there has been a significant increase in the number of scientific reports in this area.

The novelty and innovation of the research presented in this article lie in the introduction of powdered basalt into foamed geopolymers simultaneously with stabilizers of the structure of foamed geopolymers. Since there is currently no knowledge on the impact of basalt addition on foamed geopolymers, this article should be treated as an impulse for further, more detailed research. As the results below show, the addition of basalt has a positive effect on the properties of geopolymers only up to a certain amount of addition, beyond which the properties of the geopolymer mixture decrease. Therefore, further research is necessary and the presented research results are new knowledge contributing to the development of geopolymer materials, and thus far this aspect has not been solved and presented in the scientific literature.

2. Materials and Methods

Fly ash from the Skawina Combined Heat and Power Plant (Skawina, Poland) was used to produce geopolymer foams. The basalt powder used in the study came from NB Minerals (Tychy, Poland). Oxide chemical composition analysis was performed for the base materials, namely, fly ash and basalt powder. XRF oxide analysis was performed on a SCHIMADZU EDX-7200 (SHIMADZU Europa GmbH, Duisburg, Germany). The test was carried out in an air atmosphere with holders designed for bulk materials and Mylar film, and the results are shown in Table 1.

Table 1. XRF oxide analysis of fly ash (main ingredients only).

Precursor	Oxide Composition (wt.%)						
	SiO_2	TiO_2	Fe_2O_3	Al_2O_3	CaO	MgO	K_2O
Fly ash	56.64 ± 0.32	0.87 ± 0.01	4.99 ± 0.01	30.57 ± 0.41	2.79 ± 0.02	0.1 ± 0.01	2.74 ± 0.01
Basalt	46.92 ± 0.10	2.66 ± 0.03	17.48 ± 0.01	13.01 ± 0.08	10.55 ± 0.01	5.95 ± 0.11	1.20 ± 0.01

Both fly ash and basalt powder were applied to the mixture in powder form (these materials were not mechanically processed, but were applied as supplied). Figures 3 and 4 show a sample of fly ash and basalt powder. Photographs of particle morphology and others shown later related to the morphology of the finished composites were taken using a JEOL IT200 scanning electron microscope (JEOL, Akishima, Tokyo, Japan). Macroscopic images, on the other hand, were taken on a Keyence VHX-7000 digital optical microscope (KEYENCE INTERNATIONAL, Mechelen, Belgium).

Figure 3. SEM microstructure of the fly ash used in the study and visualization of the form in which it was used.

Figure 4. SEM microstructure of the basalt (basalt powder) used in the study and visualization of the form in which it was used.

Figures 5 and 6 below show the particle size distribution of fly ash and basalt powder, respectively. These materials were not subjected to additional mechanical treatment before. A similar grain size distribution can be seen for both materials. The fly ash had a slightly higher degree of fineness. Measurement of the particle size distribution was carried out using a laser particle size analyzer from Anton Paar GmbH model PSA 1190 (Anton Paar GmbH, Graz, Austria) using Kalliope Professional software (version 2.22.1).

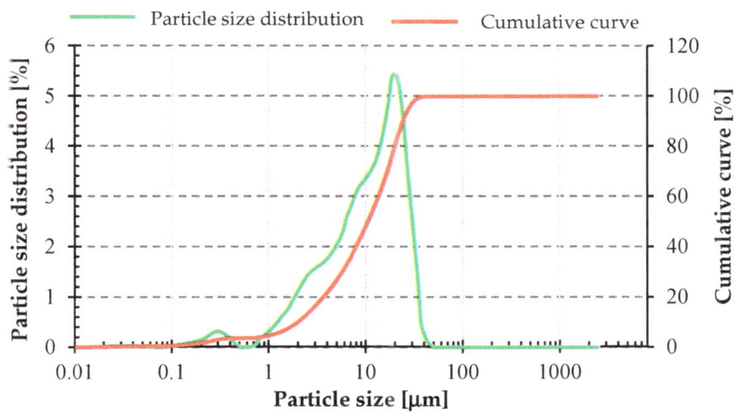

Figure 5. Particle size distribution of fly ash used in the study.

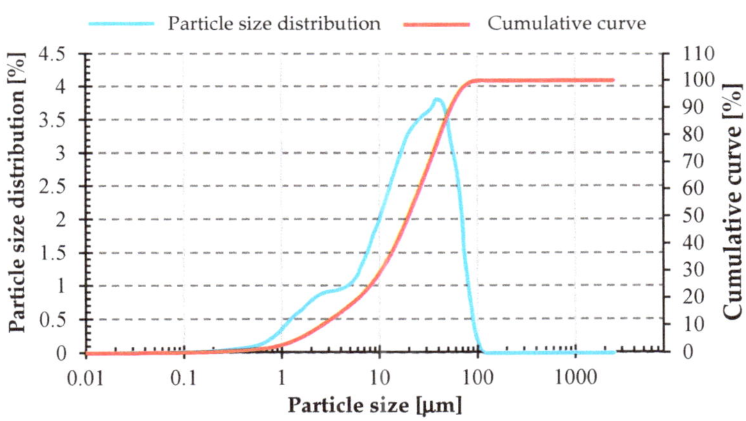

Figure 6. Particle size distribution of basalt powder used in the study.

Table 2 below shows the grain size parameters of the raw materials used in the study. The values of D_{10} for both materials were on a similar level. However, the values of D_{50} and D_{90} were already about twice as small for fly ash compared to basalt powder.

Table 2. Parameters of grain size of raw materials used for testing.

		D_{10} [µm]	D_{50} [µm]	D_{90} [µm]	Average Value [µm]
Fly ash	Average value	2.09	11.00	25.42	13.26
	Standard deviation	0.08	0.21	0.76	0.30
Basalt powder	Average value	2.62	20.48	55.71	26.72
	Standard deviation	0.01	0.14	0.30	0.15

To determine the phase composition of the fly ash and basalt powder samples used for analysis, the X-ray analysis technique (XRD) was applied. An X-ray diffractometer (PANalytical Aeris, producer; Malvern PANalytical (Lelyweg 1, Almelo, The Netherlands)) was used to carry out the study. Rietveld phase analysis was performed using the PDF-4+ database provided by the International Center for Diffraction Data (ICDD).

Figures 7 and 8 below show the phase composition of the raw materials used in the study. Based on the XRD phase analysis of the fly ash, it was determined that the fly ash used to produce the geopolymer composites studied in this paper consisted mainly of mullite (47.1 wt.%) and quartz (46.2 wt.%), with minor contributions from hematite (1.9 wt.%) and orthoclase (4.8 wt.%). In the case of basalt powder, XRD analysis conducted showed that the main phases of which it was composed were mainly anorthite (83.4 wt.%), as well as diopsite (10.6 wt.%), albite (4.8 wt.%), and quartz (1.2 wt.%). Both oxide composition and phase composition studies confirmed that fly ash and basalt powder have a suitable chemical composition and can be used as geopolymerization precursors, because they contain the appropriate amount of both SiO_2 and Al_2O_3 and the molar ratios of these compounds are consistent with the literature [1,3,35,36]. Their degree of fineness is also suitable for carrying out alkaline activation processes.

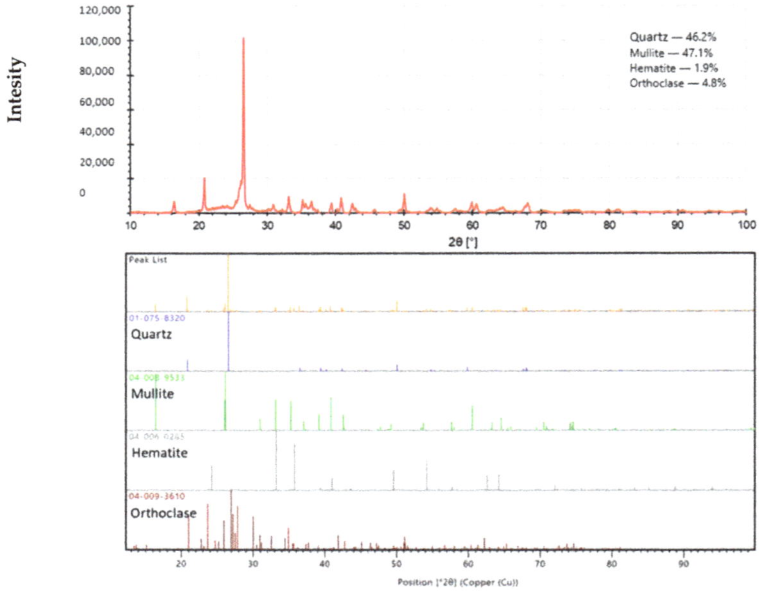

Figure 7. Diffractogram of the fly ash used in the study.

For the recorded diffractograms, calculations were made of the amount of the amorphous phase in the form of amorphous silica. Calculations were performed in the MAUD program (Version 2.998; Made on a Mac). For the fly ash sample, the amount of amorphous silica was 29.81%, while the basalt sample contained 67.32% of amorphous silica.

Five variants of samples of geopolymer compositions with additives of fly ash and basalt powder were prepared for further studies, the proportions of which, along with the designations, are shown in Table 3. Basalt powder was added, increasing its amount by 5% by mass to approximately determine its optimal proportion. The basalt powder was dosed by precise mass measurement and introduced into the fly ash for uniform mixing.

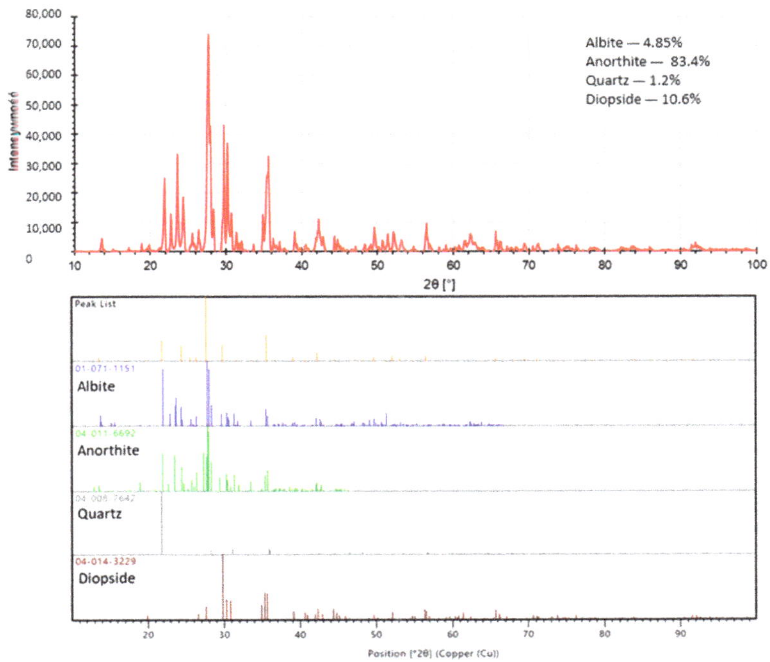

Figure 8. Diffractogram of the basalt powder used in the study.

Table 3. Variants of geopolymer compositions prepared for testing.

Sample ID	Mass Share [%]	
Fly Ash	**Basalt Powder**	
100FA_0BF	100	0
95FA_5BF	95	5
90FA_10BF	90	10
85FA_15BF	85	15
80FA_20BF	80	20

Foam stabilizers in the form of putty gypsum (Dolina Nidy, Pińczów, Poland) and cellulose–hydroxyethyl cellulose (Glentham Life Sciences, Corsham UK) were used to prepare compositions with fly ash and basalt powder. Stabilizing additives ensure that the porous structure remains for a longer time immediately after foaming and the hardening process is faster. A 10 M solution of sodium hydroxide (NaOH) and an aqueous solution of sodium silicate R-145 (water glass) (molar modulus 2.5; density about 1.45 g/cm^3), in a volume ratio of 1:2.5, were used as the activating solution. Hydrogen peroxide 36% was used as the foaming agent. The amounts of added ingredients are shown in Table 4 below.

Table 4. Additional components of geopolymer mixtures used in each composition variant.

Components of the Geopolymer Mix	Amount per 1000 g of Fly Ash
Gypsum	100 g
Cellulose	5 g
Alkaline solution	440 mL
Hydrogen peroxide	30 mL

The manufacture of geopolymers consisted of mixing the solid components and introducing the appropriate amount of additives, followed by dosing the alkali solution. After a dense plastic consistency was obtained (after about 15 min of mixing in a high-speed mixer), the foaming agent, which was hydrogen peroxide with a concentration of 36%, was dosed. Immediately after the addition of the foaming agent, the geopolymer mass was transferred to molds, sealed against moisture loss, and placed in a laboratory dryer. The curing process of the geopolymer composites was carried out at 75 °C for 24 h in an SLW 750 STD laboratory dryer (POL-EKO-APARATURA, Wodzisław Śląski, Pol-ska). After 24 h of annealing, the samples were taken out and unmolded. In each case, enough samples were produced to allow for at least five replicates. The samples were then properly prepared for further testing.

Thermal conductivity tests were carried out using the HFM 446 Lambda Series from NETZSCH (Netzsch GmbH & Co., Selb, Germany). The measurements were carried out in a temperature range of 0–20 °C. Panels with dimensions of 20 × 20 × 3 or 4 cm were prepared for the tests. An example of the appearance of the test specimen and how it was formed are shown in Figure 9 below.

Figure 9. Example of manufactured geopolymer with basalt powder—sample for testing of thermal conductivity coefficient (80FA_20BF) (**a**); sample manufacturing method—formed samples in a chamber (**b**) (samples with dimensions of 20 × 20 × 3 cm).

Compressive strength tests were carried out on a Matest 3000 kN concrete compression press (Matest, Treviolo, Italy) equipped with compression strength measuring heads and an additional force sensor up to 300 kN. The measurement was made at a speed of 0.05 MPa/s. The tests were carried out in accordance with PN-EN 12390-3:2019-07 [41]. Bending strength tests were carried out on rectangular specimens measuring 4 cm × 4 cm × 18 cm using a three-point bending test device, an Autograph AGS-X universal testing machine (Shimadzu, Kyoto, Japan), with a measuring range of up to 10 kN. The test speed was 5 mm/min, and the support spacing was 150 mm. The tests were conducted in accordance with PN-EN 12390-5:2019-08 [42].

3. Results

The density was read from a heat conduction coefficient tester. The density was determined automatically using a geometric method by measuring mass and volume. Figure 10 below presents the results of testing the density of the produced lightweight fly ash-based geopolymer structures with different proportions of basalt powder. The highest density of 357.3 kg/m^3 was characterized by samples with a 5 wt.% basalt powder addition. Their density was 14% higher than the reference sample without basalt powder addition. Samples with 20 wt.% basalt addition had the lowest density, and the density averaged 307.4 kg/m^3. No linear dependence of the density of the produced samples on the amount of introduced basalt was observed. This is most likely because the addition of basalt powder did not directly affect the density of the composition due to the similar density of the raw material itself to fly ash, but the addition did affect the consistency of the geopolymer mass and its ability to form a porous structure, as well as its stability.

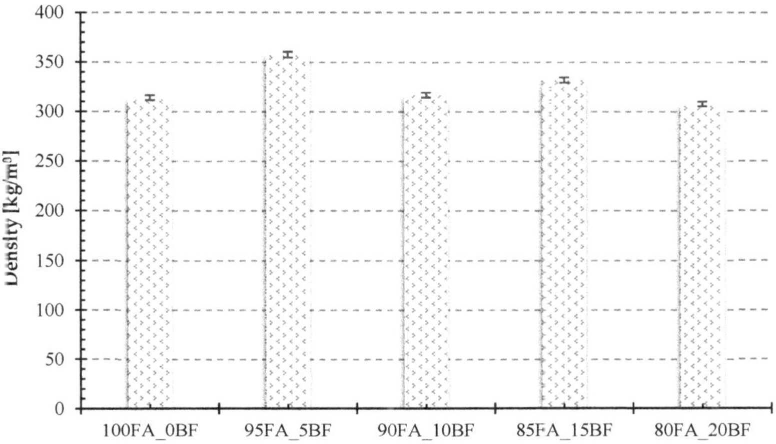

Figure 10. Results of a density study of foamed geopolymers made from fly ash with different proportions of basalt powder.

Figure 11 below shows the results of heat transfer coefficient measurements for the geopolymer foams produced. Very similar results were observed, as the obtained values did not differ significantly from each other regardless of the amount of basalt introduced. The highest values of the thermal conductivity coefficient were characterized by samples with 5 wt.% and 15 wt.% basalt additions, and these values were 0.11082 W/m × K and 0.11142 W/m × K, respectively. Comparing these values with the density test results shown in Figure 10, the dependence of the thermal conductivity coefficient on the density of the material is apparent, a dependence that is quite obvious and has been proven in many previous studies by other authors [7–11]. The sample with the lowest value of the thermal conductivity coefficient had 20 wt.% basalt mica addition and this value was 0.09254 W/m × K. The obtained results of 0.100 W/m × K are not competitive with commonly used insulation materials for construction, such as polystyrene and polyurethane foams or various types of wool, but it should be kept in mind that geopolymers are non-flammable materials capable of carrying loads even up to temperatures exceeding 1000 °C. They also have many other advantages. The literature reports that by properly controlling the foaming process of geopolymers, it is possible to obtain about twice as good results in terms of insulating properties. However, the purpose of the conducted research was not to obtain the best possible insulating parameters but to determine the suitability of the addition of basalt powder and its effect on the properties of foamed geopolymers. Obtaining very lightweight foamed structures with good insulating parameters involves a certain compromise related to their mechanical properties. Foamed geopolymers do not have to find application only in thermal insulation in construction, but can be used industrially to insulate various types of high-temperature installations. The experience of the authors of this article shows that, compared to other insulation materials commonly used, geopolymers do not lose their insulating properties as the temperature increases.

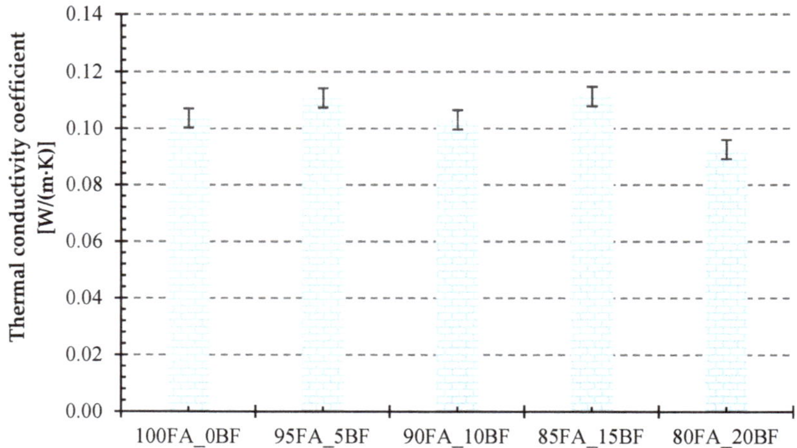

Figure 11. Thermal conductivity values for foamed geopolymers with different basalt powder content.

Figure 12 below shows the results of the compressive strength tests of manufactured geopolymer foams with basalt powder added.

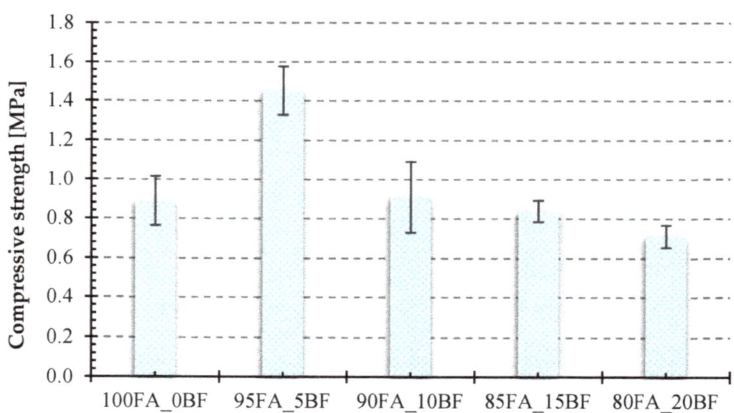

Figure 12. Compressive strength of geopolymer samples with different contents of basalt powder.

As can be seen from the graph shown in Figure 12, which compares the compressive strength results for geopolymers with different contents of basalt mica, the material with 5 wt.% basalt addition—sample 95FA_5B—had the highest strength. The strength of this material was higher than that of the reference material by about 63%. In addition, only for this sample, the compressive strength exceeded 1 MPa, which means that it met the requirements of the JC/T2200-2013 [43] standard defining acceptable compressive strengths of foam insulation panels made of ordinary Portland cement [5]. The sample with a 20 wt.% addition of basalt powder had the lowest strength. Its compressive strength was lower than that of the reference sample by about 8%. A linear decrease in compressive strength with an increase in the proportion of basalt powder is evident.

Comparing the flexural strength results shown in Figure 13, significant discrepancies in the flexural strength values for the test specimens were also apparent here. The highest flexural strength value was characterized by the sample with 5 wt.% basalt addition. Its flexural strength was 0.67 MPa. Table 5 shows all the average numerical values for the results obtained in the flexural and compressive strength tests.

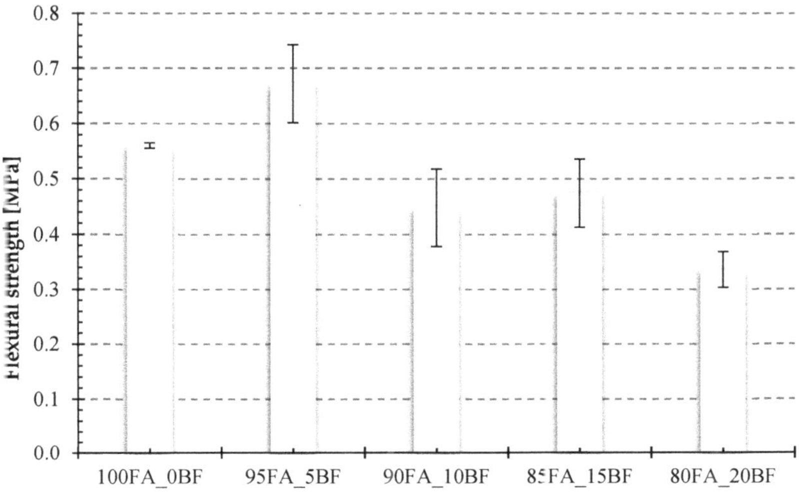

Figure 13. Flexural strength of geopolymer specimens with different contents of basalt powder.

Table 5. Flexural and compressive strength values for foamed geopolymers with basalt powder.

	100FA_0BF	95FA_5BF	90FA_10BF	85FA_15BF	80FA_20BF
Compressive strength [MPa]	0.89	1.45	0.91	0.84	0.71
Flexural strength [MPa]	0.56	0.67	0.45	0.40	0.34

A comparison of the test results presented in Figures 12 and 13 confirms that the best strength properties were obtained with the addition of 5% basalt. The addition of 5% basalt powder increased both the bending strength and compressive strength. Increasing the addition of basalt powder resulted in a decrease in compressive and bending strength, which was particularly visible in samples with 15% and 20% of basalt powder added.

Below, Figures 14–18 present microstructural images taken with a scanning electron microscope and an optical microscope. All variants of the produced samples are shown in the figures. The images show a variety of pores of different shapes and sizes. In Figure 14, the largest pore size is characterized by the sample of the reference material (without basalt addition). The visualization of the porosity of the other samples is similar. The photographs also show different wall thicknesses forming the porous geopolymer structure. It can be unequivocally stated that the addition of basalt powder caused a decrease in the pore size of the geopolymer. As the amount of basalt powder addition increased, the number of smaller pores increased, and the number of large pores decreased. This is related to the change in the consistency of the geopolymer mixture due to the addition of basalt and the change in surface tension. This causes a greater number of small pores to be produced and large pores to be annihilated due to the release of the gases that constitute them.

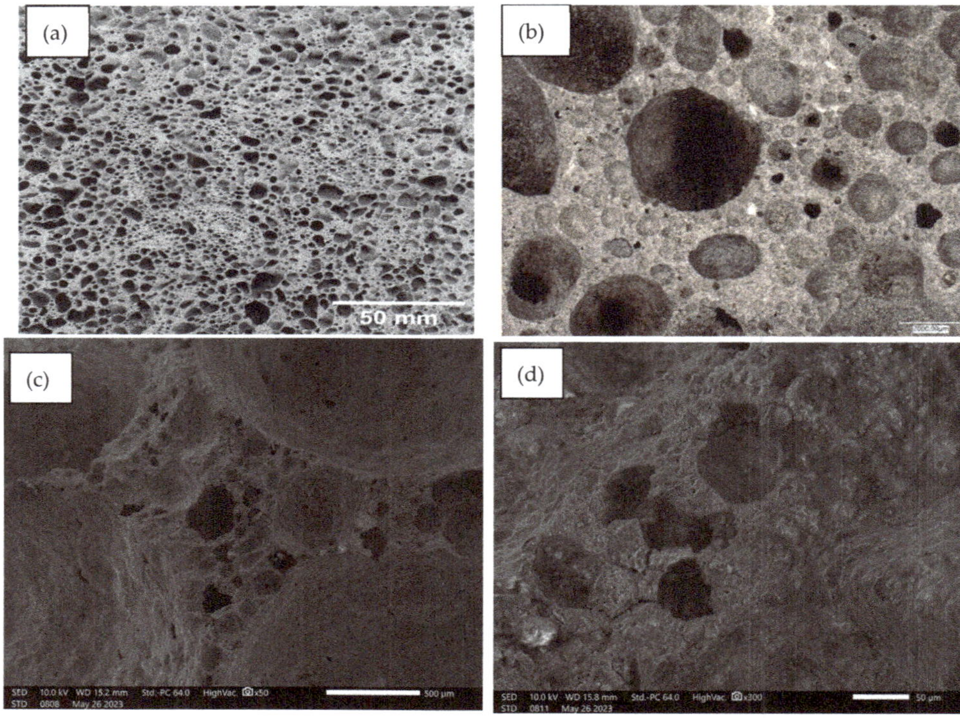

Figure 14. Images of the microstructure of foamed geopolymer 100FA_0BF: (**a**,**b**) macrophotographs taken with an optical microscope; (**c**,**d**) microphotographs taken with a scanning electron microscope.

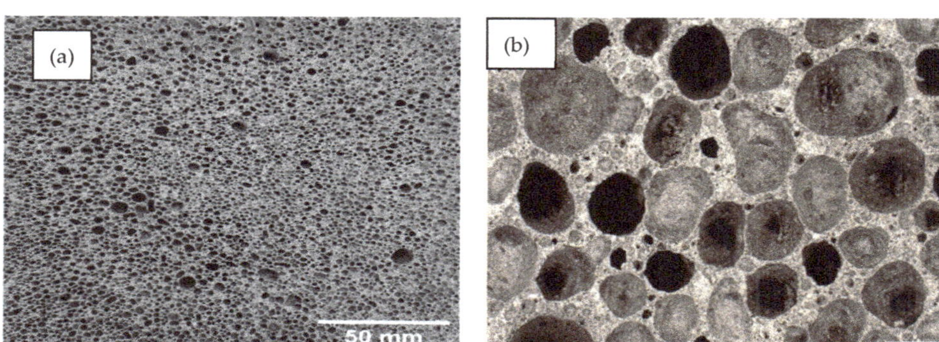

Figure 15. *Cont.*

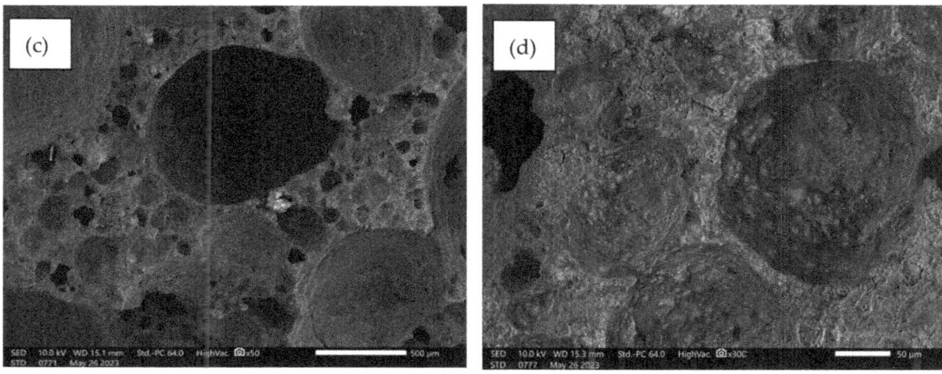

Figure 15. Images of the microstructure of foamed geopolymer 95FA_5BF: (**a**,**b**) macrophotographs taken with an optical microscope; (**c**,**d**) microphotographs taken with a scanning electron microscope.

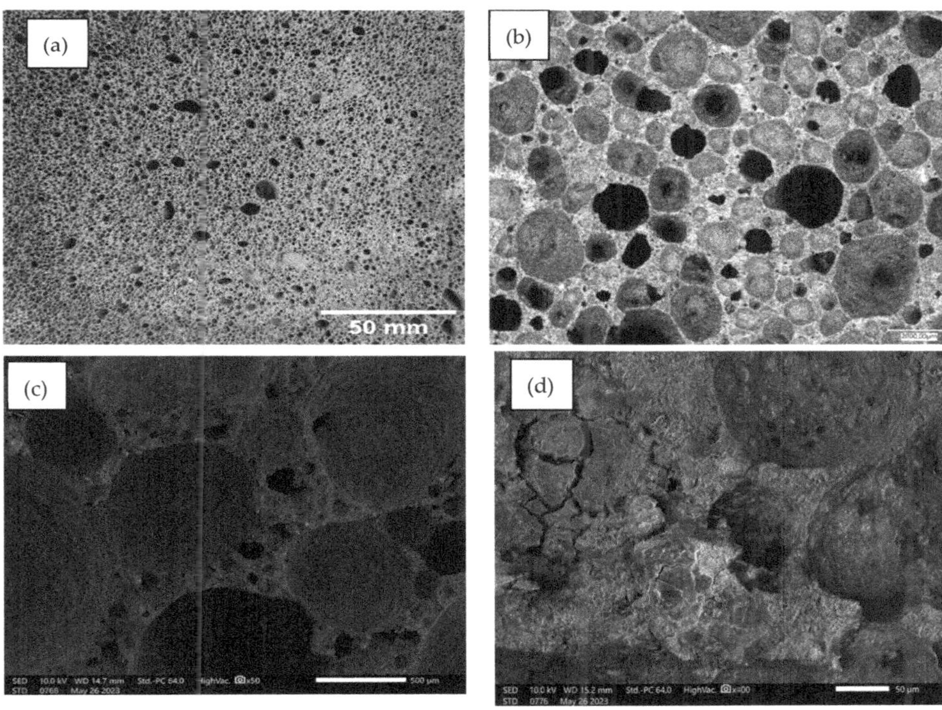

Figure 16. Images of the microstructure of foamed geopolymer 90FA_10BF: (**a**,**b**) macrophotographs taken with an optical microscope; (**c**,**d**) microphotographs taken with a scanning electron microscope.

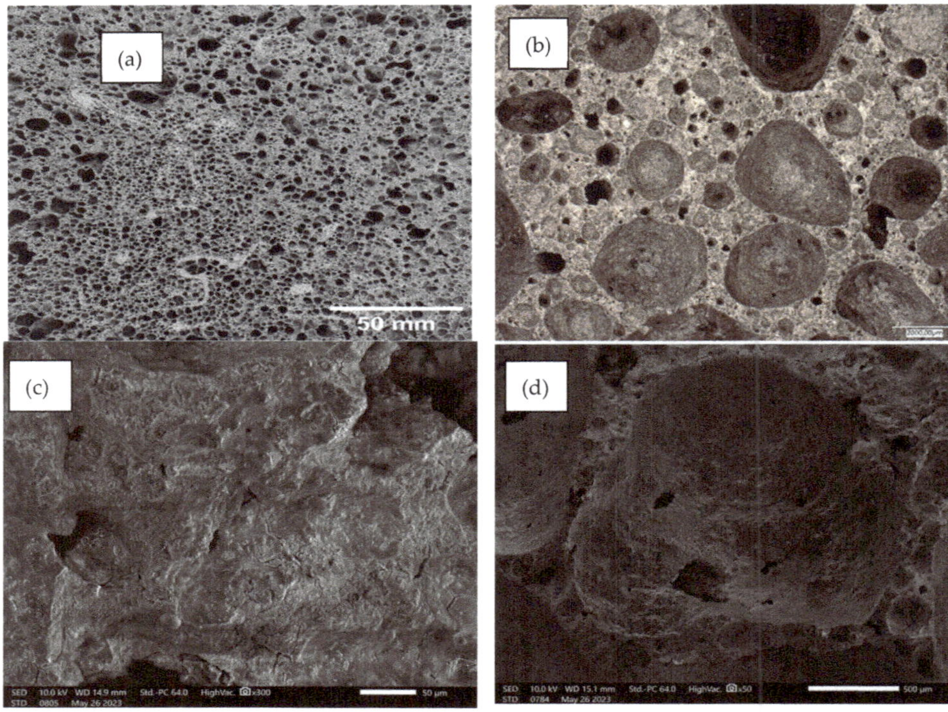

Figure 17. Images of the microstructure of foamed geopolymer 85FA_15BF: (**a**,**b**) macrophotographs taken with an optical microscope; (**c**,**d**) microphotographs taken with a scanning electron microscope.

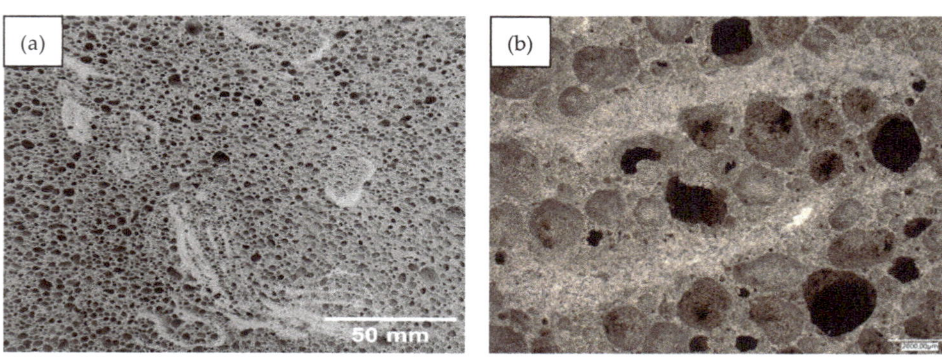

Figure 18. *Cont.*

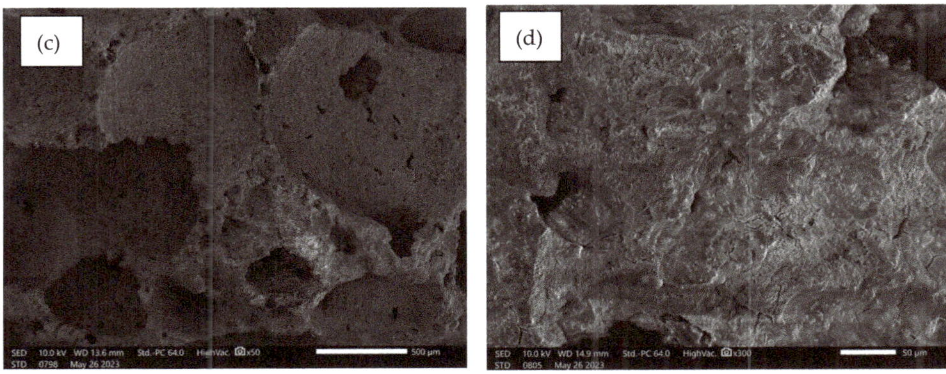

Figure 18. Images of the microstructure of foamed geopolymer 80FA_20BF: (**a**,**b**) macrophotographs taken with an optical microscope; (**c**,**d**) microphotographs taken with a scanning electron microscope.

Figure 19 below shows the results of the analysis of pore sizes in the tested samples. For the photos presented in Figures 14, 15, 16, 17 and 18a, analyses were carried out using the image analysis software "ImageJ" (https://imagej.net/ij/). The photos were properly cropped (to remove unnecessary background) and saved in shades of gray, which was necessary for analysis. Porosity was identified in the photos prepared in this way and, after appropriate graphic processing, the program calculated the average pore surface area. Samples made from mixtures with the addition of basalt flour were characterized by a much higher share of small pores and a less frequent occurrence of large pores, compared to the reference sample made from fly ash. The addition of basalt flour had a positive effect on reducing the average pore surface size compared to the reference sample 100FA_0BF.

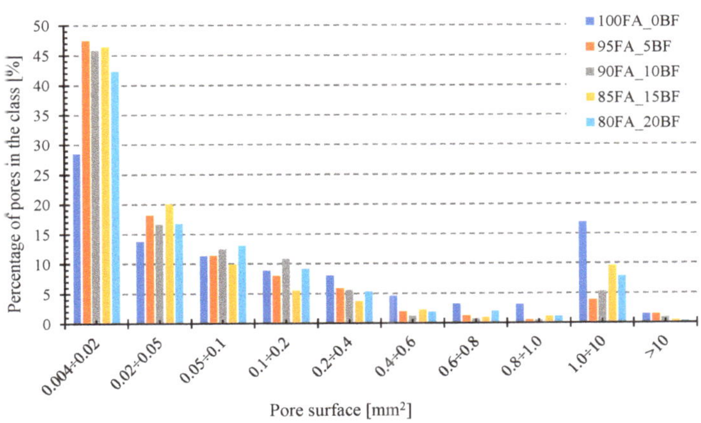

Figure 19. Dependence of the percentage of pores in classes on the pore area for geopolymer samples foamed with the addition of basalt.

4. Market Analysis and the Appropriateness of Using Basalt as an Addition to Geopolymers

The results presented in this paper illustrate the effect of basalt powder addition on the properties of foamed geopolymers. To date, basalt has been used in geopolymer materials in the form of reinforcing basalt fibers. However, it can also play the role of a precursor or stabilizing additive in the form of basalt powder with great success. Basalt processing plants report demand for basalt waste management in the form of powder or dust. This issue is particularly relevant nowadays, as many parts of the world are experiencing problems with the availability of coal combustion fly ash or smelter slag. The search for other waste sources of raw materials that can be precursors to geopolymers is of great importance.

Another very important problem that is currently causing difficulties in the implementation of geopolymer technology is the fact that most scientific studies are concerned with the use of fly ash and slag, which, as is well known, due to environmental policy and the shift away from coal-fired power generation, are running out, so their price is rising. It is now necessary to look anew for alternative waste sources other than by-products of coal combustion.

It is widely known that geopolymers can also be produced from available and chemically stable raw materials, such as metakaolins. However, it is important to note here the considerable cost of doing so. If implemented on a mass scale, products made from metakaolin-based geopolymers will not be price-competitive with traditional materials. The average cost of metakaolins in recent years has been about 400 USD per ton.

Kaolin prices on world stock exchanges have fluctuated over the last 15 years at the level of USD 130 to USD 160 [44], while the prices of kaolin after calcination (metakaolin) range from USD 300 to USD 650 depending on the quality and degree of whiteness (for example, raw material prices available in China: [45]).

It turns out that in Poland (but also in other European countries), there is a systematic problem with the availability of ash. While the problem has been dealt with differently thus far, predictions for the future are not very optimistic. Even if fly ash becomes available, its price will rise—it is estimated that it will rise by as much as 1000%. Fly ash is an attractive material for the cement and concrete industries. There is already a shortage of ash, even for these industries. If there is a need to use them for geopolymers, the situation will become even worse.

It is therefore necessary to look for other sources of raw materials for the production of geopolymers or to reduce the amount of fly ash used. The use of basalt is very attractive from this perspective. It is estimated that the geopolymer market, despite various difficulties, will develop very dynamically. Figure 20 presents forecasts for the geopolymer market (information provided at https://www.maximizemarketresearch.com/market-report/global-geopolymer-market/81356/ (accessed on 29 April 2024).

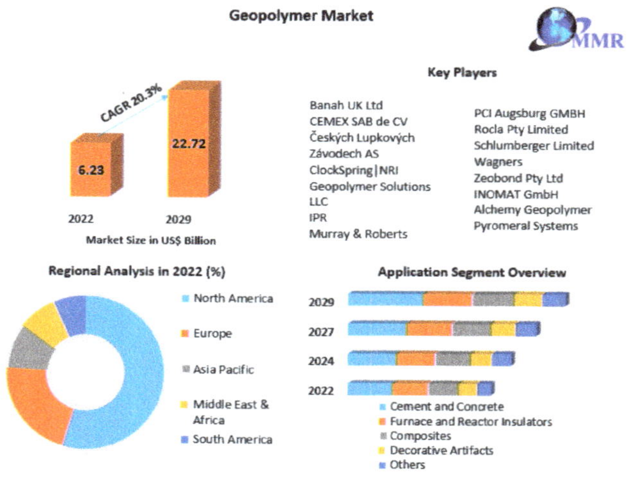

Figure 20. Geopolymer market forecasts to 2029 [46].

5. Conclusions

The studies conducted in connection with the introduction of an additive to foamed geopolymers in the form of basalt powder have led to the following conclusions:

1. As the amount of basalt powder added increases, the porosity structure changes. More spheroidal pores are formed and more pores of smaller sizes are created. This relationship was observed as a result of microscopic observations. This is probably related to the change in the consistency of the geopolymer mixture and its surface tension, which results in the formation of pores of different sizes more than in the case of a geopolymer mixture without the addition of basalt.
2. The addition of basalt powder has a positive effect on the stability of foamed structures and the ability to foam the geopolymer mass. The addition of 5% basalt powder causes an increase in density by 14%, as well as an increase in compressive strength by 63% and an increase in bending strength by 20%. The insulating properties due to the addition of 5% basalt powder decreased only by less than 7%. These dependencies result from the change in the consistency of the geopolymer mixture with the addition of basalt. The addition of 5% basalt is the optimal proportion of this addition because the highest increase in compressive strength was achieved with a slight deterioration of insulating properties (by 7%) despite an increase in density by 14%.
3. Further research should be carried out to optimize the share of basalt powder and optimize the molar ratios of activating solutions, taking into account that some of the basalt is reactive and takes part in the geopolymerization reaction and does not only act as a filler. The addition of basalt powder to geopolymers can contribute to the improvement of several parameters, such as: improvement of strength properties and abrasion resistance; improvement of thermal and insulating properties; increase in the ability to accumulate energy; porosity reduction; increased corrosion resistance in aggressive environments; reducing shrinkage and the risk of cracking. The ecological aspect is also important here because it is possible to use basalt in crushed form as waste. The effectiveness of the addition of powdered basalt will depend on many factors, including the origin of this material and its chemical and phase composition. Undoubtedly, further work should be carried out and the proportions of basalt addition should be adjusted to specific application requirements. It is also inevitable to take into account and accept a certain compromise because it is known that the addition of basalt will not improve all properties.

Author Contributions: Conceptualization, B.K.; methodology, B.K.; validation, M.Ł.; formal analysis, M.Ł.; investigation, B.K.; S.B. and M.M.; resources, M.Ł.; data curation, B.K.; writing—original draft preparation, M.Ł.; writing—review and editing, A.B. and A.M.; visualization, B.K.; supervision, B.K. and M.Ł.; funding acquisition, M.Ł. All authors have read and agreed to the published version of the manuscript.

Funding: This work was financed by the Polish National Agency for Academic Exchange under the grant BNI-UE-2023-8, and this work was also partially financed by the National Center for Research and Development in Poland under the grant "Materials for Circular Economy—industrial waste-based geopolymer composites with hybrid reinforcement" M-ERA.NET3/2021/70/GEOSUMAT/2022.

Institutional Review Board Statement: Not applicable.

Informed Consent Statement: Not applicable.

Data Availability Statement: Data are contained within the article.

Conflicts of Interest: The authors declare no conflicts of interest.

References

1. Davidovits, J. *Geopolymer Chemistry and Applications*, 4th ed.; Geopolymere Institut: Saint-Quentin, France, 2008.
2. Davidovits, J. 30 Years of Successes and Failures in Geopolymer Applications. Market Trends and Potential Breakthroughs. In Proceedings of the Geopolymer 2002 Conference, Melbourne, Australia, 28–29 October 2002

3. Provis, J.L.; van Deventer, J.S.J. *Geopolymers: Structure, Processing, Properties, and Industrial Applications*; A volume in Woodhead Publishing Series in Civil and Structural Engineering; Woodhead Publishing: Cambridge, UK, 2009.
4. Provis, J.L. Geopolymers and other alkali activated materials: Why, how, and what? *Mater. Struct.* **2014**, *47*, 11–25. [CrossRef]
5. Occhicone, A.; Graziuso, S.G.; De Gregorio, E.; Montagnaro, F.; Ricciotti, L.; Tarallo, O.; Roviello, G.; Ferone, C. Synthesis and characterization of new acid-activated red mud-metakaolin geopolymers and comparison with their alkaline counterparts. *J. Clean. Prod.* **2024**, *435*, 140492. [CrossRef]
6. Tang, W.; Pignatta, G.; Sepasgozar, S.M.E. Life-Cycle Assessment of Fly Ash and Cenosphere-Based Geopolymer Material. *Sustainability* **2021**, *13*, 11167. [CrossRef]
7. Kočí, V.; Černý, R. Directly foamed geopolymers: A review of recent studies. *Cem. Concr. Compos.* **2022**, *130*, 104530. [CrossRef]
8. Zhang, Z.; Provis, J.L.; Reid, A.; Wang, H. Mechanical, thermal insulation, thermal resistance and acoustic absorption properties of geopolymer foam concrete. *Cem. Concr. Compos.* **2015**, *62*, 97–105. [CrossRef]
9. Skvara, F.; Sulc, R.; Tisler, Z.; Skricik, P.; Smilauer, V.; Zlamalova Cilova, Z. Preparation and properties of fly as-based geopolymer foams. *Ceram. Silik.* **2014**, *58*, 188–197.
10. Łach, M.; Mierzwiński, D.; Korniejenko, K.; Mikuła, J. Geopolymer foam as a passive fire protection. *MATEC Web Conf. Fire Environ. Saf. Eng.* **2018**, *247*, 00031. [CrossRef]
11. Łach, M.; Pławecka, K.; Bąk, A.; Lichocka, K.; Korniejenko, K.; Cheng, A.; Lin, W.T. Determination of the influence of hydraulic additives on the foaming process and stability of the produced geopolymer foams. *Materials* **2021**, *14*, 5090. [CrossRef]
12. Abbas, R.; Khereby, M.A.; Ghorab, H.Y.; Elkhoshkhany, N. Preparation of geopolymer concrete using Egyptian kaolin clay and the study of its environmental effects and economic cost. *Clean. Technol. Environ. Policy* **2020**, *22*, 669–687. [CrossRef]
13. Wang, Q.; Su, H.L.; Li, C.M.; Lyu, X.J. Recycling of steel slag as an alkali activator for blast furnace slag: Geopolymer preparation and its application in composite cement. *Clean. Technol. Environ. Policy* **2023**, *25*, 1617–1629. [CrossRef]
14. Zarębska, K.; Zabierowski, P.; Gazda-Grzywacz, M.; Czuma, N.; Baran, P. Fly ash-based geopolymers with refractoriness properties. *Clean. Technol. Environ. Policy* **2022**, *24*, 2161–2175. [CrossRef]
15. Basalt: Igneous Rock—Pictures, Definition, Uses & More. Available online: https://geology.com/rocks/basalt.shtml (accessed on 15 March 2024).
16. Dobiszewska, M.; Beycioğlu, A. Physical Properties and Microstructure of Concrete with Waste Basalt Powder Addition. *Materials* **2020**, *13*, 3503. [CrossRef]
17. Dobiszewska, M.; Barnes, R.W. Properties of Mortar Made with Basalt Powder as Sand Replacement. *ACI Mater. J.* **2020**, *117*, 3–9. [CrossRef]
18. Kostrzewa-Demczuk, P.; Stepien, A.; Dachowski, R.; Krugiełka, A. The use of basalt powder in autoclaved brick as a method of production waste management. *J. Clean. Prod.* **2021**, *320*, 128900. [CrossRef]
19. Ponzi, G.G.D.; Mendes dos Santos, V.H.J.; Martel, R.B.; Pontin, D.; e Stepanha, A.S.D.G.; Schütz, M.K.; Menezes, S.C.; Einloft, S.M.O.; Vecchia, F.D. Basalt powder as a supplementary cementitious material in cement paste for CCS wells: Chemical and mechanical resistance of cement formulations for CO_2 geological storage sites. *Int. J. Greenh. Gas. Control* **2021**, *109*, 103337. [CrossRef]
20. Pavlis, R. Rock Dust: Can It Remineralize the Earth? Available online: https://www.gardenmyths.com/rock-dust-remineralize-earth/ (accessed on 15 March 2024).
21. Goll, D.S.; Ciais, P.; Amann, T.; Buermann, W.; Chang, J.; Eker, S.; Hartmann, J.; Janssens, I.; Li, W.; Obersteiner, M.; et al. Potential CO_2 removal from enhanced weathering by ecosystem responses to powdered rock. *Nat. Geosci.* **2021**, *14*, 545–549. [CrossRef]
22. Yang, H.; Liu, L.; Yang, W.; Liu, H.; Ahmad, W.; Ahmad, A.; Aslam, F.; Joyklad, P. A comprehensive overview of geopolymer composites: A bibliometric analysis and literature review. *Case Stud. Constr. Mater.* **2022**, *16*, e00830. [CrossRef]
23. Krishna, R.S.; Mishra, J.; Zribi, M.; Adeniyi, F.; Saha, S.; Baklouti, S.; Shaikh, F.U.A.; Gökçe, H.S. A review on developments of environmentally friendly geopolymer technology. *Materialia* **2021**, *20*, 101212. [CrossRef]
24. Furtos, G.; Prodan, D.; Sarosi, C.; Moldovan, M.; Korniejenko, K.; Miller, L.; Fiala, L.; Iveta, N. Mechanical Properties of MiniBars™ Basalt Fiber-Reinforced Geopolymer Composites. *Materials* **2024**, *17*, 248. [CrossRef]
25. Annadurai, S.; Baskar, P.; Elango, K.S. Geopolymer concrete reinforced with basalt fibers: An experimental investigation. *Mater. Today Proc.* 2023; *in press*. [CrossRef]
26. Punurai, W.; Kroehong, W.; SaptamongkoL, A.; Chindaprasirt, P. Mechanical properties, microstructure, and drying shrinkage of hybrid fly ash-basalt fiber geopolymer paste. *Constr. Build. Mater.* **2015**, *186*, 62–70. [CrossRef]
27. Li, M.; Gong, F.; Wu, Z. Study on mechanical properties of alkali-resistant basalt fiber reinforced concrete. *Constr. Build. Mater.* **2020**, *245*, 118424. [CrossRef]
28. Le, V.S.; Hájková, P.; Kovacic, V.; Bakalova, T.; Lukáš, V.; Le, C.H.; Seifert, K.C.; Peres, A.P.; Louda, P. Thermal conductivity of reinforced geopolymer foams. *J. Ceram.-Silik.* **2019**, *63*, 365–373. [CrossRef]
29. Le, V.S.; Szczypinski, M.M.; Hájková, P.; Kovacic, V.; Bakalova, T.; Volesky, L.; Hiep, L.C.; Louda, P. Mechanical properties of geopolymer foam at high temperature. *Sci. Eng. Compos. Mater.* **2020**, *27*, 129–138. [CrossRef]
30. Le, V.S.; Louda, P. Research of Curing Time and Temperature-Dependent Strengths and Fire Resistance of Geopolymer Foam Coated on an Aluminum Plate. *Coatings* **2021**, *11*, 87. [CrossRef]
31. Le, V.S.; Nguyen, V.V.; Sharko, A.; Ercoli, R.; Nguyen, T.X.; Tran, D.H.; Łoś, P.; Buczkowska, K.E.; Mitura, S.; Špirek, T.; et al. Fire Resistance of Geopolymer Foams Layered on Polystyrene Boards. *Polymers* **2022**, *14*, 1945. [CrossRef]

32. Wang, J.; Li, X.; Hu, Y.; Li, Y. Hu, P.; Zhao, Y. Physical and high temperature properties of basalt fiber-reinforced geopolymer foam with hollow microspheres. *Constr. Build. Mater.* **2024**, *411*, 134698. [CrossRef]
33. Gencel, O.; Nodehi, M.; Bayraktar, O.Y.; Kaplan, G. Basalt fiber-reinforced foam concrete containing silica fume: An experimental study. *Constr. Build. Mater.* **2022**, *326*, 126861. [CrossRef]
34. Venyite, P.; Makone, E.C.; Kaze, R.C.; Nana, A.; Nemaleu, J.G.D.; Kamseu, E.; Melo, U.E.; Leonelli, C. Effect of Combined Metakaolin and Basalt Powder Additions to Laterite-Based Geopolymers Activated by Rice Husk Ash (RHA)/NaOH Solution. *Silicon* **2022**, *14*, 1643–1662. [CrossRef]
35. Ismaiel Saraya, M.; El-Fadaly, E. Preliminary Study of Alkali Activation of Basalt: Effect of NaOH Concentration on Geopolymerization of Basalt. *J. Mater. Sci. Chem. Eng.* **2017**, *5*, 58–76. [CrossRef]
36. Kozub, B.; Miernik, K.; Gądek, S. A Study of Fly Ash-Based Geopolymers with Basalt Flour Addition. *Mater. Proc.* **2023**, *13*, 3. [CrossRef]
37. Dobiszewska, M.; Pichór, W. Szołdra, P. Effect of basalt powder addition on properties of mortar. *MATEC Web Conf.* **2019**, *262*, 06002. [CrossRef]
38. Ziada, M.; Erdem, S.; Tammam, Y.; Kara, S.; Lezcano, R.A.G. The Effect of Basalt Fiber on Mechanical, Microstructural, and High-Temperature Properties of Fly Ash-Based and Basalt Powder Waste-Filled Sustainable Geopolymer Mortar. *Sustainability* **2021**, *13*, 12610. [CrossRef]
39. Aktürk, B.; Kızılkanat, A.B.; Kabay, N.; Akyüncü, V. Utilization of Basalt Powder as Geopolymeric Binder. International Conference on "Cement—Based Materials Tailored for a Sustainable Future" 27–29 May 2021—Istanbul/TURKEY. Available online: https://www.researchgate.net/profile/Busra-Akturk-3/publication/357484979_Utilization_of_Basalt_Powder_as_Geopolymeric_Binder/links/61d08405da5d105e5511e3e4/Utilization-of-Basalt-Powder-as-Geopolymeric-Binder.pdf (accessed on 15 March 2024).
40. Unčík, S.; Kmecová, V. The Effect of Basalt Powder on the Properties of Cement Composites. *Procedia Eng.* **2013**, *65*, 51–56. [CrossRef]
41. *PN-EN 12390-3:2019*; Testing Hardened Concrete—Part 3: Compressive Strength of Test Specimens. PKN: Warsaw, Poland, 2019.
42. *PN-EN 12390-5:2019*; Testing Hardened Concrete—Part 5: Flexural Strength of Test Specimens. PKN: Warsaw, Poland, 2019.
43. *JC/T2200-2013*; Foamed Cement Insulation Panel. Standards Press of China: Beijing, China, 2013.
44. Available online: https://www.statista.com/statistics/248194/average-price-of-kaolin/ (accessed on 21 April 2024).
45. Available online: https://www.made-in-china.com/products-search/hot-china-products/Metakaolin_Price.html (accessed on 21 April 2024).
46. Geopolymer Market: Global Industry Analysis and Forecast (2023–2029). Available online: https://www.maximizemarketresearch.com/market-report/global-geopolymer-market/81356/ (accessed on 15 March 2024).

Disclaimer/Publisher's Note: The statements, opinions and data contained in all publications are solely those of the individual author(s) and contributor(s) and not of MDPI and/or the editor(s). MDPI and/or the editor(s) disclaim responsibility for any injury to people or property resulting from any ideas, methods, instructions or products referred to in the content.

materials

MDPI

Article

Influence of TiO_2 Nanoparticles on the Physical, Mechanical, and Structural Characteristics of Cementitious Composites with Recycled Aggregates

Carmen Teodora Florean [1,2], Horațiu Vermeșan [2], Timea Gabor [2,*], Bogdan Viorel Neamțu [2], Gyorgy Thalmaier [2], Andreea Hegyi [1,2], Alexandra Csapai [1,2,*] and Adrian-Victor Lăzărescu [1]

1 National Institute for Research and Development in Construction, Urban Planning and Sustainable Spatial Development URBAN-INCERC Cluj-Napoca Branch, 117 Calea Florești, 400524 Cluj-Napoca, Romania; carmen.florean@incerc-cluj.ro (C.T.F.); andreea.hegyi@incerc-cluj.ro (A.H.); adrian.lazarescu@incerc-cluj.ro (A.-V.L.)

2 Faculty of Materials and Environmental Engineering, Technical University of Cluj-Napoca, 103-105 Muncii Boulevard, 400641 Cluj-Napoca, Romania; horatiu.vermesan@imadd.utcluj.ro (H.V.); bodan.namtu@stm.utcluj.ro (B.V.N.)

* Correspondence: timea.gabor@imadd.utcluj.ro (T.G.); alexandra.csapai@stm.utcluj.ro (A.C.)

Abstract: The aim of this study is to analyze the effect of the addition of TiO_2 nanoparticles (NTs) on the physical and mechanical properties, as well as the microstructural changes, of cementitious composites containing partially substituted natural aggregates (NAs) with aggregates derived from the following four recycled materials: glass (RGA), brick (RGB), blast-furnace slag (GBA), and recycled textolite waste with WEEE (waste from electrical and electronic equipment) as the primary source (RTA), in line with sustainable construction practices. The research methodology included the following phases: selection and characterization of raw materials, formulation design, experimental preparation and testing of specimens using standardized methods specific to cementitious composite mortars (including determination of apparent density in the hardened state, mechanical strength in compression, flexure, and abrasion, and water absorption by capillarity), and structural analysis using specialized techniques (scanning electron microscopy (SEM) images and energy dispersive X-ray spectroscopy (EDS)). The analysis and interpretation of the results focused primarily on identifying the effects of NT addition on the composites. Results show a decrease in density resulting from replacing NAs with recycled aggregates, particularly in the case of RGB and RTA. Conversely, the introduction of TiO_2 nanoparticles resulted in a slight increase in density, ranging from 0.2% for RTA to 7.4% for samples containing NAs. Additionally, the introduction of TiO_2 contributes to improved compressive strength, especially in samples containing RTA, while flexural strength benefits from a 3–4% TiO_2 addition in all composites. The compressive strength ranged from 35.19 to 70.13 N/mm^2, while the flexural strength ranged from 8.4 to 10.47 N/mm^2. The abrasion loss varied between 2.4% and 5.71%, and the water absorption coefficient varied between 0.03 and 0.37 $kg/m^2m^{0.5}$, the variations being influenced by both the nature of the aggregates and the amount of NTs added. Scanning electron microscopy (SEM) images and energy dispersive X-ray spectroscopy (EDS) analysis showed that TiO_2 nanoparticles are uniformly distributed in the cementitious composites, mainly forming CSH gel. TiO_2 nanoparticles act as nucleating agents during early hydration, as confirmed by EDS spectra after curing.

Keywords: TiO_2 nanoparticles; physical–mechanical characteristics; cementitious composites; recycled aggregates; eco-friendly improving technologies; natural aggregates

check for updates

Citation: Florean, C.T.; Vermeșan, H.; Gabor, T.; Neamțu, B.V.; Thalmaier, G.; Hegyi, A.; Csapai, A.; Lăzărescu, A.-V. Influence of TiO_2 Nanoparticles on the Physical, Mechanical, and Structural Characteristics of Cementitious Composites with Recycled Aggregates. *Materials* **2024**, *17*, 2014. https://doi.org/10.3390/ma17092014

Academic Editors: Mengjun Chen and Jiwen Bai

Received: 4 April 2024
Revised: 16 April 2024
Accepted: 23 April 2024
Published: 25 April 2024

Copyright: © 2024 by the authors. Licensee MDPI, Basel, Switzerland. This article is an open access article distributed under the terms and conditions of the Creative Commons Attribution (CC BY) license (https://creativecommons.org/licenses/by/4.0/).

1. Introduction

In today's context, there is intense concern around the world to develop less polluting and more sustainable building materials. The reduction in construction and other waste is also a major concern, as the annual recycling rate of construction waste is less than 5% [1,2]. Therefore, integrating the recycling or reutilization of such waste materials into cementitious construction composites presents a viable strategy to reduce raw material usage and mitigate environmental impact. It is worth noting that these materials encapsulate residual energy from their production phase, further highlighting their potential for sustainability [1,3–6]. The scientific literature highlights that construction waste consists mainly of concrete, cementitious materials, and ceramic bricks, which account for over 75% of the waste, in addition to a variety of recycled aggregates that are compatible with the cementitious binder matrix [7,8]. Nevertheless, each type of waste, depending on its nature (cementitious or ceramic) and composition, as well as its source of origin, is characterized by several properties (fineness, density, water absorption, mechanical strength, etc.) that will influence the density, water absorption, compressive strength, flexural strength, abrasion resistance, freeze-thaw resistance, or other durability properties of the final cementitious composite [8–15].

Recycled ceramic brick aggregates commonly exhibit higher water absorption rates and lower mechanical strength than natural aggregates, necessitating increased water content during preparation and potentially resulting in reduced mechanical strength of the composite [9,14,16,17]. According to Xue et al. [1], the addition of waste ceramic brick ground to micrometric sizes may initially result in a decrease in the early (7-day) mechanical strengths of cementitious composites. However, when a maximum of 10% ceramic powder is added to the composites, the mechanical strengths at 28 days are higher than those of the control sample (without waste ceramic powder). Yang et al. [9] reported that the use of construction demolition waste containing 14.5% ceramic bricks resulted in a reduction in the workability of the fresh composite, with up to a 20% reduction in compressive strength at 28 days and up to a 34% reduction in tensile splitting strength. Similarly, Cachim [16] demonstrated in his work that the replacement of natural aggregates with waste ceramic brick aggregates reduces the workability of the fresh cementitious composite and the density of the hardened composite but, contrary to most reports, slightly increases the compressive strength of the hardened composite.

The effects of aggregates sourced from recycled glass on cementitious composites are diverse and depend on their granular classification. Thus, the physical–mechanical performance of the composite can be improved by using finer glass powder due to its inherent pozzolanic properties [18]. However, if the waste glass has a larger grain size, it may lead to the development of alkali–silica reactions. This, in turn, can reduce the physical and mechanical performance of the composite [19,20]. Ling and Poon [19] have shown that it is possible to replace even 100% natural aggregates with recycled glass aggregates to produce mortars, provided that the optimum particle size distribution of the recycled aggregates is maintained, with wear resistance being the most obvious improved parameter. According to Ozkan and Yuksel's study [21], replacing cement with "glass powder" can have apparently contradictory effects: compressive strength increases at low ages for a maximum of 10% replacement but decreases at high ages or for amounts of cement replaced with glass powder greater than 10%.

Incorporating industrial by-products like slag or fly ash in cement formulations frequently leads to a potential decline in early-age mechanical strengths but enhances physical–mechanical performance in later stages, possibly reducing density while enhancing durability [22]. Nevertheless, there is also evidence to suggest that replacing 90% of the sand with slag can result in an increase in capillary water absorption of over 30%, which may have a negative indirect effect on the durability of the composite [23].

Although legislation at the European level has promoted the recycling of waste from electrical and electronic equipment since 2003 [24], there has been limited research to date on the feasibility of incorporating them into cementitious composites. This is mainly due to the significant reduction in physical–mechanical strength caused by these wastes when used as aggregate, which restricts their use to a maximum of 10% as a sand substitute [25–28]. Some research [25–31] demonstrated that the replacement of sand with recycled printed circuit board (PCB) waste reduced the compressive strength of the cementitious composite by 38.7% to 95.99% (depending on the substituted NA quantity).

In another area of research, but with a complementary aim of improving the performance of cementitious composites, there are numerous reports in the literature indicating the benefits of using TiO_2 nanoparticles (NTs) as an admixture material. Thus, TiO_2 nanoparticles are used to improve some of the physical–mechanical properties of cementitious composites [32]. Additionally, they enable the development of new features such as self-cleaning and hydrophilicity [33–37], increase durability by reducing water absorption, chloride permeability, and CO_2 permeability, increase resistance to freeze–thaw cycles and sulphate attacks, and reduce the capacity of NO_x pollutant compounds [38–45]. Nevertheless, the utilization of TiO_2 nanoparticles introduces the challenge of altering the rheological properties of the fresh composite owing to their notably extensive specific surface area [35]. Thus, it has been indicated by some authors that the incorporation of 1 wt.% nano-TiO_2 increased the yield stress and viscosity of pastes by 148% and 24%, respectively [36–41]. Studies indicate that the reinforced composite's performance is improved by expediting cement hydration processes. This is achieved by TiO_2 nanoparticles acting as nucleating agents primarily in the initial stages of hydration and facilitating the formation of crystalline compounds, notably calcium silicate hydrate (CSH) and ettringite. As a result, densification of the composite matrix occurs, leading to heightened compressive strength along with diminished pore size and their even distribution within the binder mass [41–46]. Wang et al. [47] found that replacing 1–5% of cementitious composites with NTs resulted in reduced setting time, increased hydration degree, reduced porosity, and enhanced compressive and flexural strength. Different studies [48–50] identified varying optimal percentages of NT replacement, ranging from 1.5% to 10%, with corresponding increases in compressive strength. Regarding flexural strength, there are few reports in the literature, but they indicate an increase of 11% for an optimal amount of 3% NTs [50] and even 51% for an optimal amount of 4% NTs [47]. However, the literature highlights that the use of NTs presents certain challenges, such as identifying the optimal amount of NTs to be added, as excessive quantities may have adverse effects. This is particularly true when it comes to ensuring a homogeneous dispersion of NTs in the composite matrix, as agglomeration can occur, resulting in weak points in the composite [45].

The study of several industrial by-products or recycled materials, such as glass, brick, blast furnace slag, and textolite, as partial replacements for natural aggregates in cementitious composites offers several advantages over focusing on just one material. These materials can be considered aggregates in cementitious composites due to their ability to act as inert filler materials that provide bulk to the composite mixture. Aggregates typically contribute to the mechanical properties of the composite, such as strength and durability, by acting as a framework within the cementitious matrix to distribute loads and resist deformation. While these materials may also have pozzolanic or hydraulic properties, they primarily act as fillers rather than binders, like Portland cement. By replacing some of the natural aggregates with recycled materials, the overall volume of the composite can be maintained, ensuring proper workability and structural integrity [51]. Therefore, considering them as aggregates rather than additives or replacements for Portland cement emphasizes their role in improving the mechanical properties and sustainability of cementitious composites. A comparative analysis of aggregates derived from recycled waste glass (RGA), recycled ceramic brick (RBA), blast furnace slag (GBA), and textolite (RTA) derived from non-metallic waste of electronic equipment, together with the addition of TiO_2 nanoparticles, allows for the performance of different recycled materials to be assessed in terms of their physical, mechanical, and durability properties [7]. RGA, GBA, and RBA are aggregates derived from abundant sources that have been extensively investigated, yielding numerous findings regarding their potential influences on cementitious composites. In contrast, RTA is a less-explored waste material that lacks thorough documentation of its recycling potential in both the construction sector and various other domains. Previous research suggests that the use of recycled waste aggregates and the addition of TiO_2 nanoparticles can have varying effects on the properties of cementitious composites, the magnitude of which depends on the amount used and the granularity and type of crystallization. It is important to note that these effects can be both positive and negative. The challenge is to determine the optimum balance to find the most convenient solution for the use of recyclable waste aggregates while exploring the benefits of a low enough amount of TiO_2 to avoid very high additional costs but high enough to provide mechanical strength and durability benefits for cementitious composites. This comparative approach provides insight into the relative effectiveness of each material and allows the identification of the most suitable options for specific applications where TiO_2 nanoparticles are to be added. In addition, the study of multiple materials provides a more comprehensive understanding of the challenges and opportunities associated with the incorporation of recycled aggregates and TiO_2 nanoparticles into cementitious composites. Each material may exhibit unique characteristics, such as varying particle size distributions, chemical compositions, and hydration behavior, which can influence their performance within the composite matrix. Overall, studying the possibility of substituting multiple recycled materials in cementitious composites in conjunction with the addition of TiO_2 nanoparticles increases the robustness and applicability of research findings, facilitating informed decision-making in the development of sustainable building materials and practices.

Motivated by the above, the aim of this work was to perform an analysis of the influence that the addition of TiO_2 nanoparticles has on the physical–mechanical performance in correlation with microstructurally induced changes in cementitious composites in which natural aggregates are partially substituted by aggregates derived from recycled waste glass (RGA), recycled ceramic brick (RBA), blast furnace slag (GBA), and textolite (RTA) derived from the non-metallic waste of electronic equipment.

2. Materials and Methods

Several types of cementitious composites were designed, prepared, and analyzed for the purpose of the research. Based on the preliminary investigations, which aimed to assess the effect of the incorporation of recycled waste aggregates on the properties of cementitious composites, the current study extends the research initiative with a primary focus on investigating the effects of nano-TiO_2 addition on composite properties. The preliminary investigations carried out in [52] aimed to determine the optimum proportions of natural aggregates replaced by recycled waste aggregates that would produce the most favorable results in terms of the physical and mechanical properties of the composites. In addition, they highlighted the potential need for additional mixing water, depending on the use of specific types of recycled aggregate. The research hypothesis, formulated from an extensive review of the scientific literature and preliminary results, was that the incorporation of NTs would improve composite properties. However, this improvement followed a Gaussian distribution model, and efforts were focused on identifying the optimum level of NT addition. The control composition (R1) was produced using cement, natural aggregates, a superplasticizer additive, and water. In relation to this control composition, based on preliminary research, compositions (R2–R5) were identified, in which part of the natural aggregates were substituted with aggregates from recycled waste glass, brick, blast furnace slag, or textolite. To analyze the influence of TiO_2 nanoparticles on the physical–mechanical performance of cementitious composites, in the cement matrixes of the control sample, respective of the composites in which natural aggregates were substituted with recycled waste aggregates, quantities of 2%, 3%, 4%, and 5% TiO_2 nanoparticles (NTs) were introduced as admixtures, with percentages reported by mass relative to the amount of cement in the composition.

2.1. Raw Materials

The following raw materials were selected for the production of cementitious composites: Portland cement CEM I 52.5 R (HOLCIM Romania, Aleșd, Bihor County, Romania), natural aggregates (NAs) granular class 0/4 mm and 4/8 mm, recycled waste glass aggregates (RGAs) granular class 0/4 mm and 4/8 mm, recycled ceramic brick aggregates (RBAs) granular class 0/4 mm, blast furnace slag (GBA) granular class 0/2 mm, recycled textolite aggregates (RTAs) granular class 0/2 mm, MasterEase 5009 superplasticizer additive

(BASF, Ludwigshafen, Germany), water, and TiO_2 nanoparticles type AEROXIDE® TiO_2 P25 Degussa (Evonik Industries AG, Hanau, Germany). All the recycled waste aggregates were of local origin. The characteristics of the raw materials were as follows:

- Portland cement CEM I 52.5 R was purchased commercially and is characterized by a content of min. 95% Portland clinker and a compressive strength at 28 days of minimum 52.5 N/mm^2 and maximum 62.5 N/mm^2.
- MasterEase 5009 superplasticizer/strong water-reducing additive was purchased commercially.
- TiO_2 nanoparticles of type AEROXIDE® TiO_2 P25, according to the manufacturer's technical data sheet, were characterized by a purity of 99.5%, containing more than 70% anatase crystalline phase.
- Natural aggregates as well as aggregates from recycled waste were characterized by determining the particle size distribution curve according to EN 933-1 [53], bulk density and intergranular porosity according to EN 1097-3 [54], and true mass and water absorption coefficient according to EN 1097-6 [55], as shown in Figures 1–4. Additionally, for blast furnace slag (GBA), the oxide composition was determined by X-ray fluorescence (XRF) analysis (Table 1). The textolite slag was analyzed for residual metal content (Table 2) according to the methodology indicated in specific standard documents [56–59].

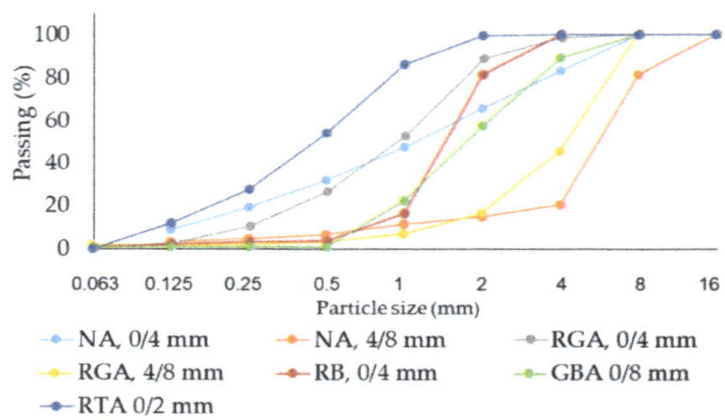

Figure 1. Particle size distribution of the aggregates [52].

Table 1. Characterization of blast furnace slag (GBA) [52].

	SiO_2	Al_2O_3	Fe_2O_3	CaO	MgO	SO_3	Na_2O	K_2O	P_2O_5	TiO_2	Cr_2O_3	Mn_2O_3	P.C.
w%	30.20	10.05	14.70	37.40	4.05	-	0.20	0.38	-	<0.52	<0.05	2.15	-

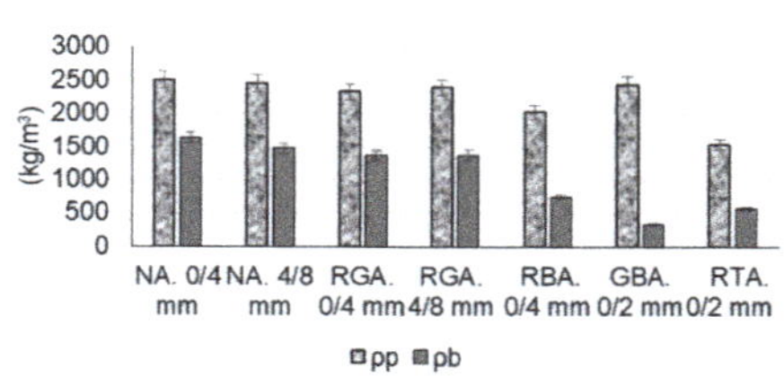

Figure 2. Bulk density (ρ_b) and true density (ρ_p) of the aggregates [52].

Table 2. Characterization of waste textolite (RTA) [52].

	As	Ba	Cd	Cr	Cu	Hg	Mo	Ni	Pb	Sb	Se	Zn
mg/kg	2.85	603.8	<0.03	18.2	1064	<0.003	<3.0	<0.20	<0.30	<0.5	<0.015	12.59

Note: the "<" sign represents values below the detection limit of the method.

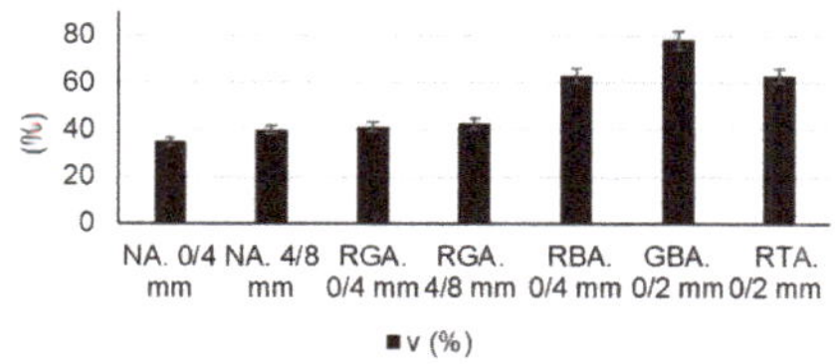

Figure 3. Intergranular bulk porosity (v) of the aggregates [52].

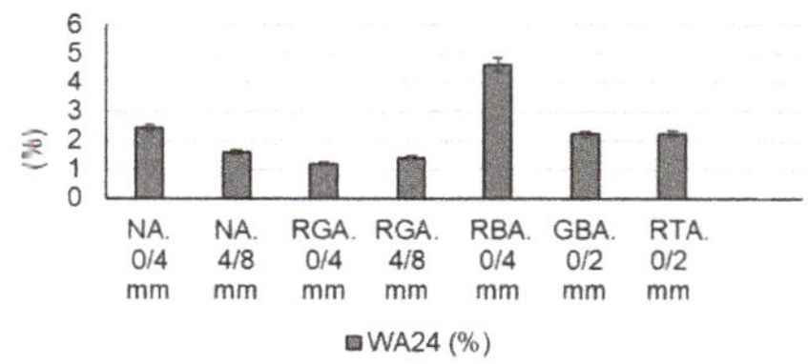

Figure 4. Water absorbtion capacity (WA_{24}) of the aggregates [52].

Example images of the raw materials are shown in Figure 5.

Portland cement CEM I 52.5 R

MasterEase 5009 superplasticizer/strong water-reducing additive

TiO_2 nanoparticles of type AEROXIDE® P25

Natural aggregates (NAs) granular class 0/4 mm

Natural aggregates (NAs) granular class 4/8 mm

Recycled waste glass aggregates (RGAs) granular class 0/4 mm

Recycled waste glass aggregates (RGAs) granular class 4/8 mm

Recycled ceramic brick aggregates (RBAs) granular class 0/4 mm

Blast furnace slag (GBA) granular class 0/2 mm

Recycled textolite aggregates (RTAs) granular class 0/2 mm

Figure 5. Photographs of the raw materials.

2.2. Production of Cementitious Composites

The control sample (R1-0) was designed as a Portland cement and natural aggregate-based mortar with a water/cement ratio of 0.6, according to Table 3 [52].

Table 3. Control sample mixture (R1-0).

Mixture Code	Design Class	Water/ Cement Ratio	Cement (kg/m^3)	Natural Aggregates, Cumulative (kg/m^3)	Natural Aggregates, 0/4 mm (% of Total Aggregates)	Natural Aggregates, 4/8 mm (% of Total Aggregates)	MasterEase 5009 Superplasticizer Additive (% Mass Ratio to Cement Quantity)
R1	C 20/25	0.6	366	1577	70	30	0.5

Subsequently, for each type of waste proposed to partially replace natural aggregates (glass, brick, slag, or textolite), specific recipes R2-0, R3-0, R4-0, and R5-0 were designed starting from the control sample (R1-0). For these mixtures, the code containing the indicator '0' represents the absence of NTs in the composition. The difference from the control sample is that in the compositions R2-0. . .R5-0, part of the amount of natural aggregates was replaced by an equal amount of recycled waste aggregates, with all other parameters remaining constant, as shown in Figure 6. The mix-design in which natural aggregates were substituted with recycled waste aggregates (R2-0. . .R5-0) was based on the condition that each aggregate cumulative distribution curve fell within the favourable range, or at least the usable range, as indicated by the concrete design and preparation standard [60–63]. Since some of the recycled aggregates used (waste ceramic brick (RBA), slag (GBA), and waste textolite (RTA)) were characterized by higher water absorption than natural aggregates, as shown in Figure 4, in order to not influence the workability of the composites and the cement hydration processes because of insufficient water, prior to preparation, these aggregates were immersed for 24 h in water, then drained, and excess water was removed by swabbing.

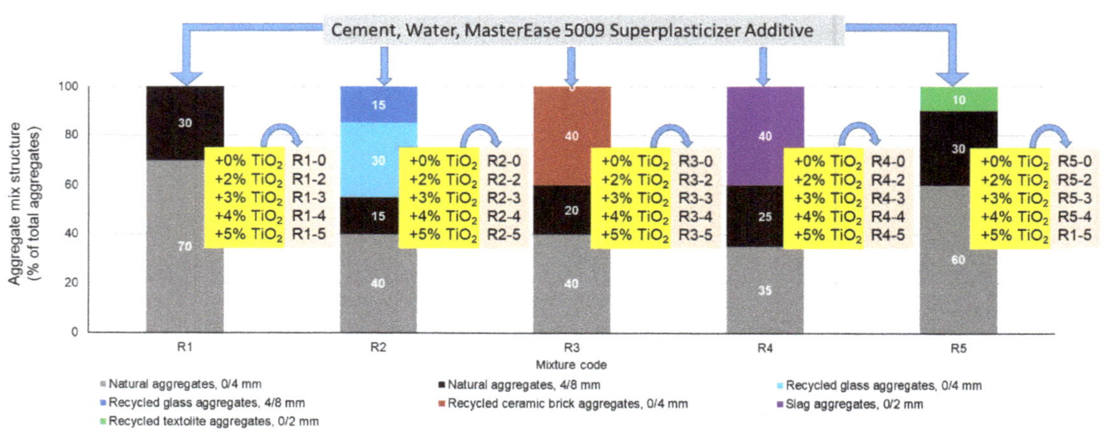

Figure 6. Raw materials used, mixture structure of aggregates, amount of NTs added, and composition identification code for the cement composite mixtures where natural aggregates were substituted with recycled waste aggregates.

In the next step, for each designed mixture in which natural aggregates were substituted by recycled waste aggregates, compositional variants were developed in which 2%, 3%, 4%, or 5% TiO_2 nanoparticles were added as a mass percentage of the cement quantity. In total, 25 mixtures of cementitious composites were designed and developed. Figure 6 shows the raw materials used, the compositional structure of the aggregates, the amount of NTs added, and the identification code of the compositions according to the types of aggregates and NT content.

For all the compositions prepared, the quantity of cement was kept constant, the quantity of superplasticizer additive used was 0.5%, mass percentages referred to the quantity of cement, and the mixing water was determined considering as a reference indicator the workability expressed by the diameter of the cake on the spreading mass for which the condition of falling within the range 175 ± 10 mm was set. The raw materials were weighed using a KERN FKB 36K0.1 balance (KERN & SOHN GmbH, Balingen, Germany) with an accuracy of 0.1 g.

The preparation of the cementitious composites was achieved by mixing the dry raw materials with water and the MasterEase 5009 superplasticizer additive using an ELE paddle mixer (ELE International Ltd., Milton Keynes, UK).

Based on literature references [36,40,42,46,64–66], it is known that NTs are also "consuming" water; therefore, in order not to jeopardize the hydration–hydrolysis reactions of cement due to insufficient water as a result of its absorption by NTs, the amount of water was adjusted so that the workability parameter of the composite remained constant and similar to that of NT-free composites, i.e., the diameter of the cake on the spreading mass, according to EN 196-3 [67], was in the range 175 ± 10 mm. Another difficulty that arose during this stage of the research was ensuring homogeneous dispersion of NTs in the cementitious matrix. Additionally, adjusting the amount of water for preparation proved to be challenging. Due to their tendency to agglomerate and form deposits or islands, which can reduce the yield of benefits induced by photo-activation and even cause negative effects on the physical–mechanical performance of the composite, representing points of vulnerability [7,34–59,64–66,68–70], a method was chosen for the incorporation of NTs. The raw materials were pre-mixed in the dry phase, and then water and the superplasticizer additive were added.

To maintain the consistency of the fresh composite, based on preliminary tests, it was determined that mixing water supplementation was necessary, both depending on the type of waste used and the amount of NTs added to the mass. Thus, for every 1% NTs added to the composite mass, the mixing water was supplemented by approximately 1.8–3.5 kg water/m^3 composite, resulting in w/c ratios of w/c = 0.625 for R1-5 and w/c = 0.65 for R5-5, with all other w/c ratio values falling within these limits.

For each casting batch, the specimens were made by casting the fresh composite in metal molds with dimensions 40 × 40 × 160 mm and in metal molds with dimensions 70 × 70 × 70 mm. After casting, the specimens were kept in the molds for 24 h in a humid air box at a constant temperature of 20 ± 1 °C and a relative humidity of min. 90%, then demolded and kept submerged in water at a temperature of 20 ± 2 °C until reaching the age of 28 days.

2.3. *Analysis of the Physical–Mechanical Performances of Cementitious Composites*

The test specimens were tested at the age of 28 days after casting. The following performance indicators were determined and analyzed for each type of cementitious composite: hardened density according to the standard method given in EN 1015-10 [71]; compressive strength and flexural strength according to the standard method given in EN 1015-11 [72] using ADR Auto 250/25 test equipment (ELE International Ltd., Milton Keynes, UK) with an accuracy of 0.01 kN; abrasion wear resistance (Bohme wear) according to the standard method given in EN 1338 [73]; capillary water absorption according to the standard method given in EN 1015-18 [70].

Weighing of specimens was conducted using a KERN FKB 36K0.1 balance (KERN & SOHN GmbH, Balingen, Germany) with an accuracy of 0.1 g and measurement of dimensions using an electronic calliper gauge with an accuracy of 0.01 mm.

Testing was carried out under laboratory conditions of 23 °C and 60% relative air humidity for a series of 3 sets of identical specimens, reporting the result as the arithmetic mean of the individual results.

2.4. Microstructural Analysis of Cementitious Composites

The visual macrostructural analysis of cementitious composites was initially conducted without optical magnification equipment to assess the uniformity of aggregate distribution in the cementitious binder matrix. Subsequently, a LEICA SAPO optical microscope (Leica Microsystems, GmbH, Wetzlar, Germany) was used for microscopic analysis to examine the distribution at the macroporosity level.

A JEOL/JSM 5600—LV scanning electron microscope (JEOL Ltd., Tokyo, Japan) operating in the secondary electron imaging (SEI) mode at 15 kV acceleration voltage was used to take SEM and EDS images. As part of the preparation process, the samples were gold coated by plasma sputtering to improve the electrical conductivity for electron microscopy analysis. Phase identification in the samples was carried out using X-ray diffraction (XRD) in the angular range $2\theta = 20-85°$. An INEL Equinox 3000 diffractometer (Thermo Fisher Scientific S.p.A., Milan, Italy) using Co-Kα radiation (λ = 1.7903 Å) was used.

3. Results and Discussions

3.1. Influence of the Addition of TiO_2 Nanoparticles on the Physical–Mechanical Characteristics of Cementitious Composites

The experimental results indicate, in terms of the density of cement composites in the hardened state (Figure 7 and Table 4), the following:

- The addition of NTs leads to the densification of the composites. This increase in bulk density occurs in all composites, regardless of whether natural aggregates have been substituted with recycled waste aggregates.
- The most significant increases in bulk density are recorded for the cases where NAs were not substituted with recycled aggregates (7.40–4.66% compared to the sample without NT content, R1-0). However, it can be observed that this increase in density is lower in the case of compositions with a higher addition of NTs.
- The smallest increases in bulk density are recorded for the cases where NAs were substituted with RTAs (0.24–1.41% compared to the NT-free sample, R5-0). This time, it was observed that this increase in density could not be correlated with the amount of NTs introduced as an addition. This non-uniform variation in the parameter could be interpreted as a sign of the inhomogeneity of the distribution of the components, i.e., the difficulty of homogeneous distribution in the composite matrix, on the one hand of RTAs and on the other hand of NTs, concomitant with the inhomogeneity of the formation of cement hydration compounds and pore distribution.
- Regarding the evolution of the parameter for the other recycled aggregate types, in the case of RGAs, there is an increase of 0.88–1.99% compared to the sample without NTs (R2-0); in the case of RBAs, the increase is within 2.11–6.92% compared to the sample without NTs (R3-0); and in the case of GBAs, the increase is within 3.47–3.92% compared to the sample without NTs (R4-0).

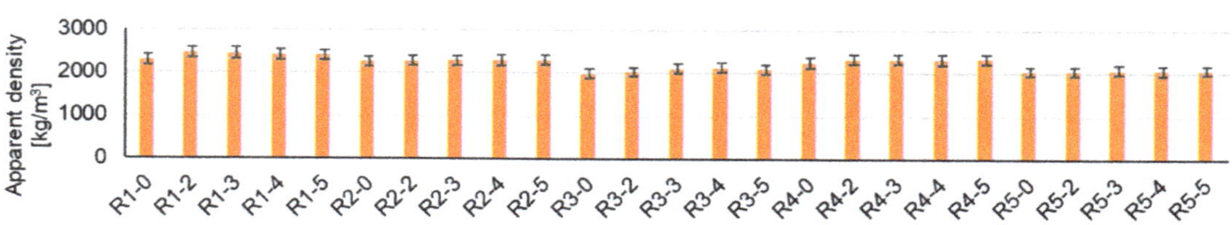

Figure 7. Apparent density.

In terms of mechanical strengths (compressive strength, Figure 8; flexural strength, Figure 9), for all cementitious composites, with or without substitution of NAs with recycled waste aggregates, a positive effect is observed due to the introduction of NTs into the composite mass (Table 4). This increase in mechanical strength is influenced both by the amount of NTs used as an admixture and by the nature of the aggregates. Thus, in general, an addition of 3% NTs (by mass, relative to the amount of cement) is favorable for increasing the compressive strength (Figure 8) for all types of composites, except for composites in which NAs have been substituted with GBAs, for which the effect is maximum for 4% NTs (by mass, relative to the amount of cement). Overall, the increase in compressive strength due to the introduction of NTs into the composite matrix is not large. Compared to the control samples specific to each type of aggregate (R1-0, R2-0, R3-0, R4-0, or R5-0), this increase in compressive strength shows maximums of: 2.62% for the case of natural aggregate compositions (R1-3); 0.95% for RGA compositions (R2-3); 1.94% for RBA compositions (R3-3); 1.70% for GBA compositions (R4-4); and 16.23% for RTA compositions (R5-3). A significant increase in compressive strength is noted for the RTA compositions. This could be interpreted as an indication of the fact that the nanoparticles present in the binder mass, through their function as nucleating agents and the positive influences they have on the formation of cement hydration compounds, probably manage to contribute significantly to mitigating the negative effect of partial substitution of NAs with RTAs.

Table 4. The average values of the experimental results.

Code	w/c Ratio	Apparent Density (kg/m^3)	Flexural Strength (N/mm^2)	Compressive Strength (N/mm^2)	Abrasion Resistance (% Mass Loss)	Coefficient of Water Absorption by Capillarity (kg/m^{2}min$^{0.5}$)
R1-0	0.60	2293	8.27	59.18	5.71	0.16
R1-2	0.61	2463	8.32	60.03	5.24	0.10
R1-3	0.62	2453	8.72	60.73	3.16	0.09
R1-4	0.62	2411	8.71	59.38	2.64	0.04
R1-5	0.63	2405	8.92	59.04	2.40	0.03
R2-0	0.60	2262	8.24	56.93	3.41	0.09
R2-2	0.61	2282	8.22	56.98	3.19	0.09
R2-3	0.62	2287	8.28	57.47	3.13	0.08
R2-4	0.62	2291	8.24	57.43	3.56	0.08
R2-5	0.63	2307	8.03	56.47	3.36	0.07
R3-0	0.61	1993	8.31	57.75	5.12	0.27
R3-2	0.62	2035	8.38	57.79	5.09	0.25
R3-3	0.63	2111	8.64	58.87	4.91	0.12
R3-4	0.64	2131	8.51	58.04	4.83	0.11
R3-5	0.64	2095	8.40	58.23	4.96	0.09
R4-0	0.61	2246	9.67	68.96	4.93	0.08
R4-2	0.62	2332	9.78	69.01	4.33	0.04
R4-3	0.63	2331	10.17	69.55	4.45	0.03
R4-4	0.64	2324	10.47	70.13	4.19	0.03
R4-5	0.65	2334	10.40	69.88	4.68	0.04
R5-0	0.62	2054	8.15	37.58	4.68	0.37
R5-2	0.64	2059	8.32	43.31	4.55	0.34
R5-3	0.64	2083	8.50	43.68	4.23	0.16
R5-4	0.65	2072	8.51	43.30	4.76	0.14
R5-5	0.65	2077	8.06	35.19	5.17	0.11

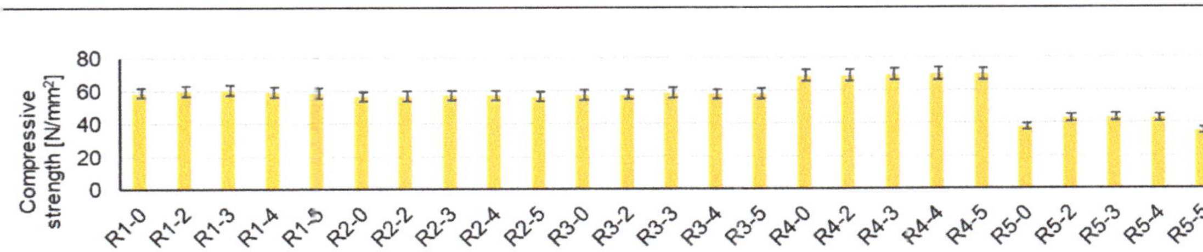

Figure 8. Compressive strength.

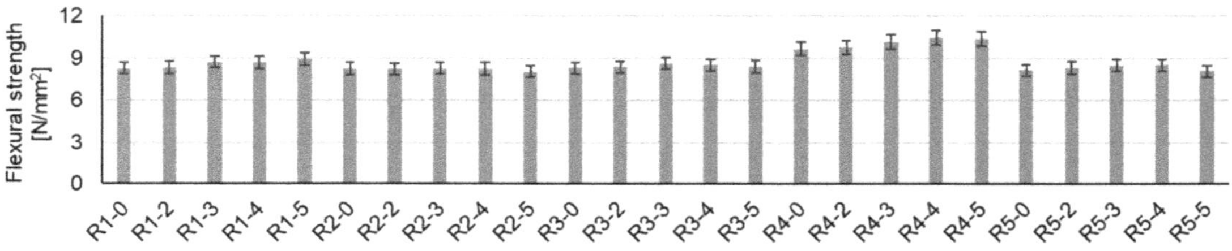

Figure 9. Flexural strength.

Although lower compared to some reports in the literature [43,68,74–77], which show compressive strength increases of 10% to 80%, depending on test age and NT content (1–4 wt.% NT), it can be said that the research results are in agreement with these reports, maintaining an increasing trend, and in contradiction with those indicated by Shekari and Razzaghi [60], who for a cementitious composite with 1.5% NTs report a reduction in compressive strength of 20.73% at the age of 28 days.

In terms of flexural tensile strength (Figure 9), the results show less obvious improvements with NTs, but in a similar trend to the compressive strength. Thus, the greatest increases in flexural strength can be identified from 8.27 N/mm^2 (R1-0) to 8.92 N/mm^2 (R1-5) for NA compositions; from 8.24 N/mm^2 (R2-0) to 8.28 N/mm^2 (R2-3) for RGA compositions; from 8.31 N/mm^2 (R3-0) to 8.64 N/mm^2 (R3-3) for RBA compositions; from 9.67 N/mm^2 (R4-0) to 10.47 N/mm^2 (R4-4) for GBA compositions; and from 8.15 N/mm^2 (R5-0) to 8.51 N/mm^2 (R2-4) for RTA compositions. As can be seen, the most favorable situations are also for additions of 3% or 4% NTs (mass percentage, relative to the amount of cement).

Abrasion mass loss, the indicator inversely proportional to abrasion resistance (Figure 10 and Table 4), is also influenced by both the nature of the aggregates and the addition of NTs. Thus, in the case of composites with NAs, there is an increasing improvement in abrasion resistance with the increasing addition of NTs, with the best performance for 5% NTs (by mass, relative to the amount of cement). However, this trend is not maintained for the composites in which NAs were partially substituted by recycled waste aggregates, with the most favorable results (lowest mass loss) for 3% or 4% NTs (mass, relative to the amount of cement) as follows: 8.21% decrease in mass loss compared to the control composition (R2-0) for 3% NTs in the composition with RGAs (R2-3); 5.66% decrease in mass loss compared to the control composition (R3-0) for 4% NTs in the composition with RBAs (R3-4); 15% decrease in mass loss compared to the control composition (R4-0) for 4% NTs in the composition with GBAs (R4-4); and 9.62% decrease in mass loss compared to the control composition (R5-0) for 3% NTs in the composition with RTAs (R5-4). A notable phenomenon was observed in the case of composites prepared using only NAs, where wear resistance increased significantly with the increase in the amount of NTs. This observation is consistent with the results reported in the literature and corresponds to the increasing trends observed for compressive and flexural strength and the decreasing trend for water absorption. These results support the hypothesis of matrix densification in the composite as a result of the addition of NTs. Despite the less pronounced improvement trends observed for compressive and flexural strength, it is noteworthy that these behaviors are underpinned by microstructural phenomena such as porosity and microcracking, which are likely to be more pronounced within the bulk rather than the surface layer of the specimen. This surface layer is subjected to abrasion, whereas the entire bulk of the composite is subjected to loading in the case of the other two strength properties.

From the point of view of water behavior and the coefficient of water absorption by capillarity (Figure 11 and Table 4), it is influenced by both the nature of the aggregates and the addition of NTs. On the one hand, the substitution of natural aggregates with those from waste induces an increase or decrease in water absorption, depending on their nature. Thus, the partial substitution of natural aggregates (NAs) with aggregates from glass waste (RGA) or slag (GBA) leads to an improvement in this performance; the water absorption coefficient by capillarity decreases compared to the composition containing only natural aggregates (R1-0), while the aggregates from ceramic brick waste (RBA) or textolite (RTA) have the reverse effect. With the introduction of TiO_2 nanoparticles in cementitious compositions, an improvement in this performance is observed for all analyzed cases, more so as the addition is higher. It is also noted that the use of NTs can counteract the negative effects of ceramic brick waste aggregates (RBAs) or textolite (RTA), the most significant reductions in the indicator being recorded in these situations. In the case of brick waste (RBA) or textolite (RTA), it is assessed that 3% NTs can lead to a composition with a water absorption coefficient approximately equal to or even slightly better compared to that of a composition with natural aggregates (0.12 kg/m^{2}min$^{0.5}$ for R3-3 and 0.16 kg/m^{2}min$^{0.5}$ for R5-3 compared to 0.16 kg/m^{2}min$^{0.5}$ for R1-0).

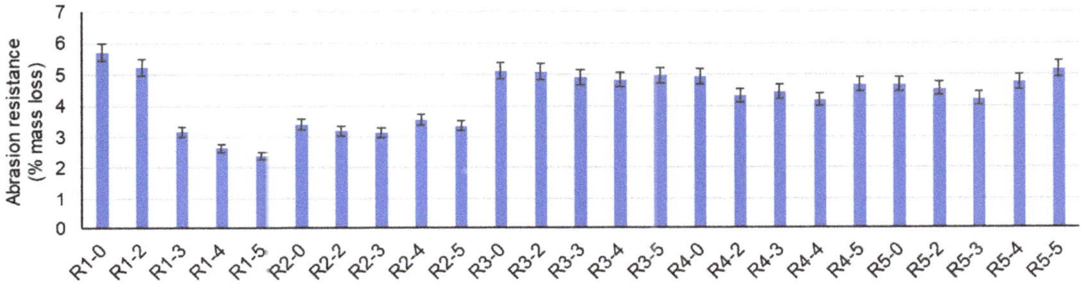

Figure 10. Abrasion resistance.

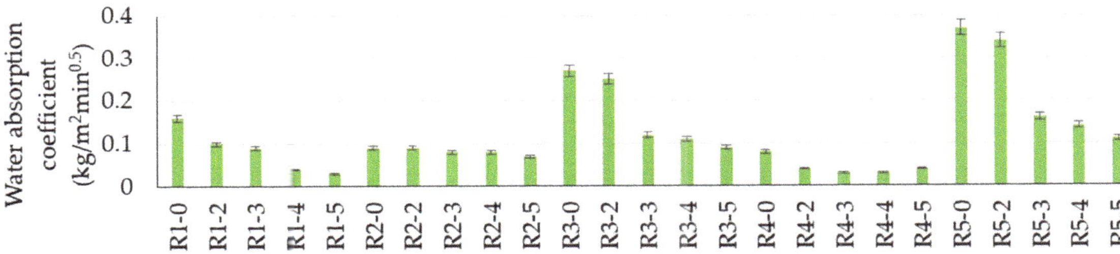

Figure 11. Water absorption coefficient.

3.2. *Influence of TiO_2 Nanoparticle Addition on the Structure and Microstructure of Cementitious Composites*

In the case of composites without NTs, visual analysis without optical magnification (Figure 12) indicates a homogeneous distribution of natural aggregates and aggregates from recycled waste in the cementitious binder mass without segregation areas. However, a clear influence of the type of recycled aggregate on the texture of the composite is identified. Thus, the most obvious change in texture is observed in the case of composites with RTAs, where, due to the poor adhesion between the cementitious binder matrix and the recycled aggregate part, the RTA granules are weakly bound, have a random orientation, and have a disorganized appearance in the crack of the composite (Figure 12e). In the case of cementitious composites with 2–5% NT content, the visual analysis records the same homogeneous distribution of aggregates in the binder matrix and the preservation of the specific appearance for the composite with RTA, regardless of the amount of NTs introduced at preparation. Figure 13 exemplifies the appearance of these composites.

Figure 12. Fracture aspect for cementitious composites made without NTs. (**a**) Cementitious composite with NA; (**b**) Cementitious composite with NA partially substituted with RGA; (**c**) Cementitious composite with NA partially substituted with RBA; (**d**) Cementitious composite with NA partially substituted with GBA; (**e**) Cementitious composite with NA partially substituted with RTA.

Figure 13. Section appearance of cementitious composites made with NT-exemplary images. (**a**) Cementitious composite with NA, R1-3; (**b**) Cementitious composite with NA partially substituted with RGA, R2-3; (**c**) Cementitious composite with NA partially substituted with RBA, R3-4; (**d**) Cementitious composite with NA partially substituted with GBA, R4-3; (**e**) Cementitious composite with NA partially substituted with RTA, R5-4.

Optical microscope analysis of NT-free composites, exemplified in Figure 14, highlights the changes that substitution of natural aggregates (NAs) with aggregates from recycled waste induces on the macroporosity of the composites. Thus, for the control composite, pores with dimensions ranging from 0.40–1.1 mm are identified in the binder matrix, with the binder evenly enclosing the aggregate grain. The substitution of NA with RGA causes a numerical increase in the pores simultaneously with the reduction in their dimensions (dimensions generally in the range 0.27–0.60 mm and rarely over 0.8 mm). Additionally, the AN or RGA granules are well embedded in the binder matrix. When RBA is used as a replacement aggregate for NAs, a good incorporation in the binder matrix is observed, with a uniform distribution of pores, more numerous compared to the control, but with smaller dimensions (0.109–0.335 mm). The use of GBA as a substituent aggregate has similar effects, with a uniform distribution of pores in the binder matrix that is more numerous, with dimensions in the range of 0.107–0.500 mm. However, the main difference is observed when RTA is used: at the RTA–cement binder interface, there are numerous areas of no contact, the distribution of RTA in the binder matrix is relatively inhomogeneous, as is the porosity, which is unevenly distributed, and the pore dimensions have large variations, with the diameter reaching almost 1 mm.

When NTs are introduced into the composite mass, a reduction in pore size is observed in the range of 0.25–0.8 mm for compositions prepared with NAs only and with 2–5% NTs. For composites with 2–5% NT and RGA content, the pore dimensions are in the range of 0.15–0.51 mm; for composites with RBA content, the pore dimensions are in the range of 0.12–0.30 mm; for composites with GBA content, the pore dimensions are in the range of 0.10–0.45 mm; and for composites with RTA content, the pore dimensions are in the range of 0.50–0.85 mm. Example images are shown in Figure 15. Based on these observations, a decrease in pore size can be seen, which is less pronounced in the case of composites with RBA or GBA and more pronounced in the case of composites with NA, RGA, and RTA.

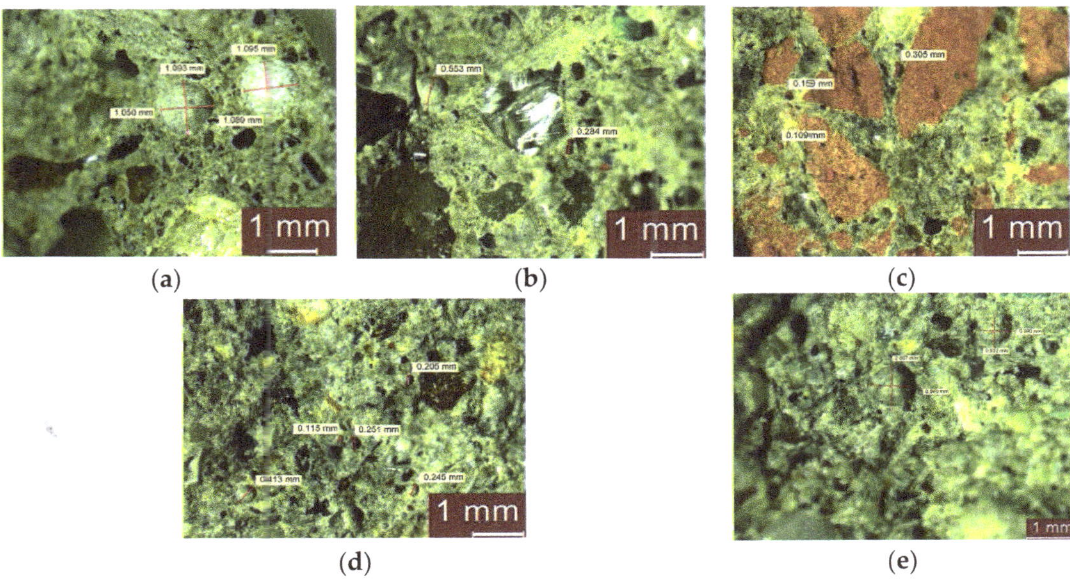

Figure 14. Microscopic analysis of cementitious composites without NTs but (**a**) with NA; (**b**) with NA partially substituted with RGA; (**c**) with NA partially substituted with RBA; (**d**) with NA partially substituted with GBA; and (**e**) with NA partially substituted with RTA.

Figure 15. Microscopic analysis of cementitious composites with NTs (**a**) with NA, R1-3; (**b**) with NA partially substituted with RGA, R2-5nt; (**c**) with NA partially substituted with RBA, R3-2nt; (**d**) with NA partially substituted with GBA, R4-2nt; and (**e**) with NA partially substituted with RTA, R5-3NT.

Figure 16 depicts the SEM images of the cementitious composite with NA (Figure 16a) and the cementitious composites with NA partially substituted with RGA (Figure 16b), RBA (Figure 16c), GBA (Figure 16d), and RTA (Figure 16e).

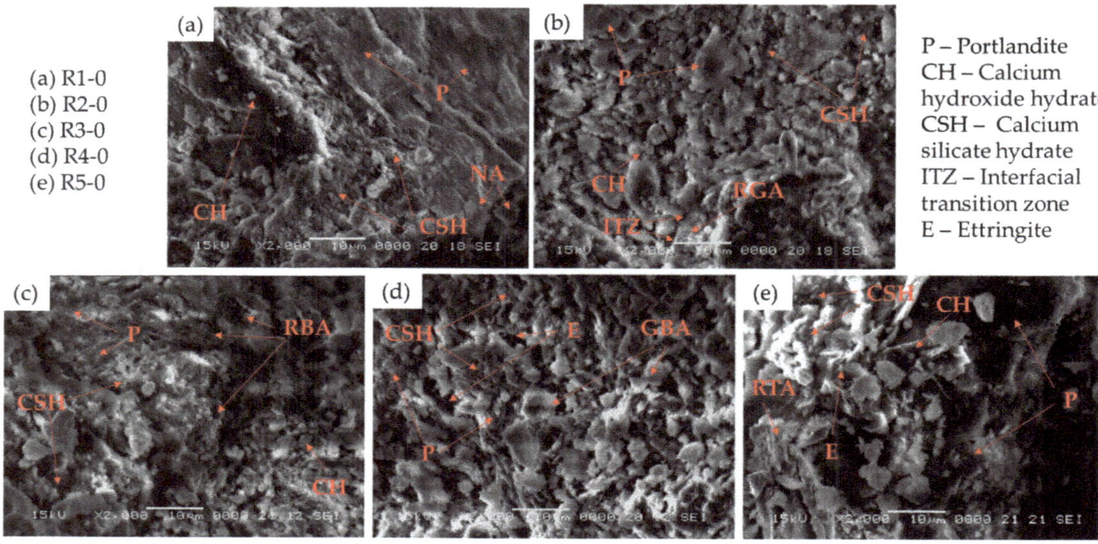

Figure 16. SEM images of the samples without NTs: (**a**) NA sample R1-0; (**b**) Cementitious composite with NA partially substituted with RGA, R2-0; (**c**) Cementitious composite with NA partially substituted with RBA, R3-0; (**d**) Cementitious composite with NA partially substituted with GBA, R4-0; (**e**) Cementitious composite with NA partially substituted with RTA, R5-0.

The compatibility of the natural aggregate, as well as RBA, GBA, and RTA, with the cement is shown to be cohesive, forming a coalesced mass with no visible cracks between the aggregates and the cement matrix. However, in the case of the sample containing RGA, there is a distinct interfacial transition zone (ITZ) between the aggregate surface and the cement matrix, indicating a weaker compatibility between RGA and the cement paste, as confirmed by the slight decrease in flexural strength and compressive strength. The SEM images indicate that the NA, RBA, and RTA samples present a finer pore structure than those containing RGA and GBA. The main hydration products observable for all samples are the rod-like crystals of ettringite (E), the calcium hydroxide hydrate (CH), and the calcium silicate hydrate (CSH), a highly porous, poorly crystalline structure. Ettringite precipitation occurs during the hydration process of Portland cement when calcium aluminate reacts with calcium sulfate, and its presence depends on the ratio of tricalcium aluminate. Variations in the ettringite ratio, correlated with its permeability to water and interaction with other chemical species, have a significant impact on the structural progression during cement hydration, which in turn affects the resulting properties of the cement. Ettringite formation, which is critical in determining the setting rate of the highly reactive aluminate phases, dominates the initial phase of cement hydration. A direct result of this process is volume expansion in fresh concrete, which has been proven to cause cracking in cured concrete during events such as delayed ettringite formation (DEF) and sulfate attack cement degradation [61].

In Figure 16a, an SEM micrograph illustrates the cementitious composite with natural aggregates (R1-0). The image shows a heterogeneous material where portlandite dominates the surface and emerges as the primary product after 28 days of concrete curing. As a result of the consumption of portlandite in the pozzolanic reaction, areas rich in CSH can be observed in the image. The RGA sample (Figure 16b) shows a relatively dense structure with no apparent cracks or pores. Extensive regions of CSH and portlandite cover most of the surface, leaving only a thin region representing the interfacial transition zone between the aggregate particle and the cement matrix. The glass granules, with sizes of 0/4 mm and 4/8 mm, are evenly dispersed within the concrete matrix. However, due to the presence of sharp particle edges and a smooth matrix surface, the possibility of insufficient bonding between the cement mortar and glass particles arises. Furthermore, the formation of CSH gel in aggregated networks with relatively small pores, combined with the limited water absorption capacity of the glass (in contrast to fine glass powder used as a concrete replacement in previous studies [62,63]), resulted in a small decrease in compressive strength.

Similarly, Figure 16c–e illustrates the morphology of the RBA, GBA, and RTA samples. There is no discernible ITZ for the RBA and GBA samples; however, an ITZ is evident in the sample containing RTA. The RBA has a porous structure with a rough, irregular surface, which greatly enhances the interlocking between the two surfaces. The compactness of the sample can also be attributed to the pozzolanic reaction between the RBA and the $Ca(OH)_2$ crystals, facilitated by the absorption of free water in the concrete resulting from the introduction of RBA as well. This reaction likely contributed to a decrease in the porosity of the hardened matrix, consequently leading to an increase in the overall flexural strength. In the sample containing GBA, the microstructure reveals the presence of several characteristic mineral phases. Larger pores with ettringite needles are distributed throughout the matrix, and the surface is predominantly covered by reticulated CSH gel. In addition, small areas show the presence of portlandite crystals. Angular particles of GBA are scattered throughout the microstructure, indicating incomplete hydration of the slag. This incomplete hydration is attributed to the lower reaction activity of the slag compared to that of the Portland cement. However, it is the foil-like, dense, crack-free, amorphous gel structure that provides the benefits of slag in increasing the compressive and flexural strength of composites. With respect to the RTA sample, the microstructure shows a dense composition with portlandite as the dominant mineral phase. Notable hydration products include ettringite and CSH gel. Thicker rod-like structures corresponding to the RTA are observed in the microstructure and appear to be well embedded in the cementitious matrix. However, the adhesion between the sleek surface of RTA and the smooth cementitious matrix is limited. This, coupled with the absence of any pozzolanic effect from RTA, has resulted in a significant reduction in compressive strength and a notable decrease in flexural strength.

The SEM micrographs of samples R1-3, R2-3, R3-3, R4-3, and R5-3 after 28 days of curing are shown in Figure 17. In the NA sample containing 3% NTs (Figure 17a), the microstructure consists mainly of reticulated CSH gel, with only small areas of portlandite visible. This phenomenon can be attributed to the TiO_2 particles acting as nucleating agents, particularly in the early stages of the hydration process, thereby accelerating cement hydration and promoting the formation of crystalline compounds. A similar trend is observed for the RGA, RBA, GBA, and RTA samples. In the case of the RGA sample (Figure 17b), the ITZ is less pronounced, with RGA particles exhibiting greater cohesion with the cementitious matrix. Pores containing needle-shaped ettringites are scattered in areas of RGA. Figure 17c shows the sample containing RGA + 3% NTs (R3-3), where portlandite crystals are rarely observed in the analyzed area and CSH gel appears as the predominant hydration product with no discernible ITZ.

Within the BGA microstructure (Figure 17d), numerous large pores filled with ettringite ($3CaO$-Al_2O_3-$3CaSO_4$-$32H_2O$) can be observed, indicating a similar hydration mechanism between GBA and Portland cement. Unreacted GBA particles, together with portlandite crystals, can be identified throughout the investigated area. In comparison, the RTA sample (Figure 17e) shows only a few areas of ettringite. CSH emerges as the predominant hydration product, with small clusters of portlandite identified throughout the observed section. The rod-shaped RTA particles are sparse and barely discernible within the cementitious matrix due to the extensive coverage by CSH, influenced by the presence of TiO_2 nanoparticles during the hydration process.

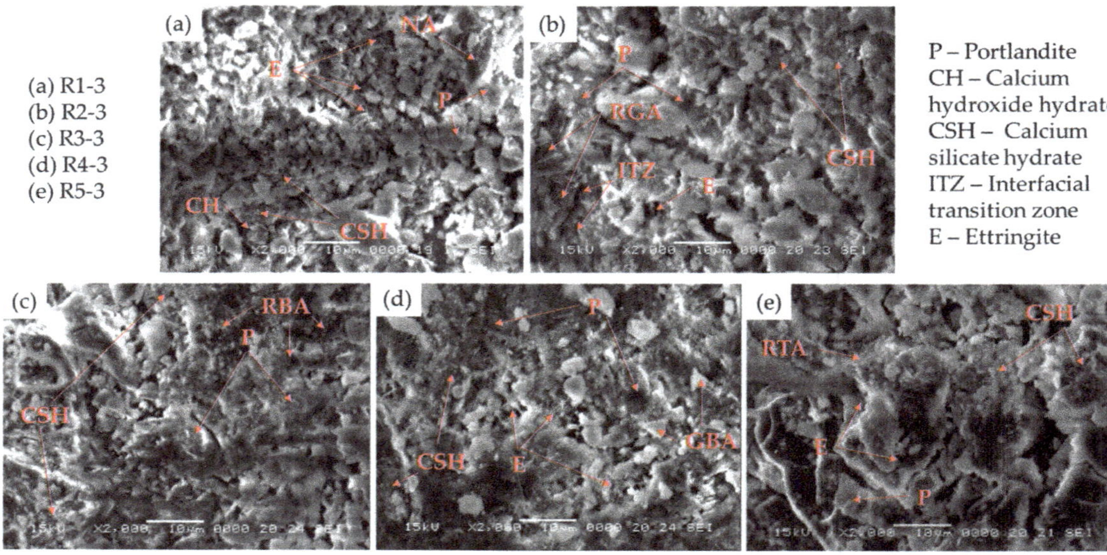

Figure 17. SEM images of the samples containing NTs: (**a**) NA sample R1-3; (**b**) Cementitious composite with NA partially substituted with RGA, R2-3; (**c**) Cementitious composite with NA partially substituted with RBA, R3-3; (**d**) Cementitious composite with NA partially substituted with GBA, R4-3; (**e**) Cementitious composite with NA partially substituted with RTA, R5-3.

The prevalent presence of CSH gel as the primary hydration product is observed, exhibiting reduced porosity compared to images of samples lacking NTs, showcasing a dense, sheet-like structure spanning considerable surface areas. The absence of distinct regions featuring portlandite, which typically exhibits lower elastic modulus and hardness, alongside the emergence of ettringite likely contributed to the enhanced compressive and flexural strength observed in the majority of samples following NT incorporation. Moreover, the increase in abrasion resistance of the samples containing NTs can be explained by their higher compressive and flexural strengths.

Figure 18 displays the EDX spectra of samples, including (a) NTs and 3% NTs (R1-3); (b) NA partially substituted with RGA + 3% NTs (R2-3); (c) NA partially substituted with RBA + 3% NTs (R3-3); (d) NA partially substituted with BGA + 3% NTs (R4-3); and (e) NA partially substituted with RTA + 3% NTs (R5-3). The spectra were recorded at different selected punctual areas to gather additional information regarding the elemental composition of specific regions. The distribution of three different elements, respectively, Ca, Si, and Ti, has been considered in all samples. Therefore, it can be seen that Ca is evenly distributed in all the R1-3 to R5-3 samples over the whole examined area. In the sample containing NA + 3% NTs (Figure 18a), Si is evenly distributed over the area examined. However, in the sample containing RGA (Figure 18b), Si appears to be preferentially distributed in certain locations due to the higher content resulting from the presence of recycled glass aggregates. Similar to R1-3, the sample containing RGB + 3% NTs (Figure 18c) shows an area of uniform Si distribution, whereas for the samples containing GBA + 3% NTs and RTA + 3% NTs, the distribution of Si appears to be less dense and more localized to specific areas of the sample. Ti appears to be uniformly scattered in all samples, suggesting a homogeneous distribution of TiO_2 in the cementitious composite.

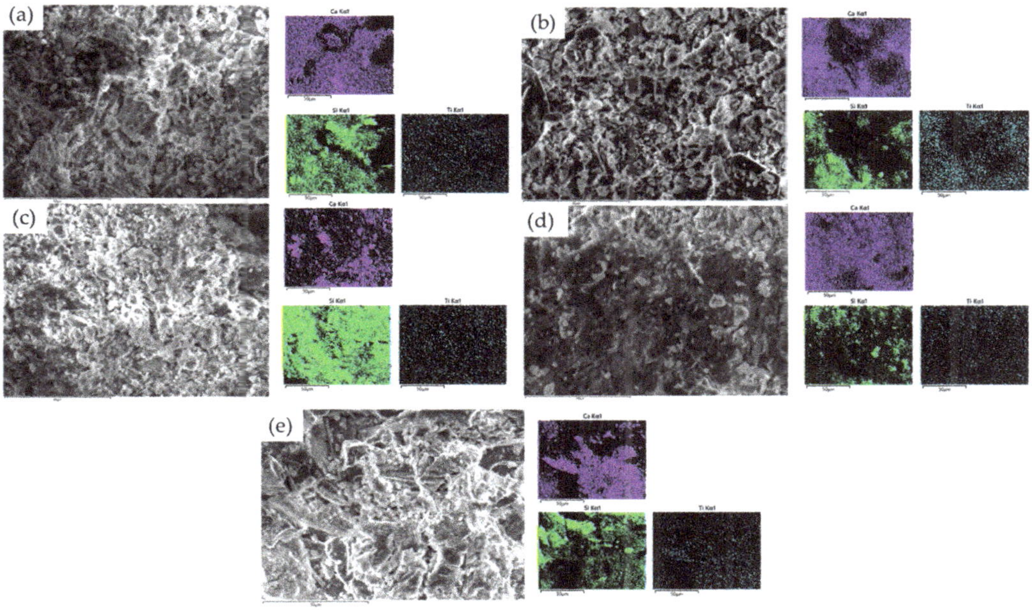

Figure 18. SEM and EDX images of the samples containing (**a**) NTs and 3% NTs (R1-3); (**b**) NA partially substituted with RGA + 3% NTs (R2-3); (**c**) NA partially substituted with RBA + 3% NTs (R3-3); (**d**) NA partially substituted with BGA + 3% NTs (R4-3); (**e**) NA partially substituted with RTA + 3% NTs (R5-3).

Figure 19 presents the comparison XRD patterns of the samples without NTs, R1-0 to R5-0 (Figure 19a), and the samples containing 3% NTs, R1-3 to R5-3 (Figure 19b). Figure 19a reveals the presence of primary peaks characteristic of ordinary Portland cement, such as calcite—$CaCO_3$ (present at 2θ = 25.2°, 31.5°, and 33.9°), aluminoferrite—$Ca_6Al_4Fe_2O_{15}$ (present at 2θ = 27.9°, 38.1°, and 55.4°), and portlandite—$Ca(OH)_2$ (present at 2θ = 21.0°, and 40.2°). In addition, Figure 19b presents the XRD pattern for the anatase and rutile phases of the TiO_2 nanoparticles. As it can be observed in the spectra for the samples R1-3 to R5-3, the presence of peaks specific for the anatase phase of the nano-TiO_2 particles is noticeable at 2θ = 29.6°, 43.1°, 57.2°, and 64.1°. Several peaks corresponding to the rutile phase of the TiO_2 nanoparticles can be observed in different spectra at 2θ = 32.5° for R3-3 and R5-3, 42.9° for R2-3, and 53.7° for R1-3 and R4-3. This underlines the lack of chemical interaction between the TiO_2 nanoparticles and the cementitious matrix and the clear presence of a predominantly anatase phase in the samples containing 3% NTs.

Summarizing the experimental results, it can be concluded that the incorporation of NTs improves the densification of the cementitious composite matrix, as demonstrated by both the physical–mechanical parameters and the microstructural investigations, potentially heralding an improvement in durability. However, an overarching observation is that, while the properties of the aggregates used significantly enhance the physical–mechanical performance, the optimum percentage of NTs to maximize the benefits varies from case to case. The increase in matrix densification is most strongly supported by the variation in water absorption coefficient and the progression of compressive, flexural, and abrasion strengths, whereas the influence on apparent density is less pronounced. This phenomenon is likely to be due to localized microstructural changes in porosity, as evidenced by SEM and EDS analyses, which pose a challenge in quantifying their representation in the high values expressed for apparent density.

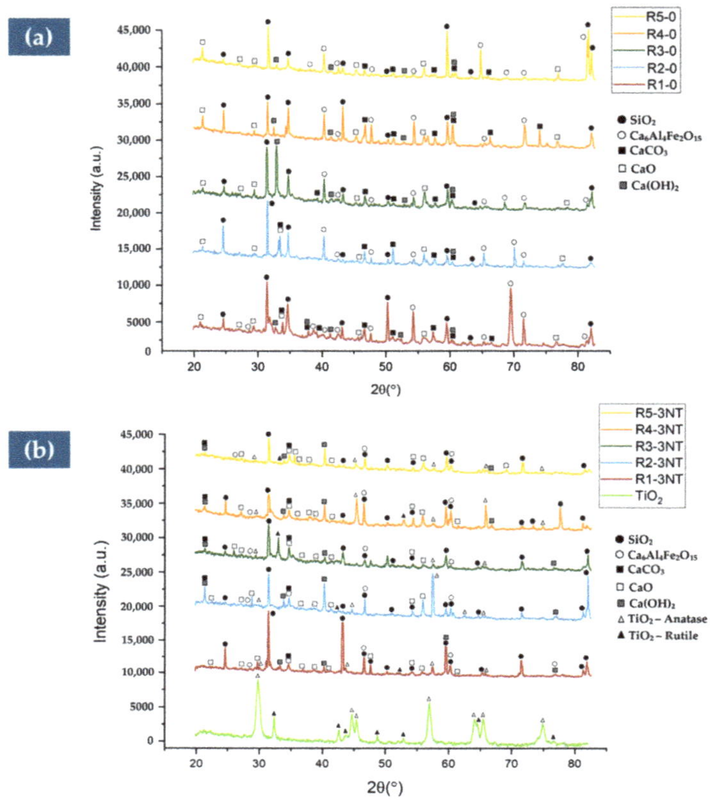

Figure 19. XRD patterns of the (**a**) samples R1-0 to R5-0, without the NTs; (**b**) samples R1-3 to R5-3, with NTs.

4. Conclusions

The study of recycled materials such as glass, brick, blast furnace slag, and textolite as partial replacements for natural aggregates in cementitious composites offers several advantages, including improved mechanical properties and sustainability. By analyzing these materials alongside TiO_2 nanoparticles, insights into their physical, mechanical, and durability properties can be gained, facilitating informed decision-making in sustainable construction practices.

- The introduction of NTs into the composite mass, regardless of the type of aggregates used, has the effect of increasing the apparent density in the hardened state.
- The introduction of NTs into the composite mass, regardless of the type of aggregates used, has the effect of increasing the compressive strength, with a maximum obtained for 3% or 4% NTs, with values between 43.3 and 70.13 N/mm^2, depending on the nature of the recycled aggregates substituted for the natural aggregates.
- The introduction of NTs into the composite mass, regardless of the type of aggregates used, has the effect of increasing the flexural strength, with a maximum obtained for 3% or 4% NTs, with values between 8.24 and 10.47 N/mm^2, depending on the nature of the recycled aggregates substituted for the natural aggregates.
- The introduction of NTs into the composite mass, regardless of the type of aggregates used, has the effect of increasing wear resistance, with a maximum obtained for 3% or

4% NTs, with values between 0.03 and 0.11 kg/m^{2}min$^{0.5}$, depending on the nature of the recycled aggregates substituted for the natural aggregates.

- The introduction of NTs into the composite mass, regardless of the type of aggregates used, has the effect of reducing water absorption by capillarity. In some cases, if recycled aggregates replacing natural aggregates induce an effect of increasing coefficient water absorption, adding NTs can reduce or even cancel this effect.
- The SEM micrographs of samples R1-3, R2-3, R3-3, R4-3, and R5-3 after 28 days show different microstructures, such as a predominantly reticulated CSH gel in the NA sample with 3% NTs, attributed to TiO_2 acting as a nucleating agent, accelerating cement hydration; a similar trend is observed for RGA, RBA, GBA, and RTA samples, with variations in ITZ, cohesion, and predominant hydration products, highlighting the strong influence of TiO_2 nanoparticles on the hydration process. The EDX spectra complete the TiO_2 nanoparticle distribution image across the investigated areas, confirming the even distribution of the nanoparticles across the sample and therefore indicating a homogenous distribution of TiO_2 in the cementitious composites.
- The XRD patterns of the samples with and without NTs reveal characteristic peaks of ordinary Portland cement (such as peaks corresponding to calcite, aluminoferrite, and portlandite) and distinct peaks for anatase and rutile phases of TiO_2 nanoparticles in the samples R1-3 to R5-3, indicating a lack of chemical interaction with the cementitious matrix and the prevalence of the anatase phase in 3% NT-containing samples.

In conclusion, this study serves as a solid foundation for future research efforts aimed at advancing waste recycling by incorporating it into innovative cementitious matrices alongside the development of highly durable materials. Such initiatives hold great promise for environmental conservation and improved structural resilience. A first avenue for such material advances could be the production of small-scale prefabricated components (e.g., paving elements, cladding units, decorative and finishing elements, urban furniture) made from cementitious composites with a blend of natural aggregates partially replaced by recycled counterparts, complemented by a surface wear layer made from a cementitious composite reinforced with NTs to increase durability.

Author Contributions: Conceptualization, C.T.F., H.V. and A.H.; methodology, C.T.F., H.V., T.G., B.V.N., G.T., A.H., A.C. and A.-V.L.; validation, H.V., A.H., B.V.N. and G.T.; formal analysis, T.G., A.C. and A.-V.L.; investigation, C.T.F., H.V., T.G., B.V.N., G.T., A.H., A.C. and A.-V.L.; data curation, C.T.F., H.V., B.V.N., G.T. and A.C.; writing—original draft preparation, C.T.F., A.H., A.C. and A.-V.L.; writing—review and editing, H.V., T.G., B.V.N. and G.T.; visualization, A.C. and A.-V.L.; supervision, H.V. and A.H. All authors have read and agreed to the published version of the manuscript.

Funding: This research received no external funding.

Institutional Review Board Statement: Not applicable.

Informed Consent Statement: Not applicable.

Data Availability Statement: Data are contained within the article.

Conflicts of Interest: Authors Carmen Teodora Florean, Andreea Hegyi, Alexandra Csapai, Adrian-Victor Lăzărescu were employed by the company NIRD URBAN-INCERC Cluj-Napoca Branch. The remaining authors declare that the research was conducted in the absence of any commercial or financial relationships that could be construed as a potential conflict of interest.

References

1. Xue, C.; Qiao, H.; Cao, H.; Feng, Q.; Li, Q. Analysis on the strength of cement mortar mixed with construction waste brick powder. *Adv. Civ. Eng.* **2021**, *2021*, 8871280. [CrossRef]
2. Chen, Y.Z. Comparison of policy about construction waste resource utilization in China & abroad. *Archit. Technol.* **2019**, *50*, 342–345.
3. Abuzaid, E.K.M.; Al-Bayati, J.K.; Mohammed, M.H. Behavior of Reinforced Concrete Beams Containing Waste Crushed Con-crete and Bricks. *Civ. Environ. Eng.* **2022**, *18*, 438–447. [CrossRef]

4. Silva, F.A.N.; Delgado, J.M.P.; Azevdo, A.C.; Lima, A.G.B.; Vieira, C.S. Preliminary Analysis of the Use of Construction Waste to Replace Conventional Aggregates in Concrete. *Buildings* **2021**, *11*, 81. [CrossRef]
5. Yang, I.H.; Park, J.; Kim, K.C.; Lee, H. Structural Behavior of Concrete Beams Containing Recycled Coarse Aggregates under Flexure. *Adv. Mater. Sci. Eng.* **2020**, *2020*, 8037131. [CrossRef]
6. Etxeberria, M.; Mari, A.R.; Vazquez, E. Recycled aggregate concrete as structural material. *Mater. Struct.* **2007**, *40*, 529–541. [CrossRef]
7. Pavlu, T.; Fortova, K.; Divis, J.; Hajek, P. The utilization of recycled masonry aggregate and recycled EPS for concrete blocks for mortarless masonry. *Materials* **2019**, *12*, 1923. [CrossRef] [PubMed]
8. Pacheco-Torgal, F.; Jalali, S. Compressive strength and durability properties of ceramic wastes based concrete. *Mater. Struct.* **2011**, *44*, 155–167. [CrossRef]
9. Yang, J.; Du, Q.; Bao, Y. Concrete with recycled concrete aggregate and crushed clay bricks. *Constr. Build. Mater.* **2011**, *25*, 1935–1945. [CrossRef]
10. Nepomuceno, M.C.S.; Isidoro, R.A.S.; Catarino, J.P.G. Mechanical performance evaluation of concrete made with recycled ceramic coarse aggregates from industrial brick waste. *Constr. Build. Mater.* **2018**, *165*, 284–294. [CrossRef]
11. Nematzadeh, M.; Dashti, J.; Ganjavi, B. Optimizing compressive behavior of concrete containing fine recycled refractory brick aggregate together with calcium aluminate cement and polyvinyl alcohol fibers exposed to acidic environment. *Constr. Build. Mater.* **2018**, *164*, 837–849. [CrossRef]
12. Khalaf Fouad, M.; DeVenny Alan, S. Properties of New and Recycled Clay Brick Aggregates for Use in Concrete. *J. Mater. Civ. Eng.* **2005**, *17*, 456–464. [CrossRef]
13. Devenny, A.; Khalaf, F.M. The use of crushed brick as coarse aggregate in concrete. *Mason. Int.* **1999**, *12*, 81–84.
14. Uddin, M.T.; Mahmood, A.H.; Kamal, M.D.R.I.; Yashin, S.M.; Zihan, Z.U.A. Effects of maximum size of brick aggregate on properties of concrete. *Constr. Build. Mater.* **2017**, *134*, 713–726. [CrossRef]
15. Cavalline, T.L.; Weggel, D.C. Recycled brick masonry aggregate concrete: Use of brick masonry from construction and demolition waste as recycled aggregate in concrete. *Struct. Surv.* **2013**, *31*, 160–180. [CrossRef]
16. Cachim, P.B. Mechanical properties of brick aggregate concrete. *Constr. Build. Mater.* **2009**, *23*, 1292–1297. [CrossRef]
17. Khatib, J.M. Properties of concrete incorporating fine recycled aggregate. *Cem. Concr. Res.* **2005**, *35*, 763–769. [CrossRef]
18. Lee, G.; Poon, C.S.; Wong, Y.L.; Ling, T.C. Effects of recycled fine glass aggregates on the properties of dry–mixed concrete blocks. *Constr. Build. Mater.* **2013**, *38*, 638–643. [CrossRef]
19. Ling, T.C.; Poon, C.S. Properties of architectural mortar prepared with recycled glass with different particle sizes. *Mater. Des.* **2011**, *32*, 2675–2684. [CrossRef]
20. Lee, G.; Ling, T.C.; Wong, Y.L.; Poon, C.S. Effects of crushed glass cullet sizes, casting methods and pozzolanic materials on ASR of concrete blocks. *Constr. Build. Mater.* **2011**, *25*, 2611–2618. [CrossRef]
21. Özkan, Ö.; Yüksel, İ. Studies on mortars containing waste bottle glass and industrial by-products. *Constr. Build. Mater.* **2008**, *22*, 1288–1298. [CrossRef]
22. Shi, C.; Day, R.L. Early strength development and hydration of alkali-activated blast furnace slag/fly ash blends. *Adv. Cement Res.* **1999**, *11*, 189–196. [CrossRef]
23. Pizoń, J.; Gołaszewski, J.; Alwaeli, M.; Szwan, P. Properties of concrete with recycled concrete aggregate containing metallurgical sludge waste. *Materials* **2020**, *13*, 1448. [CrossRef] [PubMed]
24. European Parliament. Directive 2002/96/EC of the European Parliament and of the Council of 27 January 2003 on Waste Electrical and Electronic Equipment (WEEE)—Joint Declaration of the European Parliament, the Council and the Commission relating to Article 9. *Off. J. Eur. Union* **2003**, *L37*, 24–39.
25. Premur, V.; Anić Vučinić, A.; Vujević, D.; Bedeković, G. The possibility for environmental friendly recycling of printed circuit boards. *J. Sustain. Dev. Energy Water Environ. Syst.* **2016**, *4*, 14–22. [CrossRef]
26. Niu, X.; Li, Y. Treatment of waste printed wire boards in electronic waste for safe disposal. *J. Hazard. Mater.* **2007**, *145*, 410–416. [CrossRef] [PubMed]
27. Ganesh, S.; Danish, P.; Bhat, K.A. Utilization of waste printed circuit board powder in concrete over conventional concrete. *Mater. Today Proc.* **2021**, *42*, 745–749. [CrossRef]
28. Santhanam, N.; Ramesh, B.; Pohsnem, F.K. Concrete blend with E-waste plastic for sustainable future. *Mater. Today Proc.* **2020**, *22*, 959–965. [CrossRef]
29. Mou, P.; Xiang, D.; Duan, G. Products Made from Nonmetallic Materials Reclaimed from Waste Printed Circuit Boards. *Tsinghua Sci. Technol.* **2007**, *12*, 276–283. [CrossRef]
30. Priyan, M.V.; Annadurai, R.; Onyelowe, K.C.; Alaneme, G.U.; Giri, N.C. Recycling and sustainable applications of waste printed circuit board in concrete application and validation using response surface methodology. *Sci. Rep.* **2023**, *13*, 16509. [CrossRef]
31. Vishnupriyan, M.; Annadurai, R. A study on the macro-properties of PCB fiber-reinforced concrete from recycled electronic waste and validation of results using RSM and ANN. *Asian J. Civ. Eng.* **2023**, *24*, 1667–1680. [CrossRef]
32. Bica, B.O.; de Melo, J.V.S. Concrete blocks nano-modified with zinc oxide (ZnO) for photocatalytic paving: Performance com-parison with titanium dioxide (TiO_2). *Constr. Build. Mater.* **2020**, *252*, 119120. [CrossRef]
33. Staub de Melo, J.V.; Trichês, G. Study of the influence of nano-TiO2 on the properties of Portland cement concrete for application on road surfaces. *Road Mater. Pavement Des.* **2018**, *19*, 1011–1026. [CrossRef]

34. Reches, Y. Nanoparticles as concrete additives: Review and perspectives. *Constr. Build. Mater.* **2018**, *175*, 483–495. [CrossRef]
35. De Matos, P.; Zat, T.; Corazza, K.; Fensterseifer, E.; Sakata, R.; Mohamad, G.; Rodríguez, E. Effect of TiO_2 Nanoparticles on the Fresh Performance of 3D-Printed Cementitious Materials. *Materials* **2022**, *15*, 3896. [CrossRef] [PubMed]
36. Senff, L.; Hotza, D.; Lucas, S.; Ferreira, V.M.; Labrincha, J.A. Effect of nano-SiO_2 and nano-TiO_2 addition on the rheological behavior and the hardened properties of cement mortars. *Mater. Sci. Eng. A* **2012**, *532*, 354–361. [CrossRef]
37. Senff, L.; Tobaldi, D.M.; Lemes-Rachadel, P.; Labrincha, J.A.; Hotza, D. The influence of TiO_2 and ZnO powder mixtures on photocatalytic activity and rheological behavior of cement pastes. *Constr. Build. Mater.* **2014**, *65*, 191–200. [CrossRef]
38. Casagrande, C.A.; Repette, W.L.; Hotza, D. Effect of environmental conditions on degradation of NOx gases by photocatalytic nanotitania-based cement mortars after long-term hydration. *J. Clean. Prod.* **2020**, *274*, 123067. [CrossRef]
39. Joshaghani, A.; Balapour, M.; Mashhadian, M.; Ozbakkaloglu, T. Effects of nano-TiO_2, nano-Al_2O_3, and nano-Fe_2O_3 on rheology, mechanical and durability properties of self-consolidating concrete (SCC): An experimental study. *Constr. Build. Mater.* **2020**, *245*, 118444. [CrossRef]
40. Jalal, M.; Fathi, M.; Farzad, M. Effects of fly ash and TiO_2 nanoparticles on rheological, mechanical, microstructural and thermal properties of high strength self compacting concrete. *Mech. Mater.* **2013**, *61*, 11–27. [CrossRef]
41. Jayapalan, A.R.; Lee, B.Y.; Fredrich, S.M.; Kurtis, K.E. Influence of additions of anatase TiO_2 nanoparticles on earlyage properties of cement-based materials. *Transp. Res. Rec.* **2010**, *2141*, 41–46. [CrossRef]
42. Lackhoff, M.; Prieto, X.; Nestle, N.; Dehn, F.; Niessner, R. Photocatalytic activity of semiconductor-modified cement—Influence of semiconductor type and cement ageing. *Appl. Catal. B Environ.* **2023**, *43*, 205–216. [CrossRef]
43. Nazari, A.; Riahi, S. The effect of TiO_2 nanoparticles on water permeability and thermal and mechanical properties of high strength self-compacting concrete. *Mater. Sci. Eng. A* **2010**, *528*, 756–763. [CrossRef]
44. Nazari, A.; Riahi, S. The effects of TiO_2 nanoparticles on physical, thermal and mechanical properties of concrete using ground granulated blast furnace slag as binder. *Mater. Sci. Eng. A* **2011**, *528*, 2085–2092. [CrossRef]
45. Janczarek, M.; Klapiszewski, Ł.; Jędrzejczak, P.; Klapiszewska, I.; Ślosarczyk, A.; Jesionowski, T. Progress of functionalized TiO_2-based nanomaterials in the construction industry: A comprehensive review. *Chem. Eng. J.* **2022**, *430*, 132062. [CrossRef]
46. Cerro-Prada, E.; Manso, M.; Torres, V.; Soriano, J. Microstructural and photocatalytic characterization of cement-paste sol-gel synthesized titanium dioxide. *Front. Struct. Civ. Eng.* **2016**, *10*, 189–197. [CrossRef]
47. Wang, L.; Zhang, H.; Gao, Y. Effect of TiO_2 nanoparticles on physical and mechanical properties of cement at low temperatures. *Adv. Mater. Sci. Eng.* **2018**, *2018*, 8934689. [CrossRef]
48. Zhang, R.; Cheng, X.; Hou, P.; Ye, Z. Influences of nano-TiO_2 on the properties of cement based materials: Hydration and drying shrinkage. *Constr. Build. Mater.* **2015**, *81*, 35–41. [CrossRef]
49. Gopalakrishnan, R.; Vignesh, B.; Jeyalakshmi, R. Mechanical, electrical and microstructural studies on nano-TiO_2 admixtured cement mortar cured with industrial wastewater. *Eng. Res. Express* **2020**, *2*, 025010. [CrossRef]
50. Ng, D.S.; Paul, S.C.; Anggraini, V.; Kong, S.Y.; Qureshi, T.S.; Rodriguez, C.R.; Šavija, B. Influence of SiO_2, TiO_2 and Fe_2O_3 nanoparticles on the properties of fly ash blended cement mortars. *Constr. Build. Mater.* **2020**, *258*, 119627.
51. Bianchini, G.; Marrocchino, E.; Tassinari, R.; Vaccaro, C. Recycling of construction and demolition waste materials: A chemical–mineralogical appraisal. *Waste Manag.* **2005**, *25*, 149–159. [CrossRef] [PubMed]
52. Florean, C.; Vermesan, H.; Gabor, T.; Neamțu, B.V.; Thalmayer, G.; Corbu, O.; Lazarescu, A.V.; Hegyi, A.; Csapai, A. Possibilities for Conserving Natural Resources and the Environment Through the use of Recycled Waste Aggregates as a Substitute for Natural Aggregates in Cementitious Composites. *Int. J. Conserv. Sci.* **2024**, *15*, 527–546. [CrossRef]
53. *SR EN 933-1:2012*; Tests to Determine the Geometrical Characteristics of Aggregates. Part 1: Determination of Grain Size. Granulometric Analysis by Sieving. ASRO: Bucharest, Romania, 2012. (In Romanian)
54. *SR EN 1097-3:2002*; Tests to Determine the Mechanical and Physical Characteristics of Aggregates. Part 3: Methods for the de-Termination of Bulk Density and Intergranular Porosity. ASRO: Bucharest, Romania, 2002.
55. *SR EN 1097-6:2022*; Tests to Determine the Mechanical and Physical Characteristics of Aggregates. Part 6: Determination of Density and Water Absorption of Granules. ASRO: Bucharest, Romania, 2022. (In Romanian)
56. *SR EN 14582:2017*; Waste Characterisation. Halogen and Sulphur Content. Burning in Closed Systems Containing Oxygen and Methods of Determination. ASRO: Bucharest, Romania, 2017. (In Romanian)
57. *SR EN ISO 15586:2004*; Water Quality. Determination of Trace Elements by Graphite Furnace Atomic Absorption Spectrometry. ASRO: Bucharest, Romania, 2004. (In Romanian)
58. *EPA 7000B:2007*; Method 7000B Flame Atomic Absorption Spectrophotometry. U.S. Environmental Protection Agency: Washington, DC, USA, 2007.
59. *SR ISO 11047:1999*; Soil Quality. Determination of Cadmium, Chromium, Cobalt, Copper, Lead, Manganese, Nickel and Zinc in Soil Extracts in Royal Water. Methods by Flame Atomic Absorption Spectrometry and Electrothermal Atomization. ASRO: Bucharest, Romania, 1999. (In Romanian)
60. Shekari, A.H.; Razzaghi, M.S. Influence of nano particles on durability and mechanical properties of high performance concrete. *Procedia Eng.* **2011**, *14*, 3036–3041. [CrossRef]
61. Liu, L.; Jaramillo-Botero, A.; Goddard, W.A., III; Sun, H. Development of a ReaxFF reactive force field for ettringite and study of its mechanical failure modes from reactive dynamics simulations. *J. Phys. Chem. A* **2012**, *116*, 3918–3925. [CrossRef] [PubMed]

62. Aliabdo, A.A.; Abd Elmoaty, M.; Aboshama, A.Y. Utilization of waste glass powder in the production of cement and concrete. *Constr. Build. Mater.* **2016**, *124*, 866–877. [CrossRef]
63. Ibrahim, K.I.M. The effect of using glass powder as cement substitution and its mixing method on the concrete characteristics. *J. Build. Pathol. Rehabil.* **2023**, *8*, 27. [CrossRef]
64. Chen, J.; Kou, S.; Poon, C. Hydration and properties of nano-TiO_2 blended cement composites. *Cem. Concr. Compos.* **2012**, *34*, 642–649. [CrossRef]
65. Mohseni, E.; Ranjbar, M.M.; Tsavdaridis, K.D. Durability properties of highperformance concrete incorporating nano-TiO_2 and fly ash. *Am. J. Appl. Sci.* **2015**, *8*, 519–526. [CrossRef]
66. Yu, X.; Kang, S.; Long, X. Compressive strength of concrete reinforced by TiO_2 nanoparticles. *AIP Conf. Proc.* **2018**, *2036*, 030006.
67. *SR EN 196-3:2017*; Methods of Testing Cements. Part 3: Determination of Setting Time and Stability. ASRO: Bucharest, Romania, 2017. (In Romanian)
68. Noorvand, H.; Ali, A.A.A.; Demirboga, R.; Farzadnia, N.; Noorvand, H. Incorporation of nano TiO_2 in black rice husk ash mortars. *Constr. Build. Mater.* **2013**, *47*, 1350–1361. [CrossRef]
69. *NE 012-1:2022*; Standard for the Production and Execution of Concrete, Reinforced Concrete and Prestressed Concrete Works—Part 1: Concrete Production. Ministry of Development, Public Works and Administration: Bucharest, Romania, 2022. (In Romanian)
70. *SR EN 1015-18:2003*; Test Methods for Masonry Mortars. Part 18: Determination of the Coefficient of Water Absorption due to the Capillary Action of Hardened Mortar. ASRO: Bucharest, Romania, 2003. (In Romanian)
71. *SR EN 1015-10:2002*; Test Methods for Masonry Mortars. Part 10: Determination of Bulk Density of Hardened Mortar. ASRO: Bucharest, Romania, 2002. (In Romanian)
72. *SR EN 1015-11:2020*; Test Methods for Masonry Mortars. Part 11: Determination of Flexural Strength of Hardened Mortar. ASRO: Bucharest, Romania, 2020. (In Romanian)
73. *SR EN 1338:2004*; Concrete Pavers. Conditions and Test Methods. ASRO: Bucharest, Romania, 2004. (In Romanian)
74. Nazari, A.; Riahi, S. TiO_2 nanoparticles effects on physical, thermal and mechanical properties of self-compacting concrete with ground granulated blast furnace slag as binder. *Energy Build.* **2011**, *43*, 995–1002. [CrossRef]
75. Salemi, N.; Behfarnia, K.; Zaree, S.A. Effect of nanoparticles on frost durability of concrete. *Asian J. Civ. Eng.* **2014**, *15*, 411–420.
76. Behfarnia, K.; Keivan, A.; Keivan, A. The effects of TiO_2 and ZnO nanoparticles on physical and mechanical properties of normal concrete. *Asian J. Civ. Eng.* **2013**, *14*, 517–531.
77. Fujishima, A.; Zhang, X.; Tryk, D.A. TiO_2 photocatalysis and related surface phenomena. *Surf. Sci. Rep.* **2008**, *63*, 515–582. [CrossRef]

Disclaimer/Publisher's Note: The statements, opinions and data contained in all publications are solely those of the individual author(s) and contributor(s) and not of MDPI and/or the editor(s). MDPI and/or the editor(s) disclaim responsibility for any injury to people or property resulting from any ideas, methods, instructions or products referred to in the content.

materials

MDPI

Article

Experimental Study of the Moisture Resistance of Cement Mortar Using Pozzolan Materials and Calcium Stearate

Jang Hyun Park [1] and Chang Bok Yoon [2,*]

[1] E-Moblilty Lab, Hankyong National University, Anseong 17579, Republic of Korea; parkjh@hknu.ac.kr
[2] Architectural Engineering, Seoil University, Seoul 02192, Republic of Korea
* Correspondence: all4yoon@gmail.com

Abstract: Nanosilica and diatomite are pozzolanic resources rich in SiO_2. In this study, the purpose of this study was to improve the moisture resistance of the specimen by producing a mixed material using pozzolanic materials and calcium stearate and adding it to cement mortar while stirring. The results showed that the hydration reaction was not activated when calcium stearate adhered to the fine particles of nanosilica; it existed simply in the form of a filler inside the specimen. Diatomite, due to its atypical particles and porosity, may have greater water tightness than nanosilica because of the pozzolanic reaction in particles to which calcium stearate is not attached.

Keywords: calcium stearate; water repellent; nanosilica; diatomite

check for updates

Citation: Park, J.H.; Yoon, C.B. Experimental Study of the Moisture Resistance of Cement Mortar Using Pozzolan Materials and Calcium Stearate. *Materials* **2024**, *17*, 1014. https://doi.org/10.3390/ma17051014

Academic Editors: Mengjun Chen and Jiwen Bai

Received: 15 January 2024
Revised: 18 February 2024
Accepted: 21 February 2024
Published: 22 February 2024

Copyright: © 2024 by the authors. Licensee MDPI, Basel, Switzerland. This article is an open access article distributed under the terms and conditions of the Creative Commons Attribution (CC BY) license (https://creativecommons.org/licenses/by/4.0/).

1. Introduction

Concrete has microscopic pores on the surface, which can cause damage such as water leaks when exposed to moisture. Damage due to the moisture infiltration of concrete occurs frequently, and the corrosion and expansion of reinforcing bars result in exposure to deterioration due to salt damage, freeze–thaw, etc., over time, and a decrease in durability.

Special processes are required to prevent moisture contact and penetration and improve the durability of concrete. In general, liquid-permeable paint or asphalt sheets are applied and attached to the concrete surface to install a separate waterproof protective layer to block moisture infiltration from the outside [1–4]. However, the installed protective layer may be destroyed due to external environmental factors such as cracks, impacts, and ultraviolet rays, creating a path for moisture to penetrate through the defect.

As a result, the damaged waterproofing layer may need to be partially repaired or completely rebuilt, causing inconvenience to users and requiring much time and cost [5]. Therefore, in order to compensate for these shortcomings, it is deemed necessary to conduct research on the development, and a performance evaluation, of moisture-resistant concrete. However, there is a lack of research on implementing moisture resistance in the concrete itself by using additive materials when mixing concrete instead of blocking moisture infiltration only on the concrete surface by applying materials to the surface.

Therefore, in this study, in order to develop a cement mortar with a moisture-resistant performance, an admixture was prepared using pozzolanic materials such as nanosilica and diatomite and moisture-resistant calcium stearate, and experiments were performed by mixing them at a certain ratio when manufacturing cement mortar. Naseroleslami and Chari (2019) showed that cement mortar and paste mixed with calcium stearate enhanced durability performance such as capillary water absorption under non-static pressure conditions [6]. However, when calcium stearate is used, a mixture of at least 1% of the cement weight causes changes in its physical properties, such as a decrease in compressive strength. Calcium stearate is an inorganic mixture of saturated fatty acid metal salts that is already used to manufacture hydrophobic materials, and it has disadvantages, such as the need to be preprocessed before dispersion in a solid state and the difficulty of dispersion [7–10], but fatty acid metal salts are more insoluble and are expected to be better laminated on the surface of cement mortar (Choi et al., 2010) [11]. Thus, calcium stearate is expected to create hydrophobicity in cement mortar when applied to the surface or mixed internally. Nanosilica is an ultrafine particle of cement that causes a pozzolanic reaction during the hydration reaction. Thus, the compressive strength is expected to increase in the early stages. Previous studies using nanosilica have examined dispersion to improve compressive strength in terms of durability and demonstrated that nanosilica could improve strength through a hydration reaction in mixed cement [12–16]. Gaitero et al. and Ji [17,18] discovered that water penetration decreased when using nanosilica in mixing cement due to the creation of a watertight structure with the filling of hydration products in the transition zone resulting from the pozzolanic reaction.

Diatomite is a very light and porous pozzolanic material consisting of deposited phytoplankton shells with unique physical properties, such as high porosity, water permeability, surface area, chemical stability, water absorption, and thermal resistance, owing to the irregular shapes and porous structure of diatom particles and their fragments. The principal component of the shell is opal ($SiO_2{\cdot}nH_2O$), which is amorphous silica. The content of SiO_2, the principal component, is approximately 70–80%, with the remainder consisting of Al_2O_3, Fe_2O_3, CaO, and MgO. The particle size is approximately 1 mm and takes various forms depending on the species [19]. Recently, diatomite has been used as a concrete admixture after firing to improve the durability and strength efficiency of concrete [20–24].

Calcium stearate is a powder-type material and has its own hydrophobicity, and nanosilica and diatomite have a high content of SiO_2 and also have amorphous pores. Therefore, a pozzolanic reaction occurs during the hydration stage, which has the advantage of increasing water tightness and improving durability [25,26]. Using the pores of nanosilica and diatomite, calcium stearate, a powder-like material that can reduce moisture resistance, was attached to the inside of the pores to produce a moisture-resistant mixed material, and its physical performance and durability were evaluated. Figure 1 shows SEM images of nanosilica, diatomite, and calcium stearate used in the experiment.

Figure 1. Sem analysis.

2. Materials and Methods of the Experiment

2.1. Materials

The cement used in this experiment is a domestic type 1 ordinary Portland cement specified in KS F 5201 [27] and ASTM C 150 [28], with a density of 3.15 g/cm^3 and 3000 cm^2/g. The nanosilica used is available in the domestic market (S teck company, Ansan, Gyeonggi, Republic of Korea), as well as the diatomite (Daejung company, Seoul, Republic of Korea). For the fine aggregate, a product that complies with ISO 679:2009 [29] was used, and the washed aggregate with a fineness modulus of 2.8 was used. The calcium stearate used in this experiment was obtained from the reaction of stearic acid and lime and exhibited lubricating and water-repellent properties. More specifically, it is a white powder, available in the domestic market (Daejung company, Seoul, Republic of Korea), that has a lower density than cement and a pH close to slightly alkaline or neutral. The chemical compositions of the cement, nanosilica, diatomite, and calcium stearate are shown in Tables 1 and 2 below.

Table 1. Chemical composition of materials [30].

Name	Chemical Composition (%)							
	SiO_2	Al_2O_3	Fe_2O_3	CaO	MgO	SO_3	K_2O	L.O.I
OPC	19.29	5.16	2.87	61.68	4.17	2.53	0.89	
Diatomite	91.56	1.34	3.83	1.0	0.2	0.01	0.06	
NanoSilica	99.46	0.03	0.02	0.07	0.01	0.24	0.01	0.17

Table 2. Chemical composition of metallic salts.

Name	Chemical Composition of Metallic Salts				
	Chemical Formula	Density (g/cm^3)	pH	Melting Point	Molecular Weight (g/mol)
Calcium stearate	$C_{36}H_{70}CaO_4$	1.10	7–9	147–149	607

2.2. Overview and Methods of the Experiment

2.2.1. Preparation of Hydrophobic Powder

This experiment aimed to produce moisture resistance inside cement mortar using nanosilica and diatomite, which have an excellent pozzolanic reactivity, and using calcium stearate to enhance insolubility. Owing to its unique insolubility, calcium stearate does not easily dissolve in contact with cement mortar mixing water. Accordingly, it is expected to result in bleeding. Thus, an impregnation method was applied to prevent the detachment of calcium stearate by attaching calcium stearate to the surface of each pozzolan powder using nanosilica and diatomite as carriers. To this end, calcium stearate was dissolved using isopropylene as a solvent, after which nanosilica and diatomite were added and mixed evenly in an ultrasonic stirrer for approximately 3 h so that the nanosilica, diatomite, and calcium stearate could adhere. The mixture was then completely dried for 3 days in natural conditions and 2 days at 70 °C. Subsequently, it was powdered. The powders that passed the standard screen size of 150 μm were used to obtain an even fineness. Finally, the completed powders were named NSC and DTC. The experimental formulation table is shown in Table 3.

Table 3. Experimental mixing table of cement mortar.

Specimen	W/B	C	S	W	NSC	DTC
OPC	50%	510	1530	255	-	
NSC 1%				257.5	5.1	
NSC 3%				260.1	10.2	
DTC 1%				257.5		5.1
DTC 3%				260.1		10.2

2.2.2. Method of Specimen Production and Experiment

Mixing was performed according to KS L 5109 [31] for a physical performance evaluation and microstructure analysis. For mixing, cement and binding powder were dry-mixed by adding 1% and 3% of the cement weight ratio, respectively. Next, mixing water was added and stirred for 30 s at a single speed, and then sand was added and mixed for 30 s at two speeds. It was stirred slowly for 30s at a speed of 140 ± 5 r/min, then left for 90 s, and finally stirred for 60 s at two speeds of 285 ± 10 r/min. For the compressive strength and microstructure analysis, water absorption test, and chloride penetration resistance test, the specimen was cast into a square mold 50 mm on the side and a round cylinder of ϕ 100 × 150 mm, which was demolded after 1 day and cured in water. The experiments were then conducted at the ages of 7 and 28 days. The mix proportions for this experiment are shown in Table 3.

Furthermore, this study measured the activity factor using the compressive strength at the age of 28 days and the compressive strength according to KS L 5105 [32] and KS L 5405 [33] to determine the physical properties of the specimen. Afterward, a thermal analysis (TGA) was conducted, and a scanning electron microscope (SEM) was used for microanalysis, and water absorption and permeability resistance tests were performed at the ages of 7 and 28 days based on KS F 4919 [34] to evaluate the internal moisture resistance of the specimen. In addition, the chloride ion penetration resistance was tested according to ASTM C 1202 [35] "Standard Test Method for Electrical Indication of Concrete's Ability to Resist Chloride Ion Penetration" (ASTM 1993) and KS F 2711 [36] "Standard test method for resistance of concrete to chloride ion penetration by electrical conductance" (KSA 2017).

3. Experimental Results

3.1. Thermal Analysis Measurement

$Ca(OH)_2$ is thermally decomposed at approximately 450–550 °C. A thermal analysis of the reference mortar and NSC3% and DTC3% was conducted after 7 days to determine the weight loss of the specimen using mass reduction and quantitatively evaluate the amount of $Ca(OH)_2$ produced in the hydrate. The TGA measurement results are shown in Figure 2.

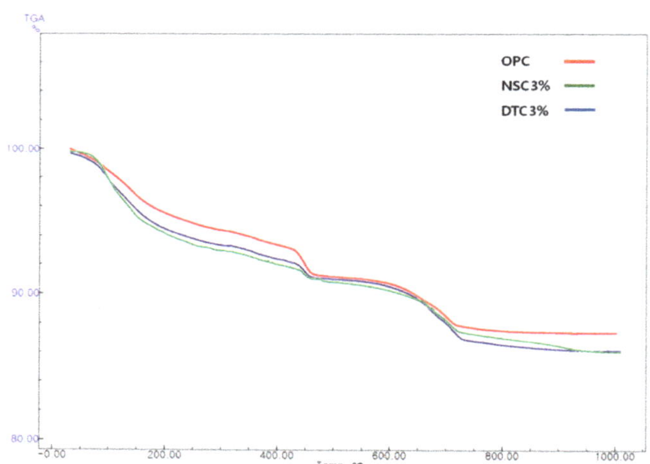

Figure 2. Results of thermogravimetry differential thermal analysis.

The amount of $Ca(OH)_2$ produced from the reference mortar was 13.4%, whereas the amounts from DTC3 and NSC3% were 2.51% and 12.05%, respectively. In the NSC specimen, the lowest mass reduction rate was determined through the endothermic peak in the section where $Ca(OH)_2$ was decomposed. Nanosilica promotes the hydration of cement at the early stage of the hydration reaction, consumes calcium hydroxide (CH) due to its high pozzolanic reaction, and then converts it to calcium silicate hydrate (CSH) gel to improve the mechanical properties of concrete. However, the pozzolanic reaction was reduced when insufficient CH was produced, as under the conditions of this experiment. The NSC specimen using nanosilica does not adhere to the surface when combined with calcium stearate, whereas calcium stearate adheres in the form of a coating due to the shape of the fine particles of nanosilica, without causing a pozzolanic reaction. Moreover, in the specimen using diatomite, the CH generated by the hydration reaction of cement and the SiO_2 present in large amounts in diatomite seems to have partially compensated for the loss of compressive strength following the mixing of calcium stearate due to the pozzolanic reaction.

3.2. Compressive Strength and Activity Factor

The following values were determined when measuring the 7-day and 28-day compressive strength. OPC, the control group, showed 28 MPa on the 7th day and 37 MPa on the 28th day, whereas NSC, which combined nanosilica and calcium stearate, exhibited a significantly lower compressive strength. The 7-day and 28-day compressive strengths of the specimen mixed with a weight ratio of 1% were 21 and 24 MPa, respectively, and those of the specimen mixed with a weight ratio of 3% were 13 and 16 MPa, respectively. The compressive strength, activity factors, and the equation used to evaluate the activity factor used in Equation (1) are shown in Figure 3 below.

$$As = \frac{C_1}{C_2} \times 100(\%) \quad (1)$$

where

As: activity factor (%);

C_1: average compressive strength of the specimen replacing admixture (MPa);

C_2: average compressive strength of OPC specimen (MPa).

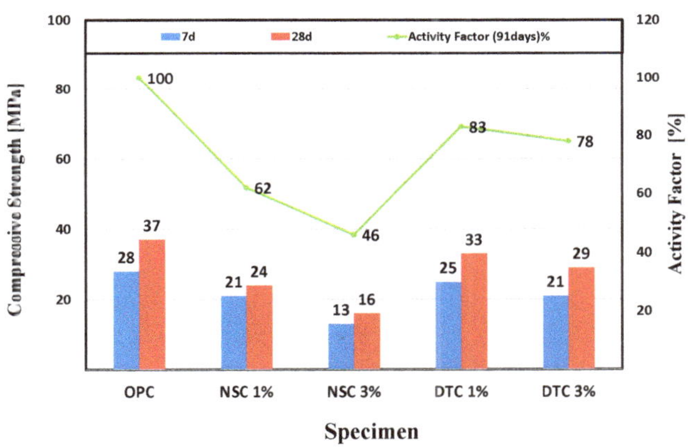

Figure 3. Results for compressive strength and activity factor.

The compressive strength increased when nanosilica was mixed because the size of the basic particles of nanosilica was 10–20 nm, and the fine particles reduced the porosity of concrete due to the void filling and particle distribution and increased the pozzolanic reaction with $Ca(OH)_2$, thereby generating CSH [37,38]. However, in this experimental condition, the dissolved calcium stearate surrounded the entire particle when attached to nanosilica; thus, the high content of SiO_2 in nanosilica could not cause a pozzolanic reaction and delayed the hydration reaction when only calcium stearate was mixed, reducing the increase in compressive strength because the transition area representing the interface between cement paste and particles of aggregate was expanded. This consequently hindered a uniform dispersion force [39,40]. The DTC specimens that combined diatomite and calcium stearate showed an increase in activity of up to 83% compared to the reference mortar. In contrast to the NSC case, calcium stearate was attached within the pores due to the characteristics of the internal pore structure of diatomite. Thus, some of the diatomite compensated for the compressive strength that was reduced through the pozzolanic reaction.

3.3. Water Absorption Measurement

Water absorption was measured at 7 days and 28 days based on KS F 4919 [34]. Absorption is typically measured by immersing the lower surface of a 70 mm × 70 mm × 20 mm test specimen coated with a waterproofing agent in water; however, in this experiment, the central part of a 50 mm × 50 mm × 50 mm square mortar plate was cut, and the cut surface was immersed to measure water absorption inside the mortar plate specimen. The initial mass (W_0) was measured after applying epoxy to the remaining surfaces, except the lower bottom, where the cut surface was immersed in water. The immersed surface was taken out after 24 h, and the mass (W_1) was measured after gently wiping the surface. Absorption was determined by calculating the means of the three specimens according to Equation (2). Moreover, a ϕ 100 × 200 circular test piece was divided into four lengthwise sections to conduct a water penetration test in pressurization. Subsequently, a water permeability test was conducted using a specimen with a height of 50 mm on the inner part. The experiment was conducted under the atmospheric pressure of 0.3 N/mm^2 to allow moisture to permeate the specimen, whereas the weight was measured after 3 h of pressurization. The equation used to measure moisture absorption is shown in Equation (2), and the hydrostatic pressure and atmospheric pressure are shown in Figure 4.

$$\text{Absorption(g)} = W_1 - W_0 \tag{2}$$

where

W_0: mass before measurement (g);
W_1: mass after measurement (g).

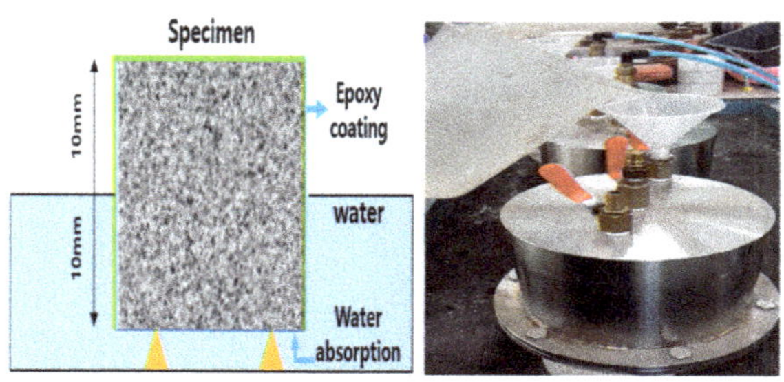

(1) Water absorption (2) Water penetration

Figure 4. Water resistance test.

The water absorption measurements revealed that the reference mortar showed a water absorption of 2.7 g, whereas the NSC specimen using nanosilica showed slightly less water absorption than the DTC specimen using diatomite. However, when a pressure of 0.3 N/mm^2 was applied, the NSC specimen showed an increase in absorption as the pressure increased compared to the reference mortar. Specifically, the NSC specimen only showed moisture resistance due to the characteristics of the calcium stearate surrounding the surface of nanosilica. The DTC specimen showed a lower compressive strength than the reference mortar; however, in contrast to the NSC specimen, the characteristics of calcium stearate attached inside the pores of the diatomite and the hydration reaction due to the pozzolanic reaction had a simultaneous effect that enhanced the moisture resistance performance. Except for the reference mortar, the pore structure was not improved by the filling of the capillary pores with the hydration product formed by the pozzolanic reaction. More precisely, moisture resistance was found to be due to the characteristics of calcium stearate. The results are presented in Tables 4 and 5, respectively.

Table 4. Results of water absorption test.

	Specimen [28 Days]				
	OPC	NSC 1%	NSC 3%	DTC 1%	DTC 3%
0 H (g, W_0)	133.4	137.7	131.5	134.9	139.5
24 H (g, W_1)	136.1	140.1	133.1	137.6	141.8
Absorption (g)	2.7	2.4	1.6	2.7	2.3

Table 5. Results of water penetration test.

	Specimen [28 Days]				
	OPC	NSC 1%	NSC 3%	DTC 1%	DTC 3%
Weight (before testing)	855.8	869.5	850.7	862.8	860.4
Weight (after the test)	870.9	888.4	875.3	879.1	876.1
Absorption (g)	15.1	18.9	24.6	16.3	15.7

The water absorption measurements revealed that the reference mortar showed a water absorption of 2.7 g, whereas the NSC specimen using nanosilica showed slightly less water absorption than the DTC specimen using diatomite. However, when a pressure of 0.3 N/mm^2 was applied, the NSC specimen's water absorption increased as the pressure increased compared to the reference mortar. Specifically, the NSC specimen only showed moisture resistance due to the characteristics of the calcium stearate surrounding the surface of nanosilica. The DTC specimen showed a lower compressive strength than the reference mortar; however, in contrast to the NSC specimen, the characteristics of the calcium stearate attached inside the pores of the diatomite and the hydration reaction due to the pozzolanic reaction had a simultaneous effect that enhanced the moisture resistance performance. Except for the reference mortar, the pore structure was not improved by the filling of the capillary pores with the hydration product formed by the pozzolanic reaction. More precisely, moisture resistance was found to be due to the characteristics of calcium stearate.

3.4. Measurement of Chloride Ion Penetration Resistance

To measure the chloride ion penetration resistance of each specimen as chloride ions moved, along with water penetration, an experiment was conducted according to ASTM C 1202 (ASTM 1993) and KS F 2711 [34,35]. The experimental measurement is shown at Figure 5.

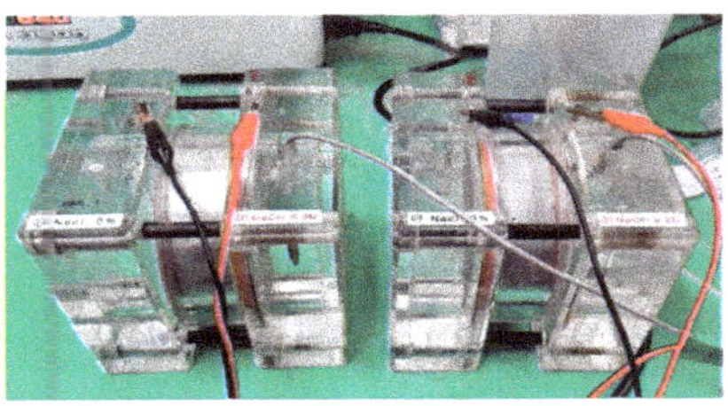

Figure 5. Testing of RCPT [41].

The specimens were retained in a desiccator under vacuum for 3 h. Subsequently, they were immersed in distilled water for 18 ± 2 h until the interiors of the specimens were completely saturated. The cathode of the applied voltage cell was then filled with a 3.0% NaCl solution and the anode with a 0.3 N NaOH solution. A direct current voltage of 60 V was maintained on both sides of the applied voltage cell and the current was recorded every 30 min for 6 h. Equation (3) and Table 6 were used to calculate the total charge that passed and the results of coulombs (C) are shown at Figure 6.

$$Q = 900(I_0 + 2I_{30} + 2I_{60} + \ldots 2I_{300} + 2I_{330} + I_{360}) \quad (3)$$

where

Q: total passing charge;
I_0: current immediately after starting test with applied voltage;
I_{360}: current 360 min after applying voltage.

Table 6. Evaluation according to chloride ion penetration [41].

Coulombs (C)	Permeability
>4000	High
2000–4000	Normal
1000–2000	Low
100–1000	Very low
<100	Negligible

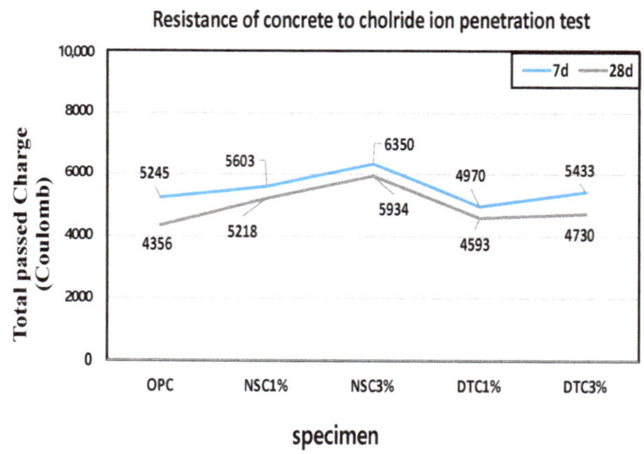

Figure 6. Mesurement of RCPT.

In the 28-day measurement, the OPC, the reference mortar in this experiment, showed a high value of approximately 4300 coulombs, whereas the C values of NSC 1% and 3% specimens were 5600 and 6300, respectively, somewhat higher than DTC 1% and 3% at 4900 and 5400. Calcium stearate generally exhibits water penetration resistance because a hydrophobic wax compound is created through contact with moisture. However, the specimen lacks water tightness, as the calcium stearate coating film formed on the nanosilica particles inhibits the formation of hydrates in the cement mortar, causing water penetration. The reaction of calcium stearate and cement may decrease chloride penetration resistance due to the deterioration in compressive strength [42]. The results for the samples with calcium stearate revealed no improvement in the pore structure inside the cement mortar.

3.5. *Scanning Electron Microscope (SEM)*

In the OPC specimen, hydration products such as CSH and CH, $Ca(OH)_2$ were evenly distributed according to the hydration process, whereas, in the NSC specimen, the hydration reaction was observed only in some parts. In the SEM image, the size of the nanosilica particles was approximately 17–18 nm, which was ultrafine. Thus, the dissolved calcium stearate seemed to have surrounded the aggregated particles instead of being attached to the nanosilica particles. Accordingly, the limited bonding between calcium oxide and nanosilica, with its high SiO_2 content, seems to have inhibited the pozzolanic reaction. As in OPC, hydration products were found in the DTC specimen. Calcium stearate attached inside the pore structure of diatomite, resisting water that had penetrated. However, its compressive strength was less than that of OPC, the reference mortar, due to the uneven adhesion of calcium stearate to diatomite and the delay in the production of hydration because even dispersion was not secured within the cement mortar. The sem measurement image was shown at Figure 7.

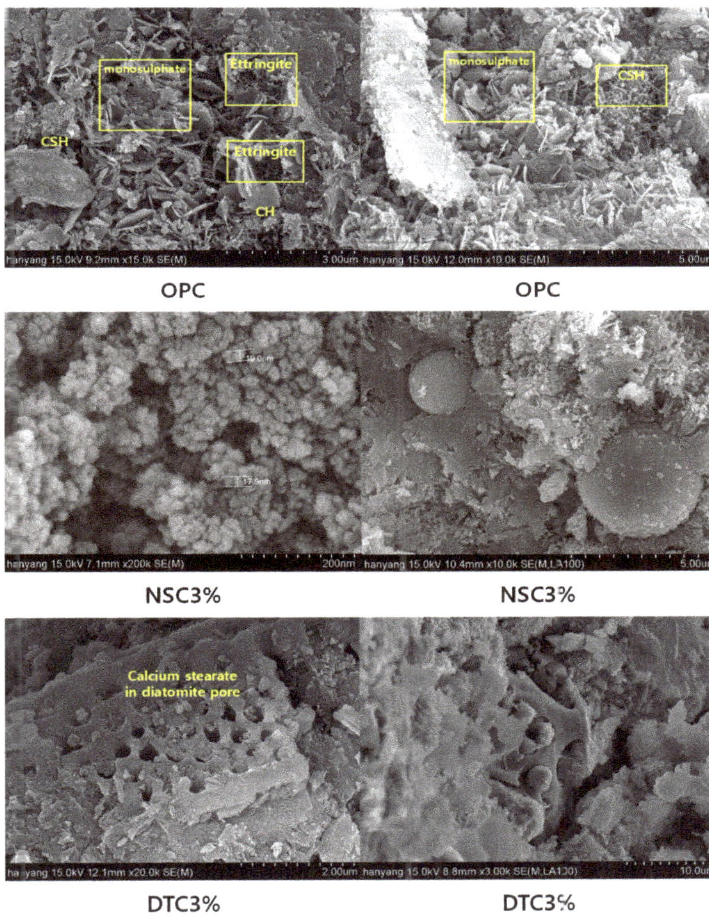

Figure 7. Result of SEM analysis.

4. Conclusions

This study used nanosilica and diatomite, which can serve as pozzolanic admixture materials, to endow concrete with a hydrophobic property through adhesion with calcium stearate, selected for its moisture resistance. It was added when mixing cement mortar, and, subsequently, we tested the internal moisture resistance. The following results were obtained:

(1) The results of the literature review showed that mixing in only nanosilica can increase compressive strength. However, the fine particles of nanosilica are coated with lique-

fied calcium stearate, thereby inhibiting the pozzolanic reaction under the conditions of this experiment.

(2) The moisture resistance measurement results were the best for the NCS3% specimen, which was rich in calcium stearate. It exhibited the best results under hydrostatic pressure, whereas its permeability was the highest under pressurization. As a simple filler, it can resist some moisture; however, water tightness cannot be expected due to the chemical reaction of nanosilica.

(3) The chloride ion penetration resistance measurements also demonstrated that the increase in the amount of mixing admixture to which calcium stearate was attached led to an increase in the total charge that passed.

(4) Diatomite, with its atypical particles and porosity, seems to have secured water tightness better than nanosilica because of the pozzolanic reaction in particles to which calcium stearate was not attached.

It is expected that it will be possible to determine the feasibility of using porous pozzolanic admixtures such as diatomite as a carrier for developing admixtures with moisture resistance. Further research should combine hydrophobic substances using pozzolanic powder with porosity and compensate for the reduction in compressive strength.

Author Contributions: C.B.Y. and J.H.P. designed the study, performed the experiments, analyzed the data, and wrote the initial draft of the manuscript. C.B.Y. was also involved in the scientific discussion, revision, and finalization of the manuscript, as well as acquiring funds. All authors have read and agreed to the published version of the manuscript.

Funding: This research was funded by the National Research Foundation of Korea (NRF) grant funded by the South Korean government (MSIT), grant number No. 2021R1F1A1061684.

Institutional Review Board Statement: Not applicable.

Informed Consent Statement: Not applicable.

Data Availability Statement: Data are contained within the article.

Conflicts of Interest: The authors declare no conflicts of interest.

References

1. Shim, H.B.; Lee, M.S. An Experimental Study on Water Resistance of Penetrating Water Repellency of Emulsified Silicon Type Exposed to The Outdoor Environment. *J. Korea Concr. Inst.* **2014**, *16*, 477–484. [CrossRef]
2. Maravelaki-Kalaitzaki, P. Hydraulic Lime Mortars with Siloxane for Waterproofing Historic Masonry. *Cem. Concr. Res.* **2007**, *37*, 283–290. [CrossRef]
3. Moradllo, M.; Sudbrink, B.; Tyler Ley, M. Determining the Effective Service Life of Silane Treatments in Concrete Bridge Decks. *Constr. Build. Mater.* **2016**, *116*, 121–127. [CrossRef]
4. Zhang, P.; Wittmann, F.; Vogel, M.; Muller, H.; Zhao, T. Influence of Freeze-thaw Cycles on Capillary Absorption and Chloride Penetration into Concrete. *Cem. Concr. Res.* **2017**, *100*, 60–67. [CrossRef]
5. Yoon, C.B.; Lee, H.S. Selection of the Optimum Carrier for Manufacturing Water-Repellent Concrete and Durability Evaluation of Cement Mortar Using It. *Appl. Sci.* **2020**, *10*, 9097. [CrossRef]
6. Naseroleslami, R.; Chari, M.N. The effects of calcium stearate on mechanical and durability aspects of self-consolidating concretes incorporating silica fume/natural zeolite. *Constr. Build. Mater.* **2019**, *225*, 384–400. [CrossRef]
7. Yao, N.; Zhang, P.; Song, L.; Kang, M.; Lu, Z.; Zheng, R. Stearic acid coating on circulating fluidized bed combustion fly ashes and its effect on the mechanical performance of polymer composites. *Appl. Surf. Sci.* **2013**, *279*, 109–115. [CrossRef]
8. Spathi, C.; Young, N.; Heng, J.Y.; Vandeperre, L.J.; Cheeseman, C.R. A simple method for preparing super-hydrophobic powder from paper sludge ash. *Mater. Lett.* **2015**, *142*, 80–83. [CrossRef]
9. Liu, W.; Xie, Z.; Yang, X.; Wu, Y.; Jia, C.; Bo, T.; Wang, L. Surface modification mechanism of stearic acid to zirconia powders induced by ball milling for water-based injection molding. *J. Am. Ceram. Soc.* **2011**, *94*, 1327–1330. [CrossRef]
10. Alonso, M.M.; Palacios, M.; Puertas, F. Compatibility between polycarboxylate-based admixtures and blended-cement pastes. *Cem. Concr. Compos.* **2013**, *35*, 151–162. [CrossRef]
11. Choi, S.S.; Chung, H.S.; Joo, Y.T.; Yang, K.M.; Lee, S.H. Appearance contamination of EPDM article from water solution. *Elastomers Compos.* **2010**, *45*, 100–105.
12. Abhilash, P.P.; Nayak, D.K.; Sangoju, B.; Kumar, R.; Kumar, V. Effect of nano-silica in concrete; a review. *Constr. Build. Mater.* **2021**, *278*, 122347.

13. Mondal, P.; Shah, S.P.; Marks, L.D.; Gaitero, J.J. Comparative study of the effects of microsilica and nanosilica in concrete. *Transp. Res. Rec.* **2010**, *2141*, 6–9. [CrossRef]
14. Ren, J.; Lai, Y.; Gao, J. Exploring the influence of SiO_2 and TiO_2 nanoparticles on the mechanical properties of concrete. *Constr. Build. Mater.* **2018**, *175*, 277–285. [CrossRef]
15. Khan, K.; Ahmad, W.; Amin, M.N.; Nazar, S. Nano-silica-modified concrete: A bibliographic analysis and comprehensive review of material properties. *Nanomaterials* **2022**, *12*, 1989. [CrossRef]
16. Chekravarty, D.S.V.S.M.R.K.; Mallika, A.; Sravana, P.; Rao, S. Effect of using nano silica on mechanical properties of normal strength concrete. *Mater. Today Proc.* **2022**, *51*, 2573–2578. [CrossRef]
17. Ji, T. Preliminary study on the water permeability and microstructure of concrete incorporating nano-SiO_2. *Cem. Concr. Res.* **2005**, *35*, 1943–1947. [CrossRef]
18. Gaitero, J.J.; Campillo, I.; Guerrero, A. Reduction of the calcium leaching rate of cement paste by addition of silica nanoparticles. *Cem. Concr. Res.* **2008**, *38*, 1112–1118. [CrossRef]
19. Jeong, G.Y. Quantitative Determination of Cristobalite Content in Diatomite and Filtered Food. *J. Mineral. Soc. Korea* **2019**, *32*, 313–321. [CrossRef]
20. Zhang, X.; Liu, X.; Meng, G. Sintering Kinetics of Porous Ceramics from Natural Diatomite. *J. Am. Soc. Ceram.* **2005**, *88*, 1826–1830. [CrossRef]
21. Sarıdemir, M.; Çelikten, S.; Yıldırım, A. Mechanical and microstructural properties of calcined diatomite powder modified high strength mortars at ambient and high temperatures. *Adv. Powder Technol.* **2020**, *31*, 3004–3017. [CrossRef]
22. Degirmenci, N.; Yilmaz, A. Use of diatomite as partial replacement for Portland cement in cement mortars. *Constr. Build. Mater.* **2009**, *23*, 284–288. [CrossRef]
23. Aydin, A.C.; Gül, R. Influence of volcanic originated natural materials as additives on the setting time and some mechanical properties of concrete. *Constr. Build. Mater.* **2007**, *21*, 1277–1281. [CrossRef]
24. Posi, P.; Lertnimoolchai, S.; Sata, V.; Chindaprasirt, P. Pressed lightweight concrete containing calcined diatomite aggregate. *Constr. Build. Mater.* **2013**, *47*, 896–901. [CrossRef]
25. Du, H.; Du, S.; Liu, X. Durability performances of concrete with nano-silica. *Constr. Build. Mater.* **2014**, *73*, 705–712. [CrossRef]
26. Wu, S.; Zhang, C.; Zhou, F.; Ma, S.; Zheng, H. The effect of nano-scale calcium stearate emulsion on the integral waterproof performance and chloride resistance of cement mortar. *Constr. Build. Mater.* **2022**, *317*, 125903. [CrossRef]
27. *KSL5201*; Portland Cement. Korean Industrial Standards: Seoul, Republic of Korea, 2017.
28. *ASTM A C150*; Standard Specification for Portland Cement. ASTM International: West Conshohocken, PA, USA, 2001.
29. *KS L ISO 679*; Cement-Test Methods-Determination of Strength (Second edition 2009-05-01). Korean Industrial Standards: Seoul, Republic of Korea, 2009.
30. Park, J.H.; Yoon, C.B. Properties and durability of cement mortar using calcium stearate and natural pozzolan for concrete surface treatment. *Mater. Sci.* **2022**, *15* 5762. [CrossRef] [PubMed]
31. *KSL5109*; Practice for Mechanical Mixing of Hydraulic Cement Pastes and Mortar of Plastic Consistency. Korean Industrial Standards: Seoul, Republic of Korea, 2017.
32. *KSL5105*; Test Method for Compressive Strength of Hydraulic Cement Mortar. Korean Industrial Standards: Seoul, Republic of Korea, 2022.
33. *KSL5405*; Fly AHY. Korean Industrial Standards: Seoul, Republic of Korea, 2018.
34. *KSL4919*; Cement-Polymer Modified Waterproof Coatings. Korean Industrial Standards: Seoul, Republic of Korea, 2017.
35. *ASTM C 1202*; Electrical Indication of Concrete's Ability to Resist Chloride Ion Penetration. Annual Book of American Society for Testing Materials Standards, Vol. C04.02. ASTM International: West Conshohocken, PA, USA, 1993.
36. *KS F 2711*; Standard Test Method for Resistance of Concrete to Chloride Ion Penetration by Electrical Conductance. Korean Industrial Standards: Seoul, Republic of Korea, 2017.
37. Fernández, J.M.; Duran, A.; Navarro-Blasco, I.; Lanas, J.; Sirera, R.; Alvarez, J.I. Influence of nanosilica and a polycarboxylate ether superplasticizer on the performance of lime mortars. *Cem. Concr. Res.* **2013**, *43*, 12–24. [CrossRef]
38. Shih, J.Y.; Chang, T.P.; Hsiao, T.C. Effect of nanosilica on characterization of Portland cement composite. *Mater. Sci. Eng. A* **2006**, *424*, 266–274. [CrossRef]
39. Li, H.; Zhang, M.H.; Ou, J.P. Abrasion resistance of concrete containing nano-particles for pavement. *Wear* **2006**, *260*, 1262–1266. [CrossRef]
40. Nemati Chari, M.; Naseroleslami, R.; Shekarchi, M. The impact of calcium stearate on characteristics of concrete. *Asian J. Civ. Eng.* **2019**, *20*, 1007–1020. [CrossRef]
41. Lee, W.G.; Yoon, C.B. Experimental Study on Physical Properties and Water Absorption Resistance Evaluation of Cement Mortar Incorporating Inorganic Metal Salt-based Water Repellent Powder. *J. Korean Recycl. Constr. Resour. Inst.* **2021**, *9*, 609–616.
42. Azarhomayun, F.; Haji, M.; Kioumarsi, M.; Shekarchi, M. Effect of calcium stearate and aluminum powder on free and restrained drying shrinkage, crack characteristic and mechanical properties of concrete. *Cem. Concr. Compos.* **2022**, *125*, 104276. [CrossRef]

Disclaimer/Publisher's Note: The statements, opinions and data contained in all publications are solely those of the individual author(s) and contributor(s) and not of MDPI and/or the editor(s). MDPI and/or the editor(s) disclaim responsibility for any injury to people or property resulting from any ideas, methods, instructions or products referred to in the content.

materials

MDPI

Article

Analysis of Durability of Watertight Concretes Modified with the Addition of Fly Ash

Janina Adamus and Bogdan Langier *

Department of Civil Engineering, Faculty of Civil Engineering, Czestochowa University of Technology, 69 Dabrowskiego St., 42-201 Czestochowa, Poland; janina.adamus@gmail.com

* Correspondence: bogdan.langier@pcz.pl

Abstract: The growing demand for watertight concrete structures is conducive to the development of research in this area, but their results are rarely published. In order to partially fill this gap, the authors of the publication present the results of research into the effect of fly ash addition on the watertightness of concrete. Prior to the tests, a recipe for a concrete mix with the addition of a sealing admixture modified with fly ash was developed. The following properties were analyzed: consistency of the concrete mix, air content in the concrete mix, compressive strength of concrete, depth of penetration of water under pressure, and frost resistance of concrete for F150 level. The work meets the expectations of the construction industry with respect to the production of concrete structures resistant not only to the penetration of water into concrete but also resistant to aggressive substances dissolved in water that accelerate the destruction of concrete and corrosion of reinforcement bars. Based on the test results, it was found that the addition of fly ash to the concrete mix enhances the positive impact of the applied sealing admixture, increasing the tightness of the concrete. It reduces the depth of penetration of water under pressure and therefore increases the frost resistance of concrete.

Keywords: watertight concrete; concrete mix; fly ash; water penetration depth; frost resistance

check for updates

Citation: Adamus, J.; Langier, B. Analysis of Durability of Watertight Concretes Modified with the Addition of Fly Ash. *Materials* **2023**, *16*, 5742. https://doi.org/10.3390/ma16175742

Academic Editor: Yuri Ribakov

Received: 31 July 2023
Revised: 18 August 2023
Accepted: 19 August 2023
Published: 22 August 2023

Copyright: © 2023 by the authors. Licensee MDPI, Basel, Switzerland. This article is an open access article distributed under the terms and conditions of the Creative Commons Attribution (CC BY) license (https://creativecommons.org/licenses/by/4.0/).

1. Introduction

Although concrete is one of the oldest building materials, it is still subjected to various modifications in order to improve its physical and mechanical properties and durability in an aggressive environment. Currently, one of the basic components of concrete is modern chemical admixtures, thanks to which it is possible to optimize its properties. The variety of available chemical admixtures allows for their selection in terms of improving both the properties of the concrete mix and the durability of concrete (improving fluidity, lowering the W/C ratio without losing fluidity, sealing, aeration, accelerating or delaying setting of the concrete, increasing early strength, improving frost resistance and many other). The rapid development of chemistry also enables the use of various additives, which are materials usually used in quantities exceeding 5% of the mass of cement. They are divided into two types; one is inert additives in the form of filler of aggregates or pigments, and the other type has pozzolanic properties (silica fume, silica fly ash) or hydraulic properties (granulated blast furnace slag). The use of admixtures and additives allows modification of the concrete mix and/or hardened concrete. Concern for the environment, in accordance with the principles of sustainable development, makes it necessary to use ecological construction products that allow reducing the consumption of cement, the production of which has a negative impact on the environment, and natural construction aggregates, whose easy to extract resources, are slowly running out. In Jura et al. [1], the possibility of using fly ash from the combustion of wood–sunflower biomass as a sand substitute for the production of concrete was analyzed. In turn, Rutkowska et al. [2,3] analyzed the possibility of using fly ash from sewage sludge as an additive to ordinary concretes. Khatib et al. [4] indicate that municipal solid waste incineration bottom ash can partially substitute fine aggregate. In [5] durability of mortars with fly ash subjected to freezing and thawing cycles and sulfate attack was tested. Kelechi et al. [6] analyzed the durability performance of self-compacting concrete containing fly ash, crumb rubber, and calcium carbide waste. Raydan et al. [7] propose the use of glass powder as a material partially replacing cement. Pietrzak and Ulewicz [8] propose to use a post-consumer thermoplastic elastomer (TPE) additive derived from used car floor mats as a substitute for sand or fine aggregate. Some of the works concern special concretes in which additives play a special role, such as absorbing harmful ionizing radiation [9,10] or improving watertightness.

In recent years, the demand for building structures made of watertight concrete has been increasing rapidly. The limited availability of building lots in large cities means that many newly erected buildings have underground parking floors, which, due to the environment and harmful external conditions, need complete protection against water penetration into their structure. In addition, the intensive development of civilization causes the formation of "urban heat islands" with a much higher temperature compared to their outskirts. In order to counteract this, more and more buildings are erected with roofs covered with vegetation, which act as natural heat accumulators [11]. According to [12], green roofs can reduce the cooling load by up to 70% and provide a significant improvement in thermal comfort conditions. The environmental benefits of green roofs focus on reducing pollutant concentrations, sequestration carbon, and reducing urban noise. The positive impact of green roofs on the urban climate was demonstrated in [13].

Mousavi et al. [14] showed that the optimally designed green roof and its proper operation could result in a 12.8% increase in comfort hours and a 14% reduction in energy consumption compared to the analyzed basic variant. Additionally, by increasing the amount of green space in cities, natural habitats for bees and other pollinating insects increase [15]. The authors of the work [16] also indicate that implementing food, energy, and water production systems on urban rooftops can potentially help cities become more self-sufficient.

However, it should be remembered that the "green roof" technology requires 100% protection of the ceiling against moisture penetration. The residents of the famous Villa Savoye, designed in 1928 by the French architect Le Corbusier, learned painfully about the consequences of not meeting this condition. After a few months after its erection, they had to move out of the building, as it turned out that water leaked through the roof, and the repair process turned out to be unprofitable and difficult to carry out [17]. Certainly, the history of this building would have been different if watertight concrete and an appropriate sealing system had been used for its construction. The presented example shows that waterproof concrete should be used not only in structures made below but also above ground level when operating conditions require protection of concrete elements against the destructive effects of water. This applies to concrete structures exposed to the pressure of groundwater, such as subways, underground passages, garages, basements of buildings, water reservoirs, sewage treatment plants, as well as flat roofs or small architectural objects such as fountains.

The impact of aggressive groundwater causes corrosion and damage to concrete structures as a result of corrosion of steel reinforcement and concrete cracks. The durability of concrete structures largely depends on the resistance to water penetration and chlorine, sulfur, or carbon dioxide compounds dissolved in it. According to [18], the processes of penetration of these substances into concrete elements take place by diffusion, penetration, absorption, or electrical migration. Basheer et al. [19] reviewed the transport mechanisms, such as water absorption, permeability, and diffusion, which are responsible for the penetration of harmful substances into concrete. It has been shown that all the transport processes are interrelated and affect the strength parameters of concrete. Thus, concrete durability can be assessed based on the transport mechanisms. Transport mechanisms occurring near the surface or in the vicinity of the reinforcement play a dominant role in concrete degradation.

Therefore, test methods assessing surface zone are of particular interest, especially in view of non-destructive evaluation of existing structures.

Currently, we are dealing with increasingly larger and deeper underground structures that are subject to destruction to a much greater extent than before. Unfortunately, classic concrete does not meet the waterproofing criteria. The thermal effects of cement hydration cause thermal stresses, which in turn cause the formation of a network of microscopic channels through which water easily migrates into the concrete. This is especially dangerous in the winter, when the freezing water increases in volume and bursts the concrete. Water leakage in concrete elements poses a significant issue as it shortens the structure's lifespan and necessitates continuous maintenance. According to [20], factors contributing to water leakage through concrete structures can be divided into three groups: design, construction, and operational factors. It is usually a combination of these factors, so the problem of water leakage should be considered from the perspective of the whole system. In the case of diaphragm walls, as emphasized by Larisch [21], the method of concrete placement plays a key role.

One of the possibilities to improve the durability and reliability of concrete structures and to increase the comfort of their use is the application of modern materials and construction technologies. Until recently, the main method of extending the durability of concrete structures was to use external insulation in the form of coatings, foils, membranes, or bituminous felts [22–25] to act as a physical barrier against water. Exterior insulation tests focus primarily on the mechanical properties and chemical resistance of the materials they are made of and their adhesion to the hardened concrete surface. In recent years, in order to prevent water intrusion into new or existing concrete structures, sealants based on sodium silicate are used, which react with portlandite in the cement matrix to form calcium-silicate hydrates, partially filling the pores of the concrete. According to [26], this reaction causes an increase in the hardness of the concrete surface of the structure by about 12%. By increasing the impermeability to water by increasing the compactness of the concrete (reducing micropores, microvoids, and microcracks), the durability of the structure is extended. X. Xue et al. [27]) claim that the water-soluble hydrophobic agent they developed for impregnating concrete elements, in addition to improving water resistance, also shows excellent thermal, low-temperature, ultraviolet, alkaline, and acid resistance. It is also resistant to chlorides. Izarra et al. [28] observed that a hydrophobic release agent containing SiO_2-CH_3 nanoparticles dispersed in vegetable oil, used to facilitate formwork demoulding, despite the small penetration depth, improves the water resistance of concrete without affecting its compressive strength. The performance of the moisture barrier system can be significantly enhanced by the use of waterproofing/dampproofing admixtures in concrete [29]. They can effectively reduce the rate of penetration of water and aggressive chemicals dissolved in it and therefore delay the negative effects of damage caused by freezing and thawing water. For this purpose, water-reducing, air-entraining, and hydrophobic admixtures are introduced into concrete mixes. In the Muhammad et al. [30], it was found that most of the work on improving the resistance of concrete to the penetration of water and harmful substances from the environment concerns the use of polymer-based materials, silicates containing compounds, silanes, siloxanes, cementing materials, as well as nanomaterials. On this basis, the authors distinguished three groups of factors determining the watertightness of concrete, taking into account the structure of materials (macro-, micro-, and nanomaterials), methods of their application (coatings applied to dry concrete or modification of the concrete mix) and their function (thin-layer coatings reducing water absorption, membranes and pore blockers). The water absorption test is most often used to assess the impact of these factors.

At work [31], the impact of a carboxylic acid-based admixture on improving the water resistance of concrete and increasing the self-sealing capacity of the cement matrix was investigated. Li et al. [32] enhanced the anti-penetration properties of the mortar prepared from cement and powder silane water repellent thanks to the nucleation of calcium silicate hydrates (C-S-H). In turn, Geng et al. [33] propose a new method of hydrophobic treatment of concrete using SiO_2 sol and silane emulsion. They showed that the hydrophobic effect was obtained due to the morphological changes of the concrete (C40), mainly the improvement of the concrete surface microstructure. Muwashee et al. [34] used bentonite and limestone dust as waterproofing admixtures. Among the hydrophobic agents for concrete, the most commonly used are metal soaps, wax emulsions, and liquid silane emulsions. The limitation of the large-scale use of hydrophobic additives is usually their high price and the fact that they are often damaged during use. In [35], an inexpensive and commercially available polydimethylsiloxane (PDMS) was proposed as a cement admixture for the hydrophobic modification of cement mortar. Thanks to this modification, a superhydrophobic material was obtained, which can be used in waterproof concrete, and additionally gives it anti-corrosion properties. The addition of PDMS increased the fluidity of the cement mortar, reduced the water requirement, and extended the setting time. Some researchers, including [36,37], see the solution to the problem of water permeability through concrete in the use of shrinkage-reducing admixtures and subsequent cracking of concrete, e.g., containing glycol ether, which reduces the diffusion of chlorides into concrete. Eamoharram et al. [38] showed a positive effect of nano-organic silicon compounds on improving concrete tightness. The authors of the work [39], in order to increase the water resistance of concrete, propose Dual-Crystallization Waterproofing Technology, combining hygroscopic crystallization, hydrophilic crystallization, and hydrophobic properties. They propose the use of a two-component reactive solution that can be sprayed on either fully cured or old concrete. As a result of chemical and physical reactions, water transport through the concrete matrix is minimized. Hygroscopic crystals block the pores of the concrete, reducing the space available for water.

Studies by Matar and Barhoun [40] on the impact of a waterproofing admixture on the properties of concrete made from recycled aggregate also deserve attention. Research conducted in this direction is particularly valuable due to the fact that the partial or complete replacement of natural aggregate with aggregate obtained by crushing demolished concrete is currently an innovative application in sustainable construction, as it reduces the landfill area required for waste disposal and protects natural resources by reducing the amount of aggregate extracted from pits or quarries, which was also noted by the authors of the work [41].

While watertight concretes, enhanced with specialized admixtures and additives, have been increasingly used in recent years and become impermeable to water after cur-ing, Chew and Silva [20] emphasize that an important factor determining the comprehensive watertightness of the structure is the prevention of water leakage through structural joints and expansion joints, requiring a special joint sealing and waterproofing system. The basic principles of sealing are described in [42].

Waterproof concrete structures, the so-called "White Box Concept," are designed and built to prevent water leakage from or into the structure. B. H. Cho et al. [43] conducted a comparison of the watertightness of underground structures sealed with the traditional method of embedding PVC tapes between individual construction elements and the modified method of attaching the tape to concrete elements by means of gluing. The authors of this work emphasize that the adhesive bonding tapes provide a much better and more durable watertightness of the structure.

The literature review indicates that, at the moment, the best solution to ensure the tightness of concrete structures is the use of watertight concrete in combination with an appropriate system for sealing expansion joints and all elements included in the structure. Despite the growing demand for waterproof concretes, there are few works on their design in the available technical literature, especially in open access. Companies protect their formulas and rarely share their knowledge in this area. Therefore, the authors of this work decided to present the design of the concrete mix as well as the results of tests of the concretes intended for structures exposed to groundwater pressure, such as garages, basements, or other types of underground technical rooms. The main goal of the work is an analysis of the effect of flay ash addition on the watertightness of concrete. Our test results showed that fly ash enhanced the effect of the sealing admixture, additionally limiting the depth of penetration of water under pressure, which is extremely important not only in the case of concrete used for underground structures but also for the construction of green roofs, which is a kind of novelty on the market. In the absence of detailed guidelines for the design of watertight concretes the test results can be used by technologists and concrete designers as guidelines in the selection of the composition of watertight concrete. Experiments allow for reducing mistakes in the future.

2. Materials and Methods

In order to study the effect of flay ash on the watertightness of concrete., the concrete mixes with the addition of sealing admixture, which was modified with fly ash, were developed. As a part of the work, the following 4 variants of concrete mixes for making watertight concrete were designed:

- V1: reference concrete mix with an admixture of plasticizer and superplasticizer,
- V2: concrete mix of variant 1 modified with the addition of a sealing admixture,
- V3: concrete mix of variant 1 modified with the addition of fly ash used as a replacement for a part of the aggregate,
- V4: concrete mix of variant 3 modified with the addition of a sealing admixture.

The adopted designations of the mixes correspond to the order of design and execution of the tested series of concretes. First, a reference series (V1) was designed experimentally, and then, the reference series was modified with the addition of a sealing admixture and marked as V2. In the next stage, the reference series was redesigned by introducing fly ash (V3), and then a sealing admixture was added to the V3 series, and thus the V4 series was created. When designing concrete mixes, it was taken into account that the technology of water-tight concrete is effective only when we are able to eliminate possible cracks that arise not only as a result of construction errors but also improper technology of concrete production. Therefore, special attention was paid to the selection of concrete mix components, especially the selection of admixtures and additives to improve the plasticity and tightness of concrete and to ensure the proper ratio of water to cement and the optimal distribution of aggregate grains.

Experimental studies of concrete mixes and hardened concrete included testing:

- consistency of the concrete mix,
- air content in the concrete mix,
- concrete compressive strength,
- depth of penetration of water under pressure,
- frost resistance of concrete for level F150.

2.1. Material Properties

Portland slag cement CEM II/B-S 42.5N NA [44] was used to produce concrete, whose composition, mechanical and physical properties are presented in Tables 1 and 2, and natural aggregate: fine with a grain size of 0–2 mm and coarse (gravel) with a grain size of 2–8 mm and 8–16 mm.

BV3M plasticizer, ViscoCrete 5 superplasticizer, and WT-200P sealing admixture were used as concrete admixtures. Silica fly ash with pozzolanic characteristics meeting the requirements of the standard PN-EN 450-1:2012 [45], i.e., loss of ignition of A category, fineness of category N, was additive to concretes. The chemical composition of fly ash is given in Table 3.

Table 1. Chemical composition of cement CEM II/B-S 42.5N NA.

Chemicals	Formula	Content [wt.%]
Calcium oxide	CaO	53.37
Silicon dioxide	SiO_2	26.73
Aluminium dioxide	Al_2O_3	7.06
Iron oxide	Fe_2O_3	2.81
Magnesium oxide	MgO	3.51
Sulfur oxide	SO_3	2.09
Chlorine	Cl	0.059
Sodium oxide	Na_2O_{eq}	0.66
insoluble parts		3.49
roasting losses		1.77

Table 2. Mechanical and physical properties of cement CEM II/B-S 42,5N NA.

Curing Time [day]	Compressive Strength [MPa]		Physical Properties of Cement		
	Average	Required			
2	21.6	≥10.0	specific surface [cm^2/g]	Soundness (expansion) [mm]	Initial setting time [min]
28	58.7	≥42.5 ≤62.5	4091.0	0.6	221.0

Table 3. Chemical composition of fly ash.

Chemicals	Formula	Content [wt.%]
Silicon dioxide	SiO_2	52.2
Aluminium dioxide	Al_2O_3	28.4
Iron oxide	Fe_2O_3	8.1
Calcium oxide	CaO	4.1
Magnesium oxide	MgO	2.4
Sulfur trioxide	SO_3	0.4
Sodium oxide	Na_2O	0.9
Potassium oxide	K_2O	2.7
Chlorine	Cl	0.008
Loss of ignition	LOI	2.6

2.2. Concrete Mix Design

When developing the recipe for concrete mixes, the following parameters were sought: water penetration depth: <30 mm, degree of frost resistance: minimum F150, consistency class after 5 min from the first contact of water with cement S2, air content in the concrete mix after 5 min from the first contact of water with cement: 2 ÷ 3%.

As part of the design of the composition of the concrete mix of variant V1, gradation tests were carried out, and then the mixing proportions were experimentally determined in order to obtain the optimal graining of the aggregate by examining its bulk density and voids. The grading curve of the aggregate mix, together with the limit curves according to PN-B-06265:2022-08 [46], is shown in Figure 1.

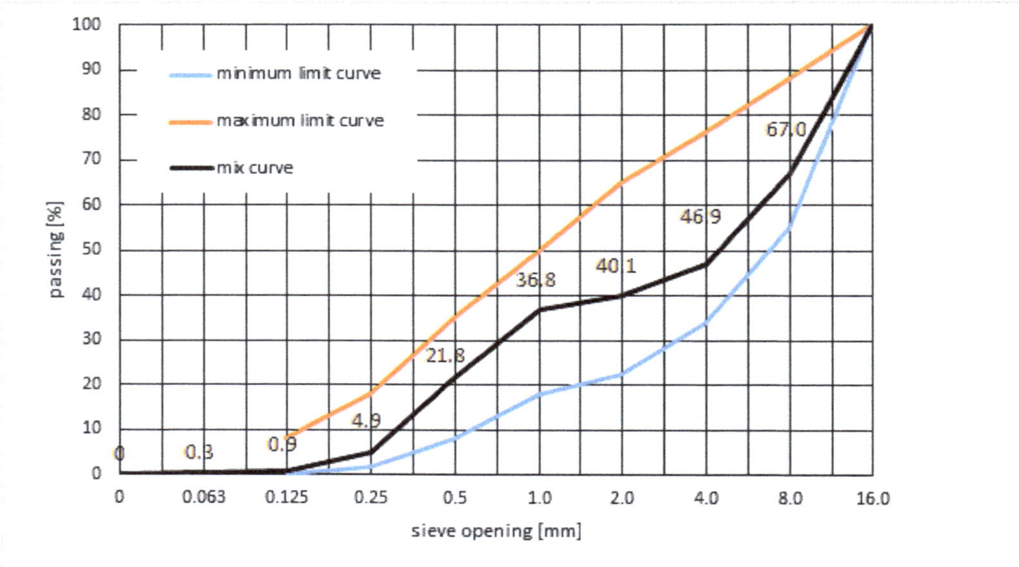

Figure 1. Grading curve of aggregate mix 0–16 mm with limit curves.

A sealing admixture in the amount of 1% of the cement mass was introduced into the designed composition of the concrete mix of variant V1 (variant V2). In variant V3 of the concrete mix, silica fly ash was introduced into the composition as a substitute for part of the aggregate without using a sealing admixture. As part of further modifications in variant V4, fly ash and a sealing admixture in the amount of 1% of the cement mass were used at the same time. The recipes of the tested concrete mixes are presented in Table 4.

Table 4. Recipes of concrete mixes per 1 m^3 of concrete.

No	Component of the Concrete Mix	Density (g/cm^3)	Mass [kg]			
			Variant of Concrete Mix			
			V1	V2	V3	V4
1.	Sand 0/2 mm	2.62	700.00	700.00	682.00	682.00
2.	Gravel 2/8 mm	2.58	501.00	501.00	488.00	488.00
3.	Gravel 8/16 mm	2.58	619.00	619.00	603.00	603.00
4.	Cement CEM II/B-S 42.5N NA	3.05	360.00	360.00	360.00	360.00
5.	Fly ash	2.20	0.00	0.00	40.00	40.00
6.	Water	1.00	156.00	153.00	156.00	153.00
7.	Plasticizer (BV3M)	1.19	1.80	1.80	1.70	1.70
8.	Superplasticizer (Visco Crete 5)	1.07	3.60	3.60	3.60	3.60
9.	Sealing admixture (WT-200P)	1.10	0.00	3.60	0.00	3.60

Fly ash in V3 and V4 concrete mixes was introduced into the composition as a substitute for part of the aggregate. All designed concrete mixes meet the requirements of concrete durability in a chemically aggressive environment.

2.3. Methods of Testing

In order to check whether the designed concrete mixes meet the design assumptions, qualifying the concrete for use in the construction of facilities exposed to groundwater, standard tests of the obtained concretes carried out, such as consistency of the concrete mix, air content in the concrete mix, concrete compressive strength and depth of water penetration under pressure. Due to the fact that concretes are also used in cold regions exposed to excessive freezing and thawing during the year, an additional frost resistance test of concrete was carried out. The purpose of such a test is to check the resistance of concrete to the destructive effects of changing temperatures. All tests were carried out in accordance with applicable standards.

The test of the consistency of the concrete mix was carried out using the concrete slump test in accordance with the standard PN-EN 12350-2:2019-07 [47]. The consistency test of the concrete mix was carried out individually for each batch of concrete mix in the series. The assessment of the change in consistency over time was performed at the same time intervals from the moment of combining the cement with water. The concrete mix was stored in a sealed container and mixed again before testing. An evaluation of the workability of freshly made concrete up to 60 min was carried out, examining their consistency after 5, 15, 30, 45, and 60 min.

In addition to affecting the strength of concrete, the air content can also affect the migration of harmful compounds and the durability of concrete in various environmental conditions. It can also impact the finish and cosmetic appearance of concrete. Therefore, air content testing is required for concretes used for structures that may be exposed to the aggressive effects of the surrounding environment.

The air content in the fresh concrete was tested using the pressure method (Figure 2.) in accordance with the standard PN-EN 12350-7:2019-08 [48]. The air content in individual concrete mixes was measured 5 min after the first contact of cement with water during the mixing process.

Figure 2. View of the device for testing air content in fresh concrete (Air Content Meter): (1) pressure gauge with aeration value indicator, (2) air chamber, (3) test container with a volume of 8 dm^3.

The compressive strength was tested on a hydraulic strength press (Figure 3) in accordance with the standard PN-EN 12390-3:2019-07 [49] using 5 cubic samples with dimensions of 150 × 150 × 150 mm and 5 cubic samples with dimensions of 100 × 100 × 100 mm, for each variant of the tested concrete.

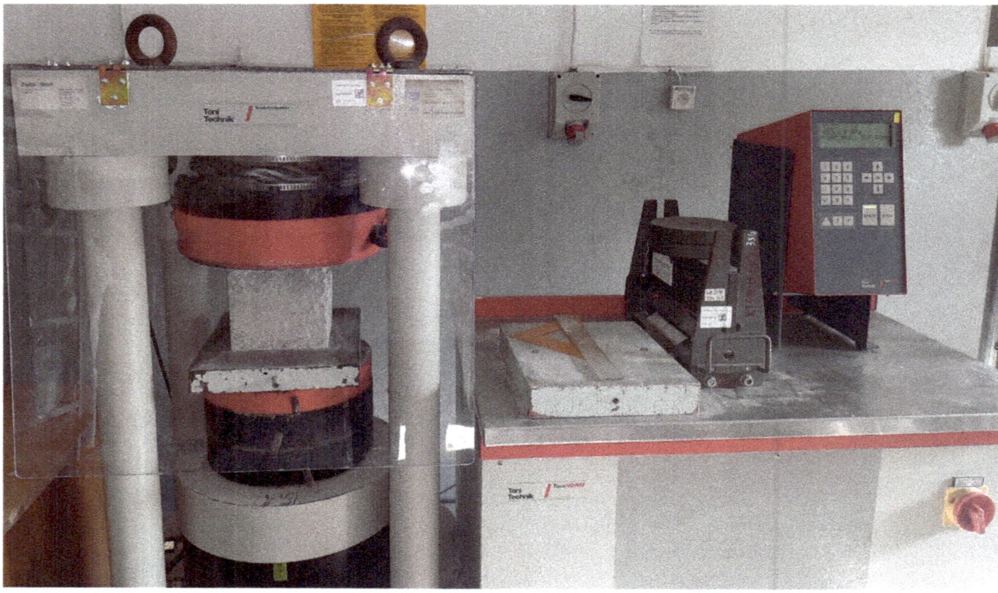

Figure 3. View of stand for compressive strength testing.

The concrete mix was placed in molds in two layers, each of which was compacted mechanically on a vibrating table. The samples remained in the forms for 24 h. After demoulding, they were placed in water, where they were cured at the temperature of 20 ± 2 °C. In the case of cubic samples with an edge of 100 mm, the compressive strength was tested after 2, 7, 28, 56, and 90 days, and in the case of the samples with an edge of 150 mm, the tests were carried out after 7, 28 and 90 days.

The depth of penetration of water under pressure into concrete specimens was tested in accordance with the standard PN-EN 12390-8:2019-08 [50]. The tests were carried out on cubic concrete samples with an edge of 150 mm. The tests were started after 56 days of curing concrete samples in water at a temperature of 20 ± 2 °C. Prior to testing, the samples were dried to constant weight. From the surface of the samples, where the water was pressed against the sample, cement laitance was removed from the area with a diameter of 75 mm. Then the samples were subjected to a stream of water at a pressure of 500 ± 50 kPa. A view of the samples during the water penetration test is shown in Figure 4.

The study was conducted continuously for 72 ± 2 h. After this time, the samples were broken (Figure 5), and the depth of penetration of water was measured.

In countries such as Poland, where subzero temperatures are common in winter, it is necessary to test concrete for frost resistance because water in concrete pores freezes under the influence of negative temperatures, increasing its volume by about 10%. This causes significant stresses, leading to cracking of the concrete and loss of its tightness. Cyclic repetition of this phenomenon can lead to the complete destruction of the concrete structure. Therefore, freeze-thaw tests were carried out in accordance with the standard PN-B-06265. The tests were carried out on cubic samples with an edge of 150 mm after 56 days. The samples were subjected to 150 cycles of freezing in the air to a temperature of −18 ± 2 °C within 4 h and thawing in water at a temperature of 18 ± 2 °C for the next 4 h. After the last cycle the samples were weighed and tested for compressive strength. According to the PN-B-06265 standard, the frost-resistant level of mature concrete is achieved when, after the cycles of freezing and thawing: (1) none of the tested concrete samples shows cracks, (2) the average weight loss of the tested samples does not exceed 5%, (3) compressive strength of samples subjected to freeze-thaw cycles is not lower than 20% compared to the control samples.

Figure 4. View of samples during water permeability test.

Figure 5. Splitting a sample after a water penetration test.

3. Test Results and Discussion

3.1. Consistency of Concrete Mix

The results of the consistency test are presented in Table 5 and graphically in Figure 6.

Table 5. Results of consistency of concrete mix made with slump test.

Time after Which the Test Is Performed [min]	Concrete Mix Cone Slump [mm]			
	V1	V2	V3	V4
5	50	60	50	60
15	80	85	85	90
30	95	95	95	100
45	90	90	90	90
60	90	90	90	90

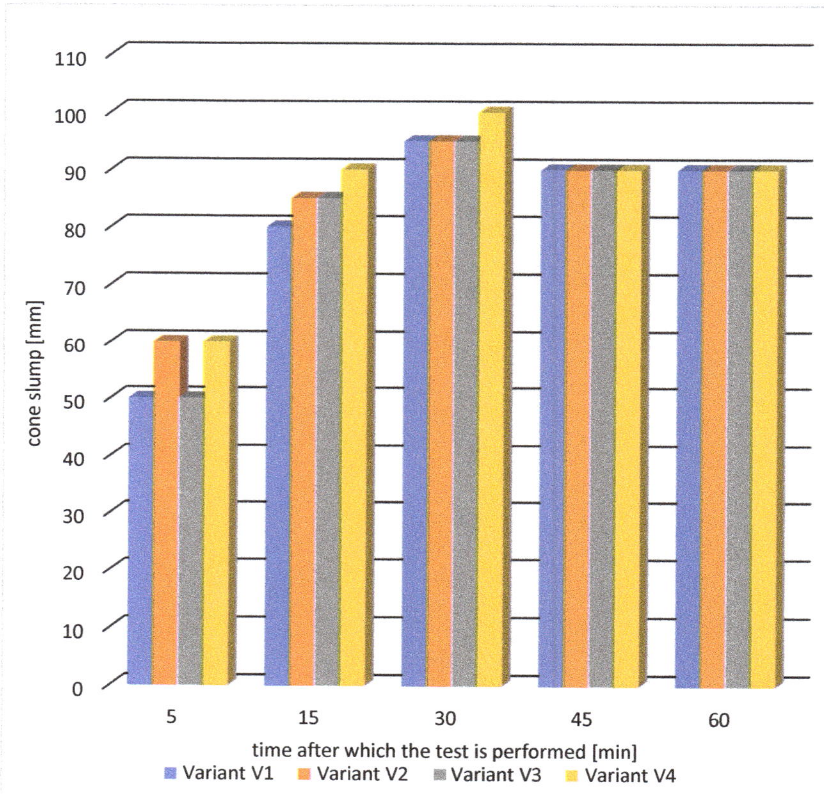

Figure 6. Results of consistency of the concrete mix.

The results of testing the consistency of concrete mixes indicate that for all variants of concrete mixes, the assumed consistency class S2 was obtained after 5 min. An increased drop of the cone of the tested mixes in the time interval of up to 30 min can be seen for all tested variants. The effective action of the fluidizing admixtures was obtained after 30 min from the moment of combining the cement with water in the mixing process. A slight decrease in consistency after 30 min should be explained by of hydration of the cement binder. The concrete mix, according to variant V4, with the addition of fly ash and sealing admixture, showed the greatest liquefaction. Between 30 and 60 min, all concrete mixes retained their workability, and the cone slump was 90 mm.

3.2. Air Content in the Concrete Mix

The results of air content in the fresh concrete are presented in Table 6.

Table 6. Air content in the concrete mix.

Air Content in Concrete Mix [%]			
Variant			
V1	V2	V3	V4
2.3	2.2	2.6	2.4

All concrete mix recipes met the assumption of air content within the limit of 2 ÷ 3%. Concrete mixes containing silica fly ash (variants V3 and V4) are characterized by a slightly higher air content. It can be seen that the addition of a sealing admixture reduces the air content in the tested mixes, both in the case of its introduction to the reference concrete mix (variant V1) and after its introduction to the concrete mix of variant V3 (with the addition of fly ash). In the concrete mix of the V1 variant, compared to the V2 variant, the air content decreased from 2.3% to 2.2%, whereas in the concrete mix of the V3 variant, compared to V4, there was a decrease from 2.6% to 2.4%.

3.3. Compressive Strength Test of Concrete

The test results of compressive strength are presented in Table 7.

Table 7. Compressive strength.

Variant	Average Compressive Strength [MPa]				
	Cubic Samples with Side of 100 mm				
	2 Days	7 Days	28 Days	56 Days	90 Days
V1 SD *	28.0 1.49	48.4/↑72.9% 1.15	69.9/↑44.4% 1.55	72.6/↑3.9% 1.54	72.7/↑0.1% 1.86
V2 SD *	26.5 1.09	47.0/↑77.4% 0.88	68.5/↑45.7% 1.62	73.3/↑7.0% 1.03	73.5/↑0.3% 1.91
V3 SD *	25.6 0.99	47.6/↑85.9% 0.99	69.1/↑45.2% 1.40	72.1/↑4.3% 1.42	73.8/↑2.4% 1.12
V4 SD *	24.5 1.11	45.6/↑86.1% 0.86	70.7/↑55.0% 1.51	71.7/↑1.4% 1.42	74.7/↑4.2% 1.76
	Cubic Samples with Side of 150 mm				
	2 Days	7 Days	28 Days	56 Days	90 Days
V1 SD *	-	48.6 1.22	68.6/↑41.0% 1.48	-	70.9/↑3.9% 1.38
V2 SD *	-	52.0 1.65	68.3/↑31.4% 1.58	-	71.4/↑4.5% 1.84
V3 SD *	-	46.2 1.35	69.6/↑50.7% 1.22	-	73.8/↑6.0% 1.22
V4 SD *	-	48.5 1.37	71.0/↑46.4% 1.49	-	75.2/↑5.9% 1.57

*—Standard deviation; ↑increase in compressive strength [%] is shown in green

The tests showed that after 28 days of concrete curing, the compressive strength class C50/60 was obtained for all four recipes, and the strengths were similar to each other. The largest difference occurred between variants V2 and V4 and amounted to about 4%. The concrete of variant V4, with the addition of fly ash and sealing admixture, obtained the highest value of compressive strength, which was 71 MPa. This may be due to the synergistic effect of the fly ash with the sealing admixture, which has an impact on the elimination of micro-cracks in concrete.

The addition of fly ash reduced the compressive strength in the first days of concrete maturation (variants V3 and V4), but in the later period, concretes with the addition of fly ash achieve a greater increase in strength, specifically the concrete according to variant V4 obtained the highest compressive strength after 90 days of maturation.

Figure 7 shows the change in compressive strength during the maturation of the tested variants from the 2nd to the 90th day of maturation of the cubic samples with a side of 100 mm. While Figure 8 graphically demonstrates statistical data on the results of the static compression test in the form of a box plot.

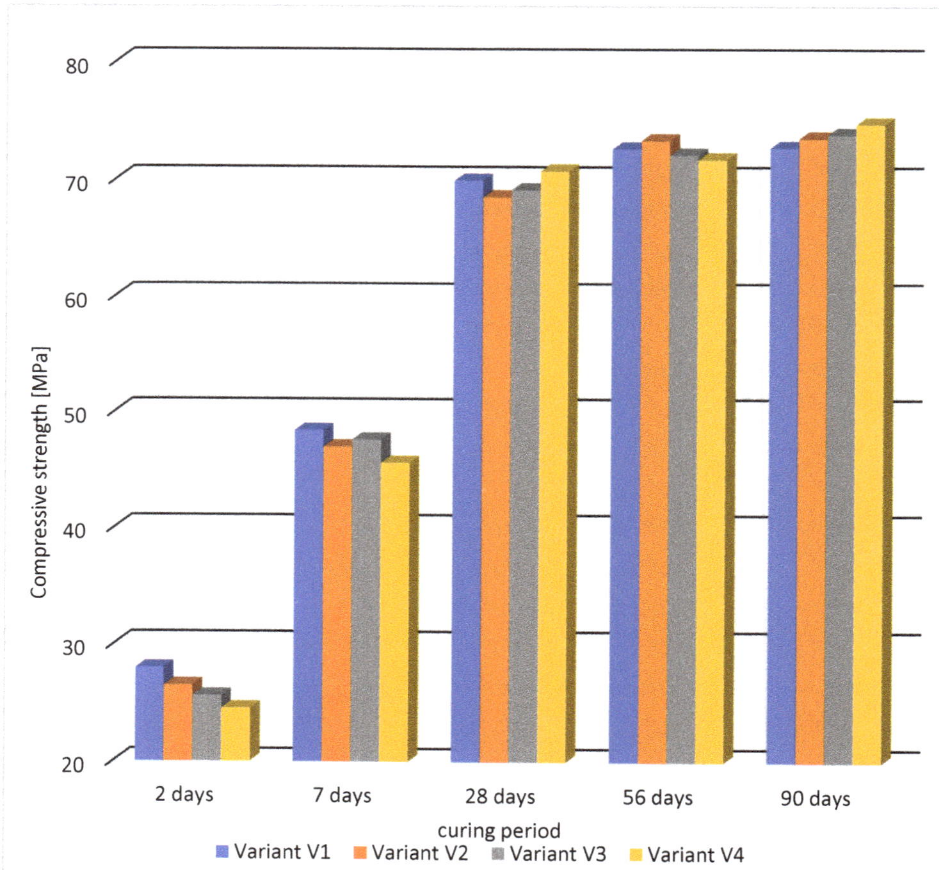

Figure 7. Compressive strength of concrete at various ages for samples with a side of 100 mm.

After 2 days of concrete curing, the highest strength of 28 MPa was obtained in the reference series, while in the variants with the addition of fly ash, the strengths were the lowest (variants V3 and V4). Between the 2nd and 7th day of maturation, concretes with the addition of fly ash achieved a higher increase in compressive strength compared to the series without ash, but the strengths were still slightly lower. After 28 days, very similar results of compressive strength were obtained in all variants, and the greatest increase in strength was obtained for the concrete variant V4. In the further period of concrete curing between 56 and 90 days, a further increase in compressive strength was observed for variants V3 and V4 containing fly ash.

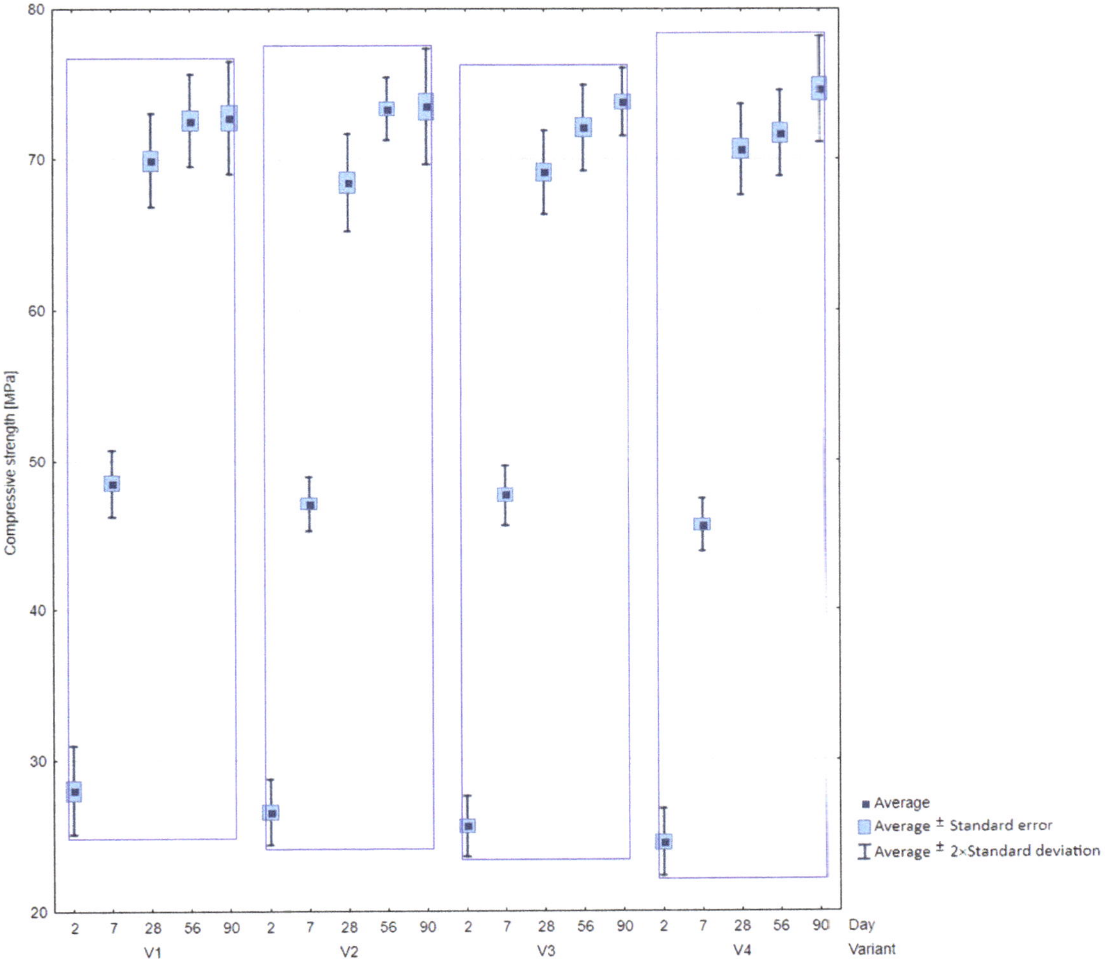

Figure 8. Box-plot for compressive strength results.

3.4. Water Penetration Test

The results of water penetration, i.e., the depth at which water penetrated the concrete sample, are shown in Figure 9, while an example of the appearance of the sample after fracture is shown in Figure 10.

The depth of water penetration into the concrete of the reference series (V1) was 41 mm. For the remaining modified concrete mix recipes (variants V2 ÷ V3), the assumed water tightness of concrete was obtained, i.e., the depth of penetration of water under pressure did not exceed the assumed limit of 30 mm. The analysis shows that the sealing admixture (variant V2) and fly ash (variant V3) affect the reduction in the penetration depth. Modification of the reference series of concrete (variant V1) by introducing fly ash into the concrete mix (variant V3) resulted in a reduction in water penetration by 39%, while modification of variant V1 with sealing admixture (variant V2) resulted in the reduction in water penetration by 56%. In the case of variant V4, the addition of fly ash enhanced the effect of sealing admixture, reducing water penetration by 61%. The synergy of both components effectively seals the concrete structure, creating a barrier that is hardly permeable to water.

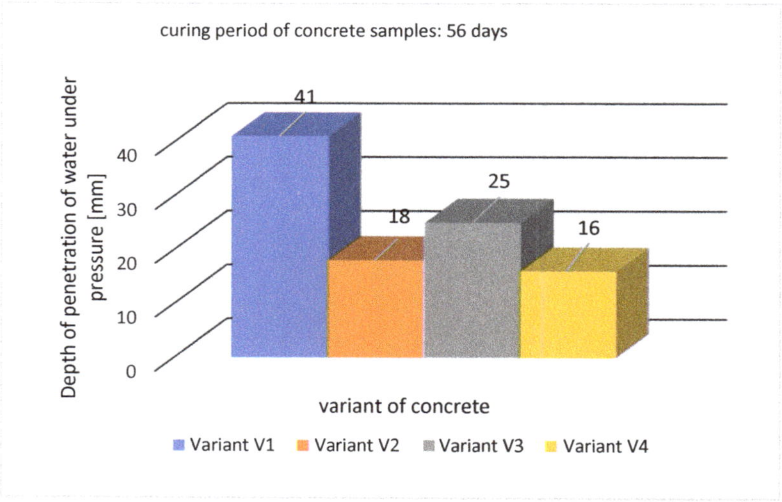

Figure 9. Depth of penetration of water under pressure for analyzed concretes.

Figure 10. View of the concrete sample after the depth of penetration test.

Such concrete reduces not only the water penetration into the concrete but also prevents the ingress of aggressive substances dissolved in water, which in turn decreases the destruction of concrete and corrosion of reinforcing bars.

3.5. *Freeze-Thaw Test*

In all tested variants, no loss of mass for samples subjected to freezing and thawing cycles was recorded. The results of the strength decrease tests are shown in Figure 11.

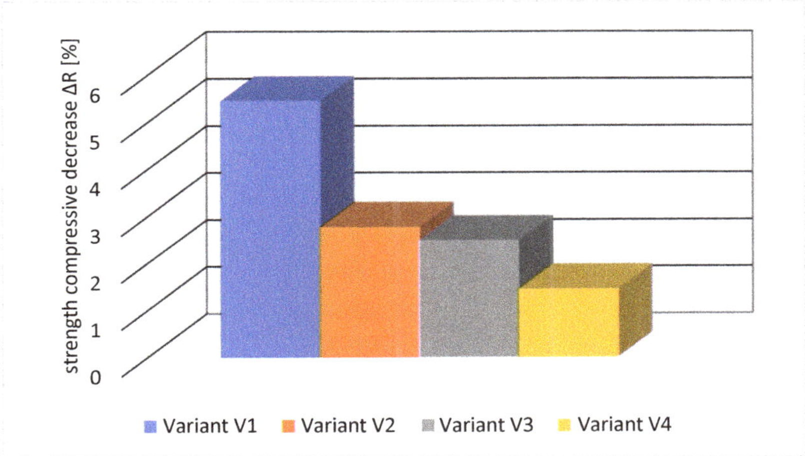

Figure 11. The average decrease in strength of tested concrete samples.

The analysis of the freeze-thaw tests showed that the assumed F150 class was obtained for all four concrete mix recipes. None of the tested samples was cracked or scratched. Concrete, according to variant V1, shows the greatest decrease in compressive strength, i.e., 5.46%. The smallest decrease in strength, i.e., 1.45%, was observed for concrete according to variant V4. The reason for the better results in the case of variant V4 is a more airtight structure compared to other concretes due to the use of both a sealing admixture and fly ash, which reduces the access of water to the interior of the concrete.

4. Conclusions

Waterproof concrete is a modern building material that allows for replacing traditional solutions using external insulation in the form of coatings or membranes. Appropriate design of the concrete mix and execution of the concrete ensures the extension of the service life of the concrete structures. Based on the obtained results of the conducted tests, it can be stated that:

1. The applied sealing admixture had a positive effect on the tightness of the concrete and thus improved the frost resistance of the concrete. A 56% decrease in water penetration from 41 mm for the V1 series to 18 mm for the V2 series was observed.
2. Fly ash enhanced the effect of the sealing admixture, additionally limiting the depth of water penetration under pressure. For the V4 series, the depth of water penetration was 16 mm, which is a reduction in this parameter by 61%.
3. The addition of fly ash to the concrete mix improved its workability and increased the air content in the concrete mix. It reduced the compressive strength in the first stage of maturation but increased it later, i.e., after 90 days.
4. The sealing admixture has a positive effect on the tightness of the concrete, which is reflected in the compressive strength. After 90 days of curing, it was found that in concrete without fly ash, the strength increased by 1.1% (series V1 and V2), while in the presence of fly ash by 1.2% (series V2 and V3).
5. Analysing the properties of the tested concretes, it can be concluded that the most favorable results were obtained for the V4 series, which contained the addition of fly ash and a sealing admixture.

In the absence of detailed guidelines for the design of watertight concretes the test results can be used by technologists and concrete designers as guidelines in the selection of the composition of watertight concrete.

Future research will include an analysis of the possibility of using fly ash from municipal waste incineration in the composition of watertight concrete.

Author Contributions: Conceptualization, J.A.; methodology, J.A. and B.L.; formal analysis, J.A. and B.L.; investigation, J.A. and B.L.; resources, J.A. and B.L.; writing—original draft preparation, J.A. and B.L.; writing—review and editing, J.A. and B.L.; visualization, B.L.; supervision, J.A. All authors have read and agreed to the published version of the manuscript.

Funding: This work was financed by Czestochowa University of Technology under research project No BS/PB-500-301/2023.

Institutional Review Board Statement: Not applicable.

Informed Consent Statement: Not applicable.

Data Availability Statement: The data presented in this study are available on request from the corresponding author.

Conflicts of Interest: The authors declare no conflict of interest.

References

1. Jura, J.; Ulewicz, M. Assessment of the possibility of using fly ash from biomass combustion for concrete. *Materials* **2021**, *14*, 6708. [CrossRef]
2. Rutkowska, G.; Chalecki, M.; Zółtowski, M. Fly ash from thermal conversion of sludge as a cement substitute in concrete manufacturing. *Sustainability* **2021**, *13*, 4182. [CrossRef]
3. Rutkowska, G.; Zółtowski, M.; Liss, M. The use of modal analysis in addition percentage differentiation, and mechanical properties of ordinary concretes with the addition of fly ash from sewage sludge. *Materials* **2021**, *14*, 5039. [CrossRef] [PubMed]
4. Khatib, J.M.; Jahami, A.; Kordi, A.E.; Sonebi, M.; Malek, Z.; Elchamaa, R.; Dakkour, S. Effect of municipal solid waste incineration bottom ash (MSWI-BA) on the structural performance of reinforced concrete (RC) beams. *J. Eng. Des. Technol.* **2021**, *21*, 862–882. [CrossRef]
5. Jaworska-Wedzinska, M.; Jasinska, I. Durability of mortars with fly ash subject to freezing and thawing cycles and sulfate attack. *Materials* **2022**, *15*, 220. [CrossRef] [PubMed]
6. Kelechi, S.E.; Adamu, M.; Mohammed, A.; Ibrahim, Y.E.; Obianyo, I.I. Durability performance of self-compacting concrete containing crumb rubber, fly ash and calcium carbide waste. *Materials* **2022**, *15*, 488. [CrossRef]
7. Raydan, R.; Khatib, J.; Jahami, A.; Hamoui, A.K.E.; Chamseddine, F. Prediction of the mechanical strength of concrete containing glass powder as partial cement replacement material. *Innov. Infrastruct. Solut.* **2022**, *7*, 311. [CrossRef]
8. Pietrzak, A.; Ulewicz, M. Influence of post-consumer waste thermoplastic elastomers obtained from used car floor mats on concrete properties. *Materials* **2023**, *16*, 2231. [CrossRef]
9. Lehner, P.; Gołaszewski, J. Relationship of different properties from non-destructive testing of heavy concrete from magnetite and serpentinite. *Materials* **2021**, *14*, 4288. [CrossRef]
10. Badarloo, B.; Lehner, P.; Bakhtiari Doost, R. Mechanical properties and gamma radiation transmission rate of heavyweight concrete containing barite aggregates. *Materials* **2022**, *15*, 2173. [CrossRef]
11. Manso, M.; Teotonio, I.; Silva, C.M.; Cruz, C.O. Green roof and green wall benefits and costs: A review of the quantitative evidence. *Renew. Sustain. Energy Rev.* **2021**, *135*, 110111. [CrossRef]
12. Mihalakakou, G.; Souliotis, M.; Papadaki, M.; Menounou, P.; Dimopoulos, P.; Kolokotsa, D.; Paravantis, J.A.; Tsangrassoulis, A.; Panaras, G.; Giannakopoulos, E.; et al. Green roofs as a nature-based solution for improving urban sustainability: Progress and perspectives. *Renew. Sustain. Energy Rev.* **2023**, *180*, 113306. [CrossRef]
13. Huang, J.; Kong, F.; Yin, H.; Middel, A.; Liu, H.; Meadows, M.E. Green roof effects on urban building surface processes and energy budgets. *Energy Convers. Manag.* **2023**, *287*, 117100. [CrossRef]
14. Mousavi, S.N.; Gheibi, M.; Wacławek, S.; Behzadian, K. A novel smart framework for optimal design of green roofs in buildings conforming with energy conservation and thermal comfort. *Energy Build.* **2023**, *291*, 113111. [CrossRef]
15. Jacobs, J.; Beenaerts, N.; Artois, T. Green roofs and pollinators, useful green spots for some wild bee species (Hymenoptera: Anthophila), but not so much for hoverflies (Diptera: Syrphidae). *Sci. Rep.* **2023**, *13*, 1449. [CrossRef]
16. Toboso-Chavero, S.; Montealegre, A.L.; García-P'erez, S.; Sierra-P'erez, J.; Munoz-Liesa, J.; Durany, X.G.; Villalba, G.; Madrid-Lopez, C. The potential of local food, energy, and water production systems on urban rooftops considering consumption patterns and urban morphology. *Sustain. Cities Soc.* **2023**, *95*, 104599. [CrossRef]
17. Uluçay, N.O. A method proposal for interior design analysis via Villa Savoye. *J. Art Arch. Stud.* **2020**, *9*, 5–13.
18. Zhang, Y.; Zhang, M. Transport properties in unsaturated cement-based materials—A review. Constr. *Build. Mater.* **2014**, *72* 367–379. [CrossRef]
19. Basheer, L.; Kropp, J.; Clelandc, D.J. Assessment of the durability of concrete from its permeation properties: A review. *Constr. Build. Mater.* **2001**, *15*, 93–103. [CrossRef]

20. Chew, M.; De Silva, N. Benchmarks to minimize water leakages in basements. *Struct. Surv.* **2003**, *21*, 131–145. [CrossRef]
21. Larisch, M.D. Modern concrete technology and placement methods and their influence on waterproofing performance of Diaphragm walls. In Proceedings of the New Zealand Concrete Industry Conference, Auckland, New Zealand, 6–8 October 2016.
22. Song, J.; Oh, K.; Kim, B.; Oh, S. Performance evaluation of waterproofing membrane systems subject to the concrete joint load behavior of below-grade concrete structures. *Appl. Sci.* **2017**, *7*, 1147. [CrossRef]
23. Mazzotta, F.; Lantieri, C.; Vignali, V.; Simone, A.; Dondi, G.; Sangiorgi, C. Performance evaluation of recycled rubber waterproofing bituminous membranes for concrete bridge decks and other surfaces. *Constr. Build. Mater.* **2017**, *136*, 524–532. [CrossRef]
24. Vogel, F.; Sovják, R.; Pešková, Š. Static response of double shell concrete lining with a spray-applied waterproofing membrane. *Tunn. Undergr. Space Technol.* **2017**, *68*, 106–112. [CrossRef]
25. Mendes, P.; Lopes, J.G.; De Brito, J.; Feiteira, J. Waterproofing of concrete foundations. *J. Perform. Constr. Facil.* **2014**, *28*, 242–249. [CrossRef]
26. Song, Z.; Xue, X.; Li, Y.; Yang, J.; He, Z.; Shen, S.; Jiang, L.; Zhang, W.; Xu, L.; Zhang, H.; et al. Experimental exploration of the waterproofing mechanism of inorganic sodium silicate-based concrete sealers. *Constr. Build. Mater.* **2016**, *104*, 276–283. [CrossRef]
27. Xue, X.; Li, Y.; Yang, Z.; He, Z.; Dai, J.G.; Xu, L.; Zhang, W. A systematic investigation of the waterproofing performance and chloride resistance of a self-developed waterborne silane-based hydrophobic agent for mortar and concrete. *Constr. Build. Mater.* **2017**, *155*, 939–946. [CrossRef]
28. Izarra, I.; Cubillo, J.; Serrano, A.; Rodriguez, J.F.; Carmona, M. A hydrophobic release agent containing SiO_2-CH_3 submicron-sized particles for waterproofing mortar structures. *Constr. Build. Mater.* **2019**, *199*, 30–39. [CrossRef]
29. Fleming, J.P. Secretary. ACI Committee 212.3R-91 (reapproved 1999) Chemical admixtures for concrete. *ACI Mater. J.* **1989**, *212*, 212.3R-1–212.3R-31.
30. Muhammad, N.Z.; Keyvanfar, A.; Majid, M.Z.A.; Shafaghat, A.; Mirza, J. Waterproof performance of concrete: A critical review on implemented approaches. *Constr. Build. Mater.* **2015**, *101*, 80–90. [CrossRef]
31. Coppola, L.; Coffetti, D.; Crotti, E. Innovative carboxylic acid waterproofing admixture for self-sealing watertight concretes. *Constr. Build. Mater.* **2018**, *171*, 817–824. [CrossRef]
32. Li, H.; Xu, C.; Dong, B.; Chen, Q.; Gu, L.; Yang, X. Enhanced performances of cement and powder silane based waterproof mortar modified by nucleation C-S-H seed. *Constr. Build. Mater.* **2020**, *246*, 118511. [CrossRef]
33. Geng, Y.; Li, S.; Hou, D.; Chen, X.; Jin, Z. Effect of SiO_2 sol/silane emulsion in reducing water and chloride ion penetration in concrete. *Coatings* **2020**, *10*, 682. [CrossRef]
34. Muwashee, R.S.; Al-Jameel, H.A. Studying the effect of waterproofing admixtures on some properties of cement mortar. *IOP Conf. Ser. Mater. Sci. Eng.* **2020**, *737*, 012060. [CrossRef]
35. Wang, F.; Lei, S.; Ou, J.; Li, W. Effect of PDMS on the waterproofing performance and corrosion resistance of cement mortar. *Appl. Surf. Sci.* **2020**, *507*, 145016. [CrossRef]
36. Aldykiewicz, A.; Berke, N.; Callander, I.; Bentur, A. Use of concrete admixtures to produce "waterproof" concrete. In Proceedings of the Superplasticzers and Other Admixtures in Concrete CANMET ACI, Sorento, Italy, 1 January 2006; Volume Supplementary.
37. Berke, N.S.; Dallaire, M.P.; Hicks, M.C.; Kerkar, A. New Developments in Shrinkage-Reducing Admixtures. In Proceedings of the ACI SP 173—Superplasticizers and Other Chemical Admixtures in Concrete: Proceedings, Fifth CANMET/ACI International Conference, Rome, Italy, 7–10 October 1997; American Concrete Institute: Farmington Hills, MI, USA, 1997; pp. 971–998.
38. Bamoharram, F.F.; Heravi, M.M.; Saneinezhad, S.; Ayatic, A. Synthesis of a nano organo-silicon compound for building materials waterproofing. using heteropolyacids as a green and eco-friendly catalyst. *Prog. Org. Coat.* **2013**, *76*, 384–387. [CrossRef]
39. Al-Rashed, R.; Jabari, M. Dual-Crystallization Waterproofing Technology for Topical Treatment of Concrete. *Case Stud. Constr. Mater.* **2020**, *13*, e00408. [CrossRef]
40. Matar, P.; Barhoun, J. Effects of waterproofing admixture on the compressive strength and permeability of recycled aggregate concrete. *J. Build. Eng.* **2020**, *32*, 101521. [CrossRef]
41. Hrabová, K.; Niedoba, J.; Vymazal, T.; Lanik, J.; Teply, B. The assessment of structural concrete with recycled aggregates in terms of sustainability. *Int. Multidiscip. Sci. GeoConf. SGEM* **2021**, *21*, 287–294. [CrossRef]
42. Hohmann, R. Planning 21and execution of joints and joint sealing and waterproofing solutions for watertight concrete structures. *Beton- Stahlbetonbau* **2018**, *113*, 83–99. [CrossRef]
43. Cho, B.H.; Nama, B.H.; Seo, S.; Kim, J.; An, J.; Youn, H. Waterproofing performance of waterstop with adhesive bonding used at joints of underground concrete structures. *Constr. Build. Mater.* **2019**, *221*, 491–500. [CrossRef]
44. *PN-EN 197-1*; Cement—Part 1 Composition, Specifications and Conformity Criteria for Common Cements. European Parliament: Strasbourg, France, 2011.
45. *PN-EN 450-1:2012*; Fly Ash for Concrete—Part 1: Definitions, Specifications and Conformity Criteria. European Parliament: Strasbourg, France, 2012.
46. *PN-B-06265:2022-08*; Concrete—Requirements, Performance, Production and Conformity. National Supplement to PN-EN 206+A2:2021-08. Polish Committee for Standardization: Warsaw, Poland, 2022.
47. *PN-EN 12350-2:2019-07*; Testing Fresh Concrete. Part 2. Slump Test. European Parliament: Strasbourg, France, 2019.
48. *PN-EN 12350-7:2019-08*; Testing fresh concrete. Part 7: Air content—Pressure methods. European Parliament: Strasbourg, France, 2019.

49. *PN-EN 12390-3:2019-07*; Testing hardened concrete—Part 3: Compressive strength of test specimens. European Parliament: Strasbourg, France, 2019.
50. *PN-EN 12390-8:2019-08*; Testing hardened concrete—Part 8: Depth of penetration of water under pressure. European Parliament: Strasbourg, France, 2019.

Disclaimer/Publisher's Note: The statements, opinions and data contained in all publications are solely those of the individual author(s) and contributor(s) and not of MDPI and/or the editor(s). MDPI and/or the editor(s) disclaim responsibility for any injury to people or property resulting from any ideas, methods, instructions or products referred to in the content.

MDPI AG
Grosspeteranlage 5
4052 Basel
Switzerland
Tel.: +41 61 683 77 34

Materials Editorial Office
E-mail: materials@mdpi.com
www.mdpi.com/journal/materials

Disclaimer/Publisher's Note: The title and front matter of this reprint are at the discretion of the Guest Editors. The publisher is not responsible for their content or any associated concerns. The statements, opinions and data contained in all individual articles are solely those of the individual Editors and contributors and not of MDPI. MDPI disclaims responsibility for any injury to people or property resulting from any ideas, methods, instructions or products referred to in the content.

www.ingramcontent.com/pod-product-compliance
Lightning Source LLC
Chambersburg PA
CBHW061508210926
51850CB00008B/1851
* 9 7 8 3 7 2 5 8 3 7 9 4 6 *